Programming with Threads

Steve Kleiman

Devang Shah

Bart Smaalders

SunSoft Press
A Prentice Hall Title

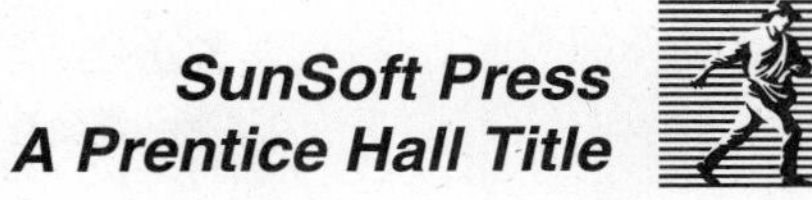

The publisher offers discounts on this book when ordered in bulk quantities. For more information, contact: Corporate Sales Department, Prentice Hall PTR, One Lake Street, Upper Saddle River, NJ 07458. Phone: 800-382-3419 or 201-236-7156, Fax: 201-236-7141, email: corpsales@prenhall.com

Cover designer: *M & K Design, Palo Alto, California*
Manufacturing manager: *Alexis R. Heydt*
Acquisitions editor: *Gregory G. Doench*
Cover Design Director: *Jerry Votta*
Production Supervisor: *Joanne Anzalone*

10 9 8 7 6 5 4 3 2

ISBN 0-13-172389-8

SunSoft Press
A Prentice Hall Title

Table of Contents

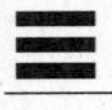

Figures

Tables

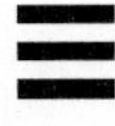

Code Examples

Acknowledgments

The chapter on parallel programing was written by Robert Sproull and was inspired by [Rao 91]. Dan Stein, a member of the threads development team, helped with the original SunSoft *Guide to Multithreaded Programming*, which was our starting point. Notes for a multithreading course prepared by Tom Doeppner and a paper on using threads with distributed objects by Bob Hagmann were also helpful. A talk by Dado Vrsalovic provided additional material.

Thanks to Mike Jones, Nick Sterling, and Steve Jankowski for providing some excellent review comments.

Lastly, thanks to Karin Ellison from SunSoft Press for supporting us all along.

Preface

Threads are a new[1] and powerful tool. As with most powerful tools, programmers must apply threads with discretion lest they do more harm than good. Part of the art of good multithreaded programming is knowing when *not* to use threads. Keep in mind that UNIX® has gotten along for many years without them. The real impetus toward using threads has been the increasing popularity of multiprocessors and client-server computing. Typically, programs are expected to handle many requests simultaneously in these situations.

This book is for programmers interested in a practical guide to developing multithreaded programs. This book concentrates on teaching when and how to apply threads, what problems to expect and how to deal with them. It covers concurrency theory relatively lightly as there are many other books and papers that do better justice to the topic[2]. This book also can be used as reference for the practicing threads programmer.

We assume that you are generally familiar with both UNIX programming concepts and the C programming language. It will be helpful if you have some experience with asynchronous programming using signal handlers or with programs that respond to multiple events, such as window or network programs.

This book is designed to be a general guide to programming with threads, not a tutorial on a specific set of interfaces. The two main UNIX threads interfaces are the IEEE Portable Operating System Interface (POSIX) standard P1003.1c[3] (also called "Pthreads" and ISO/IEC 9945-1:1990c) and the UNIX International (UI) threads standard (see Appendix B, "UNIX International Threads"). Both have the same basic model of threads, though the actual function definitions tend to use different styles. The coding examples in this book use the thread and operating system interfaces specified by the POSIX standards.

1. Threads are relatively new to UNIX though they have been around in various forms in other operating systems for a long time. The general issue of dealing with concurrency has been discussed in the literature since the 1960s, if not before.

2. For those of you who are familiar with such books, we promise that there are no "dining philosophers" examples here.

3. Formerly P1003.4a.

The POSIX thread standard specifies the threads application programming interfaces and the ways in which the other POSIX interfaces behave with respect to threads. In practice, threads programming also involves using other, non-standard aspects of the threads programming environment such as debuggers, performance tools, and non-standard libraries. In addition, effective threads programming requires some knowledge of the potential ways that the interfaces may be implemented within the standard. This book explains some of the tools available in the threads programming environment and some of the potential threads implementation strategies. In-depth examples of tools and implementation strategies are taken from the Solaris™ programming environment from Sun Microsystems.

In many cases, a threads programmer will be asked to convert existing applications and libraries to be multithreaded. This book covers potential approaches to threading existing code.

Using This Book

The chapters in this book are grouped into sections that can be skipped or skimmed depending on your interests.

Introduction

This section introduces the basic thread interfaces, thread creation, thread synchronization, libraries, and how threads interact with the UNIX process model. It covers some techniques for applying threads and constructing correct multithreaded programs. After reading this section, you should be able to construct useful multithreaded programs.

- Chapter 1, "Introduction to Threads"
- Chapter 2, "Getting Started"
- Chapter 3, "Synchronization"
- Chapter 4, "Using Libraries in Multithreaded Programs"
- Chapter 5, "Threads and Process Resources"
- Chapter 6, "Synchronization Strategies"
- Chapter 7, "Using Threads"

Programmers who are already familiar with general thread concepts can simply browse this section to become familiar with the POSIX interfaces.

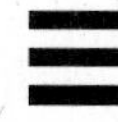

Advanced Interfaces

This section introduces the interfaces and strategies that are appropriate in more unusual or performance-critical situations.

- Chapter 8, "Thread-Specific Data"
- Chapter 9, "Signals"
- Chapter 10, "Advanced Synchronization"
- Chapter 11, "Thread Cancellation"
- Chapter 12, "Threads Scheduling"
- Chapter 13, "Threads and Processes: Advanced Topics"
- Chapter 14, "Advanced Synchronization Strategies"
- Chapter 15, "Multiprocessor Issues"
- Chapter 16, "Parallel Computation"

You can skip this section on a first reading, but it is a good idea to at least skim it at some point so you know what's there if you need it.

Using Threads in the Real World

This section covers techniques for applying threads and constructing correct multithreaded programs and libraries.

- Chapter 17, "Multithreading Existing Code"
- Chapter 18, "Threads Development Environment"

Reference material

This section contains reference material for the practicing thread programmer on a variety of subjects.

- Appendix A, "Example Programs"
- Appendix B, "UNIX International Threads"
- Appendix C, "Manual Pages"
- Appendix D, "Annotated Bibliography"

There is a World Wide Web site for threads examples, errata and other materials at:

http://www.sun.com/smi/ssoftpress/threads/

This site also contain most of the larger code examples in this book in full running form.

Coding Conventions

In many of the smaller coding examples, full declarations, included files, and full testing for errors are deleted for clarity. In these examples you should generally assume that the line:

```
#include <pthread.h>
```

appears somewhere before the code. Since this book concentrates on threads more than the other aspects of POSIX, you should understand that the newer POSIX interfaces (as well as the newer UNIX International interfaces) no longer rely on the global variable `errno` to return error codes. Instead, they mostly return zero if the function was successful, or a non-zero error code (found in the include-file `<errno.h>`).

Introduction to Threads 1

What Are Threads?

A thread of control, or more simply a *thread*, is an independent sequence of execution of program code inside a UNIX process. A traditional UNIX process has a single thread that has sole possession of the process's memory and other resources. The interfaces in the POSIX Pthreads interface standard and the UNIX International (UI) interface standard[1] allow more than one thread of control to be active in a process simultaneously. The threads share all of the process's memory. Each thread reads or writes process memory or makes requests for system services as directed by the program code. When one thread writes to memory, other threads can read the results. The threads also share all of the process's resources, such as file descriptors, so more than one thread can write to the same file. Like other process resources, threads within a process are generally invisible from outside the process, except, of course, by debuggers and other tools.

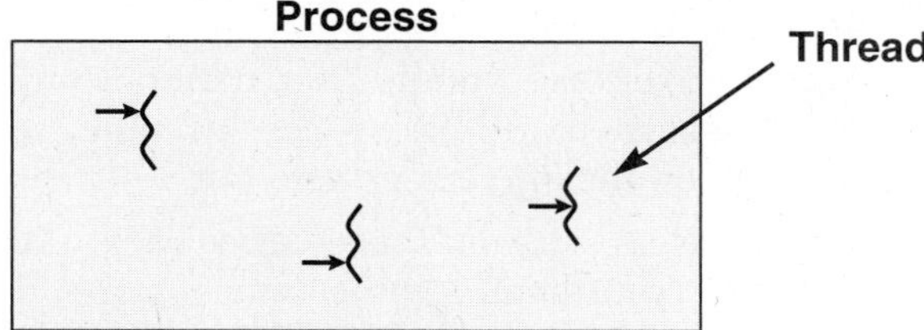

Figure 1-1 Threads in a Process

The threads within a process are scheduled and execute independently in the same way as different single-threaded UNIX processes. For example, when a thread executes an I/O request that waits until completion, it does not prevent other threads from executing. On multiprocessors, different threads may execute on different processors. On uniprocessors, threads may interleave their execution arbitrarily. Typically, another thread can run when the current thread blocks or uses up its allotted time interval (also called a timeslice or time quantum) as shown in Figure 1-2.

1. The official name for the POSIX threads standard is P1003.1c. The UI standard that contains the threads interfaces is the System V Interface Definition (SVID) Issue 4.

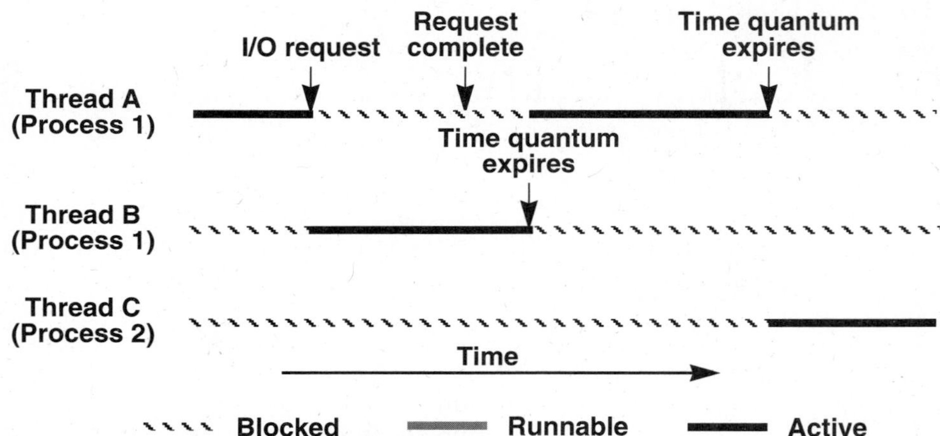

Figure 1-2 Threads Interleaving Execution on a Uniprocessor

With traditional UNIX processes, programmers who wanted more than one function to be active at any one time used several processes. The processes would communicate with each other using one or more of the available interprocess communications (IPC) facilities, such as pipes or sockets. Data would usually be copied from the transmitting process, then sent over a connection or pipe to the receiver where it would be copied into the receiving process. The flow of data is implicitly controlled by the IPC facility, and errors in the different processes are isolated. However, using these mechanisms implies a relatively large amount of setup and data copying overhead. In addition, maintaining the additional processes, with their associated address spaces and other resources, represents a relatively heavy burden on the operating system in both memory and processing.

If, instead of using processes, threads are used for each independent function, communicating data between them becomes much easier; they can simply pass pointers to the data instead of copying. In addition, threads represent a much lighter burden on the system than using separate processes, as separately protected address spaces and other process resources need not be maintained. In fact, it is possible to execute certain thread functions completely without operating system intervention.

Programming with more than one thread in a process opens up the possibility that one thread will interfere with memory or other process resources another thread is using. Using threads allows you to trade off the protection of heavyweight processes and heavyweight IPC mechanisms for lightweight threads and high speed communication. Controlling threads so that they don't interfere with each other is what requires your attention.

The Benefits of Threads

Threads bring a variety of benefits as a payoff for added programming complexity. Let's explore some of the situations where threads can help.

Throughput

A program with only one thread of control must wait each time it requests a service from the operating system. On a uniprocessor as well as on a multiprocessor, using more than one thread lets a process overlap processing with one or more I/O requests. The thread making a request waits, but another thread in the process can continue. This lets a process have many pending I/O requests. Threads provide this overlap of I/O requests although each request is coded in the usual synchronous style (unlike the various asynchronous I/O techniques).

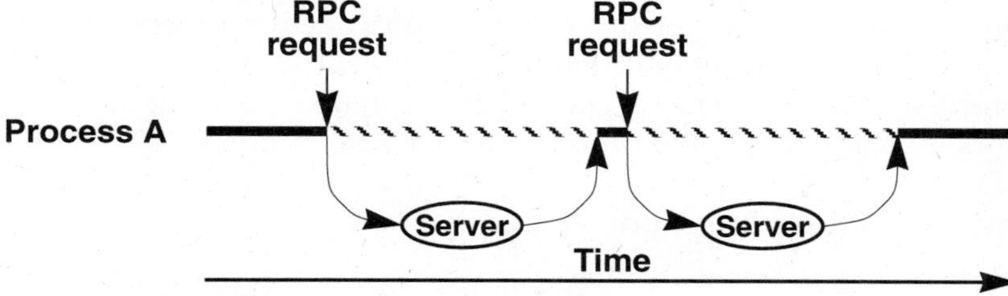

Figure 1-3 Remote Procedure Call Using a Single Thread

An example is a program that does several remote procedure calls (RPCs) to different hosts to obtain a result. In a single-threaded program, the RPCs must be done serially. The program must send a request to a host and wait for the response before sending the next request (see Figure 1-3).

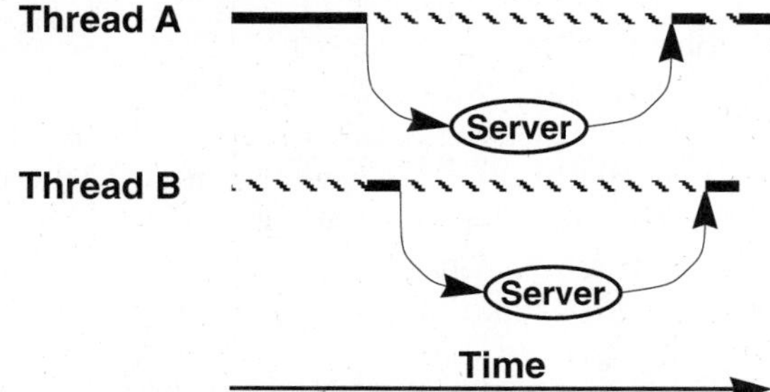

Figure 1-4 Remote Procedure Call Using a Thread Per Server (On a Uniprocessor)

In a multithreaded program, a thread can be created to issue each RPC request. Each thread makes an independent request to a server using the usual RPC interfaces. On a uniprocessor, the requests are generated serially, since there is only one processor. However, the threads wait concurrently for the replies, as illustrated in Figure 1-4.

Multiple Processors

Computers with more than one processor provide multiple simultaneous points of execution. Multiple threads are an efficient way for application developers to utilize the parallelism of the hardware. A good example is a process that does a matrix multiplication. A thread can be created for each available processor. Each of the threads repeatedly computes a unique element of the result matrix by repeatedly doing the appropriate vector multiplication.

Another example is in discrete event simulations, such as process or logic simulations. These typically have many independent activities that are capable of being processed simultaneously. The program can take advantage of the available processors by using threads to process each independent activity.

User Interface Responsiveness

Single-threaded applications having a graphical user interface (GUI) typically display a "wait cursor" (e.g., a watch or hourglass) and freeze when a button corresponding to a time-consuming operation is pressed. If such an application were multithreaded, the pressing of a button associated with a long operation could cause the operation to be done by an independent thread while the thread servicing the user interface continues on (see Figure 1-5). This enables the application and its user interface to remain responsive to more requests.

Another way an application can increase user interface responsiveness is to use separate threads to perform operations that can be deferred. For example, most word processors automatically save to a backup file. Single-threaded word processors freeze (and usually display a "wait cursor") when it's time to do the auto-save. A multithreaded word processor can use a separate thread to write out the file. This allows the thread servicing the user interface to remain active while the document is being auto-saved.

Server Responsiveness

Server programs in client/server applications may get multiple requests from independent clients simultaneously. These requests must be handled serially if the server has only one thread of control. This causes long requests to block the servicing of other pending requests. Multithreaded servers can be more adaptive to variations in user demands than the single-threaded equivalents, because each

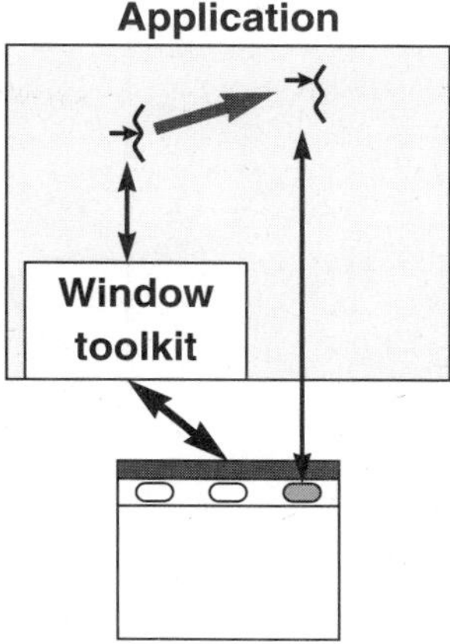

Figure 1-5 Graphic Application Using Threads

individual request can be independently scheduled according to its importance. Requests that involve lengthy computations or that are simply less important do not block the execution of other activities. A good example of this is a database server where each concurrent user of the database has a separate thread. Users making long database queries won't block out other users since threads are independently scheduled by the system according to their priority.

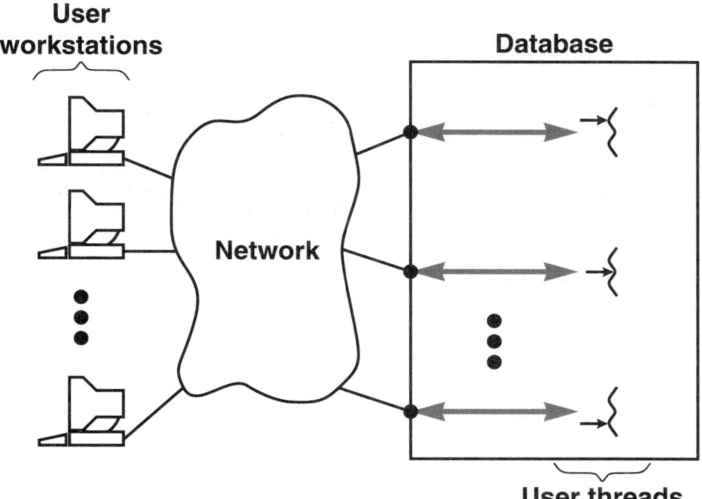

Figure 1-6 Multithreaded Database Server

The only alternative for single threaded programs is to intersperse polls for new requests throughout the code that processes long requests. For example:

```
long_request()
{
    ... do some of the request
    if (there is a pending request that is more important){
        save the current request state
        process pending request
        restore request state
    }
    ...do some more of the request
}
```

Server Deadlock Avoidance

In some client/server applications, servers can also be clients of other servers or even of themselves. Suppose a database server calls a naming service that stores its information in the database server. A single-threaded database server will deadlock (i.e., will not make further progress) in this situation since its single thread is already occupied servicing the original request. A multithreaded server can create (or reuse) a separate thread for each request, as shown in Figure 1-7.

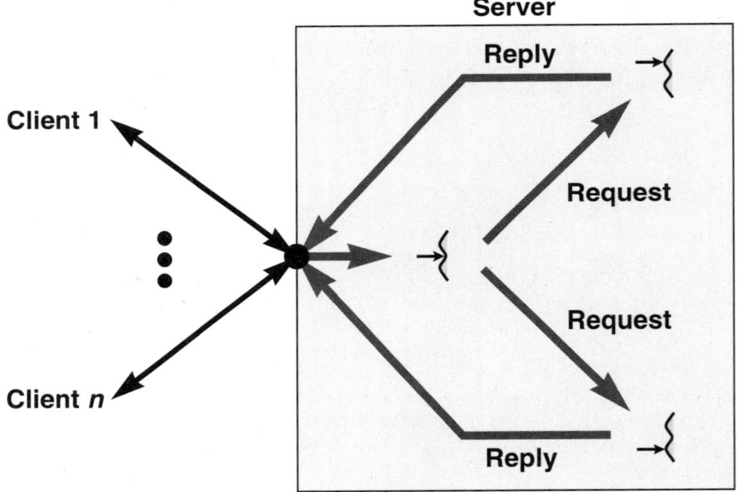

Figure 1-7 Multithreaded Server

This not only increases server responsiveness (i.e., long requests cannot completely lock out other requests), but it also allows the server to be re-entered because new requests are not blocked by existing requests, as shown in Figure 1-8.

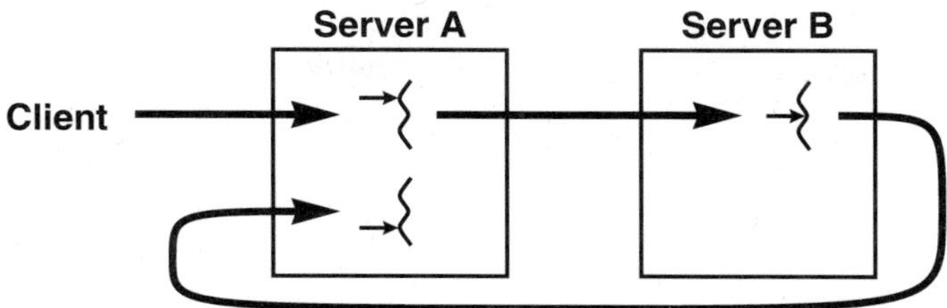

Figure 1-8 Avoiding Server Deadlock

Program Structure

Threads can also be used to simplify the structure of a program. A simple example is a spreadsheet application which typically recomputes the results of spreadsheet formulas when a change is made, without stopping the user from interacting with the application while this is in progress. With a single thread of control, the application must do some recomputation and then check for more user input before doing more, as follows:

```
spreadsheet()
{
    for (;;) {
        while (formula_update_required() &&
            !user_input_available()) {
                recompute_one_formula();
        }
        cmd = get_user_input();
        process_user_input(cmd);
    }
}
```

Code Example 1-1 Spreadsheet Recomputation Without Threads

With more than one thread available, the application can break this into two independent threads: one that takes care of user input and one that takes care of recomputation, which is created as required:

```
spreadsheet_thread()
{
    for (;;) {
        cmd = get_user_input();
        process_user_input(cmd);
    }
}
```

```
recompute_thread()
{
    for (;;) {
        wait_for_cell_change();
        for (each formula) {
            recompute_one_formula();
        }
    }
}
```

Code Example 1-2   Spreadsheet Recomputation with Threads

Programs that use multiple threads can have subroutines that concentrate on handling a particular function. Multiplexing between several activities is handled by the threads package. The independent operations are now separated into independent routines. The spreadsheet thread does not have to remember to process the recomputation at appropriate intervals. The operations can proceed independently with the importance of each operation reflected in the thread's scheduling priority. This usually results in more understandable and maintainable code.

Some programs are naturally expressed as independent activities. A classic example of this is discrete event simulation where each independent activity to be simulated is naturally expressed as an independent thread. For example, in a simulation of a computer system (see Figure 1-9) each client can be represented by an independent thread that generates network requests. The network can be expressed as a thread that services the queued network requests and sends them on to the correct server. Similarly, the behavior of servers and disks can be modeled as threads. Each thread can be customized to have specific, independent behavior, without affecting the behavior of other threads.

Communication

Threads can also benefit an application that uses more than one process and communicates large amounts of data between its processes through traditional interprocess communication (IPC) facilities (for example, pipes or sockets). Much of the communication between processes that would otherwise require setup and extensive use of system resources is done implicitly in a multithreaded application through memory that is shared by all the threads. As shown in Figure 1-10, the sending threads can simply pass pointers to the appropriate data to receiving threads.

Alternatively, programs can use two or more processes that access common data through shared memory. In effect, such programs are using more than one thread of control. The problem with this approach is that each process has a full address space and operating systems state. The cost of creating and maintaining this large

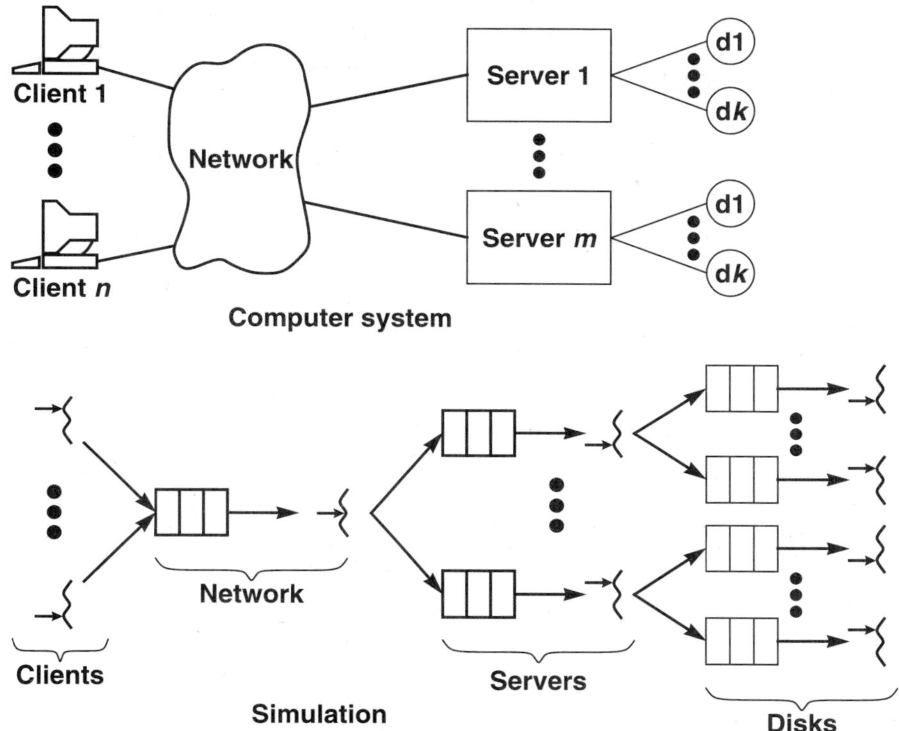

Figure 1-9 Computer System and Simulation

amount of state makes each process much more expensive than a thread in both time and space. In addition, the inherent separation between processes may require a major programming effort to communicate between the threads in different processes or to synchronize their actions.

A Warning

Threads are not appropriate for all programs. For example, an application that must accelerate a single compute-bound algorithm will not benefit from multithreading when run on uniprocessor hardware. For some I/O-bound programs, the system may already provide the required degree of I/O concurrency (for example, read-ahead and write-behind to regular files in the primary file system). It would also be a bad idea to compute every statement in a program that could possibly be executed in parallel in separate threads. Threads

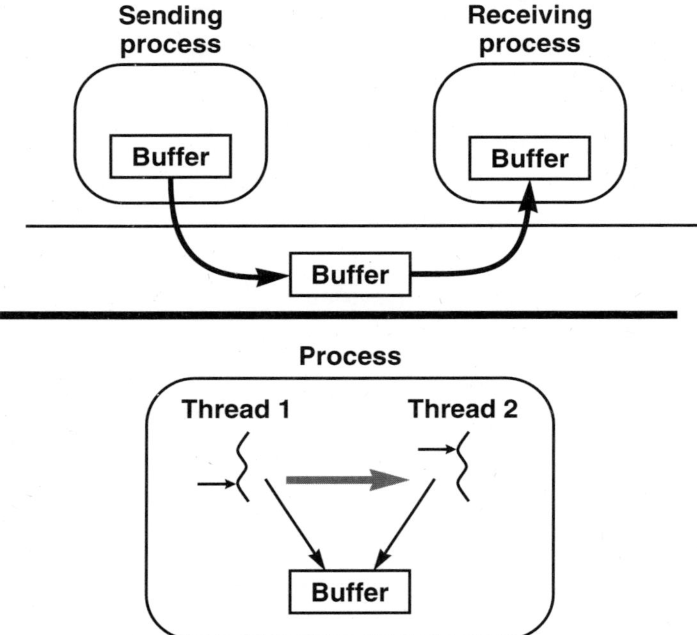

Figure 1-10 Communicating with Processes and Threads

are lightweight when compared to processes, but they are inappropriate for such a "data flow" programming model. Some of the art of multithreaded programming consists of knowing when and how to apply threads.

Fortunately, many multithreaded programs have similar forms. This book explains a number of paradigms or templates for a variety of multithreaded programs. These templates are similar in spirit to different forms of parsers and lexical analyzers explained in books on compiler writing, or to the general "event-loop" paradigm used by programs with window-based graphical user interfaces. You can use the paradigms in different situations, much like selecting a tool from a toolkit, once you understand them. For most situations, you can pick out the appropriate template and apply it relatively easily.

Controlling Concurrency

Even appropriate multithreaded applications can be difficult to design and debug. It is relatively easy for threads to interfere with each other, since they share memory and other process resources. In addition, many programmers are not trained to think about how to deal with situations where there can be many things going on simultaneously. For example, a simple statement that increments a counter, such as:

```
counter++;
```

can fail to operate correctly if executed concurrently. Such statements are normally decomposed into a series of operations either by the compiler or the processor's microcode. For example:

1. Load the value of `counter` into a register
2. Increment the register
3. Store the contents of the register into `counter`

If two threads execute the statement simultaneously, the following series of events is possible:

Thread 1	Thread 2
1. Load `counter` into register	
	1. Load `counter` into register
	2. Increment register
	3. Store register into `counter`
2. Increment register	
3. Store register into `counter`	

In this case, Thread 1 will overwrite the value stored by Thread 2, so the counter will be incremented once instead of twice.

Over the years, programmers have developed a number of techniques, such as structured and object-oriented programming, to control program complexity. Similarly, concurrent programmers have developed a number of techniques to help deal with the complexity of concurrent programs. The techniques are based on a number of concurrency control interfaces defined by the Pthreads standard, in addition to the interfaces that create and destroy threads. A significant portion of this book is devoted to explaining these techniques and showing how to apply them in practical situations.

The concurrency control techniques are in the form of a set of programming rules. They are similar in spirit to the set of rules used to develop structured or object-oriented programs, such as information hiding or block structure.

Concurrent Programming

Once you understand how to apply threads and the techniques for structured concurrency control, concurrent programming becomes much easier. You can write programs without using these techniques, just as you can write programs without using structured programming techniques. However, it will be more difficult to write and maintain correct concurrent programs without using structured techniques, especially for larger or more complex programs, just as unstructured "spaghetti" code is more difficult to write and maintain. The techniques explained in this book are not specific to any programming language, though some languages support them more directly[2]. Programming in such "concurrent" languages still requires a thorough knowledge of structured concurrency control techniques[3]. This book concentrates on concurrency in C and C++.

Summary

You've seen some of the ways in which threads can benefit applications. The next chapter gets started using threads by introducing an example application that uses threads to increase user interface responsiveness.

2. For example, Modula-3 and Ada.

3. As the old programmer's saying goes: You can write bad Fortran in any language.

Getting Started 2 

This chapter presents a simple example using threads and introduces the basic thread creation and destruction programming interfaces. The chapter also explains some common pitfalls encountered in using these interfaces. Readers who are familiar with the basic threads interfaces may want to skip this chapter.

A Simple Example Using Threads

Consider an application that displays compressed pictures from a series of files. Normally such a program would decompress a picture, display it and then wait for the user to signal that he or she is finished viewing by pressing a button or typing a character. The program would begin decompressing the next picture when the user has finished with the current picture. The user must wait until the decompression process is complete before seeing the next picture. By using a thread to decompress the next picture while the user is viewing the current one, the program can eliminate some or all of the waiting time.

In Code Example 2-1, the function `get_next_picture()` opens the file specified by its argument, allocates a buffer of appropriate size, and decompresses the picture in the file into the buffer. When the display program starts, it calls `get_next_picture()` to decompress the first picture and display it. Rather than immediately waiting for the user to signal that he or she wants to see the next picture, it calls `pthread_create()` to create a new thread which will be responsible for concurrently decompressing then next picture while the main thread displays the current picture and waits for user input. `pthread_create()` stores the thread-id of the new thread in `pic_thread` before it returns. The thread-id can be used in subsequent Pthreads routines to refer to the new thread.

The first thing the new thread does is call `get_next_picture()` with the next file as an argument. The thread exits when `get_next_picture()` returns. When the user types a character to display the next picture, the program must ensure that the decompression process for the next picture has finished. The program calls `pthread_join()` to wait for the decompressing thread to finish its job and exit. The main thread can now repeat the process for the next picture if any.

```
int
main(int argc, char *argv[])
{
    pthread_t pic_thread;
    int fileno;
    pic_buf_t *buf;

    for (fileno = 1; fileno < argc; fileno++) {
        if (fileno == 1) {
            /* do the first file w/o a thread */
            buf = get_next_picture((void *)argv[fileno]);
        } else {
            /* wait for decompression thread to finish */
            pthread_join(pic_thread, (void **)&buf);
        }
        if (fileno < argc-1) {
            /* launch thread to do next picture, if any */
            pthread_create(&pic_thread, NULL,
                get_next_picture, (void *)argv[fileno + 1]);
        }
        display_buf(buf);       /* display current picture */
        free(buf);              /* free picture*/
        if (getchar() == EOF)   /* wait for user to finish looking */
            break;
    }
    return (0);
}

void *
get_next_picture(void *arg)
{
    int fd;
    pic_buf_t *buf;

    fd = open((char *) arg, O_RDONLY);
    if (fd < 0)
            return (NULL);
    buf = (pic_buf_t *) malloc(...)
    while ((nbytes = read(fd,...)) != 0) {
        decompress data into buf
    }
    close (fd);
}
```

Code Example 2-1 Displaying a Series of Pictures Using Threads

Threads Interfaces

Now that we've seen a simple threads example, let's go into more detail about the interfaces a programmer uses to manipulate threads.

Creating Threads

The interface for creating a thread is:

```
#include <pthread.h>

int
pthread_create(
    pthread_t *threadp,
    const pthread_attr_t *attr,
    void *(*start_routine)(void *), void *arg);
```

`pthread_create()` creates a new thread of control that calls the function *`start_routine()`*, with a single argument, *`arg`*. If `pthread_create()` successfully creates a new thread, the thread-id for the new thread is stored in the location pointed to by *`threadp`*, and `pthread_create()` returns zero. If there was some problem with creating the thread, `pthread_create()` returns an error code found in `errno.h`. The *`attr`* argument to `pthread_create()` is used to modify the attributes of the new thread (see "Thread Attributes," below). If *`attr`* is `NULL`, the new thread is created using a default set of attributes.

Note – Threads are an optional feature in POSIX. Threads are supported if the `_POSIX_THREADS` macro is defined in `<unistd.h>` (such macros are called feature test macros in POSIX). This can be tested dynamically by calling `sysconf()` using the `_SC_THREADS` macro from `<unistd.h>` as an argument. `sysconf()` returns `-1` if the feature is not supported.

The Pthreads implementation may have some internal limit on the number of threads it can create for one process. The minimum number the implementation supports is available as the macro value `PTHREAD_THREADS_MAX` defined in `<limits.h>`. This value must be greater than or equal to 64 (64 is also the value of the `_POSIX_THREAD_THREADS_MAX` macro). The actual limit when the program is run may be greater. This number may be retrieved by calling `sysconf()` using the `_SC_THREAD_THREADS_MAX` macro from `<unistd.h>` as an argument.

Using the Thread Start Routine Argument

The argument that is passed to the start routine for the new thread is a single pointer. If more arguments are required, it is easy to set up a structure and have the argument point to it:

```
struct two_args {
    int arg1;
    int arg2;
};
void *needs_2_args(void *);

void
a()
{
    pthread_t t;
    struct two_args *ap;
    int error;

    ap = (struct two_args *) malloc(sizeof (struct two_args));
    ap->arg1 = 1;
    ap->arg2 = 2;
    error = pthread_create(&t, NULL, needs_2_args, (void *) ap);
    if (error != 0)
        handle the error
    ...
}

void *
needs_2_args(void *ap)
{
    struct two_args *argp = (void *) ap;
    int a1, a2;

    a1 = argp->arg1;
    a2 = argp->arg2;
    free(argp);
    ...
}
```

Code Example 2-2   Passing More Than One Argument to a Thread Start Routine

A warning about passing arguments

Be careful not to allocate the argument structure on the stack of a routine that may return before the new thread is done referencing it. Why is this a problem? As an example, consider the following code.

```
/* Warning: this code contains a bug */
pthread_t
a()
{
    pthread_t t;
    struct two_args args;
    int error;

    args.arg1 = 1;
    args.arg2 = 2;
    error = pthread_create(&t, NULL, needs_2_args, (void *) &args);
    if (error != 0)
        handle the error
    return (t);         /* ERROR! destroys args while in use */
}
```

Remember, threads share all memory in a process. Automatic local variables, such as `args`, are created when the function is entered (usually in the current stack frame) and are destroyed when the function returns. The routine `a()` may have already returned, destroying `args`, by the time the new thread begins execution. Typically, this memory will be reused by other routines called after `a()` returns, overwriting the new thread's arguments.

Destroying Threads

When a thread has completed its job, it should be destroyed so its resources can be reclaimed. The usual way to destroy a thread is to simply return from the start routine, as illustrated in Code Example 2-1. However, if this is not convenient you can also call:

```
void
pthread_exit(void *status);
```

which destroys the calling thread. The single pointer value in *`status`* will be made available to another thread that waits for the thread to exit (see "Waiting for Threads to Exit" below). When the thread is destroyed by returning from the thread's start routine, the thread's *completion status* is set to the return value. The completion status is a pointer value that is available to other threads. The completion status should not point to data allocated on the exiting thread's stack, as this memory may be freed and reused when the thread exits.

Waiting for Threads to Exit

One way of determining that another thread has completed its function is to wait for it to exit. The function:

```
int
pthread_join(pthread_t thread, void **statusp);
```

waits for a thread (whose thread-id is *thread*) to exit. When *thread* exits (or if it has already exited), its *completion status* is stored into the location pointed to by *statusp*, and pthread_join() returns 0. For example, in Code Example 2-1 the main thread used the completion status to return a pointer to the buffer containing the decompressed picture. If *statusp* is NULL, then pthread_join() returns without storing the status. If there is some problem, pthread_join() returns an error code. Once a thread has been joined, it no longer exists and its thread-id is no longer usable. It is an error for more than one thread to join with the same thread simultaneously.

An active thread can also be destroyed at the request of another thread in the same process. This mechanism is called *thread cancellation* and is explained in Chapter 11, "Thread Cancellation." A thread cannot return status when it has been canceled, and pthread_join() sets the location pointed to by *statusp* to the value PTHREAD_CANCELED.

Note – A thread's completion status and its argument are both of type (void *). The ANSI definition of the C programming language states that the results of casting integral types (e.g., int, unsigned int, etc.) to (void *) are dependent on the implementation. However, most popular computer architectures and language implementations allow integral types and (void *) to be cast freely between each other, and an integral type can be passed directly as an argument or completion status at the cost of some portability. Keep in mind that non-pointer values may conflict with PTHREAD_CANCELED.

Using the thread completion status

The completion status is a convenient way of returning the results of a thread's execution to another thread. For example, in Code Example 2-1, the thread running get_next_picture() returns a pointer to the buffer that contains the decompressed picture as its thread exit status.

A warning about passing completion status

Be careful to ensure that the thread completion status does not point to data allocated in the automatic storage of the exiting thread. This is a problem whether the exiting thread calls `pthread_exit()` or whether it returns from the start routine.

This is similar to the problem of passing a pointer to automatic data as an argument to the thread start routine. Once `pthread_join()` completes, the target thread will be completely destroyed, including any automatic data it may have allocated.

Getting the Current Thread-id

`pthread_create()` returns the thread-id of the newly created thread to the thread that called `pthread_create()`. The new thread does not know its thread-id, by default. This is somewhat similar to the process creation interface, `fork()`, which returns the process-id of the new process to the parent but not the child. The child gets its process-id by calling `getpid()`. Similarly, a thread can also get its thread-id by calling:

```
pthread_t
pthread_self();
```

Comparing Thread-ids

You should treat thread-ids as opaque objects. For example, it is perfectly reasonable for a system to implement a thread-id as a structured data type. For this reason it is not possible to compare thread-ids using C comparison operators. Instead, you can determine whether two thread-ids are equivalent by calling:

```
int
pthread_equal(pthread_t t1, pthread_t t2);
```

`pthread_equal()` returns a non-zero value if the two thread-ids reference the same thread. If they reference different threads, it returns zero.

Thread Attributes

Threads have a set of attributes that can be specified at the time the thread is created. Thread attributes are specified by setting up a thread attributes structure of type `pthread_attr_t`. The structure contains the values of various thread creation attributes, possibly including some that are not defined by POSIX and are specific to the underlying threads implementation. The members of the thread attributes structures are never referenced directly. Instead, POSIX defines a set of routines that are used to set up and retrieve the values of the various structure members. We'll see examples of this later.

A threads attributes structure is allocated by the program and then initialized by calling:

```
int
pthread_attr_init(pthread_attr_t *attr);
```

This initializes the attributes structure's thread attributes to the system's default values. Individual thread attributes are then set up by calling functions that get and set the value of specific attributes. Once an attributes structure has been set up, it can be repeatedly referenced in calls to `pthread_create()`. In many cases, a program creates several types of threads, with each type having the same attributes. The attributes structure for these types can be set up when the program starts and then used in thread creation as required. See Code Example 2-3 for an example of using thread attributes.

A threads attributes structure is deinitialized by calling:

```
int
pthread_attr_destroy(pthread_attr_t *attr);
```

This deletes any hidden storage associated with the threads attributes structure, allowing the program to free the attributes structure itself.

Detached Threads

Normally, when a thread exits, the threads system must remember at least the thread's completion status and thread-id in case the application joins with the thread some time later. When the application doesn't require the thread's completion status and doesn't need to know when a thread has exited, the application can create a *detached* thread. This simply means that the system will silently throw away the thread's completion status and thread-id when the thread exits. Detached threads cannot be the target of `pthread_join()`. If the thread-id of a detached thread is passed to `pthread_join()`, it will return with an error.

The `detachstate` attribute specifies whether the thread is to be detached. The `detachstate` attribute can have one of two values: `PTHREAD_CREATE_DETACHED` or `PTHREAD_CREATE_JOINABLE`. The default value for `detachstate` is `PTHREAD_CREATE_JOINABLE`. The `detachstate` attribute is manipulated by calling:

```
int
pthread_attr_setdetachstate(pthread_attr_t *attr, int detachstate);
```

```
int
pthread_attr_getdetachstate(const pthread_attr_t *attr,
    int *detachstatep);
```

pthread_attr_setdetachstate() sets the value of detachstate in *attr* and pthread_attr_getdetachstate() fetches it. Both return errors if something goes wrong. For example:

```
int
main()
{
    pthread_attr_t detached_attr;
    pthread_t t;
    void *detached_func(void *);

    pthread_attr_init(&detached_attr);
    pthread_attr_setdetachstate(&detached_attr,
        PTHREAD_CREATE_DETACHED);
    pthread_create(&t, &detached_attr, detached_func, NULL);
    ...
    return (0);
}
```

Code Example 2-3 Creating a Detached Thread

A running thread may also be detached if the program subsequently becomes uninterested in its results. For example, if a thread is doing a remote procedure call (see Figure 1-4 on page 3) and the program is no longer interested in the results, the program might simply detach the thread to let its resources be reclaimed when the remote procedure call completes and the thread exits. Threads may detached by calling:

```
int
pthread_detach(pthread_t thread);
```

which detaches a joinable thread. It returns an error if it cannot find the thread or if the thread is already detached.

Summary

Threads can be easily created and destroyed. They essentially behave like asynchronously running functions in Pthreads. Threads can be given a number of different attributes when they are created via the extensible attributes mechanism. We've seen one example already: detached threads that are used when the created thread does not return a value and other threads do not need to synchronize with the thread's termination.

Synchronization 3

This chapter gives an introduction to synchronizing threads so that they don't conflict while operating on memory and other process resources. We will discuss the basic synchronization primitives: mutual exclusion locks and condition variables, and give simple examples of using each. The chapter also describes the conditions under which synchronization must be used in order to correctly access memory. An interface that allows a package of functions to dynamically initialize themselves while potentially being called by multiple threads is also discussed.

Readers who are familiar with the basic threads interfaces may want to skip most of this chapter. However, you should still at least skim the section on "Data Races." In addition, you may not be familiar with the "Dynamic Package Initialization" interface. The synchronization primitives are a powerful facility that require some discipline. Be sure to read Chapter 6, "Synchronization Strategies," which covers some techniques to use when applying these primitives.

The Synchronization Problem

So far, we've seen how to create new threads and use them to do some independent activity, such a decompressing a picture. The independent activities can be coordinated using `pthread_create()` and `pthread_join()`. We also need the ability to have more than one thread cooperate on some activities, such as multiplying two matrices. This is difficult, as threads that run simultaneously can interfere with each other when they access the same memory. To illustrate this interference, consider the following code:

```
struct account {
    int checking;
    int savings;
};

void
savings_to_checking(struct account *ap, int amount)
{
    ap->savings -= amount;
    ap->checking += amount;
}
```

```
int
total_balance(struct account *ap)
{
    int balance;

    balance = ap->checking + ap->savings;
    return (balance);
}
```

Code Example 3-1 Example Requiring Synchronization

If Thread 1 calls `total_balance()` while Thread 2 calls `savings_to_checking()`, the following events can happen:

Thread 1	**Thread 2**
	`savings -= amount;`
`balance = checking + savings;`	
	`checking += amount;`
`return (balance);`	

Clearly, in this case the value returned by `total_balance()` will be less than the intended total amount of money in the account by `amount`.

The source of the problem is that more than one thread of control is trying to manipulate the same data at the same time. This is generally referred to as a *data race*[1]. A solution to this problem is to allow only one thread at a time to execute the code that manipulates the shared data. In the last example, only one thread should be allowed to execute either `total_balance()` or `savings_to_checking()` at any one time. This is called *mutual exclusion* as the presence of one thread in a section of code excludes all others. The section of code that may be executed by only one thread at a time is sometimes called the *critical section*. Mutual exclusion can be achieved by using a *mutex*. A mutex is a data structure of type `pthread_mutex_t` allocated in memory. There are two main operations on a mutex: locking and unlocking. For example:

```
struct account {
    int checking;
    int savings;
};
pthread_mutex_t lock = PTHREAD_MUTEX_INITIALIZER;
```

1. For a more precise definition of data races see "Data Races" on page 30.

```
void
savings_to_checking(struct account *ap, int amount)
{
    pthread_mutex_lock(&lock);
    ap->savings -= amount;
    ap->checking += amount;
    pthread_mutex_unlock(&lock);
}

int
total_balance(struct account *ap)
{
    int balance;

    pthread_mutex_lock(&lock);
    balance = ap->checking + ap->savings;
    pthread_mutex_unlock(&lock);
    return (balance);
}
```

Code Example 3-2 Using Mutexes to Protect a Critical Section

The function `pthread_mutex_lock()` "locks" the mutex. Other threads that attempt to lock the mutex will be forced to wait until it is unlocked. When the mutex is unlocked, by calling `pthread_mutex_unlock()`, one of the threads that was waiting for the lock to be released will lock the mutex and return from `pthread_mutex_lock()`.

Synchronization Variables

Mutexes are one example of a synchronization variable. There are several other types. All synchronization variable types are allocated in memory just like ordinary data structures. Once allocated, they must be initialized before use. The initialization can also set up attributes of the particular instance of the synchronization variable. Initialization can be done using an initialization function for that synchronization variable type. Certain synchronization variable types can be statically initialized to a specific initializer value when allocated and don't require further initialization. Statically initialized synchronization variables use default attributes. Synchronization variables must be explicitly destroyed before their memory is freed or reused. This allows any associated data structures to be cleaned up.

As illustrated in Code Example 3-2, a synchronization variable works by preventing threads from proceeding past a synchronization operation according to a policy set by the synchronization variable. When this happens the thread is said to be *blocked* on the synchronization variable. In the case of mutexes, the policy is to allow only one thread to proceed past `pthread_mutex_lock()` until the mutex is unlocked.

By default, the method used to block the thread is dependent on the thread scheduling discipline, the synchronization variable's attributes, and the implementation of the threads package. For example, blocking may cause the thread to test the synchronization variable continually until it is allowed to proceed (this is called spin blocking). Alternatively, it might put the thread on a queue associated with the synchronization variable and deschedule the thread (called sleeping), or it might use a combination of these two techniques (e.g., spin for awhile, then sleep). No matter which implementation technique is used, a thread's being blocked does not prevent other unblocked threads from running.

Similarly, when an operation on a synchronization variable allows one of the threads blocked on it to proceed, which of the waiting threads is allowed to proceed is also dependent on the thread scheduling discipline, the synchronization variable's attributes, and the implementation of the threads package. For example, if the thread scheduling and synchronization variable attributes permit a spin blocking technique, then the first spinning thread to check the synchronization variable will be the one allowed to proceed.

Thread synchronization variable attributes are set up using an attributes structure in a manner similar to thread attributes. Like thread attributes, the members of synchronization variables attributes structures are only referenced using a set of special routines. An attributes structure is allocated, initialized, set up, and then can be used repeatedly in synchronization variable initialization.

Mutual Exclusion

As we saw in Code Example 3-2, mutexes provide a "locking" mechanism that will allow only one thread at a time to execute a section of code. However, locking and unlocking are not the only operations; like all synchronization variables, they must be carefully initialized and destroyed.

Initializing and Destroying Mutexes

Mutexes are allocated like any other data structure. They can be defined as a static or automatic data structure of type `pthread_mutex_t`, as in:

```
pthread_mutex_t lock;
```

They can also be dynamically allocated:

```
pthread_mutex_t *mp;

mp = (pthread_mutex_t *) malloc(sizeof (pthread_mutex_t));
```

Once a mutex is allocated, it must be properly initialized before further use. One way to do this is to call:

```
int
pthread_mutex_init(pthread_mutex_t *mp,
    const pthread_mutexattr_t *attr);
```

The *attr* argument points to a data structure containing attributes to be used for the mutex. If *attr* is NULL, default attributes are used. `pthread_mutex_init()` can return an error if the implementation detects that an active mutex is being reinitialized.

Mutexes can also be statically initialized by setting them to a special value, as follows:

```
pthread_mutex_t mutex = PTHREAD_MUTEX_INITIALIZER;
```

This allows the mutex to be initialized without additional programming or execution overhead.

Mutexes are destroyed by calling:

```
int
pthread_mutex_destroy(pthread_mutex_t *mp);
```

The mutex that is destroyed must have been initialized either statically or by using `pthread_mutex_init()`. This should be done whenever the memory associated with the mutex is freed or reused. `pthread_mutex_destroy()` can return an error if the implementation detects that the mutex is being waited for.

Here's an example of how `pthread_mutex_init()` and `pthread_mutex_destroy()` are used:

```
struct data_record {
    pthread_mutex_t data_lock;
    char data[128];
};
```

```
/* Create and initialize a new data record. */
struct data_record *
new_record()
{
    struct data_record *recp;

    recp = (struct data_record *)malloc(sizeof (struct data_record));
    pthread_mutex_init(&recp->data_lock, NULL);
    return (recp);
}

/*
 * Delete a data record. The caller must ensure that no threads
 * are waiting to acquire this record's data_lock.
 */
void
delete_record(struct data_record *recp)
{
    pthread_mutex_destroy(&recp->data_lock);
    free((void *)recp);
}
```

Code Example 3-3   Using Mutexes

Mutex attributes

Mutex attributes structures are allocated by the program and are initialized by:

```
int
pthread_mutexattr_init(pthread_mutexattr_t *attr);
```

The specific mutex attributes are set by calling functions that modify the initialized `pthread_mutexattr_t`. Non-default attributes which are usually applied in more specialized situations will be covered later. Mutex attributes are destroyed by calling:

```
int
pthread_mutexattr_destroy(pthread_mutexattr_t *attr);
```

Locking and Unlocking Mutexes

Locking and unlocking are the primary mutex operations. A mutex is locked and unlocked via:

```
int
pthread_mutex_lock(pthread_mutex_t *mp);

int
pthread_mutex_unlock(pthread_mutex_t *mp);
```

The thread that locks the mutex is considered its *owner.* Only the thread that owns a mutex may unlock it. If the mutex is not locked or is not owned by the calling thread, calling `pthread_mutex_unlock()` may return an error. Both these functions can return errors if the mutex is not properly initialized either statically or dynamically.

Mutexes can be used to control access to many types of resources in addition to data in memory. For example:

```
void
write_strings(char *strings[], int nstrings)
{
    int i;
    static pthread_mutex_t file_lock = PTHREAD_MUTEX_INITIALIZER;

    pthread_mutex_lock(&file_lock);
    for (i = 0; i < nstrings; i++) {
        write(1, strings[i], strlen(strings[i]));
    }
    pthread_mutex_unlock(&file_lock);
}
```

Code Example 3-4   Using a Mutex to Synchronize Access to a File

In this case, access to a file is being controlled so that only one thread can write data to a file at any one time. Sequences of strings will not be interleaved on output when more than one thread calls `write_strings()`.

Sometimes it is convenient to attempt to lock a mutex without blocking. Usually this is done when blocking would cause a deadlock (see "Deadlock" on page 91). The function:

```
int
pthread_mutex_trylock(pthread_mutex_t *mp);
```

acquires the lock if it is free or returns an `EBUSY` error (and does not block) if the mutex is locked.

Data Races

Up to this point, we've been relying on an intuitive notion about what constitutes a data race. Threads programmers require a precise definition of data races in order to prevent them. Before we go into that, let's explore the ways threads can interact with memory on multiprocessors.

In older multiprocessors, access to memory is strictly multiplexed. This means that a processor executing program code reads or writes memory in the order specified by the code. All memory operations of all processors in the system appear to happen in some global order, though the operation histories of different processors are interleaved arbitrarily. The memory operations of such machines are called *sequentially consistent*. This is similar to the way threads operate on uniprocessors in the presence of timeslicing. In this case memory access by different threads is strictly interleaved on instruction boundaries, though the interleaving may occur at arbitrary times.

In a sequentially consistent environment, threads can synchronize using ordinary memory operations. For example, a producer thread and a consumer thread can synchronize access to a circular data buffer as follows:

```
#define next(x)     (((x) + 1) % NENT) /* NENT >= 2 */
int rdptr = 0;
int wrptr = 0;
data_t buf[NENT];
```

Thread 1: Producer

```
while (work_to_do) {
    buf[wrptr] = produce();
    while (next(wrptr) == rdptr)
        ;  /*buffer full, wait */
    wrptr = next(wrptr);
}
```

Thread 2: Consumer

```
while (work_to_do) {
    while (wrptr == rdptr)
        ;  /*buffer empty, wait*/
    consume(buf[rdptr]);
    rdptr = next(rdptr);
}
```

Code Example 3-5 Producer/Consumer Example for Sequentially Consistent Memory

In current multiprocessors, the ordering of memory operations issued by different processors in the system is relaxed for greater performance. So, if one processor stores values in location *A* and then location *B*, another processor that loads data from location *B* and then location *A* may see the new value of *B* but the old value of *A*. The memory operations of such machines are called *weakly ordered*. On these machines, the circular buffer technique shown in Code Example 3-5 fails because the consumer may see the new value of `wrptr` but the old value of the data in the buffer.

In such machines, full synchronization can be achieved only through the use of special instructions that force an order on memory operations. Most high level language compilers generate only ordinary memory operations to take advantage of the increased performance. Compilers usually cannot determine when memory operation order is important and generate the special ordering instructions. The programmer must correctly use synchronization primitives to ensure that modifications to a location in memory are ordered with respect to modifications and/or access to the same location in other threads.

Synchronization is still important even when accessing a single primitive variable (e.g., an integer). On machines where an integer or other primitive data type may not be aligned to the data bus width or may be larger than the data bus width, a single memory load may require multiple memory cycles. This means that loading the value of a primitive data type may return some bits that represent an old value while other bits represent a newer value. On some processor architectures, primitive variable access is "atomic" and this cannot happen (for example, SPARC®), but portable programs can't rely on this. For example:

```
pthread_mutex_t count_mutex;
int count;

void
increment_count()
{
    pthread_mutex_lock(&count_mutex);
    count = count + 1;
    pthread_mutex_unlock(&count_mutex);
}

int
get_count()
{
    int c;

    pthread_mutex_lock(&count_mutex);
    c = count;
    pthread_mutex_unlock(&count_mutex);
    return (c);
}
```

Code Example 3-6 Using a Mutex to Ensure Atomic Variable Access

The two functions in the example use the mutex for different purposes. `increment_count()` uses the mutex simply to ensure that `count` is incremented *atomically*. In other words, if threads call `increment_count()` simultaneously, each one will begin and end the increment operation without other threads being allowed to access intermediate values, as we saw in "Controlling Concurrency" on page 10. `get_count()` uses the mutex to guarantee that memory is synchronized when it refers to `count`, i.e. the entire current value of `count` will be fetched from memory, not mixed old data and new data (e.g., if two independent bus operations were required to load the value of `count`). In both cases, the compilation system must recognize that it cannot optimize the code by moving access to global variables, like `count`, from between the calls to `pthread_mutex_lock()` or `pthread_mutex_unlock()`. However, it may do code optimization between these calls.

You can see from the above discussion that unsynchronized simultaneous access to memory can cause problems. Let's carefully define the situation that causes these problems to see how they might be avoided.

Definition of a data race

> A program has a data race if it is possible for a thread to modify an addressable location at the same time that another thread is accessing the same location.

As we've seen, POSIX provides thread synchronizing routines that threads programmers use to prevent simultaneous access.

The POSIX Memory Model

POSIX threads can access all addressable locations in a process. This includes all allocated data, whether it is statically allocated, dynamically allocated (e.g., by `malloc()`) or automatically allocated as part of a routine's stack frame. However, memory that is not addressable, such as variables that are allocated in registers, cannot be portably shared among threads.

Table 3-1 shows the list of POSIX functions that ensure that the order of memory operations is preserved with respect to the execution of the function[2]. The list contains all the POSIX synchronization primitives and several other system routines.

Table 3-1 POSIX Functions That Synchronize Memory with Respect to Threads

`fork()`	`pthread_cond_signal()`	`sem_post()`
`pthread_create()`	`pthread_cond_broadcast()`	`sem_trywait()`
`pthread_join()`	`pthread_mutex_lock()`	`sem_wait()`
`pthread_cond_wait()`	`pthread_mutex_trylock()`	`wait()`
`pthread_cond_timedwait()`	`pthread_mutex_unlock()`	`waitpid()`

2. For a list of additional UNIX International and SVR4 functions that have this property, see "Avoiding Data Races" on page 377.

A portable POSIX program must ensure that it is not possible for a thread to write to a particular location at the same time that another thread is either reading or writing it. A program does this by using the blocking, thread creation, or thread destruction characteristics of the functions listed in Table 3-1. Such programs are said to be *data race free*. Portable programs cannot rely on modifications to memory being observed by other threads in the order written in the program.

When more than one thread reads a location in memory, it is not a data race. Variables that are statically initialized and are not subsequently modified may be read by multiple threads without synchronization. In general, no further synchronization is required as long as any threads modifying a particular memory location are prevented (by using the functions in Table 3-1) from executing at the same time as the threads that are only reading that location. For example, memory locations that are dynamically initialized, and are not subsequently modified, before any of the reading threads are created require no further synchronization for access.

Optimizing compilers sometimes reorder memory accesses to achieve a gain in performance. However, such compilers also avoid changing the order of access to addressable locations with respect to calls to the routines in Table 3-1 so the programmer can reliably control when memory is modified with respect to other threads. Keep in mind that the compiler need not retain the program order of memory operations if there are no intervening calls to synchronization routines (and the accesses are not to locations marked with the type-qualifier `volatile`; see "Memory model" on page 265).

There are other functions than those listed in Table 3-1 which may allow threads to affect each other's execution, such as sending data over a pipe or sending and receiving a signal. However, a portable program can only rely on the functions listed in the table to synchronize addressable memory with respect to threads. On multiprocessors that are not sequentially consistent, these routines execute the appropriate special memory synchronization instructions (see "Shared Memory Multiprocessors" on page 263).

Condition Variables

Threads must be able to wait for other threads to complete an activity. For example, a thread might wait for a buffer to be filled by another thread. Mutexes alone can't do this; they can only ensure serialization of an activity. A synchronization variable called a condition variable solves this problem. Condition variables are used in conjunction with mutexes, allowing a thread to wait until an arbitrary condition has occurred. For example, a condition variable can allow a thread to wait until an element is added to a list rather than simply ensuring that adding or deleting items from a list is done atomically.

There are two basic operations on a condition variable: signalling and waiting for it to be signalled. First, one or more threads wait on a condition variable. Then, when a condition variable is signalled, one or all of the threads (as specified by the signaller) waiting for the condition variable are allowed to proceed. A signal on a condition variable that does not have any waiting threads is not remembered. The next thread that waits on the condition variable will block until the condition variable is again signalled. In other words, condition variables are "stateless."

Initializing and Destroying Condition Variables

Like a mutex, a condition variable can be defined as a static or automatic data structure, or it can be dynamically allocated and initialized. The data type for a condition variable is `pthread_cond_t`. Here's an example definition:

```
pthread_cond_t cond;
```

Condition variables are dynamically initialized by calling:

```
int
pthread_cond_init(pthread_cond_t *cond,
    const pthread_condattr_t *attr);
```

The *attr* argument points to a data structure containing attributes to be used for the condition variable. If *attr* is `NULL`, default attributes are used. `pthread_cond_init()` can return an error if the implementation detects that a condition variable is being reinitialized before it has been destroyed.

Condition variables may also be statically initialized by setting them to a special value, as follows:

```
pthread_cond_t cond = PTHREAD_COND_INITIALIZER;
```

Condition variables are destroyed by:

```
int
pthread_cond_destroy(pthread_cond_t *cond);
```

The condition variable that is destroyed must have been initialized. This should be done whenever the memory associated with the condition variable is freed or reused. `pthread_cond_destroy()` can return an error if the implementation detects that the condition variable is being waited for.

Condition attributes structures are allocated by the program and are initialized by:

```
int
pthread_condattr_init(pthread_condattr_t *attr);
```

The specific condition variable attributes are set by calling functions that modify the initialized `pthread_condattr_t`. Non-default attributes usually apply in more specialized situations and will be covered later.

Waiting for and Signalling Conditions

As we said, the two main operations on condition variables are waiting and signalling. These operations are done by calling:

```
int
pthread_cond_wait(pthread_cond_t *cond, pthread_mutex_t *mutex);

int
pthread_cond_signal(pthread_cond_t *cond);

int
pthread_cond_broadcast(pthread_cond_t *cond);
```

`pthread_cond_wait()` blocks the calling thread from proceeding until the condition variable is signaled. It unlocks the associated mutex before blocking the calling thread and locks it before returning after the condition is signalled via `pthread_cond_signal()` or `pthread_cond_broadcast()`. The action of unlocking the mutex and blocking is atomic; that is, another thread cannot acquire the mutex and signal the condition between the time the mutex is released and the calling thread blocks. `pthread_cond_broadcast()` unblocks all of the threads blocked on the condition variable. `pthread_cond_signal()` causes at least one of the threads blocked on the condition variable to become unblocked.

Notice that an implementation of `pthread_cond_signal()` is allowed to wake up more than one thread. Pthreads specified this relaxed semantic because requiring `pthread_cond_signal()` to wake up exactly one thread can be expensive to implement on multiprocessors. However, the extra wake-ups should happen rarely in most implementations.

Using Condition Variables

Code Example 3-7 shows an implementation of a first-in, first-out (FIFO) queue for passing data pointers. The queue is implemented by a fixed size circular buffer. In this example, the thread retrieving data from the queue must wait until there is data in the queue, and the thread that enters new data into the queue must wait until some data is removed if the queue is currently full. The code uses two condition variables, `notempty` and `notfull`, to represent these two logical conditions.

Code Example 3-7 also illustrates a different style of using mutexes than was shown in Code Example 3-2. Here, a different mutex is used for each circular buffer, while Code Example 3-2 uses a single mutex that is shared by all accounts. Another way of thinking about it is that in Code Example 3-2 the mutex protects the code, and in Code Example 3-7 the mutexes protect consistent sets of data. In Code Example 3-2, threads would have to wait to get access to any account, while in Code Example 3-7, threads would wait only if they are accessing the same circular buffer. The basic locking strategies are explained in Chapter 6, "Synchronization Strategies."

```
#define QSIZE  10                  /* number of pointers in the queue */
typedef struct {
    pthread_mutex_t buf_lock;      /* lock the structure */
    int start_idx;                 /* start of valid data */
    int num_full;                  /* # of full locations */
    pthread_cond_t notfull;        /* full -> not full condition */
    pthread_cond_t notempty;       /* empty -> notempty condition */
    void *data[QSIZE];             /* Circular buffer of pointers */
} circ_buf_t;

/*
 * new_cb() creates and initializes a new circular buffer.
 */
circ_buf_t *
new_cb()
{
    circ_buf_t *cbp;

    cbp = (circ_buf_t *) malloc(sizeof (circ_buf_t));
    if (cbp == NULL)
        return (NULL);
    pthread_mutex_init(&cbp->buf_lock, NULL);
    pthread_cond_init(&cbp->notfull, NULL);
    pthread_cond_init(&cbp->notempty, NULL);
    cbp->start_idx = 0;
    cbp->num_full = 0;
    return (cbp);
}
```

```
/*
 * delete_cb() frees a circular buffer.
 */
void
delete_cb(circ_buf_t *cbp)
{
    pthread_mutex_destroy(&cbp->buf_lock);
    pthread_cond_destroy(&cbp->notfull);
    pthread_cond_destroy(&cbp->notempty);
    free(cbp);
}

/*
 * put_cb_data() puts new data on the queue.
 * If the queue is full, it waits until there is room.
 */
void
put_cb_data(circ_buf_t *cbp, void *data)
{
    pthread_mutex_lock(&cbp->buf_lock);
    /* wait while the buffer is full */
    while (cbp->num_full == QSIZE)
        pthread_cond_wait(&cbp->notfull, &cbp->buf_lock);
    cbp->data[(cbp->start_idx + cbp->num_full) % QSIZE] = data;
    cbp->num_full += 1;
    /* let a waiting reader know there's data */
    /* exercise: can cond_signal be moved after unlock? see text */
    pthread_cond_signal(&cbp->notempty);
    pthread_mutex_unlock(&cbp->buf_lock);
}
```

```
/*
 * get_cb_data() gets the oldest data in the circular buffer.
 * If there is none, it waits until new data appears.
 */
void *
get_cb_data(circ_buf_t *cbp)
{
    void *data;

    pthread_mutex_lock(&cbp->buf_lock);
    /* wait while there's nothing in the buffer */
    while (cbp->num_full == 0)
        pthread_cond_wait(&cbp->notempty, &cbp->buf_lock);
    data = cbp->data[cbp->start_idx];
    cbp->start_idx = (cbp->start_idx + 1) % QSIZE;
    cbp->num_full -= 1;
    /* let a waiting writer know there's room */
    /* exercise: can cond_signal be moved after unlock? see text */
    pthread_cond_signal(&cbp->notfull);
    pthread_mutex_unlock(&cbp->buf_lock);
    return (data);
}
```

Code Example 3-7 FIFO Queue Using Circular Buffers

In typical use, an expression that represents a logical condition is evaluated under the protection of a mutex. If the condition expression is true, the thread blocks on the condition variable, which releases the mutex. Some time later, another thread acquires the mutex and makes a change that may cause the condition expression to change, in which case it signals the condition variable. This causes at least one of the threads waiting on the condition (or all, if the signalling thread uses `pthread_cond_broadcast()`) to unblock and to relock the mutex. Since reacquiring the mutex can be blocked by other threads that get the mutex and potentially change the result of the condition expression, the condition expression that caused the wait must be reevaluated when `pthread_cond_wait()` returns. Also, even `pthread_cond_signal()` is allowed to wake up more than one thread, so the condition must be reevaluated to make sure it wasn't changed by another awakened thread. In other words, `pthread_cond_wait()` must be used in a loop, so most instances of waiting for a condition variable look like the following example.

```
...
pthread_mutex_lock(&mutex);
/* condition can't change after lock is acquired */
while (condition expression) {     /* must loop to retest condition */
    /* mutex is released during wait */
    pthread_cond_wait(&condvar, &mutex);
    /* mutex is reacquired at this point */
}
... do whatever needs to be done assuming condition is true
pthread_mutex_unlock(&mutex);
...
```

Code Example 3-8 Code for a Typical Condition Wait

In Code Example 3-7, there are several logical conditions and condition expressions associated with them. The implementation associated a separate condition variable with each of these conditions, as shown in Table 3-2.

Table 3-2 Conditions in Code Example 3-7

Condition	Expression	Condition Variable
FIFO queue is empty	`cbp->num_full == 0`	`cbp->notempty`
FIFO queue is full	`cbp->num_full == QSIZE`	`cbp->notfull`

You need not use a separate condition variable for each condition. It is possible to share a condition variable across many conditions, though this results in extra wake-ups from `pthread_cond_wait()`. A condition variable can be associated with only one mutex at any one time, so all such condition expressions must be evaluated under the same mutex. Also, there is not much incentive to share conditions, as they are relatively lightweight.

It's not critical that the condition expression actually change before the condition is signalled while the mutex protects the condition expression. For example, the following two code segments are equivalent:

```
Segment 1:
    ...
    pthread_mutex_lock(&mutex);
    ... change memory such that the condition expression might change
    pthread_cond_signal(&cond);/* or pthread_cond_broadcast() */
    pthread_mutex_unlock(&mutex);
    ...
```

```
Segment 2:
    ...
    pthread_mutex_lock(&mutex);
    pthread_cond_signal(&cond);/* or pthread_cond_broadcast() */
    ... change memory such that the condition expression might change
    pthread_mutex_unlock(&mutex);
    ...
```

In segment 2, the result of the condition expression is changed after the condition is signalled. This is not a problem. The mutex protects the condition expression from being reevaluated by a thread that was awakened by the signal until the mutex is released. This is because the awakened thread must first reacquire the mutex (in `pthread_cond_wait()`).

Signalling the condition variable after the condition expression has been changed under the mutex is also correct:

```
Segment 3:
    ...
    pthread_mutex_lock(&mutex);
    ... change memory such that the condition expression might change
    pthread_mutex_unlock(&mutex);
    pthread_cond_signal(&cond);/* or pthread_cond_broadcast() */
    ...
```

Signalling the condition variable after the condition has been changed under the mutex has a performance benefit: any thread waking up as a result of the condition variable being signalled will likely acquire the mutex. Signaling the condition while holding the mutex means that if a waiting thread wakes up immediately it will always block on the mutex until the signalling thread releases it. In addition, this technique has the added benefit of shortening the critical section, which shortens the time that other threads are locked out. As an exercise, try moving the condition variable signalling in the `put_cb_data()` and `get_cb_data()` routines in Code Example 3-7 until after the mutex is released.

It is important to understand that the condition variable must either be signalled while the mutex is held or *after* the result of the condition expression is changed while holding the mutex. Failing to acquire the mutex before signalling can lead to *lost wake-up* bugs. A lost wake-up occurs when a thread calls `pthread_cond_signal()` or `pthread_cond_broadcast()` when another thread is between the test of the condition and the call to `pthread_cond_wait()`.

Consider the following situation:

Thread 1 / **Thread 2**

```
Thread 1                             Thread 2
                                     pthread_mutex_lock(&mutex);
                                     while (condition == 0)
condition = 1;
pthread_cond_signal(&cond);
                                         pthread_cond_wait(&cond);
                                         ... waits forever
```

In this case, the thread has not begun waiting on the condition variable and will miss the signal. When the thread calls `pthread_cond_wait()` it may never wake up since the signal already happened.

Changing the condition under the mutex before signalling does not cause a lost wake-up. The mutex ensures that the testing thread will either sleep or see the new condition (in which case the signal is ignored) as shown:

```
Thread 1                             Thread 2
pthread_mutex_lock(&mutex);
condition = 1;
pthread_mutex_unlock(&mutex);
                                     pthread_mutex_lock(&mutex);
                                     while (condition == 0)
                                     ... condition is true
                                     pthread_mutex_unlock(&mutex);
pthread_cond_signal(&cond);
```

```
Thread 1                             Thread 2
                                     pthread_mutex_lock(&mutex);
                                     while (condition == 0)
                                         pthread_cond_wait(&cond);
pthread_mutex_lock(&mutex);
condition = 1;
pthread_mutex_unlock(&mutex);
pthread_cond_signal(&cond);              ... condition wait returns
                                     while (condition == 0)
                                     ... condition is true
                                     pthread_mutex_unlock(&mutex);
```

Figure 3-1 Signalling Condition after Releasing Mutex

Using pthread_cond_broadcast()

Since pthread_cond_broadcast() causes all threads blocked on the condition to contend again for the mutex, it should be used only in situations where unblocking all the waiting threads is required. For example, you can use pthread_cond_broadcast() to allow threads to contend for variable amounts of resources when the resources are freed.

```
pthread_mutex_t rsrc_lock = PTHREAD_MUTEX_INITIALIZER;
pthread_cond_t rsrc_add = PTHREAD_COND_INITIALIZER;
unsigned int resources, waiting;

void
get_resources(int amount)
{
    pthread_mutex_lock(&rsrc_lock);
    while (resources < amount) {
        waiting++;
        pthread_cond_wait(&rsrc_add, &rsrc_lock);
    }
    resources -= amount;
    pthread_mutex_unlock(&rsrc_lock);
}

void
add_resources(int amount)
{
    pthread_mutex_lock(&rsrc_lock);
    resources += amount;
    if (waiting > 0) {
        waiting = 0;
        pthread_cond_broadcast(&rsrc_add);
    }
    pthread_mutex_unlock(&rsrc_lock);
}
```

Code Example 3-9 Condition Variable Broadcast

Note that in add_resources(), it does not matter whether resources is updated first or pthread_cond_broadcast() is called first inside the mutex.

Waiting with time-outs

Sometimes it is convenient to set a time limit on waiting for a condition to become true. A timed wait could be achieved by using timer_settime() (or setitimer() in UNIX International or BSD) and signal handlers (see Chapter 9, "Signals"), but it is much more convenient to use a timed condition wait:

```
int
pthread_cond_timedwait(pthread_cond_t *cond,
    pthread_mutex_t *mutex,
    const struct timespec *abstime);
```

`pthread_cond_timedwait()` blocks until the condition is signaled or until the time of day specified by *abstime* has passed. If the time limit is passed, `pthread_cond_timedwait()` returns an `ETIMEDOUT` error. The time-out is specified as an absolute time of day (instead of a relative time interval) so the condition can be retested efficiently without recomputing the time-out value, as shown in Code Example 3-10.

```
#define MYTIMEOUT 10

struct timespec to;
pthread_mutex_t m;
pthread_cond_t c;
int err;

pthread_mutex_lock(&m);
to.tv_sec = time(NULL) + MYTIMEOUT;
to.tv_nsec = 0;
while (condition == FALSE) {
    err = pthread_cond_timedwait(&c, &m, &to);
    if (err == ETIMEDOUT) {
        /* time-out do something */
        break;
    }
}
pthread_mutex_unlock(&m);
```

Code Example 3-10 Condition Wait with Time-out

Dynamic Package Initialization

Implementors of libraries or other "packages" of related routines sometimes initialize internal data structures the first time a package routine is called rather than requiring the caller to explicitly call an initialization routine before any other package routine. For example, a package may open a package database file the first time a package routine is called. This situation takes a bit of thought to implement as the routines can be entered by several threads simultaneously. This problem can be solved using statically initialized mutexes, but it is such a common synchronization problem that POSIX provides a special interface for it[3]. Consider the following code:

3. Older drafts of the Pthreads standard did not allow static initialization of mutexes. This made the dynamic package initialization interface the only way to accomplish reliable initialization. The current standard allows static initialization and so the dynamic package initialization interface is now a bit redundant. It remains for convenience and for historical reasons.

```
static int initialized = 0;
static pthread_mutex_t init_lock = PTHREAD_MUTEX_INITIALIZER;

static void
pkg_init_func(void)
{
    /* initialize the package */
}

pkg_func1()
{
    pthread_mutex_lock(&init_lock);
    if (initialized == 0) {
        initialized = 1;
        pkg_init_func();
    }
    pthread_mutex_unlock(&init_lock);
    ... remainder of pkg_func1
}

pkg_func2()
{
    pthread_mutex_lock(&init_lock);
    if (initialized == 0) {
        initialized = 1;
        pkg_init_func();
    }
    pthread_mutex_unlock(&init_lock);
    ... remainder of pkg_func2
}
```

Code Example 3-11 Dynamic Package Initialization Using Mutexes

The `init_lock` mutex protects access to `initialized` and prevents `pkg_init_func()` from being entered more than once when a package function is simultaneously entered. It is a common mistake to attempt to only acquire the mutex the first time, as follows:

```
/* Warning: this code has a bug */
if (initialized == 0) {    /* ERROR! data race */
    pthread_mutex_lock(&init_lock);
    pkg_init_func();
    initialized = 1;
    pthread_mutex_unlock(&init_lock);
}
```

This is a data race: the testing of `initialized` may be concurrent with its modification as the lock is not held during the testing. If two threads were to call a package routine simultaneously, they could both see `initialized == 0` and then both call `pkg_init_func()` serially, due to the mutex.

Dynamic initialization can be simplified by using:

```
pthread_once_t once_control = PTHREAD_ONCE_INIT;

int
pthread_once(pthread_once_t *once_control,
    void (*init_routine)(void));
```

`pthread_once()` calls *`init_routine()`* only once for a given *`once_control`* variable. The *`once_control`* variable must be non-local (i.e., statically allocated or global) and must be initialized to `PTHREAD_ONCE_INIT`.

Using `pthread_once()`, the package entry routine in Code Example 3-11 can be simplified as shown in Code Example 3-12.

```
static pthread_once_t pkg_once = PTHREAD_ONCE_INIT;

pkg_func1()
{
    pthread_once(&pkg_once, pkg_init_func);
    ... remainder of pkg_func1
}
```

Code Example 3-12 Dynamic Package Initialization Using `pthread_once()`

Notice that the self-initialization synchronization is now isolated in the single call to `pthread_once()`.

Summary

Up to this point you've been introduced to the basic routines for creating and synchronizing threads. These are the fundamental tools in programming with threads. You've also seen how these primitives must be used to avoid having the threads you create interfere with each other. You're almost to the point where you can begin writing a fairly wide variety of threads programs. However, there are a couple of things left to cover before you jump in, such as how the system libraries and process resources interact with threads. We'll cover these issues in the next two chapters.

Using Libraries in Multithreaded Programs

4 

This chapter explains how system calls and other libraries are used in multithreaded programs. Threads can affect both the semantics and the interfaces of function packages, and packages can have restrictions on how processes with multiple threads are allowed to use the package. Routines with no restrictions are said to be *thread-safe*. The chapter includes a taxonomy of the common types of restrictions placed on multithreaded programs and the common interface modifications used to accommodate multithreaded programs.

Readers who are familiar with the basic threads interfaces should skim the chapter to make sure they understand the thread-safety issues.

System Calls

Threads execute system calls the same way (single-threaded) processes do. The kernel handles these requests independently and with the same atomicity guarantees as system calls issued by independent processes. For example, if one thread extends a file with a `write()` system call, another thread that detects the new end of file will also be able to read the new data.

System calls that block (e.g., `wait()`, `read()`, and `open()`) only block the thread that issued the call.

`errno`

Each thread has its own independent version of the `errno` variable. This allows different threads to make system calls that may change the value of `errno` without interfering with each other. Source code must include:

```
#include <errno.h>
```

in order to access the thread-private `errno` value.

Of course, since threads share the process they can make calls that change user or kernel state in a way that affects each other. For example, there is only one user ID for each process that all threads share. Changing it affects the credentials of system calls issued by any thread in the process. The kernel maintains a consistent system and process state in the presence of potentially simultaneous system calls, but the threads within a process must still cooperate to use the state properly.

Thread-Safe Functions

A function or set of functions is said to be thread-safe (also multithread-safe or MT-safe), or reentrant[1] when the functions may be called by more than one thread at a time without requiring any other action on the caller's part. The functions synchronize among themselves, as appropriate, keeping any synchronization hidden from the caller. Good examples are the memory allocation functions in `libc`, `malloc()` and `free()`. These functions may be freely called by many threads simultaneously. As usual, it is an error to free the same memory twice: for example, by calling `free()` on the same memory in two different threads simultaneously.

Thread-safe functions are not required to protect access to unstructured memory under the control of the caller. For example, two threads calling the memory copy function `memcpy()` with an overlapping destination area simultaneously creates a data race. In this case, the caller must synchronize to ensure that only one `memcpy()` or any other access is active for any destination location. Another example of a data race would be when the source region in a call to `memcpy()` is modified by another thread (via `memcpy()` or otherwise) while the copy is still in progress.

Thread-safe functions synchronize to protect the data pointed to by references to "objects" manipulated by a set of functions and whose structure is opaque to the caller (i.e., cannot legally be manipulated by the caller)[2]. A good example of this is the `FILE` "object" in `stdio`. Functions like `fprintf()` may be called simultaneously on the same `FILE` without synchronization.

Serializability

In most cases, calls to thread-safe functions behave "atomically" as viewed by the caller. In other words, simultaneous calls behave as if they were executed in some (arbitrary) serial order. For example, if thread *A* calls `malloc((size_t) 1)` and

1. A function can be "reentered" via several mechanisms: being called by more than one thread, being called by an asynchronous signal handler that interrupts the function, or by direct or indirect recursion. The term "thread-safe" is used when reentrance with respect to multiple simultaneous calls by different threads is supported. Similarly, a function that is reentrant with respect to asynchronous signals is "async-safe" (see "Async-Safe Functions" on page 164).

2. We use the term "object" to refer to any data structure that is manipulated by a set of functions and whose structure is opaque to callers of the set of functions, since C does not directly support objects like C++ does. For C++ this notion corresponds to language supported objects as well as C-style ones.

thread *B* calls `malloc((size_t) 2)` simultaneously (without restriction by synchronization), the calls will either behave as if `malloc((size_t) 1)` was called and returned and then `malloc((size_t) 2)` was called and returned, or it will behave as if the functions were called and returned in the opposite order. This property is called *serializability*.

However, thread-safe functions are not required to be serializable. A function that adds two items to a list may add each item individually, allowing other additions to interleave. For example, a call that adds items *A* and *B* and another call that adds items *C* and *D* may cause the list to have the new items in the order *A,C,B,D*. This ordering is not possible in any serial execution of the call to add two items. There can be other, more subtle effects such as simultaneous calls causing a different flushing of cached data, or sampling a file at different times. The documentation of a thread-safe function should specify any behaviors that are not serializable.

Restrictions on Concurrency

Pure functions, such as `sin()`, that access no global data or access only read-only global data or other state (e.g., files) are trivially thread-safe. Such functions can be executed by any number of threads simultaneously. Functions that do modify global state must be made thread-safe at the cost of some potential concurrency. In other words, these functions must use synchronization or the other functions listed in Table 3-1 on page 32 to restrict the concurrent execution of the calling threads and ensure there are no data races (see "Data Races" on page 30) and the function works properly. In other words, a thread that calls such a function may be momentarily blocked though the caller will be oblivious to it.

In most cases, such restrictions on concurrency are minor. However, in some cases, the restrictions are severe enough that the user of the function must be cognizant of the limitation. For example, a Remote Procedure Call (RPC) library may allow only one call at a time to be outstanding to each host, while simultaneous calls to different hosts are allowed to proceed concurrently. If the limitation is severe, as in the RPC example, it will usually be described in the function's documentation.

Note – Most of the manual pages supplied in Solaris note whether the function is thread-safe. Solaris uses the term "MT-safe" to denote thread-safety.

POSIX Thread-Safe Functions

POSIX defines almost all its interfaces to be thread-safe. This includes the interfaces in the C language standard. There are two exceptions: functions that have problems in being made thread-safe inherent in their interfaces, and functions designed to be explicitly locked. We'll cover the former first; explicitly locked functions will be covered later.

A good example of a function interface that has inherent thread-safety problems is `getpwuid()` (get password file entry for a user). `getpwuid()` returns a pointer to a data structure that is allocated in a static, global buffer area used to hold several entries read in from a file. Returning a pointer to data in the buffer area is safe and efficient when there is only one thread of control. When more than one thread is allowed to call such an interface, the data in the buffer may be overwritten while another thread is still referencing it. POSIX (and UNIX International) have defined alternative interfaces for these functions. The alternatives have the name of the original function with "`_r`" (for reentrant[3]) appended, as shown in Table 4-1. The original functions are not thread-safe. See Appendix C, "Manual Pages," for more information on these interfaces.

Table 4-1 POSIX Thread-Safe Functions

`asctime_r()`	`getpwnam_r()`	`readdir_r()`
`ctime_r()`	`getpwuid_r()`	`strtok_r()`
`getgrgid_r()`	`gmtime_r()`	`ttyname_r()`
`getgrnam_r()`	`localtime_r()`	
`getlogin_r()`	`rand_r()`	

In some cases, an older interface can be made thread-safe with restrictions on the values of its arguments. In POSIX the functions `ctermid()` and `tmpnam()` may not be called with a `NULL` argument when used by more than one thread (i.e., the caller must pass in a data area instead of using the static buffer). All other interfaces defined by POSIX and the C standard are thread-safe (see [IEEE 95A] and [Kernighan 88]).

Note – The thread-safe functions in Table 4-1 are an optional feature in POSIX. Threads are supported if the `_POSIX_THREAD_SAFE_FUNCTIONS` macro is defined in `<unistd.h>`. This can be tested dynamically by calling `sysconf()` using the `_SC_THREAD_SAFE_FUNCTIONS` macro from `<unistd.h>` as an argument. `sysconf()` returns `-1` if the feature is not supported. `_POSIX_THREAD_SAFE_FUNCTIONS` is always defined when `_POSIX_THREADS` is defined (i.e., for Pthreads).

---

3. The term "reentrant" rather than "thread-safe" was used early in the POSIX threads standardization process and so the "`_r`" convention remains.

While the POSIX functions are either thread-safe or have thread-safe versions, this is not quite enough information to use all of them effectively. Let's look at some specific functions.

Memory Allocation

The memory allocation routines `malloc()`, `calloc()`, and `realloc()` are thread-safe and allocate memory from a heap shared by all the threads in the process. For example, it is perfectly legal for a thread to free memory allocated by a different thread.

`stdio`

The standard I/O functions are thread-safe. Simultaneous calls on the same `FILE` are serialized. For example:

Thread 1	Thread 2
`printf("Now is the time\n");`	`printf("for all good people\n");`

will print either:

```
Now is the time
for all good people
```

or:

```
for all good people
Now is the time
```

on the standard output, but not some intermingling of the two phrases.

A series of calls to `stdio` functions can be made "atomic" by using the following functions:

```
void
flockfile(FILE *file);

int
ftrylockfile(FILE *file);

void
funlockfile(FILE *file);
```

These calls behave in a manner similar to mutexes. They act on locks internal to `stdio` and used by other `stdio` functions. For example:

Thread 1

```
flockfile(stdout);
printf("Brian Kernighan\n");
printf("Dennis Ritchie\n");
funlockfile(stdout);
```

Thread 2

```
printf("Bill Joy\n");
```

will print either:

```
Brian Kernighan
Dennis Ritchie
Bill Joy
```

or

```
Bill Joy
Brian Kernighan
Dennis Ritchie
```

on the standard output, but not some intermingling of the two sets of names. Calls to `flockfile()` and `funlockfile()` must "bracket." In other words the thread that called `flockfile()` on a particular `FILE` must also be the one that calls `funlockfile()`.

Note – You must ensure that `FILE`s are always locked in the same order (e.g., `stdin` before `stdout`) when more than one `FILE` is locked at the same time (see "Lock Ordering" on page 91). POSIX does not mandate a lock ordering, so use the following convention: order the locking of `FILE`s by their associated file descriptor, locking the lowest first.

C++ `iostream` Library

Warning – Currently POSIX does not define any interfaces specific to C++. The following describes what is available in the Solaris/SunPro™ environment[4].

The C++ language provides a technique, called scoped locking, that allows locks to be acquired and released automatically whenever a lexical scope is entered or exited (see "Scoped Locking" on page 96). The C++ `iostream` library supports

4. SPARCompiler™ C++ Language System version 4.0

this technique by providing a special I/O stream locker class, `stream_locker`, that can be used instead of explicit calls to locking functions like `flockfile()` and `funlockfile()`. As show in Code Example 4-1, an instance of `stream_locker` is created in an enclosing lexical scope of a series of operations on an I/O stream. The I/O stream is locked when the instance is created. When the scope is exited by exception, `return`, `break`, `goto`, or simply executing to the end of the scope, the instance of `stream_locker` is destroyed and the I/O stream lock is automatically released.

```
#include <iostream.h>

void
a(int flag)
{
    stream_locker lockp(cout);

    cout << func1() << func2();
    if (flag)
        return;
    cout << func3();
}
```

Code Example 4-1 Using the `stream_locker` *Class*

This will keep the output of `func1()`, `func2()`, and `func3()` together if the entire function is executed and will properly release the lock if any of the called functions throw an exception or if the `a()` returns in the middle of the locked scope.

The public declaration of `stream_locker` is shown in Code Example 4-2. The `stream_locker` class also provides two additional operations, `lock()` and `unlock()`, that explicitly acquire and release the stream lock. Notice that the actual declaration of the constructor includes a flag that defers locking so that the critical section is protected by the use of `lock()` and `unlock()`.

```
class stream_locker {
public:
    enum lock_choice { lock_defer=0, lock_now=1 };
    stream_locker(iostream& obj, lock_choice lock_flag=lock_now);
    stream_locker(iostream* ptr, lock_choice lock_flag=lock_now);
    ~stream_locker();
    void lock();
    void unlock();
}
```

Code Example 4-2 `stream_locker` *Public Declaration*[5]

Explicitly Locked Functions

Synchronization imposes some overhead. This overhead can add up for functions that are called often in an inner loop. In these cases it may be desirable for the library to provide explicit locking primitives that allow the caller to acquire any required locks outside the inner loop. POSIX has defined explicitly locked versions of the stdio functions putc(), putchar(), getc(), and getchar() for this reason. The explicitly locked functions are:

```
int
getc_unlocked(FILE *file);

int
getchar_unlocked(void);

int
putc_unlocked(int c, FILE *file);

int
putchar_unlocked(int c);
```

Calls to these functions must be bracketed by calls to flockfile() and funlockfile() for the FILE to be operated on. For example:

```
int i;
char buf[1024];
...
flockfile(stdout);
for (i = 0; i < sizeof(buf); i++) {
    putc_unlocked(buf[i], stdout);
}
funlockfile(stdout);
```

Code Example 4-3 *Using* putc_unlocked()

Thread-Unsafe Functions

In general, thread-unsafe functions provide no guarantees about safety in the presence of more than one thread. The safest approach is to call thread-unsafe functions only from the initial thread (i.e., the thread that called main()).

5. This is a simplified version. Some of the intermediate classes have been deleted.

Warning – It may seem that you can use your own locking when using thread-unsafe functions, and thus be able to call them from different threads, albeit only one at a time. However, thread-unsafe functions can share unknown global state with any other thread-unsafe functions. For example, single-threaded libraries are usually compiled with references to a single global `errno` variable. Calling supposedly unrelated thread-unsafe functions from different threads can still fail due to interactions on hidden, shared state such as the compiled-in global `errno`.

Other Thread-Safety Variations

There are several useful variations of thread-safety between completely thread-safe and thread-unsafe that are not defined or used in POSIX. Typically, these are applied to older libraries that either cannot be made thread-safe (due to lack of source availability) or are simply not worth making thread-safe. These variations do not have generally accepted names, but the following names are used in Solaris.

Package-Unsafe Functions

A package (library or other group) of functions that is known to share no global state (such as `errno`[6]) with a function external to the package can be called by different threads provided the caller ensures that only one thread at a time will enter any of the package functions. Such functions are called *package-unsafe*. The usual technique for using package-unsafe functions is to associate a single mutex with the package and to consistently acquire the mutex before calling any of the package functions. For convenience, you can replace calls to package functions with calls to "wrapper" functions that acquire and release the associated mutex around a call to a package function.

Object-Unsafe Functions

The caller of a function in an *object-unsafe* package (either a C++ class or a C package that operates on object-like pointers to data structures) must ensure that not more than one thread operates the same instance of an object at any one time. The caller is free to operate on different instances of the same class simultaneously. See "Object-Unsafe Functions" on page 261.

---

6. This can be as simple as ensuring that the source includes `<errno.h>` and recompiling the package in the threads environment if there is no other shared state.

Summary

Library implementors have a variety of common techniques to deal with concurrent access by threads. The techniques presented in this chapter allow users (and implementors) of libraries to quickly understand the allowable interface usage in a multithreaded program. Some techniques, such as alternate, thread-safe versions of functions or explicitly locked functions, affect library interfaces. In other cases, the library implementor may also choose not to allow multithread access (i.e., thread-unsafe) or to simply restrict multithread access, such as in package-unsafe or object-unsafe. Most techniques impose some restriction on concurrency. Sometimes the restriction is severe enough to be worth documenting.

Threads and Process Resources 5

This chapter discusses how threads within a process interact with the process's resources such as file descriptors, user ID, and timers. The chapter pays particular attention to ways the file offset of a file descriptor may be affected by multiple threads. A positioned I/O primitive is discussed that helps deal with this issue. In addition, the chapter introduces how the process creation and destruction interfaces affect processes with multiple threads.

Process Resources

Threads within a process can share almost all resources (e.g., the process address space, file descriptor table, timers, and user ID) in the process. For example, if one thread opens a file, all the threads in the process can manipulate the resulting file descriptor. However, the results of doing so may not be what the programmer expects.

Consider the program in Code Example 5-1, which prints the number of *newline* characters in the file attached to file descriptor zero (the standard input) using the number of threads specified by the command-line argument. Each thread reads file descriptor zero repetitively. Each `read()` independently moves the shared seek offset. However, POSIX only requires that the operating system moves the seek offset to reflect the number of bytes read before `read()` returns. Many implementations (including Solaris) will only move the seek offset after the I/O completes and the number of bytes read has been determined. In this case, several threads sharing a file description may see identical seek offsets when the `read()` call is issued and read the same portion of the file. This is not unique to threads; processes sharing a file description via inheritance will also see this behavior.

```
/* Warning: this code contains a bug */
void *
countlines(void *result)
{
    int i, nbytes;
    char buffer[8192];
    int sum = 0;

    while ((nbytes = read(0, buffer, sizeof(buffer))) > 0) {
        for (i = 0; i < nbytes; i++) {
            if (buffer[i] == '\n')
                sum++;
        }
    }
    *(int*) result = sum;
    return (NULL);
}

int
main(int argc, char *argv[])
{
    int nthreads;
    pthread_t t[10];
    int sum[10];
    int i;
    int n = 0;

    nthreads = atoi(argv[1]);

    for (i = 0; i < nthreads; i++)
        pthread_create(&t[i], NULL, countlines, &sum[i]);
    for (i = 0; i < nthreads; i++)
        pthread_join(t[i], NULL);
    for (i = 0; i < nthreads; i++)
        n += sum[i];
    printf("using %d threads, counted %d newlines\n", nthreads, n);
    return (0);
}
```

Code Example 5-1 Threads Reading a File Serially, Causing Unexpected Results

Unshared Resources

In general, all resources are shared except that each thread has an independent machine state (e.g., general registers, program counter, and stack pointer) and signal mask (see Chapter 9, "Signals"). In addition, each thread has a private version of the errno variable. This allows independent threads to make system calls that may change the value of errno without interfering with each other. Each thread also has a private array of pointers called thread-specific data (see Chapter 8, "Thread-Specific Data").

Positioned I/O

Suppose you would like to have more than one thread operate on individual records within a file. In order to read or write a particular record, the seek offset associated with the file must be positioned to the record's start before the I/O is done. Consider the following code:

```
void
write_record(int fd, struct record *recp, int recno)
{
    lseek(fd, (offset_t)(sizeof (struct record) * recno), SEEK_SET);
    write(fd, (char *)recp, sizeof (struct record));
}

void
read_record(int fd, struct record *recp, int recno)
{
    lseek(fd, (offset_t)(sizeof (struct record) * recno), SEEK_SET);
    read(fd, (char *)recp, sizeof (struct record));
}
```

Code Example 5-2   Reading and Writing Records (Code Has Threading Error)

The code shown will work when called from a single-threaded program. However, if a multithreaded program tries to call either read_record() or write_record() on a particular file from several threads simultaneously, the following sequence of events can occur:

```
Thread 1                                Thread 2

write_record(fd, &record, 5);
   lseek(fd, (offset_t)
     sizeof (struct record) * 5,
     SEEK_SET);
                                        write_record(fd, &record, 10);
                                           lseek(fd, (offset_t)
                                             (sizeof (struct record) * 10,
                                             SEEK_SET);
                                           write(fd, recp,
                                             sizeof (struct record));
   write(fd, recp,
     sizeof (struct record));
```

Thread 1 will wind up writing record 11 even though it was supposed to write record 5 since the file's seek offset is shared. The obvious solution is to prevent more than one thread from changing the seek offset by using a mutex lock as follows:

```
pthread_mutex_t file_lock = PTHREAD_MUTEX_INITIALIZER;

void
write_record(int fd, struct record *recp, int recno)
{
    pthread_mutex_lock(&file_lock);
    lseek(fd, (offset_t)(sizeof (struct record) * recno), SEEK_SET);
    write(fd, (char *)recp, sizeof (struct record));
    pthread_mutex_unlock(&file_lock);
}

void
read_record(int fd, struct record *recp, int recno)
{
    pthread_mutex_lock(&file_lock);
    lseek(fd, (offset_t)(sizeof (struct record) * recno), SEEK_SET);
    read(fd, (char *)recp, sizeof (struct record));
    pthread_mutex_unlock(&file_lock);
}
```

Code Example 5-3 Reading and Writing Records (Suboptimal)

This code will behave properly when called with the same file descriptor simultaneously. Notice that the lock is held from before the call to `lseek()` until after the `read()` or `write()` completes. This will allow only one I/O operation to be outstanding at any one time. An improvement is to allocate one mutex with each file descriptor, though this will misbehave if it turns out that the file descriptor is a duplicate (`dup()`) of another and therefore shares the seek offset. A better solution is to use positioned I/O operations like the following:

```
ssize_t
pread(int fd, void *buf, size_t nbytes, size_t offset);

ssize_t
pwrite(int fd, void *buf, size_t nbytes, size_t offset);
```

Caution – The `pread()` and `pwrite()` operations are *not* defined in POSIX; they are defined in the UNIX International system interface and are a part of Solaris 2. However, they are extremely useful and they can be implemented using other POSIX interfaces. See below.

`pread()` and `pwrite()` behave like `read()` and `write()` except that they take an additional offset argument. The I/O takes place at the specified offset from the beginning of the file and does not affect the seek offset associated with the file descriptor. The `read_record()` and `write_record()` routines become:

```
void
write_record(int fd, struct record *recp, int recno)
{
    pwrite(fd, (char *)recp, sizeof (struct record),
        (offset_t)(sizeof (struct record) * recno));
}

void
read_record(int fd, struct record *recp, int recno)
{
    pread(fd, (char *)recp, sizeof (struct record),
        (offset_t)(sizeof (struct record) * recno));
}
```

Code Example 5-4 Reading and Writing Records (Best)

Implementing positioned I/O in POSIX

As mentioned previously, positioned I/O is not currently directly available through the POSIX interfaces. However, if the underlying system supports POSIX asynchronous I/O[1], the positioned I/O interfaces can be simulated, as follows:

```
#include <errno.h>
#include <sys/types.h>
#include <aio.h>

ssize_t
pread(int fd, caddr_t buf, size_t nbytes, size_t offset)
{
    struct aiocb io;
    const struct aiocb *list[1];
    int err;

    io.aio_fildes = fd;
    io.aio_offset = offset;
    io.aio_buf = buf;
    io.aio_nbytes = nbytes;
    io.aio_reqprio = 0;
    io.aio_sigevent.sigev_notify = SIGEV_NONE;
    err = aio_read(&io);    /* atomically reads at offset */
    if (err != 0)
        return (err);       /* errno is set */
    list[0] = &io;
    err = aio_suspend(list, 1, NULL); /* wait for I/O to complete */
    if (err != 0)
        return (err);       /* errno is set */
    return (aio_return(&io));          /* return I/O status */
}
```

1. Defined in the POSIX Realtime standard: P1003.1b [IEEE 95A].

```
ssize_t
pwrite(int fd, caddr_t buf, size_t nbytes, size_t offset)
{
    struct aiocb io;
    const struct aiocb *list[1];
    int err;

    io.aio_fildes = fd;
    io.aio_offset = offset;
    io.aio_buf = buf;
    io.aio_nbytes = nbytes;
    io.aio_reqprio = 0;
    io.aio_sigevent.sigev_notify = SIGEV_NONE;
    err = aio_write(&io);  /* atomically reads at offset */
    if (err != 0)
        return (err);      /* errno is set */
    list[0] = &io;
    err = aio_suspend(list, 1, NULL); /* wait for I/O to complete */
    if (err != 0)
        return (err);      /* errno is set */
    return (aio_return(&io));          /* return I/O status */
}
```

Code Example 5-5   Positioned I/O Using POSIX Asynchronous I/O

This implementation depends on the asynchronous I/O interfaces to atomically read or write at the specified offset. Unlike the positioned I/O interfaces the asynchronous I/O interfaces may affect the file offset.

Arguments and Environment Variables

Command arguments passed to `main()` via `argv` and environment values passed through the `environ` variable and accessed using `getenv()` are stored in global process memory. Most programs don't modify these values and therefore require no special locking to simply read the values (see "The POSIX Memory Model" on page 32). However, you must provide synchronization if you intend to modify these values while other threads may be accessing them.

Timers and Waiting

There is only one set of timers in a process. Calls to `alarm()` or `timer_settime()`[2] (or `setitimer()` in the UNIX International interfaces) sets a process-wide timer. When a timer expires, a signal is sent to the process that generated it, not to any particular thread. Threads must cooperate to set individual, per-thread timers.

When a thread calls `pause()`, `sleep()`, `nanosleep()`, or any other blocking system call, the calling thread blocks and other threads are unaffected.

Signals

Signals are a relatively complex topic even in single-threaded programs. For now, we'll explore the case where a multithreaded process does not set up signal handlers or block signals using a signal mask. Signal handling will be covered in Chapter 9, "Signals."

Each thread has an independent signal mask. However, all the threads in the process share the set of actions to be taken in response to each signal. When the process is initialized via `exec()`, the initial thread inherits the signal mask of the thread that called `exec()`, and any signal actions that had specified signal handling routines are reset to default processing (`SIG_DFL`, just like single-thread `exec()`). The signal actions that specify default processing or to ignore the signal (`SIG_IGN`) remain unchanged.

Each new thread inherits the signal mask of the thread that created it. Therefore if the process never changes the signal mask, all the threads in the process will have the same signal mask. A signal sent to such a process will be blocked if the original mask specified blocking for that signal. If the mask does not block the signal and if the signal action is `SIG_IGN` or `SIG_DFL`, the normal default operation takes place to the process as a whole. The operations are one of the following: terminate the process, take a core dump and terminate the process, stop the entire process (i.e., *all* of the threads), or ignore the signal. In essence, in this simple scenario, a multithreaded process's reaction to signal is identical to a single-threaded process. The situation gets much more complicated when the process actually specifies signal handlers or sets the signal masks differently in its threads, as we'll see in Chapter 9, "Signals."

2. Defined in the POSIX Realtime standard: P1003.1b [IEEE 95A].

Process Creation and Destruction

When a process executes `fork()`, the operating system creates a duplicate of the process except that only the thread that called `fork()` is duplicated in the child process[3]. All other threads don't exist in the child.

Both the `exit()`, `_exit()`, and `exec()` system calls work as they do in single-thread processes except that they also destroy all the threads in the process. When `exec()` rebuilds the process, it creates a single thread which calls `main()`. As usual, if this *initial thread* returns from `main()`, it calls `exit()` using the return value as the exit status. The initial thread can also terminate by calling `pthread_exit()`. This destroys only the initial thread. If all the threads in a process exit, the process itself exits with a status of zero.

Modifying environment variables by directly dereferencing the `environ` variable is, of course, not safe with respect to other threads accessing environment variables (even by calling `getenv()` or other functions that depend on the environment). If you do this, you must take care that no other thread can access the environment while you are changing it.

Using `fork()`

There are several potential problems when a process executes `fork()`:

- Threads that may have been holding mutexes in the parent no longer exist in the child. These locks can never be released since it is illegal for a thread to release a mutex held by another. A thread in the child that calls a routine requiring such a lock will wait forever.
- There may be "helper" threads in the parent that some routines rely on to function. These will either have to be recreated in the child and placed in similar state, or such routines cannot be called in the child.

These problems are not encountered if the child does not require locks or helper threads that were used by the parent. It is also allowable to call routines that are explicitly documented as being safe with respect to calls to `fork()` (or *fork-safe*, see Table 5-1)[4]. Calling `exec()` reinitializes the process and eliminates this problem. So a general strategy is to have the child only execute code with the above restrictions after it returns from `fork()` and then quickly call `exec()`.

---

3. In the UNIX International standard, `fork()` duplicates all parent threads in the child. Another interface, `fork1()`, has the same behavior as Pthreads. See Appendix B, "UNIX International Threads."

4. The fork-safe functions are also safe with respect to signals. See "Async-Safe Functions" on page 164.

Table 5-1 Fork-Safe Functions (Same as Table 9-1 on page 165)

_exit()	fdatasync()	read()	tcflow()
access()	fork()	rename()	tcflush()
aio_error()	fstat()	rmdir()	tcgetattr()
aio_return()	fsync()	sem_post()	tcgetpgrp()
aio_suspend()	getegid()	setgid()	tcsendbreak()
alarm()	geteuid()	setpgid()	tcsetattr()
cfgetispeed()	getgid()	setsid()	tcsetpgrp()
cfgetospeed()	getgroups()	setuid()	time()
cfsetispeed()	getpgrp()	sigaction()	timer_getoverrun()
cfsetospeed()	getpid()	sigaddset()	timer_gettime()
chdir()	getppid()	sigdelset()	timer_settime()
chmod()	getuid()	sigemptyset()	times()
chown()	kill()	sigfillset()	umask()
clock_gettime()	link()	sigismember()	uname()
close()	lseek()	sigpending()	unlink()
creat()	mkdir()	sigprocmask()	utime()
dup2()	mkfifo()	sigsuspend()	wait()
dup()	open()	sleep()	waitpid()
execle()	pathconf()	stat()	write()
execve()	pause()	sysconf()	
fcntl()	pipe()	tcdrain()	

Of course, these restrictions may not be viable for all programs, such as programs that don't call `exec()` in the child. The strategies that can be used to solve these problems are beyond the scope of this chapter. The strategies to deal with more complex situations are described in Chapter 13, "Threads and Processes: Advanced Topics."

Waiting for Processes to Exit

Calling `wait()` or `waitpid()` to wait for a child process will only block the thread executing the call. If more than one thread waits for the same process, one of the waiting threads returns from `waitpid()` with the child process status. The other threads will return an `ECHILD` error.

Summary

At this point we've got all the tools to begin writing multithreaded programs. The next few chapters deal with strategies for applying these new tools.

Synchronization Strategies 6

This chapter explains strategies for synchronization in multithreaded applications. The chapter covers the strategies that are applied in most common situations. The *monitor* style (structured locking) is covered in depth as well as techniques for reasoning about program correctness such as *invariants*.

There are several general synchronization strategies to use in multithreaded programming. All of them must avoid data races (see "Data Races" on page 30). The strategies vary in the degree to which they allow threads to overlap operation.

Single Global Lock

One strategy is to have a single, application-wide mutex that is acquired whenever any thread in the application is running and is released before it must block. Since only one thread can be accessing shared data at any one time, each thread sees a consistent view of memory. This strategy can be quite effective on a uniprocessor, provided care is taken to ensure that shared memory is put into a consistent state before the lock is released and that the lock is released often enough so that other threads can run. In fact, many multi-tasking, uniprocessor operating system implementations have taken this approach.

Code Example 6-1 shows an example of a file copy program that uses a single, global lock. The lock must be carefully released while the I/O is being done. In this particular case the double buffering technique and the single lock ensure that two I/O operations cannot operate on the same buffer simultaneously. Otherwise, releasing the lock during the I/O may cause a data race.

```
/*
 * Program to copy standard input to standard output. The program
 * uses two threads. One reads the input and puts the data into a
 * double buffer. The other reads the buffer contents and writes to
 * standard output. A single lock is used and is released during I/O.
 *
 * The mutex lock protects the data buffers and the full buffer
 * count. The some_full condition indicates that some buffers have
 * been filled. The some_empty condition indicates that some buffers
 * have been emptied.
 *
 * Note: performance increase over single-threaded utilities will
 * usually onlybe seen for "raw" devices, since the operating system
 * usually suppliesinternal read-ahead and write-behind for other
 * types of files.
 */
pthread_mutex_t lock = PTHREAD_MUTEX_INITIALIZER;
pthread_cond_t some_full = PTHREAD_COND_INITIALIZER;
pthread_cond_t some_empty = PTHREAD_COND_INITIALIZER;
struct {
    char data[BSIZE];
    int nbytes;                 /* number of bytes in this buffer */
} buf[2];                       /* double buffer */
int full_bufs = 0;              /* number of buffers that are full */

main()
{
    pthread_t t_reader;
    int err;
    extern void reader(), writer();

    /* Create reader */
    err = pthread_create(&t_reader,NULL,
        (void *(*)(void *))reader,NULL);
    if (err)
        exit (1);
    /* Do the writer operation in this thread */
    writer();
    return (0);
}
```

```
void
reader()
{
    int i = 0;
    size_t nbytes;

    pthread_mutex_lock(&lock);
    do {
        while (full_bufs == 2)
            pthread_cond_wait(&some_empty, &lock);
        pthread_mutex_unlock(&lock);
        nbytes = read(0, buf[i].data, BSIZE);
        pthread_mutex_lock(&lock);
        buf[i].nbytes = nbytes;
        i = (i + 1) % 2;
        if (full_bufs == 0)
            pthread_cond_signal(&some_full);
        full_bufs += 1;
    } while (nbytes > 0);
    pthread_mutex_unlock(&lock);
}

void
writer()
{
    int i = 0;
    size_t nbytes;

    pthread_mutex_lock(&lock);
    do {
        while(full_bufs == 0)
            pthread_cond_wait(&some_full, &lock);
        nbytes = buf[i].nbytes;
        if (nbytes > 0) {
            pthread_mutex_unlock(&lock);
            write(1, buf[i].data, nbytes);
            pthread_mutex_lock(&lock);
            full_bufs -= 1;
            if (full_bufs == 0)
                pthread_cond_signal(&some_empty);
            i = (i + 1) % 2;
        }
    } while (nbytes > 0);
    pthread_mutex_unlock(&lock);
}
```

Code Example 6-1 File Copy Using a Single Lock

The single global lock approach can be simple. However, applications relying on a single lock cannot take advantage of more than one processor. In addition, even uniprocessor concurrency can be impaired if the lock is not dropped during some I/O. Perhaps the main drawback of the single global lock strategy is that it requires cooperation from all the modules and libraries in the system to synchronize on the single lock.

Thread-Safe Functions

An alternate approach is to make the functions that make up a module or library thread-safe (see "Thread-Safe Functions" on page 48). The functions that make up the module or library may be called by more than one thread at a time. The functions synchronize among themselves as appropriate, keeping any synchronization hidden from the caller. This keeps the contract between the calling and called functions simple and is in keeping with good modular programming practices.

Structured Code Locking

Structured code locking (or code locking, for short) assumes that a shared set of data is accessed only by calling a function or set of functions. Usually the function or set of functions is within one module. Code locking restricts the concurrency of calling threads based on which function or section of code is being executed. Typically, the module has a single mutex that is acquired before entering a *critical section* of code (i.e., code that accesses the module's shared data) in all the functions in the module and is released after leaving it. Here's a simple example:

```
/*
 * Simple FIFO message queue.
 */
struct mq_elt {
    struct mq_elt *next;        /* next elt towards the tail */
    struct mq_elt *prev;        /* next elt towards the head */
    msg_t msg;                  /* the message */
};

struct mq {
    pthread_cond_t notempty;    /* messages exist */
    struct mq_elt *head;        /* first message */
    struct mq_elt *tail;        /* last message */
};
typedef struct mq *mq_t;        /* opaque msg queue ptr */
```

```
/* the msg queue monitor lock */
pthread_mutex_t mq_lock = PTHREAD_MUTEX_INITIALIZER;

/* Internal functions */

/*
 * Add a message queue element to the tail of the message queue
 */
static void
add_tail(mq_t mq, struct mq_elt *new)
{
    new->prev = mq->tail;
    new->next = NULL;
    if (mq->tail == NULL)
        mq->head = new;
    else
        mq->tail->next = new;
    mq->tail = new;
}

/*
 * Delete an element from the head of the message queue
 */
static struct mq_elt *
delete_head(mq_t mq)
{
    struct mq_elt *head;

    head = mq->head;
    if (head->next == NULL)
        mq->tail = NULL;       /* last element on q */
    else
        head->next->prev = NULL;
    mq->head = head->next;
    return (head);
}
```

```
/* External functions */

/*
 * Create a new message queue.
 * Note:no locking is required because no other thread has a pointer
 * to the new message queue yet!
 */
mq_t
mq_new()
{
    mq_t mq;

    mq = (mq_t) malloc(sizeof (struct mq));
    mq->head = mq->tail = NULL;
    pthread_cond_init(&mq->notempty, NULL);
    return (mq);
}

/*
 * Put a new message at the tail of the queue.
 */
void
mq_put(mq_t mq, msg_t m)
{
    struct mq_elt *new;

    new = (struct mq_elt *) malloc(sizeof (struct mq_elt));
    new->msg = m;
    pthread_mutex_lock(&mq_lock);
    add_tail(mq, new);
    pthread_cond_signal(&mq->notempty);
    pthread_mutex_unlock(&mq_lock);
}
```

```
/*
 * Get the oldest message in the queue. Wait if there is none yet.
 */
msg_t
mq_get(mq_t mq)
{
    struct mq_elt *old;
    msg_t m;

    pthread_mutex_lock(&mq_lock);
    while ((old = mq->head) == NULL)
        pthread_cond_wait(&mq->notempty, &mq_lock);
    old = delete_head(mq);
    m = old->msg;
    pthread_mutex_unlock(&mq_lock);
    free(old);
    return (m);
}

/*
 * Flush the queue
 */
void
mq_flush(mq_t mq)
{
    pthread_mutex_lock(&mq_lock);
    while (mq->head != NULL) {
        free(delete_head(mq));
    }
    pthread_mutex_unlock(&mq_lock);
}
```

Code Example 6-2 FIFO Message Queue Using Code Locking

The message queue uses one lock for all message queues. The mutex is held around any section of code that accesses or modifies any global state (in this case either a message queue or queue element). The mutex need not be held when data that cannot be accessed by other threads is manipulated. For example, `mq_new()` does not require any locking because the queue it is creating cannot be visible to other threads until it returns. In addition, `mq_new()` assumes that `malloc()` is thread-safe and does no special locking before calling it. The implementation of `malloc()` has its own internal locking hidden inside.

Monitors

The above example shows that, for the most part, only one thread at a time can be executing any of the functions that manipulate global state in the message queue "module." This is similar to the monitor concept [Hoare 74] supported by some concurrent programming languages such as Mesa [Mitchell 79]. When using monitors, the compiler automatically locks a mutual exclusion lock whenever a function inside the monitor (i.e. the externally visible functions that make up the module) is called and releases it when it returns. The mutual exclusion lock is called the monitor lock. The compiler also directly supports condition variables that release and acquire the monitor lock when waiting and awakening.

Monitors are a structured concept. Modules are designed so that access to shared state is controlled exclusively by the module's externally visible functions. In general, this is good "information hiding" programming practice. The compiler ensures that only one thread can be executing monitor functions at any one time. The programmers cannot forget to acquire the monitor lock at the beginning of a function nor can they forget to release it before returning. A programmer can imitate the monitor style of programming by using code locking without requiring compiler support. Conversely, programmers are also free to violate the monitor discipline; however, this increases the difficulty of ensuring that the routine is thread-safe in much the same way that `goto` statements increase the difficulty in understanding that a routine functions correctly.

Internal Functions

The functions `add_tail()` and `delete_head()` in Code Example 6-2 are examples of *internal functions*. Internal functions are called only from within the module while the monitor lock is held. They are different from the external functions of the monitor in that they don't acquire the monitor lock on entry; they assume it is already held.

The external functions in a module programmed in the monitor style cannot call other external functions while holding the monitor lock. Otherwise, the second external function would attempt to acquire a lock that is already held by the calling thread, which would result in deadlock. This problem can be remedied by having internal versions of the external function that does not acquire the lock. For example:

```
internal_func(...)
{
    ...
}
```

```
external_func(...)
{
    pthread_mutex_lock(&monitor_lock);
    internal_func(...);
    pthread_mutex_unlock(&monitor_lock);
}
```

Invariants

The queue in Code Example 6-2 is assumed to have a certain form:

- The `head` member of the `mq` structure points to the first element on the queue or is `NULL` if there are no elements.
- The `tail` member of the `mq` structure points to the last element on the queue or is `NULL` if there are no elements.
- Each element in the queue except the one at the head has a `prev` member that points to the element that was placed on the queue before this one (i.e., toward the head). This element has a `next` member that points to the original element.
- The element at the head of the queue has a `NULL prev` member.
- The element at the tail of the queue has a `NULL next` member.

Both `mq_put()` and `mq_get()` assume that the queue is in this form before they begin operating on it and they leave the queue in this form when they are done. These restrictions on the form of the queue is an example of an *invariant*. Notice that invariants associated with the queue may not be true while the queue is being operated on. For example, between line 33 and line 34 in `delete_head()` an element that is not the head of the queue has a `NULL prev` member.

More generally, an invariant is an expression evaluating the shared state associated with the monitor that is always true when the monitor lock is *not* held by any thread. Therefore, the code within the monitor lock can assume that the invariant is true immediately after it acquires the monitor lock. Similarly, the code must ensure that the invariant is true immediately before releasing the monitor lock. This action is sometimes called restoring the invariant. The invariant must also be restored before waiting on condition variables, as they also release the monitor lock.

Invariants can be programmed and used as debugging aids. An example invariant for the message queue code would be as follows.

```
int
check_queue(mq_t mq)
{
    struct mq_elt *elt;

    if (mq->head == NULL && mq->tail == NULL)
        return (1);
    if (mq->head == NULL || mq->tail == NULL)
        return (0);
    if (mq->head->prev != NULL || mq->tail->next != NULL)
        return (0);
    for (elt = mq->tail; elt != mq->head; elt = elt->prev) {
        if (elt->prev->next != elt)
            return (0);
    }
    return (1);
}
```

Code Example 6-3 Message Queue Invariant

This invariant can be used to check the form of the queue after the monitor lock is acquired and before it is released. A typical way of doing this is to evaluate the invariant function using the `assert()` macro (in `<assert.h>`). The `assert()` macro prints a diagnostic message and aborts the program if its argument evaluates to zero. Assertion checking can be disabled by defining the `NDEBUG` flag at the time that `assert.h` is included. For example, in `mq_get()`:

```
msg_t
mq_get(mq_t mq)
{
    struct mq_elt *old;
    msg_t m;

    pthread_mutex_lock(&mq_lock);
    assert(check_queue(mq));
    while ((old = mq->head) == NULL) {
        assert(check_queue(mq));
        pthread_cond_wait(&mq->notempty, &mq_lock);
        assert(check_queue(mq));
    }
    old = delete_head(mq);
    m = old->msg;
    assert(check_queue(mq));
    pthread_mutex_unlock(&mq_lock);
    free(old);
    return (m);
}
```

Code Example 6-4 Checking the Invariant

Releasing the Monitor Lock

Another way of looking at the monitor style is as implementing a state machine. Calls to the external functions of the module make changes to the shared memory that represents the state of the module (e.g., a message queue) so that it transitions from one valid state to another valid state. Valid states are ones in which the invariant is true. The state transitions usually require several changes so that the shared values can be in invalid states (i.e., the invariant is false) during the transition. Holding the monitor lock prevents other threads from seeing these invalid states, therefore making the transition from one state to another seem atomic.

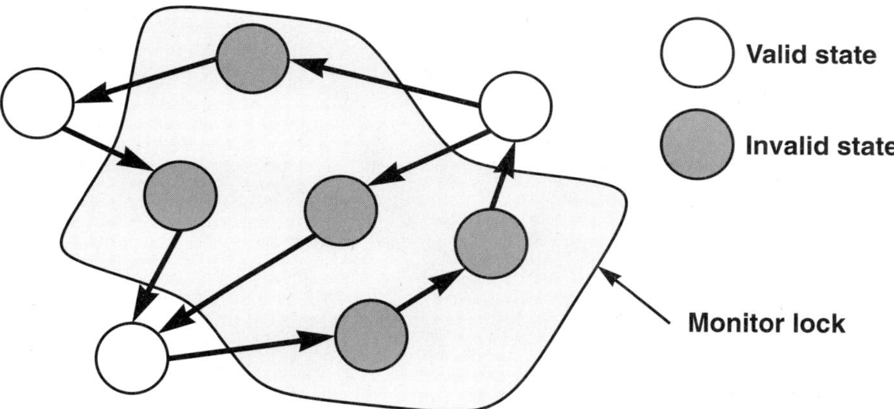

Figure 6-1 State Machine View of Monitors

Between the times that a thread acquires the monitor lock, other threads may call module functions. Therefore, the state of the module can potentially change to any other valid state. Any assumptions about the state the module was in must be discarded or reverified. A good example of this situation is when the monitor lock is released while waiting for a condition. Any values in local variables that were computed based on the module state while the monitor lock was held must be discarded and recomputed or revalidated when the monitor lock is reacquired after the condition wait.

As an example, consider the following simple implementation of a read-only record buffer.

```
/*
 * Simple fixed size read-only cache of fixed size records.
 * Note: on systems with mapped file capability, such caches are only
 * useful for large backing files containing small records (< page)
 * that have poor spatial reference locality. Otherwise, it is more
 * efficient to simply map the file and let the VM system cache the
 * pages for you.
 * Warning: there are potential performance bugs in this code.
 */

struct rec_buf {                /* Record cache buffer element */
    struct rec_buf *forw;       /* next element */
    struct rec_buf *back;       /* previous element */
    char busy;                  /* indicates record is in use */
    pthread_cond_t notbusy;     /* signals buf is no longer in use */
    int recno;                  /* record number */
    rec_t record;               /* record data */
};

/*
 * rc_lock is the monitor lock. The rc_notbusy condition signals
 * that some buffer may not be busy.
 */
pthread_mutex_t rc_lock = PTHREAD_MUTEX_INITIALIZER;
pthread_cond_t rc_notbusy = PTHREAD_COND_INITIALIZER;
struct rec_buf rc_cache[CACHESIZE];   /* the buffer cache */
struct rec_buf *rc_bucket[NBUCKETS]; /* the hash lists by rec no */
int rc_file_fd;                 /* the file behind the cache */
int end_rec_no;                 /* the last rec number in file + 1 */

/* Internal functions */
#define HASH(r) ((r) % NBUCKETS)/* simple hash function example */

/*
 * Find the list element associated with record number recno.
 */
static struct rec_buf *
find_rec(int recno)
{
    struct rec_buf *bufp;

    bufp = rc_bucket[HASH(recno)];
    while (bufp != NULL) {
        if (bufp->recno == recno)
            return(bufp);
        else
            bufp = bufp->forw;
    }
    return (NULL);
}
```

```
/*
 * Search the cache for a non-busy buffer. If there is none, wait.
 * Note: this is a poor implementation as it always finds buffers at
 * the front of the cache.
 */
static struct rec_buf *
alloc_rec(int recno)
{
    struct rec_buf *bufp;
    struct rec_buf *headp;
    int hash;

    for (;;) {
        for (bufp = &rc_cache[0]; bufp < &rc_cache[CACHESIZE];
          bufp++) {
            if (bufp->busy == 0) { /* Buf not busy */
                if (bufp->recno != NOREC) {
                    /*
                     * Buf is already on a record list.
                     * Remove it from the list it is on.
                     */
                    hash = HASH(bufp->recno);
                    if (rc_bucket[hash] == bufp) { /*at head of list */
                        if (bufp->forw == bufp) {
                            rc_bucket[hash] = NULL;
                        } else {
                            rc_bucket[hash] = bufp->forw;
                            bufp->forw->back = bufp->back;
                        }
                    } else {
                        bufp->back->forw = bufp->forw;
                        bufp->forw->back = bufp->back;
                    }
                }
                /* Now put it on new list */
                hash = HASH(recno);
                headp = rc_bucket[hash];
                if (headp == NULL) {
                    if (bufp->recno != NOREC) {
                        bufp->forw = bufp;
                        bufp->back = bufp;
                    }
```

```
                } else {
                    /* Add to front of list */
                    bufp->forw = headp;
                    bufp->back = headp->back;
                    headp->back->forw = bufp;
                    headp->back = bufp;
                }
                rc_bucket[hash] = bufp;
                bufp->recno = recno;
                memset(&bufp->record, 0, sizeof(bufp->record));
                return (bufp);
            }
        }
        /* wait for any non-busy buf */
        pthread_cond_wait(&rc_notbusy, &rc_lock);
    }
}

/* External functions */

/*
 * Initialize the buffer cache. Must be called first.
 */
void
rec_init(int fd)
{
    struct rec_buf *bufp;
    int i;

    for (bufp = &rc_cache[0]; bufp < &rc_cache[CACHESIZE]; bufp++) {
        bufp->forw = bufp->back = bufp;
        bufp->busy = 0;
        bufp->recno = NOREC;
    }
    for (i = 0; i < NBUCKETS; i++) {
        rc_bucket[i] = NULL;
    }
    rc_file_fd = fd;
    end_rec_no = (lseek(fd, 0, SEEK_END) / sizeof (rec_t)) + 1;
}
```

```
/*
 * Find record by record number. If not in cache, read it in.
 * Caller must call rec_done() when finished with the record.
 */
struct rec_buf *
rec_get(int recno)
{
    struct rec_buf *bufp;
    int bytesread;

    if (recno >= end_rec_no)
        return (NULL);
    pthread_mutex_lock(&rc_lock);
    /*
     * Keep checking until the non-busy recno is found. The search
     * must be restarted if we must release the monitor because the
     * buffer is busy.
     */
    while ((bufp = find_rec(recno)) != NULL && bufp->busy)
        pthread_cond_wait(&bufp->notbusy, &rc_lock);
    if (bufp == NULL) {
            /* recno not in cache, read it in */
        bufp = alloc_rec(recno);/* allocate buffer */
        bytesread = pread(rc_file_fd, &bufp->record, sizeof (rec_t),
            sizeof (rec_t) * bufp->recno);
        if (bytesread <= 0) {
            end_rec_no = recno;
            bufp->recno = RECINVAL;
            pthread_mutex_unlock(&rc_lock);
            return (NULL);
        }
    }
    bufp->busy = 1;
    pthread_mutex_unlock(&rc_lock);
    return (bufp);
}
```

```
/*
 * Give up ownership of the record (i.e., done reading).
 */
void
rec_done(struct rec_buf *bufp)
{
    pthread_mutex_lock(&rc_lock);
    assert(bufp->busy);           /* check for protocol violation */
    bufp->busy = 0;
    pthread_mutex_unlock(&rc_lock);
    pthread_cond_signal(&bufp->notbusy); /* wake waiters for this buf */
    pthread_cond_signal(&rc_notbusy); /* wake waiters for any buf */
}
```

Code Example 6-5 Read-Only Record Cache

Notice the condition variable wait loop in `rec_get()`. The loop first searches for the record and if the record is found but is busy, it waits for the `notbusy` condition to be signalled. This releases the monitor lock. When the thread wakes up after getting the signal, it searches for the record number *again*. It does not simply check the buffer's busy bit. The reason for this is that the buffer pointed to by `bufp` may not be the same record by the time the thread reacquires the monitor lock: another thread may have caused the buffer to be overwritten with a different record number before the calling thread reacquired it. The local state, `bufp->recno == recno`, must be discarded when the monitor lock is released and recomputed when the monitor is reacquired.

The condition variable wait loop in `rec_get()` can be optimized as follows in this particular implementation:

```
while ((bufp = find_rec(recno)) != NULL && bufp->busy) {
    pthread_cond_wait(&bufp->notbusy, &rc_lock);
    if (bufp->recno == recno && !bufp->busy)
        break;
}
```

This loop would call `find_rec()` again only when the record got overwritten or the buffer is being used by another thread. This optimization is possible because the actual buffer cache (`rc_cache`) is statically allocated so that `bufp` will always point to a buffer. The condition `bufp->recno == recno` must be re-evaluated, not `bufp`. This optimization would not be possible if cache buffers were dynamically allocated and freed because the memory pointed to by the local variable `bufp` may have already been freed.

Multiple Conditions

Sometimes a routine must wait for more than one condition to be true. Programmers may be tempted to do the following:

```
/* Warning: this code contains bugs! */
func()
{
    mutex_enter(&monitor_lock);
    while (!cond1)
        pthread_cond_wait(&cond1_cv, &monitor_lock);
    while (!cond2)
        pthread_cond_wait(&cond2_cv, &monitor_lock);
    /* Assume both cond1 and cond2 are true. Wrong! */
    ...
    mutex_unlock(&monitor_lock);
}
```

Code Example 6-6 The Wrong Way to Wait for Two Conditions

If `cond2` is not true the first time, then the routine must wait on `cond2_cv` and release the monitor lock. When `cond2_cv` is signalled, `cond2` may be true, but `cond1` may no longer be, as the monitor lock has been released since it was last tested. Both conditions must be retested:

```
func()
{
    pthread_mutex_lock(&monitor_lock);
    while (!cond1 || !cond2)
        if (!cond1)
            pthread_cond_wait(&cond1_cv, &monitor_lock);
        if (!cond2)
            pthread_cond_wait(&cond2_cv, &monitor_lock);
    }
    /* Assume both cond1 and cond2 are true */
    ...
    pthread_mutex_unlock(&monitor_lock);
}
```

Code Example 6-7 A Correct Way to Wait for Two Conditions

Structured Data Locking

Like structured code locking, structured data locking (data locking, for short) assumes that shared data is accessed only though functions in a module. However, it also assumes that the shared data can be grouped into independent "objects" that share no state. For example, there is no shared data between independent message queues in Code Example 6-2. We could have just as easily written:

```
/*
 * Simple FIFO message queue, using data locking.
 */
struct mq_elt {
    struct mq_elt *next;       /* next element */
    struct mq_elt *prev;       /* previous element */
    msg_t msg;                 /* the message */
};

struct mq {
    pthread_mutex_t mq_lock;   /* monitor lock for this msg queue */
    pthread_cond_t notempty;   /* messages exist */
    struct mq_elt *head;       /* first message */
    struct mq_elt *tail;       /* last message */
};
typedef struct mq *mq_t;       /* opaque msg queue representation */

/*
 * Internal functions and mq_new() are the same as Code Example 6-2
 * and have been omitted.
 */

void
mq_put(mq_t mq, msg_t m)
{
    struct mq_elt *new;

    new = (struct mq_elt *) malloc(sizeof (struct mq_elt));
    new->msg = m;
    pthread_mutex_lock(&mq->mq_lock);
    add_tail(mq, new);
    pthread_mutex_unlock(&mq->mq_lock);
    pthread_cond_signal(&mq->notempty);
}
```

```
/*
 * Get the oldest message in the queue. Wait if there is none yet.
 */
msg_t
mq_get(mq_t mq)
{
    struct mq_elt *old;
    msg_t m;

    pthread_mutex_lock(&mq->mq_lock);
    while ((old = mq->head) == NULL)
        pthread_cond_wait(&mq->notempty, &mq->mq_lock);
    old = delete_head(mq);
    m = old->msg;
    pthread_mutex_unlock(&mq->mq_lock);
    free(old);
    return (m);
}

/*
 * Flush the queue
 */
void
mq_flush(mq_t mq)
{
    pthread_mutex_lock(&mq->mq_lock);
    while (mq->head != NULL) {
        free(delete_head(mq));
    }
    pthread_mutex_unlock(&mq->mq_lock);
}
```

Code Example 6-8   FIFO Message Queue Using Data Locking

This is a slightly different point of view than code locking. The data locking approach examines the independent *objects* that are manipulated by a module and associates a lock with each object. The associated lock is held whenever the data in the object is manipulated. The lock can be said to "protect" its associated object. Notice that the structured monitor approach is preserved. In fact, languages that support monitors usually also support *object monitors* that have an independent monitor lock embedded in each object manipulated by a module.

The most obvious advantage in using this approach is that operations on independent queues can proceed concurrently, without losing the structuring of monitors. However, it becomes much more difficult to use this technique when there is data shared between objects.

Object Deletion

Consider the following implementation of a function, `mq_delete()`, that deletes a message queue from Code Example 6-8:

```
void
mq_delete(mq_t mq)
{
    mq_flush(mq);                   /* flush out remaining messages */
    pthread_mutex_destroy(&mq->mq_lock);
    pthread_cond_destroy(&mq->notempty);
    free(mq);
}
```

Code Example 6-9   Deleting a FIFO Message Queue

Notice that the implementation does not acquire the object monitor lock or wake up any waiting threads before destroying the synchronization variables or freeing the queue. If other threads are waiting for messages or to acquire the object monitor lock, it will cause a serious and hard-to-detect bug. It may seem reasonable to attempt to wake up other threads waiting for messages, but this would still not protect against threads waiting for the monitor lock or about to call `mq_put()` or `mq_get()`. In fact, the calling thread must ensure that no other thread has an active reference to the queue to be deleted by using external synchronization[1]. In some sense, this is the same requirement as in single-thread programming that a reference to an object not be used after it is deleted. In multithreaded programming the requirement can be restated as: a reference to an object may not be used after or at the same time that an object is being deleted.

Locking and Modularity

In Code Example 6-5 the interface to the record cache has an explicit call, `rec_done()`, that tells the cache the user of the record is done operating on it. An equivalent module implemented for single-threaded programs would probably not require such a protocol. Instead there would be the usually implicit assumption that the caller would not attempt to read in a new record while it was still operating on the previous result. After all, the caller has complete control over the pattern of calls to the interface. Multithreaded programming makes it likely that the caller cannot totally control the usage of the interface. Similarly, the blocking behavior of the implementation of an interface can affect both the

1. Maintaining reference counts works, provided the caller adheres to the reference count protocol. A garbage collector also works. There is still an external synchronization protocol in both these cases.

 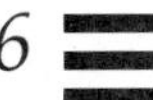

performance and correctness of the caller. Unfortunately, this means that interfaces and interface specifications may have to change to accommodate the new "contract" between the caller and callee.

Nested Monitors

Suppose module *A* calls a function in module *B* while *A* still holds the monitor lock. If the module *B* function blocks on some condition, its monitor lock will be released, but the monitor lock in module *A* will remain held, perhaps for a long time. More importantly, if the path to signal the condition that the thread in the module *B* function is waiting for is through a function in module *A*, we have a deadlock. The thread that may signal the condition is waiting for the monitor lock held by the thread waiting for the condition.

Object monitors can reduce this problem since the monitor lock only locks one object. This means that only one object in module *A* is blocked when the nested call blocks in module *B* and only that particular object must not be in the path to signal a thread waiting in the nested call. However, the problem is not eliminated.

The solution to this problem is to avoid holding the monitor lock when calling functions with unknown blocking behavior. In many cases, the blocking behavior of any particular function is pretty clear. For example, it is clear that functions like `strcmp()` or `memcpy()` probably don't have much blocking (aside from the occasional page fault). On the other hand, it is clear that functions such as `getc()` or `mq_get()` (from Code Example 6-2) have definite blocking behavior that is explicit in their semantics. If it is isn't obvious for a particular function, then it is best to assume the worst and don't hold the monitor lock while calling it.

In many cases, it will be easy to move the call to either before the monitor lock is acquired or after it is released. In Code Example 6-2, the call to `malloc()` in `mq_put()` was moved to before the monitor lock is acquired, and the call to `free()` in `mq_get()` was moved to after the monitor lock was released. In other cases, the monitor lock will have to be dropped and reacquired. As we've seen in "Releasing the Monitor Lock this can cause some extra work.

Unfortunately, this means that interface specifications may have to detail the allowed blocking behavior of any implementation of the interface.

Long Operations

A function that does a long operation while holding the monitor lock prevents other threads from accessing the shared state for the time the monitor lock is held. This can be particularly bad if the operation can take an unbounded amount of time, as in waiting for a packet or typed input. It is good practice to release the monitor lock while doing I/O or other long operations. For example, `rec_get()` in Code Example 6-5 holds the monitor lock while reading in the record. It could be rewritten as follows:

```
/*
 * Find record by record number. If not in cache find, read it in.
 * Caller must call rec_done() when finished with the record.
 */
struct rec_buf *
rec_get(int recno)
{
    struct rec_buf *bufp;
    int bytesread;

    if (recno >= end_rec_no)
        return (NULL);
    pthread_mutex_lock(&rc_lock);
    /* Keep checking till the non-busy recno is found. */
    while ((bufp = find_rec(recno)) != NULL && bufp->busy)
        pthread_cond_wait(&bufp->notbusy, &rc_lock);
    if (bufp == NULL) {
        /*
         * recno not in cache, read it in. The buffer is marked
         * busy so that no other thread will get it after we release
         * the monitor lock to read in the data.
         */
        bufp = alloc_rec(recno);
        bufp->busy = 1;
        pthread_mutex_unlock(&rc_lock);
        bytesread = pread(rc_file_fd, &bufp->record, sizeof (rec_t),
            sizeof (rec_t) * bufp->recno);
        if (bytesread <= 0) {
            end_rec_no = recno;
            bufp->recno = RECINVAL;
            rec_done(bufp);
            return (NULL);
        }
    } else {
        bufp->busy = 1;
        pthread_mutex_unlock(&rc_lock);
    }
    return (bufp);
}
```

Code Example 6-10 Releasing the Monitor Lock for I/O in Record Cache

Note that the buffer busy bit is set before the lock is dropped. In effect, the busy bit also serves to protect the buffer across the call to `pread()`, a function previously performed by the lock. Also note that the code on the failure of `pread()` changes slightly from the previous version — the busy bit has to be cleared and any waiters woken up by calling `rec_done()`, as shown.

Reentrant Monitors

A similar problem occurs when a function in module *A* calls a function outside module *A* while it holds the monitor lock. A deadlock will happen if the called function eventually calls a function in module *A* that requires the monitor lock. A module using its own functions is a special case of this problem.

As in the nested monitor problem, object monitor can reduce, but not eliminate, the problem. The reentrant call to module *A* must manipulate the same object that called outside module *A*.

The solution is similar to the nested monitor problem; avoid holding the monitor lock when calling outside functions that may depend on this module through some path. As in nested monitors, the external dependencies of any particular function are clear in many cases. For example, it is clear that a system routine like `malloc()` does not depend on your new window widget. Such problems tend to happen with functions at the same level of abstraction in sometimes surprising and unintentional ways. For example, a list module may use a memory allocator module that may use lists. Releasing the monitor lock (and therefore restoring) the invariant allows a module to participate multiple times in a call stack.

The reentrant monitor problem is similar to the single-threaded reentrance problem. In single-threaded programming, if a function in a module recurses, calls an external module function, or calls a function outside the module in a way that the module might be reentered, it must ensure that any non-local data that may be shared with the reentering call is in a form the subsequent calls can use. Essentially, a function must do the equivalent of restoring the invariant before making the external call. Similarly, the function must discard or revalidate any values in local variables that depend on the shared state when the external calls return. The only difference in multithreaded programming is that attempting to reenter the monitor lock produces a deadlock. This is, in some sense, more desirable than going ahead and operating on inconsistent data.

Monitors Revisited

After the previous discussion, let's step back and review. The code examples show that structured code or data locking deviates slightly from the strict compiler-supported monitor. In particular, various actions that don't directly manipulate the shared data are done outside the monitor lock. The general form of a function in the structured data locking version of the monitor is:

```
type_t
external_func(struct obj *objectp)
{
    type_t return_val;

    Setup locals. Call functions outside monitor.

    pthread_mutex_lock(&objectp->monitor_lock);

    Evaluate state of shared data.

    while (! some condition)
        pthread_cond_wait(&objectp->some_cv, &objectp->monitor_lock);

    Reevaluate shared data, assuming some_condition is true and
    transform it as required. Call functions internal to monitor.
    If transformation makes (or may make)a signalable condition true
    then:
    pthread_cond_signal(&objectp->some_other_cv);

    return_val = ...;       /* save rtn val before monitor release */
    pthread_mutex_unlock(&objectp->monitor_lock);

    Call outside monitor.
    Can also signal conditions changed under monitor lock

    return(return_val);
}
```

Code Example 6-11 General Form of Structured Data Locking Monitor

Not all the actions in Code Example 6-11 need be done in all functions. For example, a particular function may wait on a condition variable but not signal (and vice versa), or it may not return a value. However, the example shows the overall pattern. This coding discipline yields several advantages:

- The shared data goes through well-defined transformations from one valid state to another only while the monitor lock is held.
- An invariant expression can be written that evaluates the condition of the shared state and should always be true while no thread holds the lock.
- It is easy to identify the particular lock that protects shared data.

- The monitor style is easy to understand and to apply to well-structured, object-based, or object-oriented modules[2].

Like most structured techniques, these advantages may seem mundane or obvious. It's worth comparing this to other techniques. Compare the monitor style with the double buffered file copy using semaphores in Code Example 10-4 on page 184. Notice that it is more difficult to determine that the reader and write thread are not accessing the same buffer at the same time. There is no monitor lock to ensure that the shared data is being protected. The example is fairly simple so it is not all that difficult to convince yourself that it works, but you can imagine a more complex situation where using semaphores in this manner would be significantly worse.

Deadlock

Deadlock is the permanent blocking of further progress. We've already seen two forms of it: *self-deadlock* or *recursive deadlock*, when a thread attempts to acquire a mutex (or other type of lock) that it already owns (usually due to a reentrant monitor), and the nested monitor deadlock, where module *A* blocks in module *B*, but the path to wake up module *B* is through module *A*. Another form of deadlock is due to the order in which locks of various forms are acquired.

A simple case is where a thread in module *A* calls module *B* while holding module *A*'s monitor lock. Meanwhile, another thread in module *B* calls module *A* while holding module *B*'s monitor lock. Each thread owns one lock and is blocked waiting for the other. The solution to this is the same as in nested monitor calls: avoid holding the monitor lock when calling outside functions.

Lock Ordering

Unfortunately, this is not a complete solution because there is something more fundamental going on here. This form of deadlock can happen whenever there is:

- more than one thread,
- there are resources that can be reserved for exclusive use by a thread,
- other threads block when attempting to reserve a resource reserved by another thread, and
- a thread may own more than one resource.

---

2. We use the term "object based" modules to mean modules that hide their implementation and the structure of their internal state by only allow state modifications by calling module functions that operate on "objects" that are opaque to the caller. "Object oriented" modules also use inheritance.

As an example, suppose a process with several threads uses the record cache in Code Example 6-5. Assume thread *A* gets record 1 and tries to get record 2 before it releases record 1. Meanwhile, thread *B* has record 2 and tries to get record 1 before it releases record 2. Again, each thread has a resource that the other "owns." This deadlock can also happen with any of the blocking synchronization primitives, file and record locking system calls, or any other routine that exclusively reserves a resource or blocks until the resource is available. We call this situation a *lock-ordering deadlock* because it occurs when two threads attempt to "lock" two resources in different orders.

The general strategy to avoid this problem is first to avoid holding two blocking resources at any one time, even if they seem unrelated. If more than one thread can own more than one blocking resource, then one thread can own *A* and want *B* while another thread owns *B* and wants *A*. If owning two resources can't be avoided, then establish a well-defined order in which the resources are acquired. This order is sometimes called a *lock hierarchy.* If all threads acquire the resource in the same order, this form of deadlock can't happen.

For example, assume a process with several threads uses a writable version of the record cache in Code Example 6-5 to store accounts and wants to transfer some money from record *i* to record *j* atomically, and that similar operations can happen in more than one thread at a time. We establish the rule that the lower-numbered record must be acquired before the higher-numbered record, as shown in Code Example 6-12. This prevents the lock-ordering deadlock.

```
void
transfer(int source_recno, int dest_recno, int amount)
{
    struct rec_buf *source_rb, *dest_rb;

    if (source_recno < dest_recno) {
        source_rb = rec_get(source_recno);
        dest_rb = rec_get(dest_recno);
    } else {
        dest_rb = rec_get(dest_recno);
        source_rb = rec_get(source_recno);
    }
    transfer amount
    rec_done(source_rb);
    rec_done(dest_rb);
}
```

Code Example 6-12   Ordering the Locking of Records

Sometimes adhering to a lock hierarchy can be tricky, for example, if a thread using the record cache had reserved a record to operate on an account and sometime later the user requests a transfer to a lower-numbered account. One solution is to immediately release the higher-numbered account and reacquire the two accounts in the proper order. This may incur a large cost if only because the state of the initial account will have to be reverified since it may have changed while it was released. In fact, the account may no longer exist; another thread may have deleted it while the lock was released! An alternative strategy is to attempt to reserve the lower-numbered account using a new, non-blocking call that returns an error if the record is currently reserved. Code Example 6-13 shows an implementation and use of `get_tryget()` that doesn't wait if the buffer is busy. If the record is successfully locked, the thread may continue. However, if the non-blocking reservation attempt indicates the record is busy, the thread must release the record it owns and do the more lengthy process of reacquiring the records in the correct order and reverifying their state.

```
/* Try to get the record. Don't wait if it is busy */
struct rec_buf *
rec_tryget(int recno)
{
    struct rec_buf *bufp;
    int bytesread;

    if (recno >= end_rec_no)
        return (NULL);
    pthread_mutex_lock(&rc_lock);
    /* Keep checking till the non-busy recno is found. */
    bufp = find_rec(recno);
    if (bufp == NULL) {
        /* recno not in cache, read it in */
        bufp = alloc_rec(recno);/* Warning! potential deadlock */
        bufp->busy = 1;
        pthread_mutex_unlock(&rc_lock);
        bytesread = pread(rc_file_fd, &bufp->record, sizeof (rec_t),
            sizeof (rec_t) * bufp->recno);
        if (bytesread <= 0) {
            end_rec_no = recno;
            bufp->recno = RECINVAL;
            rec_done(bufp);
            return (NULL);
        }
    } else {
        if (bufp->busy)
            bufp = NULL;        /* buffer is busy, don't wait */
        else        bufp->busy = 1;
        pthread_mutex_unlock(&rc_lock);
    }
    return (bufp);
}
```

```
void
do_something()
{
    struct rec_buf *rb1;
    struct rec_buf *rb2;
    int recno1, recno2;

    rb1 = rec_get(recno1);

    operate on rb1
    discover you need to work on recno2

    if (recno2 < recno1) {
        /* try to violate the lock hierarchy */
        if ((rb2 = rec_tryget(recno2)) == NULL) {
            /* the try failed. do it the hard way */
            rec_done(rb1);
            rb2 = rec_get(recno2);
            rb1 = rec_get(recno1);
            /*
             * recno1 may have changed since we last acquired it.
             * If deletion is allowed, it may have even disappeared!
             */
            recheck that recno1 exists and is in the correct state.
        }
    } else
        rb2 = rec_get(recno2);

    operate on rb1 and rb2

    rec_done(rb1);
    rec_done(rb2);
}
```

Code Example 6-13 Violating the Lock Hierarchy

The pthread_mutex_trylock() and sem_trywait() synchronization functions are provided for similar purposes.

Resource Deadlocks

The rec_tryget() function in Code Example 6-13 illustrates another form of deadlock. Suppose an application has as many threads as there are cached buffers (i.e., CACHESIZE threads) and they all call do_something() simultaneously. When do_something() calls rec_tryget(), each thread will have one buffer (rb1) and must get another in order to progress, because alloc_rec() in rec_tryget() blocks waiting for a non-busy buffer. The threads cannot make further progress since they already have all the available buffers and no thread is willing to give any up.

A solution to this deadlock is for each thread to acquire all the resources it needs to progress first before continuing. If it cannot acquire the resource it must give them up and start again.

C++

Programs written in the C++ programming language can take directly take advantage of all the strategies outlined above. However, the C++ language can cause more opportunities for pitfalls. For example, C++ exceptions can cause the flow of control to change in unexpected ways. For example:

```
pthread_mutex_t m = PTHREAD_MUTEX_INITIALIZER;// f's monitor lock

f()
{
    pthread_mutex_lock(&m);
    ...
    g();                    // throws exceptions
    ...
    pthread_mutex_unlock(&m);
}
```

When the function, g(), throws an exception that is handled by a caller of f(), the flow of control will bypass the lock release. An obvious alternative is to catch exceptions to release the lock:

```
f()
{
    pthread_mutex_lock(&m);
    try {
        ...
        g();                // throws exceptions
        ...
    } catch (...) {
        pthread_mutex_unlock(&m);
        throw;
    }
    pthread_mutex_unlock(&m);
}
```

Scoped Locking

The defensive programming style forced by attempting to catch unexpected exceptions is both ugly and error prone. However, the programmer can take advantage of C++ language features to provide a more elegant, robust, and structured mechanism. Code Example 6-14 shows an example of structured code locking that uses a special internal class, `a::locker`, that acquires the monitor lock when created and releases it when destroyed. The first statement in `f()` instantiates an `a::locker`, `mon`. The instantiation calls the constructor for `mon` that acquires the monitor lock. C++ ensures that the destructor for `mon` is called when the scope of the instantiation of `mon` is exited by any means[3]. This not only releases the lock properly when an exception occurs, but it also does so when the scope is exited by `return`, `break`, `goto`, or simply executing the last statement in the scope.

```
class a {
private:
    static pthread_mutex_t am; // monitor lock
    // lock and unlock monitor. for internal functions
    static void lock(void)      {pthread_mutex_lock(&am);}
    static void unlock(void)    {pthread_mutex_unlock(&am);}
    class locker;
    friend class a::locker;
    class locker {
    public:
        // constructor: acquire monitor lock when created
        locker()                {a::lock();}
        // destructor: release monitor lock when destroyed
        ~locker()               {a::unlock();}
    };
    void g()                    {throw ("error");}
    // other private functions
public:
    void f();
    // other public functions
};

pthread_mutex_t a::am = PTHREAD_MUTEX_INITIALIZER;
```

3. Exiting the scope by calling `longjmp()` is not detected by C++. However, exception handling is a more appropriate mechanism than `setjmp()/longjmp()` and should be used instead.

```
void
a::f()
{
    locker mon;              // monitor is held as long as mon exists
    ...
    g();                     // throws exceptions
    ...
}
```

Code Example 6-14 C++ Scoped Code Locking

Object monitors require a slightly different locker class:

```
class b {
private:
    pthread_mutex_t bm;    // object monitor for b
    // constructor: initialize object monitor lock when created
    b()                      {pthread_mutex_init(&bm, NULL); ...}
    // destructor: destroy object monitor lock
    ~b()                     {pthread_mutex_destroy(&bm); ...}
    // lock and unlock monitor. for internal functions
    void lock(void)          {pthread_mutex_lock(&bm);}
    void unlock(void)        {pthread_mutex_unlock(&bm);}
    class locker;
    friend class b::locker;
    class locker {
        b* bp;
    public:
        // constructor: acquire monitor lock when created
        locker(b* objp)          {bp = objp; bp->lock();}
        // destructor: release monitor lock when destroyed
        ~locker()                {bp->unlock();}
    };
    void g()                 {throw ("error");}
    // other private functions
public:
    void f();
    // other public functions
};

void
b::f()
{
    locker mon(this);        // monitor is held as long as mon exists
    ...
    g();                     // throws exceptions
    ...
}
```

Code Example 6-15 C++ Scoped Object Locking

The implementation of `b::f()` in Code Example 6-14 also shows that the locker class can be instantiated in interior scopes.

This "resource acquisition is object initialization" technique can also be applied to situations other than locking. It is useful in any case where operations must be bracketed in a lexical scope. Examples of this could be acquiring and releasing buffers, or opening and closing devices.

Locking Guidelines

The structured locking discipline makes it easier to construct correct multithreaded programs. This is similar to the way structured programming techniques help make it easier to construct correct programs.

Here are some simple guidelines for structured locking:

- Try to use the structured locking style: use a single mutex associated with the module functions. If more concurrency is required, use a mutex associated with each data object implemented by the module functions.
- Define and use invariants.
- Don't hold locks when calling functions outside the module that may reenter the module.
- Try not to hold locks across long duration operations like I/O where this can impact performance.

Using Threads 7

Threads are a powerful new tool for programmers, and in many ways they can completely change the familiar programming paradigms. As a result, the best approach to solving a particular problem using threads is not always immediately obvious even to experienced programmers. This chapter will help you determine when threads are a good solution to a programming problem (and hopefully when they're not!) and introduces a number of threading paradigms that are used to solve common programming problems. This chapter also introduces routines that implement some thread-safe versions of basic data structures and provide practical illustrations of several of the thread programming paradigms. You will find Chapter 16, "Parallel Computation" a necessary follow-up to this chapter if you are interested in the details of using multiprocessors more effectively.

Creating Threads

As in all new technologies, one of the most significant pitfalls encountered by early adopters of threads is over-use. Just as those learning to use C++ have learned to avoid creating large object hierarchies, those learning threaded programming are advised to keep the use of threads as simple as possible. Novices can be unaware of the typical costs of creating or synchronizing threads, or they may apply threads to every independent operation even though there is little opportunity for concurrency or gain in program structuring.

Threads are useful for a variety of situations, which roughly correspond to "The Benefits of Threads" on page 3. A programmer should ask a series of questions (as shown in the next few sections) to determine whether threads are appropriate to the situation at hand. These questions are not independent; there can be more than one reason to use (or not use) threads.

Improving I/O Throughput

Question

Is the application I/O bound? Would overlapping I/O operations help?

Even uniprocessors are capable of generating many I/O operations simultaneously. I/O operations can be active on all attached devices such as networks, disks, tapes, serial lines, etc. In most cases, it is also more efficient to queue several requests to individual devices as this allows the next I/O to be computed and queued while the current I/O request is being serviced, as shown in Figure 7-1.

Single Thread	compute (n)	wait for I/O (n)	compute (n+1)	wait for I/O (n+1)
Thread 1	compute (n)	wait for I/O (n)	compute (n+2)	wait for I/O (n+2)
Thread 2	wait for I/O (n-1)	compute (n+1)	wait for I/O (n+1)	compute (n+3)

Figure 7-1 I/O Overlap

The file copy program shown in Code Example 10-4 on page 184 is an example of a situation where multiple threads may not be appropriate. If the input file and the output file are regular UNIX files there will probably be little performance improvement in most situations. Most UNIX file systems recognize serial access patterns and automatically generate read-ahead and write-behind operations to an in-memory cache, in effect, automatically providing threads. However, if the program is intended to be used with raw devices (e.g., tapes and disk drives), there would be much improvement, as the input and output operations would now overlap.

By using threads, I/O overlap can be achieved using the normal, synchronous programming paradigms. For example, a Remote Procedure Call (RPC) client can call several servers simultaneously as shown in Figure 1-4 on page 3.

Asynchronous I/O vs. threads

POSIX P1003.1b includes interfaces for asynchronous I/O. Asynchronous I/O interfaces split the process of reading or writing into two phases: submission and completion. In the submission phase, an I/O operation is submitted to the system which then queues the request. The system returns control to the user program once the request is queued. The program may then continue computing, submit further I/O operations, or it may wait for previously submitted I/O operations to complete. When a queued I/O operation completes, it may signal the requesting process and/or wake up a waiting requester. The POSIX asynchronous I/O also allows I/O operations to be prioritized, I/O operations to be cancelled after submission, and a list of I/O operations to be submitted.

Asynchronous I/O operations can be used in place of threads if the only desired benefit is an increase in throughput. However, there are several limitations. First, asynchronous I/O can force the program to poll for I/O completion or to use an *event loop* style of programming (familiar to programmers of applications with window system based graphical user interfaces):

```
for (;;) {
    wait for I/O completion
    switch (I/O that completed) {
        ...
    }
}
```

Code Example 7-1 Using Asynchronous I/O in an Event Loop

This style may either be simpler for the program (e.g., the window tool kit requires using an event loop anyway) or it may introduce more complexity (e.g., the event loop must know about and coordinate all asynchronous program events). The main disadvantage of this style is that it tends to force the response to all events through the single-threaded event loop. This makes it difficult for the program to take advantage of any of the other thread benefits, where applicable. For example, in the event loop style it is difficult to defer the computation of the response to a low priority I/O operation completion or to take advantage of a multiprocessor to compute in parallel.

Another disadvantage of using asynchronous I/O is that higher level I/O libraries, such as `stdio` or remote procedure call, cannot be accessed using the POSIX asynchronous I/O interfaces since they operate only on file descriptors. Threads, on the other hand, easily accommodate such interfaces.

One fundamental advantage of asynchronous I/O over threads is in situations where it is important to have multiple outstanding I/O operations that must be done in a particular order. Consider an application that is trying to write out the contents of a memory buffer to a tape drive as quickly as possible. On most UNIX systems the character device (raw) interface to tapes is most efficient[1] for this purpose. This interface typically does not provide random access. Instead, the tape is initially positioned to the beginning of the tape or the tape file, then subsequent `write()` or `read()` operations stream[2] record data to or from the tape serially (see Figure 7-2).

---

1. This bypasses any buffer cache and usually causes the device to transfer directly from the requesting program's data buffer, without additional copying.

2. Many newer tape drives are most efficient when they *stream*; that is, when they read or write continuously forward. The system must keep up with the data transfer rate, otherwise the drive mechanism must stop and reposition itself. This slows the reading or writing process.

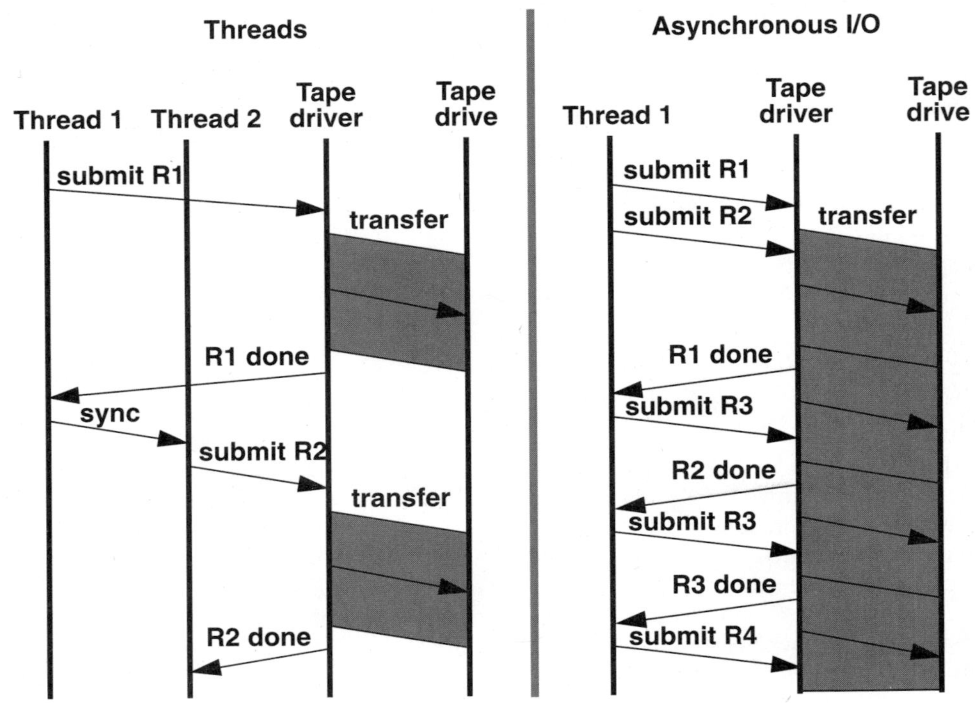

Figure 7-2 *Writing a Tape: Asynchronous I/O vs. Threads*

Using Multiple Processors

Question

Is this operation compute bound? Would taking advantage of more than one processor help?

The obvious candidates are operations that take several seconds or longer and can be split into relatively independent units. Computations that are structured as units with a high degree of interdependency may not see much performance improvement due to waiting for results between the units and inherent synchronization overhead.

When evaluating the performance of a computation, we often speak of *speedup* and *scalability*. Speedup is the ratio of the elapsed time of a single-threaded implementation of a computation to that of a multithreaded implementation executing on a multiprocessor. Ideally, the multithreaded implementation would be *N* times faster on an *N* processor machine. However, the speedup is usually less than linear because of limited parallelism opportunities in the algorithm, synchronization overhead, data sharing, and other effects. The term "scalability" describes how well a multithreaded implementation of a computation meets this ideal.

Amdahl's Law

In most computations there is some portion that can take advantage of the available processors (i.e., can be parallelized) and some portion that must be executed serially. If the portion of the computation that must be executed serially dominates the execution time, the speedup gained by multithreading the parallel portion will not be significant. Suppose the ratio of the serial execution times for the parallelizable portion of the code to the total serial execution time is *P*:

$$P = \frac{\text{Execution time of parallelizable code}}{\text{Total execution time}}$$

Then Amdahl's Law gives the maximum *speedup* achievable for *N* processors:

$$Speedup = \frac{1}{(1 - P) + \frac{P}{N}}$$

Figure 7-3 Amdahl's Law

For example, suppose a program executes for 10 minutes on a uniprocessor. After evaluating the code, you estimate that the code consuming 5 minutes of the uniprocessor execution time can be parallelized using threads and therefore *P* is 0.5. The following table gives the maximum speedup for different numbers of processors:

Processors	Execution Time (minutes)	Speedup Ratio
1	10	1
2	7.5	1.333
4	6.25	1.6
8	5.625	1.777
∞	5	2

Amdahl's Law gives only a theoretical maximum speedup. The parallelizable portion of the code may not speed up in proportion to the number of processors for many reasons, such as the overhead of the synchronization primitives, additional cache misses for maintaining a coherent shared memory on a multiprocessor, blocking due to contention on synchronization variables, and interference from other activities being scheduled on the system (see Chapter 15, "Multiprocessor Issues").

Improving User Interface Responsiveness

Question

> Are there long operations that "freeze" the user interface while they are in progress (i.e., display a "wait cursor")? Does it make sense to allow the user to do something else while the operation is taking place (including cancelling it)?

A typical example is automatic saving of a document (shown in Code Example 2-1 on page 14) where each automatic save is done in the background by a separate thread. Another example is the spreadsheet recomputation shown in Code Example 1-2 on page 8 where the recomputation is done in the background by a thread while the main thread runs the user interface. Any operation that can take long enough to be noticeable to the user is a candidate for being executed in a separate thread. In some cases the operations can simply be done by separate threads in the "background" and the user interface can proceed (e.g., auto-save). In other cases the user must wait for the operation to complete before proceeding. Threads are useful in this case simply because the operation can proceed in the background while the user interface thread allows the user to enter a request to cancel the operation, if desired.

One actual example is an X11 window manager that monitors the state of certain files with a `stat()` system call. These files might represent the user's root menu definitions or the user's mail spool. The files may actually be on remote systems, and when those systems are even temporarily unavailable due to failure or overload, the entire window system may well block. By performing the `stat()` call in a separate thread, the window manager can continue to handle user requests despite the remote outage.

Here are some common situations in which threads can be useful to applications with user interfaces. The list is by no means exhaustive. It intended as food for thought for programmers with similar situations:

- Automatic, periodic save to file
- Printing
- Recalculating a spreadsheet
- Word processor repagination
- Rendering the next page or image to be displayed
- Prefetching file data
- Long computations
- Database queries
- Remote file system delays

Improving Server Responsiveness

Question

Is this application a server? Does it mostly wait for requests from several clients or several requests from one client? If so, would servicing more than one request at the same time help?

For example, multiple requests to the server to compute some value cannot be accelerated on a uniprocessor if the computation requires only use of the CPU. It may still be advantageous to use more than one thread even when the operation is compute bound, if some requests are long and it would be undesirable to have the computing of the response for these prevent response to short requests.

Program Structure

Question

Does the program contain several independent, active entities?

The classic example of this is discrete event simulation where each independent entity is represented by an independent thread (see Figure 1-9 on page 9). However, many programs that maintain state of multiple pending operations may be much simplified with the use of threads. For example, a process monitor that follows all the children of a single parent process can be written in several ways: the monitor can fork each time the process it is monitoring forks, but this is expensive in terms of system resources. A clever programmer may be able to monitor all the processes using a single process and a way of multiplexing all the various events, but this can be extremely awkward if the various transitions are complex. Threads provide a convenient technique for allowing such a process monitor to keep the state of each monitored process encoded in its monitor thread's state.

Server Deadlock Avoidance

Question

Is this application a server? If so, is it also a client of other servers that in turn may be clients of this server? Is it a client of itself?

Suppose a Remote Procedure Call server, *A*, makes a call to another RPC server, *B*, in the process of servicing a request. If server *B*, in turn, calls server *A* in order to process server *A*'s request, the call cannot proceed if server *A* has only one thread: the only thread in server *A* is already occupied (see Figure 1-8 on page 7).

This situation can be caused by any chain of calls to servers that calls back to a server somewhere in the chain. This can also happen if the server is a client of itself.

Failure Attributes

Question

What happens to the application when unusual events occur? Do failed operations block inside library or system calls?

A good example of the need to take failure models into account is the changes caused by distributing an application across multiple machines. Here, the application may find portions of itself unresponsive (due to crashes, network outages, etc.). If the programmer has not considered the possible effect of partitioned operation, the application may well freeze and/or malfunction badly. In this case, threads provide an easy way of isolating the application from the immediate effects of remote machine unavailability, as they both allow and force the programmer to deal with the asynchronous nature of a distributed application.

A simple example is the perfmeter, a small graphical application that monitors the various performance characteristics of a local or remote host. In the case of a local host, the perfmeter may directly call into the kernel for performance statistics. No particular care is needed on the part of the programmer; if the system call doesn't return promptly the user is faced with worse problems than an unresponsive GUI, as the system has probably crashed! However, once the perfmeter supports monitoring remote hosts (presumably through a synchronous RPC protocol such as that employed by `rstatd`), the programmer needs to take into account the various failure modes that are now possible. For example, the remote host may not respond to initial RPC requests, or it may stop responding sometime later. In either case, the display will freeze until the RPC time-outs expire or the remote machine responds. While the more technically astute user will quickly associate an unresponsive perfmeter GUI with a machine in trouble, the programmer would do well to anticipate the unresponsive failure mode and use threads to allow the GUI to be updated or manipulated regardless of remote machine status. In this case, the addition of threads allows the programmer to add the feature of monitoring multiple machines at once; without threads, the first machine to fail would prevent the status of the others from being displayed.

Threads vs. Event Loops

Question

Do portions of the application assume or require an event-loop programming style?

Using threads in a process often generates very asynchronous behavior, which may be incompatible with the assumptions made by library developers. The popular X window system tool kits and 3-D graphics libraries are examples of event-loop programming, where much of the state of the application is maintained in data structures. One of the principal structural advantages of threaded programs is the ability to maintain transitional state information directly within the state of each of the threads. This contrast means that integrating threads with event-driven libraries can be a daunting and less than completely successful undertaking; see *[Smaalders 92]*. A reasonable solution with most GUI libraries is to keep all operations that need to deal with the event-loop libraries confined to a single thread, and perform long running operations in separate threads. This is covered in detail in "Multithreading a Graphical User Interface" on page 333.

Processes vs. Threads

Question

Do the independent units in a program need to be protected from each other?

It may be desirable for program units coded by different organizations to reside in different address spaces (processes) and communicate via pipes, files, or sockets. The restricted interface between the processes allows failure in a unit to be detected and isolated from the others much more readily than if the units were implemented by independent threads inside a single process. As we have seen, threads inside a process can easily interfere with each other in numerous ways that are difficult to detect.

A possible compromise is to use independent processes that communicate via shared memory or shared mapped files. This limits the damage that one process can do to another to the shared region. The processes can still pass data quickly and synchronize with each other using the synchronization primitives.

Another situation where using processes may be better than threads is where the independent operation must be done using different user or group IDs. A process can have only one user and group ID that is shared by all its threads. Operations that are sensitive to the processes' credentials must be completely serialized. This can easily destroy any concurrency.

If this sounds negative with respect to using threads, remember that using processes has a cost. They typically slow down communication, context switch more slowly, are created and destroyed much more slowly, and are a far larger burden on memory than are threads.

Thread Paradigms

From the situations outlined above we can see that threads are commonly used in a few prototypical styles. The following section describes threading strategies that are often employed when solving general programming problems (see [Hauser 93] for a case study). These approaches are applicable in a wide variety of situations, whether on uniprocessor or multiprocessor machines. For a detailed discussion of techniques targeted at using threads with multiple processors to improve performance, see Chapter 16, "Parallel Computation."

Deferring Work

Deferring work is a very common use of threads. A thread executing some critical request can defer to another thread work that can be done after the request is serviced. The work can be done by a thread that is created on demand, or it can be given to a pre-existing thread. The former is preferable on systems that support local contention scope and have low thread creation costs (see Chapter 12, "Threads Scheduling"). The priority of the thread doing the deferred work can be adjusted depending on its importance. A low priority means the work can be deferred until the system is less busy.

We've seen examples of this in the section on "Improving User Interface Responsiveness", above. However, it can also be useful in any situation where the response time to a request is critical. For example, RPC servers can defer work not critical to a request, or a tree insertion routine can defer the work of rebalancing a tree. Another typical use of the deferred work paradigm is the execution of things typically seen as background tasks in applications. Printing a document, saving a file, reading data from slow devices such as tapes or disks — all of these tasks can be good examples of deferred work. Note that in an end-user application the most important work at hand is responding to user input immediately. This is critical in order to maintain the carefully crafted metaphors placed in the user interface — if the scroll bar doesn't move when the slider is moved, the illusion is broken and the user perceives the system as being slow. Deferring work with threads allows the programmer to maintain that shared illusion. Once the deferred work has completed, the display can be updated to reflect the status change. For printing, for example, a small gauge or slider displaying percentage completion with frequent updates would alert users as to when they might expect their printouts to be ready.

Anticipating Work

This paradigm is sometimes useful in those cases where we have enough extra CPU resources to be able to afford speculative execution. A good example is an image-viewing program that starts uncompressing and building images while the user is busy viewing earlier images — it isn't clear whether the user will actually request to see all the files, but if he does the program will appear to provide them much more quickly than would otherwise be the case. Another example is the thumbnail sketches built by some postscript viewers; the odds are good that the user may never request them, but building them takes a long time and the CPU is often unloaded while the user reads the document. The principle disadvantage of doing this is the highly variable response rates seen by the user.

Pipelines, Pumps, and Serializers

Pipelines are a very familiar paradigm for anyone who has programmed Unix shell scripts; they consist of a series of filters or data pumps (see *[Rao 91]* and [Hauser 93]). Each pipeline component processes and transfers the data to the next component in the pipeline. Pipelines can be used for such tasks as providing for delayed or queued message delivery, combining multiple pending messages into a single one to reduce transport costs, and utilizing multiple processors to increase data throughput. This last case is perhaps the trickiest to implement and it is covered in more detail in Chapter 16, "Parallel Computation." Another significant advantage of using pipelines is that they often greatly simplify program structure and provide all needed synchronization in the low-level data handling routines, freeing most programmers from dealing with complex data locking issues.

Serializers are like tees in the pipeline, in that they combine two streams of data or control into a single stream, imposing an order on the previously disparate streams. Serializers are often implemented in single-threaded programming via the `select()` or `poll()` calls; they allow the programmer to combine different streams of data into a single, ordered one. Note that with threads it is possible to combine events or data sets from different domains. For example, it is feasible to construct a server that handles local requests via shared memory and synchronizes using semaphores and at the same time accepts remote requests via a TCP socket connection; with multiple threads we can easily block on a `select()` or `poll()` system call and a `sem_wait()` call at the same time.

Sleepers and One-Shots

Sleepers are a familiar programming technique for those conversant with window system or event-loop programming; a sleeper is simply a thread that repeats an action periodically, sleeping between tasks. Typical examples include blinking a cursor in a terminal emulator, checking whether new mail has been delivered or adding yet another data point onto a scrolling performance monitor. Threads can greatly simplify programming tasks of this sort.

One-shots are simply a degenerate case of a sleeper; they make only one iteration through the internal flow of control loop — sleeping, running, and then exiting. A good example might be a thread spawned to print a copy of the current document without blocking the user interface.

Deadlock Avoiders

Deadlock avoiders are a rather sophisticated thread programming paradigm, and even experienced thread programmers may find them difficult to use correctly. A deadlock avoider is a thread that is used to defer work until the necessary locks can be acquired. For example, a database engine might find itself holding some of the locks necessary to complete a particular task, but not all of them. Acquiring the remaining locks could prove difficult without violating the proper locking order. It might be far simpler to create another thread to handle the task. This "deadlock avoider" could then acquire the locks in the correct order as they are released by the parent thread, perform the task, release the locks, and exit.

Task Rejuvenation

Task rejuvenation, or error recovery, is an attempt by the programmer to overcome errors by resetting some or all of the program back into a known state by restarting threads. This can be a powerful technique for handling unexpected state transitions in a program, but its use tends to hide problems rather than solve the root cause. It has been used to good effect in recovering from external device failures and resets, and allows one to avoid programming for "blue moon conditions." However, it is not clear at present that the effort involved in supporting such "restarts" would not be better spent in anticipating and coding around unusual error conditions, especially given the limited support for error and exception handling in C and C++.

Threading Data Structures

Programmers have long relied on a common, widely understood set of data structures to help organize their programs. Good examples of such data structures are linked lists or hash tables. Multithreaded programmers need a similar armamentarium. Below, we provide thread-safe versions of three familiar data structures including a singly linked list, a queue, and a hash table. In the following section we'll use these routines in an example program that illustrates some of the common threading paradigms.

Linked Lists

The first example is a linked list. Linked lists are relatively simple, though the basic techniques used can be applied to much more complicated examples. The interface is as follows:

```
int
list_init(list_t *list);
```

This function initializes the `list` data structure.

```
int
list_add(list_t *list, void *item);
```

This routine adds `item` to the `list`. It doesn't check for duplicates.

```
int
list_traverse(list_t *list, int (*func)(void *, void *), void *arg);
```

This function traverses the `list`, calling the caller-supplied function once for each item, passing the item and a caller-supplied pointer, *arg*, as arguments. If *func()* returns `1`, traversal stops and `list_traverse()` returns. If it returns `0`, traversal continues, while if `-1` is returned, the item is deleted from the `list`.

```
int
list_remove(list_t *list, void *item);
```

This function removes the first instance of `item` from the `list`.

```
int
list_destroy(list_t *list);
```

This function destroys the `list` structure.

This example, shown in Code Example 7-2, includes checks for internal consistency — in other words, tests to see that the *invariant* is maintained. This is a useful technique during debugging, and helps find subtle errors; attempts to write more complex threaded code without such checks usually results in having to retrofit them later.

```
void
ll_init(llh_t *head)
{
    head->back = &head->front;
    head->front = NULL;
}
```

```
void
ll_enqueue(llh_t *head, ll_t *data)
{
    data->n = NULL;
    *head->back = data;
    head->back = &data->n;
}

ll_t *
ll_peek(llh_t *head)
{
    return (head->front);
}

ll_t *
ll_dequeue(llh_t *head)
{
    ll_t *ptr;
    ptr = head->front;
    if (ptr && ((head->front = ptr->n) == NULL))
        head->back = &head->front;
    return (ptr);
}

ll_t *
ll_traverse(llh_t *ptr, int (*func)(void *, void *), void *user)
{
    ll_t *t;
    ll_t **prev = &ptr->front;

    t = ptr->front;
    while (t) {
        switch (func(t, user)) {
        case 1:
            return (NULL);
        case 0:
            prev = &(t->n);
            t = t->n;
            break;
        case -1:
            if ((*prev = t->n) == NULL)
                ptr->back = prev;
            return (t);
        }
    }
    return (NULL);
}
```

```
/* Make sure the list isn't corrupt and returns number of list items */
int
ll_check(llh_t *head)
{
    int i = 0;
    ll_t *ptr = head->front;
    ll_t **prev = &head->front;

    while (ptr) {
        i++;
        prev = &ptr->n;
        ptr = ptr->n;
    }
    assert(head->back == prev);
    return (i);
}

typedef struct list_entry {
    struct ll list;
    void *data;
} list_entry_t;

typedef struct list {
    int count;
    pthread_mutex_t lock;
    llh_t head;
} list_t;

static int
list_check(list_t *ptr)                    /* call while holding lock */
{
    assert(ptr->count == ll_check(&ptr->head));
    return (1);
}

int
list_init(list_t *ptr)
{
    ptr->count = 0;
    ll_init(&ptr->head);
    pthread_mutex_init(&ptr->lock, NULL);
    assert(pthread_mutex_lock(&ptr->lock) == 0 &&
          list_check(ptr) &&
          pthread_mutex_unlock(&ptr->lock) == 0);
    return (0);
}
```

```
int
list_add(list_t *ptr, void *item)
{
    /* we call malloc w/o holding lock to save time */
    list_entry_t *e = (list_entry_t *) malloc(sizeof (*e));

    if (e == NULL)
        return (-1);
    e->data = item;
    pthread_mutex_lock(&ptr->lock);
    assert(list_check(ptr));
    ptr->count++;
    ll_enqueue(&ptr->head, &e->list);
    assert(list_check(ptr));
    pthread_mutex_unlock(&ptr->lock);
    return (0);
}

struct wrap {
    int (*func)(void *, void *);
    void *user;
};

static int
wrapper(void *e, void *u)
{
    list_entry_t *q = (list_entry_t *) e;
    struct wrap *w = (struct wrap *)u;
    return (w->func(q->data, w->user));
}
```

```
int
list_traverse(list_t *ptr, int (*func)(void *, void *), void *user)
{
    list_entry_t *ret;

    struct wrap wrap;
    wrap.func = func;
    wrap.user = user;
    pthread_mutex_lock(&ptr->lock);
    assert(list_check(ptr));
    ret = (list_entry_t *)
        ll_traverse(&ptr->head, wrapper, (void *) &wrap);
    if (ret) {
        free(ret);
        ptr->count--;
    }
    assert(list_check(ptr));
    pthread_mutex_unlock(&ptr->lock);
    return (0);
}

static int
matchit(void *data, void *compare)
{
    return ((data == compare)? -1: 0);
}

int
list_remove(list_t *ptr, void *item)
{
    return (list_traverse(ptr, matchit, item)? -1: 0);
}

int
list_destroy(list_t *ptr)
{
    list_entry_t *e;

    while ((e = (list_entry_t *) ll_dequeue(&ptr->head)) != NULL)
        free(e);
    return (pthread_mutex_destroy(&ptr->lock));
}
```

Code Example 7-2 Linked List Routines

The list routines are easy to apply, but the alert programmer will notice that the list is only locked during a call to one of the above functions. As a result, modifications to the memory referenced by the data pointers stored in the list at other times will cause a data race.

Queues

The next example is a simple queue, which allows threads to enqueue and dequeue pointers. This type of synchronization device is very useful and easy to use, and is a natural way of implementing a pipeline. The only caveat is that the producer thread(s) (the one enqueuing data) cannot reclaim the storage associated with the pointers; this is left to the consumer thread(s).

The interfaces for the queue routines are straightforward:

```
int
dataq_init(dataq_t *dataq);
```

The initialization prepares the *dataq* structure for use.

```
int
data_enqueue(dataq_t *dataq, void *ptr);
```

This routine places *ptr* at the end of the queue. It returns `0` if successful, `-1` if it was unable to allocate the necessary memory.

```
void *
data_dequeue(dataq_t *dataq);
```

This routine removes the pointer at the head of the queue. If the queue is empty, the routine blocks until data is added.

```
int
dataq_destroy(dataq_t *dataq);
```

This routine destroys the *dataq* structure.

Note that as with all synchronization primitives, some sort of external synchronization is required to allow the safe use of `dataq_destroy()`; destruction of an object with other threads still attempting to use it is a common source of obscure bugs.

```
typedef struct dataq_data {
    ll_t list;
    void *data;
} dataq_data_t;

typedef struct dataq_waiter {
    ll_t list;
    pthread_cond_t cv;
    int wakeup;
} dataq_waiter_t;

typedef struct dataq {
    pthread_mutex_t lock;
    int num_data;
    int num_waiters;
    llh_t data;
    llh_t waiters;
} dataq_t;

static int
dataq_check(dataq_t *ptr)     /* call while holding lock! */
{
    assert(ptr->num_data == ll_check(&ptr->data));
    assert(ptr->num_waiters == ll_check(&ptr->waiters));
    return (1);
}

int
dataq_init(dataq_t *ptr)
{
    ptr->num_data = 0;
    ptr->num_waiters = 0;
    ll_init(&ptr->data);
    ll_init(&ptr->waiters);
    pthread_mutex_init(&ptr->lock, NULL);
    assert((pthread_mutex_lock(&ptr->lock) == 0) &&
          (dataq_check(ptr) == 1) &&
          (pthread_mutex_unlock(&ptr->lock) == 0));
    return (0);
}
```

```
int
dataq_enqueue(dataq_t *dataq, void *in)
{
    dataq_data_t *ptr = (dataq_data_t *) malloc(sizeof (*ptr));
    dataq_waiter_t *sleeper = NULL;

    if (ptr == NULL)
        return (-1);
    ptr->data = in;
    pthread_mutex_lock(&dataq->lock);
    assert(dataq_check(dataq));
    ll_enqueue(&dataq->data, &ptr->list);
    dataq->num_data++;
    if (dataq->num_waiters) {
        sleeper = (dataq_waiter_t *) ll_peek(&dataq->waiters);
        sleeper->wakeup = 1;
    }
    assert(dataq_check(dataq));
    pthread_mutex_unlock(&dataq->lock);
    if (sleeper)
        pthread_cond_signal(&sleeper->cv);
    return (0);
}
```

```
int
dataq_dequeue(dataq_t *dataq, void **outptr)
{
    dataq_data_t *dptr;
    dataq_waiter_t *sleeper = NULL;

    pthread_mutex_lock(&dataq->lock);
    if ((dataq->num_waiters > 0) ||
         ((dptr = (dataq_data_t *) ll_dequeue(&dataq->data)) == NULL)) {
        dataq_waiter_t wait;
        wait.wakeup = 0;
        pthread_cond_init(&wait.cv, NULL);
        dataq->num_waiters++;
        ll_enqueue(&dataq->waiters, &wait.list);
        while (wait.wakeup == 0)
            pthread_cond_wait(&wait.cv, &dataq->lock);
        ll_dequeue(&dataq->waiters);
        dataq->num_waiters--;
        pthread_cond_destroy(&wait.cv);
        dptr = (dataq_data_t *) ll_dequeue(&dataq->data);
    }
    dataq->num_data--;
    if (dataq->num_data && dataq->num_waiters) {
        sleeper = (dataq_waiter_t *) ll_peek(&dataq->waiters);
        sleeper->wakeup = 1;
    }
    pthread_mutex_unlock(&dataq->lock);
    if (sleeper)
        pthread_cond_signal(&sleeper->cv);
    *outptr = dptr->data;
    free(dptr);
    return (0);
}

int
dataq_destroy(dataq_t *dataq)
{
    pthread_mutex_destroy(&dataq->lock);
    return (0);
}
```

Code Example 7-3 Queue Routines

As is typical of such synchronization structures, the data queue code uses a lock to protect the internal data structures during their modification. Note that since we want to enforce queuing, each thread that is blocked due to an empty queue sleeps on its own condition variable (created on its own stack), inserting and removing itself from the list. This is a very useful technique when you wish to enforce sequential access.

Hash Tables

Another common programming tool is the hash table, but it can be more complicated to use in a threaded environment since the locking techniques are more complex. The fundamental problem is that a thread that looks up data in the hash table usually wants to use the data after retrieval. This is not difficult if the amount of data is small and known; we can simply copy the data into a buffer supplied by the calling thread while holding a lock on the table. However, as the amount of data increases this is no longer practical, and other problems remain. For example, suppose we wish to implement a cache for some data that is slow to obtain. We can use a hash table to cache the results of previous lookups; for new requests, threads will look for data in the cache, fail to find it, and begin obtaining the information the hard way. We clearly don't want to lock the hash table while we're waiting for results as this would prevent the retrieval of other information, but if we drop the lock, multiple threads requesting the same information at nearly the same time will all make expensive requests for the same information and all will attempt to insert the data once they obtain it, which isn't desirable. Both the copy-out and the insertion problems argue for the ability to lock each entry in the hash table individually.

Continuing our cache daemon example, we can also anticipate the need to traverse all the hash table entries, either to collect and print out statistics or to invalidate all the entries in the cache. In this case we find ourselves having to hold a lock on the entire table for those cases where we wish to operate on the entire table at once. This is a situation roughly analogous to a read/write lock (see "Read/Write Locks" on page 248).

The interface routines are as follows:

```
hash_t *
hash_make(int bucket_size, int hash_type);
```

This routine constructs a hash table with *bucket_size* buckets. A *hash_type* of 0 specifies that the hash key is a string, otherwise hash keys are treated as opaque values.

```
void **
hash_get(hash_t *tbl, void *key);
```

This routine gets the address associated with *key* where a pointer may be stored. If the entry doesn't exist, it is created. It also atomically locks the entry, so that it may be modified or read without a data race.

```
void **
hash_find(hash_t *tbl, void *key);
```

This routine gets the address associated with `key` where a pointer may be stored. If the entry doesn't exist, `NULL` is returned. It also atomically locks the entry, so that it may be modified or read without a data race.

```
int
hash_operate(hash_t *tbl,
    void (*func)(void *key, void **data, void *arg), void *arg);
```

This routine obtains an exclusive lock over the entire table and calls `func()` for each entry in the hash table, passing `key`, the data pointer storage location, and `arg` with each call.

```
int
hash_delete(hash_t *tbl, void **data);
```

This routine deletes the entry that was obtained and locked earlier with either `hash_get()` or `hash_find()`.

```
int
hash_release(hash_t * tbl, void ** data);
```

This routine releases the entry lock that was obtained via the `hash_find()` and `hash_get()` routines. Note that all such locks must be released before a `hash_operate()` call can proceed.

```
int
hash_destroy(hash_t *tbl);
```

This routine destroys `tbl`.

```
#define ENTRY_LOCKED 1
#define STRING_HASH_KEY 0
#define INT_HASH_KEY 1

#include "llt.h"

typedef struct hash_entry {
    void *data;                     /* data storage */
    void *key;                      /* key (either int or char*) */
    unsigned int hash_signature;    /* speeds up lookups for strings*/
    short status;                   /* holds locked bit */
    short num_waiters;              /* number of threads waiting */
    pthread_t holder;               /* for debugging checks */
    llh_t waiters;                  /* threads waiting for entry */
    struct hash_entry *next_entry;/* ptr to next entry in bucket */
    struct hash_entry *right_entry;/* next entry in master chain */
    struct hash_entry *left_entry;/* previous entry in master */
} hash_entry_t;

typedef struct hash_waiter {
    ll_t list;                      /* list pointer */
    int wakeup;                     /* flag for cv */
    hash_entry_t *entry;            /* which entry we're waiting for */
    pthread_cond_t cv;              /* condition variable we block on */
} hash_waiter_t;

typedef struct hash {
    pthread_mutex_t lock;           /* mutext to protect hash table */
    int size;                       /* number of buckets */
    int hash_type;                  /* 0 == string, else int */
    int operator_wait_count;        /* #threads waiting to op */
    int get_wait_count;             /* #threads waiting to use get */
    int lock_status;                /* -1 op, 0 unused + get count */
    pthread_cond_t operate_cv;      /* waiters for operate */
    pthread_cond_t get_cv;          /* waiters for get during op */
    hash_entry_t **table;           /* buckets */
    hash_entry_t *start;            /* first entry in master chain */
} hash_t;

extern hash_t *hash_make(int size, int key_type);
extern void **hash_get(hash_t *tbl, char *key);
extern void **hash_find(hash_t *tbl, char *key);
extern int hash_release(hash_t *tbl, void **data);
extern void *hash_delete(hash_t *tbl, void **dataptr);
extern int hash_operate(hash_t *tbl, void (*ptr)(void *,void *,void *),
      void *usr_arg);
```

```
static int
hash_check(hash_t *ptr)             /* call while lock is held! */
{
    int i, count1, count2;
    hash_entry_t *tmp;

    count1 = 0;
    for (i = 0; i < ptr->size; i++) {
        tmp = ptr->table[i];
        while (tmp) {
            int waiters = ll_check(&tmp->waiters);
            assert(waiters == tmp->num_waiters);
            count1++;
            tmp = tmp->next_entry;
        }
    }
    tmp = ptr->start;
    count2 = 0;
    if (tmp) {
        count2++;
        assert(tmp->right_entry == NULL);
        tmp = tmp->left_entry;
    }
    while (tmp) {
        if (tmp->left_entry != NULL)
            assert(tmp->left_entry->right_entry == tmp);
        count2++;
        tmp = tmp->left_entry;
    }
    assert(count2 == count1);
    return (1);
}

static unsigned
hash_string(char *s)
{
    unsigned result = 0;

    while (*s)
        result += (result << 3) + *s++;
    return (result);
}
```

```
hash_t *
hash_make(int size, int key_type)
{
    hash_t *ptr;

    ptr = (hash_t *) malloc(sizeof (*ptr));
    ptr->size = size;
    ptr->table = (hash_entry_t **)
                    malloc((size_t)(sizeof (hash_entry_t *) * size));
    ptr->start = NULL;
    ptr->hash_type = key_type;
    ptr->lock_status = 0;
    (void) memset((void *) ptr->table, (char) 0,
          sizeof (hash_entry_t *) * size);
    pthread_mutex_init(&ptr->lock, NULL);
    pthread_cond_init(&ptr->operate_cv, NULL);
    pthread_cond_init(&ptr->get_cv, NULL);
    assert((pthread_mutex_lock(&ptr->lock) == 0) &&
          (hash_check(ptr) == 1) &&
          (pthread_mutex_unlock(&ptr->lock) == 0));
    return (ptr);
}
```

```
void **
hash_get(hash_t *tbl, char *key)
{
    unsigned int sig;
    unsigned int bucket;
    hash_entry_t *tmp;
    hash_entry_t *new;

    if (tbl->hash_type == STRING_HASH_KEY)
        bucket = (sig = hash_string(key)) % tbl->size;
    else
        bucket = (sig = (unsigned int) key) % tbl->size;
    pthread_mutex_lock(&tbl->lock);
    assert(hash_check(tbl));
    while (tbl->operator_wait_count || tbl->lock_status < 0) {
        tbl->get_wait_count++;
        pthread_cond_wait(&tbl->get_cv, &tbl->lock);
        tbl->get_wait_count--;
    }
    tmp = tbl->table[bucket];
    if (tbl->hash_type == STRING_HASH_KEY)
        while (tmp != NULL) {
            if ((tmp->hash_signature == sig) &&
               (strcmp(tmp->key, key) == 0))
                break;
            tmp = tmp->next_entry;
        } else {
            while (tmp != NULL) {
                if (tmp->key == key)
                    break;
                tmp = tmp->next_entry;
            }
        }
    if (tmp) {
        if (tmp->num_waiters || (tmp->status & ENTRY_LOCKED)) {
            hash_waiter_t wait;
            hash_waiter_t *tst;

            wait.wakeup = 0;
            wait.entry = tmp;
            pthread_cond_init(&wait.cv, NULL);
            tmp->num_waiters++;
            ll_enqueue(&tmp->waiters, &wait.list);

            while (wait.wakeup == 0) {
                pthread_cond_wait(&wait.cv, &tbl->lock);
```

```
            }

            tst = (hash_waiter_t *)ll_dequeue(&tmp->waiters);
            assert(tst == &wait);
            tmp->num_waiters--;
            pthread_cond_destroy(&wait.cv);
        }
        tbl->lock_status++;
        tmp->status |= ENTRY_LOCKED;
        tmp->holder = pthread_self();
        assert(hash_check(tbl));
        pthread_mutex_unlock(&tbl->lock);
        return (&tmp->data);
    }

    /* not found. insert new entry into bucket. */
    new = (hash_entry_t *) malloc(sizeof (*new));
    new->key = ((tbl->hash_type == STRING_HASH_KEY)?
                 strdup(key): key);
    new->hash_signature = sig;
    /* hook into chain from tbl */
    new->right_entry = NULL;
    if ((new->left_entry = tbl->start) != NULL) {
        assert(tbl->start->right_entry == NULL);
        tbl->start->right_entry = new;
    }
    tbl->start = new;
    /* hook into bucket chain */
    new->next_entry = tbl->table[bucket];
    tbl->table[bucket] = new;
    new->data = NULL;               /* so we know that it is new */
    new->status = ENTRY_LOCKED;
    new->holder = pthread_self();
    new->num_waiters = 0;
    ll_init(&new->waiters);
    tbl->lock_status++;
    assert(hash_check(tbl));
    pthread_mutex_unlock(&tbl->lock);
    return (&new->data);
}
```

```
void **
hash_find(hash_t *tbl, char *key)
{
    hash_entry_t *tmp;
    unsigned int sig;

    if (tbl->hash_type == STRING_HASH_KEY)
        sig = hash_string(key);
    else
        sig = (unsigned int) key;
    pthread_mutex_lock(&tbl->lock);
    assert(hash_check(tbl));
    while (tbl->operator_wait_count || tbl->lock_status < 0) {
        tbl->get_wait_count++;
        pthread_cond_wait(&tbl->get_cv, &tbl->lock);
        tbl->get_wait_count--;
    }
    tmp = tbl->table[ sig % tbl->size];
    if (tbl->hash_type == STRING_HASH_KEY) {
        for ( ;tmp != NULL; tmp = tmp->next_entry) {
            if (sig== tmp->hash_signature && strcmp(tmp->key, key)==0)
                break;
        }
    } else {
        for (; tmp != NULL; tmp = tmp->next_entry) {
            if (tmp->key == key)
                break;
        }
    }
```

```
    if (tmp) {
        if (tmp->num_waiters || (tmp->status & ENTRY_LOCKED)) {
            hash_waiter_t wait;

            wait.wakeup = 0;
            wait.entry = tmp;
            pthread_cond_init(&wait.cv, NULL);
            tmp->num_waiters++;
            ll_enqueue(&tmp->waiters, &wait.list);
            while (wait.wakeup == 0)
                pthread_cond_wait(&wait.cv, &tbl->lock);
            tmp->num_waiters--;
            ll_dequeue(&tmp->waiters);
            pthread_cond_destroy(&wait.cv);
        }
        tmp->status |= ENTRY_LOCKED;
        tmp->holder = pthread_self();
        tbl->lock_status++;
        assert(hash_check(tbl));
        pthread_mutex_unlock(&tbl->lock);
        return (&tmp->data);
    }
    assert(hash_check(tbl));
    pthread_mutex_unlock(&tbl->lock);
    return (NULL);
}
```

```
int
hash_release(hash_t *tbl, void **data)
{
    hash_entry_t *tmp = (hash_entry_t *)data;
    hash_waiter_t *sleeper = NULL;
    int op_wait;

    pthread_mutex_lock(&tbl->lock);
    assert(hash_check(tbl));
    assert(tbl->lock_status > 0);
    assert(tmp->status & ENTRY_LOCKED);
    assert(tmp->holder == pthread_self());
    tmp->holder = 0;
    tmp->status &= ~ENTRY_LOCKED;
    tbl->lock_status--;
    op_wait = (tbl->operator_wait_count && tbl->lock_status == 0);
    if (tmp->num_waiters) {
        sleeper = (hash_waiter_t *) ll_peek(&tmp->waiters);
        sleeper->wakeup = 0xdeadbeef;
    }
    assert(hash_check(tbl));
    pthread_mutex_unlock(&tbl->lock);
    if (op_wait)
        pthread_cond_broadcast(&tbl->operate_cv);
    if (sleeper)
        pthread_cond_signal(&sleeper->cv);
    return (0);
}
```

```
void *
hash_delete(hash_t *tbl, void **dataptr)
{
    hash_waiter_t *sleeper = NULL;
    hash_entry_t *act, *tmp, **prev;
    unsigned int sig;
    char *old;
    int bucket;
    int op_wait;

    act = (hash_entry_t *) dataptr;
    pthread_mutex_lock(&tbl->lock);

    assert(hash_check(tbl));
    assert(act->status & ENTRY_LOCKED);
    assert(act->holder == pthread_self());
    if (tbl->hash_type == STRING_HASH_KEY)
        sig = hash_string(act->key);
    else
        sig = (unsigned int) act->key;
    tmp = tbl->table[ bucket = sig % tbl->size];
    prev = tbl->table + bucket;
    for (; tmp != NULL; tmp = tmp->next_entry) {
        if (tmp == act)
            break;
        prev = &tmp->next_entry;
    }
    assert(tmp != NULL);
    old = tmp->data;
    tbl->lock_status--;
    op_wait = (tbl->operator_wait_count && tbl->lock_status == 0);
    if (tmp->num_waiters) {     /*others are waiting so keep entry here*/
        tmp->holder = 0;
        if (tmp->num_waiters) {
            sleeper = (hash_waiter_t *) ll_peek(&tmp->waiters);
            sleeper->wakeup = 0xbadbeef;
            tmp->data = NULL;
            tmp->status &= ~ENTRY_LOCKED;
            tmp->holder = 0;
            tmp = NULL;             /* so we don't free it later */
        }
```

```
    } else {
        hash_entry_t *r, *l;
        /*
         * tmp now points to entry marked for deletion,prev to address
         * of storage of next pointer pointing to tmp.
         * remove from bucket chain first.
         */
        assert(hash_check(tbl));
        if (tbl->hash_type == STRING_HASH_KEY)
            free(tmp->key);
        *prev = tmp->next_entry;
        /* now remove from dbly linked tbl chain */
        r = tmp->right_entry;
        l = tmp->left_entry;
        if (r != NULL)
            r->left_entry = l;
        else
            tbl->start = l;
        if (l != NULL)
            l->right_entry = r;
        assert(hash_check(tbl));
    }
    assert(hash_check(tbl));
    pthread_mutex_unlock(&tbl->lock);
    if (tmp)
        free(tmp);
    if (op_wait)
        pthread_cond_broadcast(&tbl->operate_cv);
    if (sleeper)
        pthread_cond_signal(&sleeper->cv);
    return (old);
}
```

```
int
hash_operate(hash_t *tbl,
    void (*ptr)(void *, void *, void *),void *usr_arg)
{
    hash_entry_t *tmp;
    int c = 0;
    int sleepers;

    pthread_mutex_lock(&tbl->lock);
    while (tbl->lock_status != 0) {
        tbl->operator_wait_count++;
        pthread_cond_wait(&tbl->operate_cv, &tbl->lock);
        tbl->operator_wait_count--;
    }
    tmp = tbl->start;
    while (tmp) {
        (*ptr)(tmp->data,usr_arg, tmp->key);
        tmp = tmp->left_entry;
        c++;
    }
    if (tbl->get_wait_count)
        pthread_cond_broadcast(&tbl->get_cv);
    pthread_mutex_unlock(&tbl->lock);
    return (c);
}
```

Code Example 7-4 Hash Table Routines

Note that a hash table can be a straightforward way of locking objects that don't support locks internally; using the address of the object as the key in an integer hash table provides a lock per object in a reasonably efficient, scalable way.

An Example

Let's use the data structures and routines shown in the previous section and several of the more common thread paradigms to write a threaded program.

The example program implements a multithreaded daemon for caching the result of name service requests. The name cache daemon has the following design features and constraints:

- It needs to support multiple types of connections. In this case we've chosen to support both UDP and TCP sockets. This is typical of more and more system services as the various types of IPC mechanisms have multiplied.
- We assume that the actual name service requests take a long time (~1 second) to complete, so providing multithreaded access to the information is important.

- The daemon has to support some method of cache invalidation; in this case it invalidates the cache if a `SIGHUP` is received. However, we've decided to not trust any data older than 30 minutes; this will "age" the cache and prevent the long-term retention of possibly erroneous data.
- In order to keep response time reasonable at the start of the day and after lunch, we'll determine the most popular entries periodically and revalidate the data for those entries before they expire, and discard any data we find that is out of date.

There are many other features and ideas that might be incorporated in a realistic cache daemon; however, these are sufficient for our example. Figure 7-4 illustrates the basic program structure. Note the following:

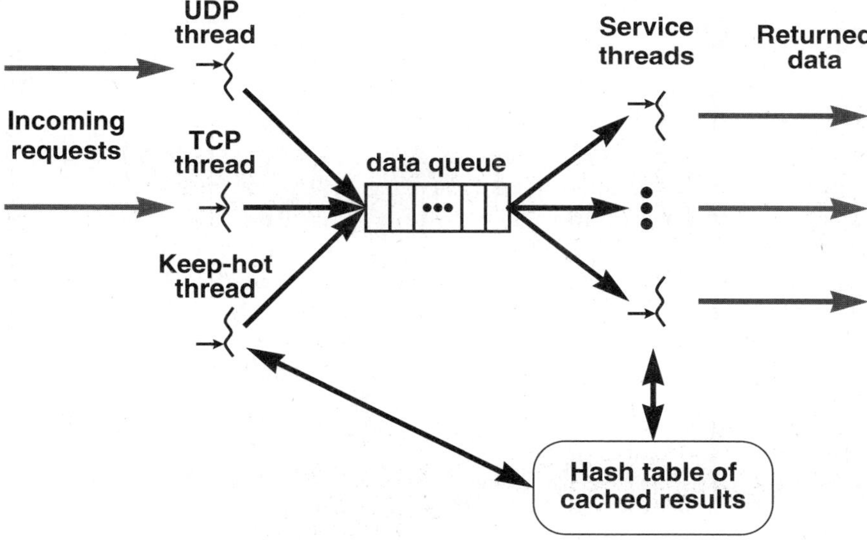

Figure 7-4 Cache Daemon Structure

- There is a thread associated with each transport. This is often required if the wait paradigms for the transports are not compatible; an example might be a shared memory transport using semaphores and a socket-based transport such as TCP.
- The various transports use a single data queue to order requests, forming an example of the serializer paradigm discussed earlier. If desired, we could easily use multiple queues here for high and low priority requests. The keep-hot thread also issues requests through the same queue.

- The service threads block on the queue waiting for requests rather than blocking on a read() or select() (poll()) system call. This allows us to support many connections without the undue resource consumption involved in using a thread per connection. The service threads form a classic Pipeline architecture, each waiting for work in the data queue.
- The hash table provides a "blackboard" of available information. This is accessed by the service threads for data lookup and update. The keep-hot thread accesses the hash table periodically when scanning for the most popular entries to keep active in the cache. The keep-hot thread is a typical example of the sleeper paradigm. Its queuing of update and deletion requests for the service threads is an example of both the deferred work and deadlock avoidance paradigms. The keep-hot thread defers the work of actually looking up the data again to the service threads in order to enable traversing the list quickly. Even if we could accept a longer traversal time, any attempt to delete the data during traversal with the existing hash table interfaces would cause deadlock, so we use the service threads as deadlock avoiders as well.

Note that this example is rather complex and assumes a certain familiarity with sockets, networking, and other aspects of Unix system programming. The complexities are interesting in that they are typical of the issues encountered when writing a multi-threaded server. The code in this example does indeed run and does effectively cache the requested data. The easiest way to use this example is to run it and use the mconnect program (available on Unix systems) to connect to port 6666 using TCP. There is a program at the World Wide Web site[3] (udp_client.c) that will allow you to exercise the UDP thread as well.

Cache daemon data structures

Since the two communication protocols (UDP and TCP) need different techniques for reading and writing the data, we use a set of function pointers to allow the requesting thread to specify the function used to read the query, write back the results, and handle any errors that occur. This allows for easy expansion to other communication domains that don't use read() or write() (providing a third transport that uses shared memory makes an interesting programming exercise). In order to reduce memory usage, we allocate different data structures for the TCP and UDP cases; the first part of the data structures are the same, so this causes no problems.

3. http://www.sun.com/smi/ssoftpress/threads/

```
#include <pthread.h>
#include <stdlib.h>
#include <string.h>
#include <stdio.h>
#include <unistd.h>
#include <errno.h>
#include <memory.h>
#include <signal.h>
#include <sys/types.h>
#include <sys/socket.h>
#include <netinet/in.h>
#include <arpa/inet.h>
#include <netdb.h>

#include "hash.h"
#include "dataq.h"

#define WORK_LOOKUP 1
#define WORK_UPDATE 2
#define WORK_DELETE 3

static char *named_ops[] = {NULL, "Lookup", "Update", "Delete"};

#define NAMESIZE 255
#define RESULTSSIZE 255

typedef struct work {
    int todo;
    int (*rfunc)(struct work *, char *name);
    int (*wfunc)(struct work *, char *results);
    int (*efunc)(struct work *);
} work_t;

typedef struct tcp_work {
    work_t work;
    int fd;
} tcp_work_t;

typedef struct udp_work {
    work_t work;
    char name[NAMESIZE];
    int len;
    struct sockaddr addr;
    int addrlen;
} udp_work_t;
```

```
typedef struct update_work {
    work_t work;
    char name[NAMESIZE];
} update_work_t;

typedef struct nsdata {
    char *answer;
    int hits;
    time_t time;
} nsdata_t;

static dataq_t *q;
static hash_t *h;
static int ttl = 15;        /* time to live for data */

void service_thread(void *);
void update_thread(void *);
void udp_thread(void *);
void tcp_thread(void *);
char *getanswer(char *);
```

The service threads perform all the lookup, update, and delete functionality. We've kept this generic by using function pointers. Locking is handled by the hash routines; we just need to take into account copying the results of a lookup operation before we release the entry lock.

```
void
service_thread(void *arg)
{
    work_t *w;
    nsdata_t *d;
    nsdata_t **dptr;
    time_t now;
    char name[NAMESIZE];
    char results[RESULTSSIZE];

    for (;;) {
        dataq_dequeue(q, (void **)&w);     /* get data */
        now = time(NULL);
        /* perform the transport specific read operation */
        if (w->rfunc(w, name) != 0) {
            w->efunc(w);                    /* whoops. error handler */
            continue;
        }
        /* look up and acquire lock */
        dptr = (nsdata_t **) hash_get(h, name);
        d = *dptr;
        switch (w->todo) {
        case WORK_LOOKUP:
            if (d) {
                d->hits++;
                if (d->time + ttl > now)
                    break;
            }
            /* fallthrough */
        case WORK_UPDATE:
            if (!d) {
                d = *dptr = (nsdata_t *) malloc(sizeof (**dptr));
                d->hits = 1;
                d->answer = NULL;
            }
            if (d->answer)
                free(d->answer);
            d->time = now;
            d->answer = getanswer(name);
            break;
```

```
        case WORK_DELETE:
            if (d) {
                if (d->answer)
                    free(d->answer);
                d->answer = 0;
                free(d);
                *dptr = NULL;
                hash_delete(h, (void**)dptr);
            }
            break;
        }
        if (w->todo == WORK_LOOKUP)
            strcpy(results, d->answer);
        if (w->todo != WORK_DELETE)
            hash_release(h, (void**)dptr);     /* release lock */
        w->wfunc(w, results);
    }
}
```

We install an empty `SIGPIPE` handler during setup since we can receive a `SIGPIPE` if the process we're returning the results to exits in the middle of a write. We setup the data structures, install the handler and start our service threads, and then pause. The `getanswer()` function makes the actual name service request and formats up a single string response in a fresh buffer.

```
static void
do_nothing()
{
}
```

```
void
main(int argc, char *argv[])
{
    int i;
    static dataq_t qstruct;
    pthread_t thread;
    struct sigaction act;

    h = hash_make(1117, STRING_HASH_KEY);
    q = &qstruct;
    dataq_init(q);
    act.sa_handler = do_nothing;
    sigemptyset(&act.sa_mask);
    act.sa_flags = 0;
    sigaction(SIGPIPE, &act, NULL);

    for (i = 0; i < 10; i++)
        pthread_create(&thread, NULL,
            (void *(*)(void *))service_thread, NULL);
    pthread_create(&thread, NULL,
        (void *(*)(void *))tcp_thread, NULL);
    pthread_create(&thread, NULL,
        (void *(*)(void *))udp_thread, NULL);
    pthread_create(&thread, NULL,
        (void *(*)(void *))update_thread, NULL);
    for (;;)
        pause();
}

char *
getanswer(char *name)
{
    char buffer[4096];
    struct hostent result;
    int herrno;

    if (gethostbyname_r(name, &result, buffer,
            sizeof (buffer), &herrno) == NULL) {
        sprintf(buffer, "%d:%d\n", -1, herrno);
    } else {
        struct in_addr in;
        memcpy(&in.s_addr, *(result.h_addr_list), sizeof (in.s_addr));
        sprintf(buffer, "%d:%s\n", 0, inet_ntoa(in));
    }
    return (strdup(buffer));
}
```

The following functions implement the TCP transport. Since TCP has a file descriptor per connection, we can defer reading any data until the service threads receive the work request. This tends to simplify data handling, but we need to do more work in connection management. The most interesting portion of this is the use of the accept thread to accept connection requests as fast as possible. It sends the file descriptor returned from the accept system call to the `tcp_thread`, which is parked in a poll system call on all the active TCP connections and the pipe. When any data is received on the pipe, it is interpreted as an integer file descriptor and added to the list of descriptors to be polled. Once `poll()` returns and the `revents` field indicates that data is available on that descriptor, the descriptor is passed to a service thread as part of a `tcp_work` request and is removed from the list of descriptors to be polled, not returning until read again from the pipe. This technique allows us to handle a large number of active connections without having a thread per connection. This can result in significant savings in kernel resources, since we minimize the number of threads parked in blocking system calls in the kernel.

Note that `tcp_read()` reads one character at a time; this keeps things simple, for this example, since we can use new-lines as a message boundary. This is typical of many simple TCP protocols such as SMTP for mail and NNTP for news.

```
/*
 * The following routines implement the tcp thread. Note the use of a
 * pipe to handle waking the main tcp thread when either a new
 * descriptor is ready or an existing one has had the request serviced.
 */
#define MAXCONS 20
#define PORT_NUM 6666

static int fd_write_return;
static int fd_read_return;
static struct pollfd pfds[MAXCONS];
static int tcp_read(tcp_work_t *, char *);
static int tcp_write(tcp_work_t *, char *);
static int tcp_error(tcp_work_t *);
```

```
static int
tcp_read(tcp_work_t *w, char *name)
{
    int i, rc;

    i = 0;

    /* the following isn't efficient, but it is simple and brief */
    while (i++ < NAMESIZE-1 && (rc = read(w->fd, name, 1)) == 1) {
        if (*name == '\n') {
            *name-- = 0;
            if (*name == '\r')      /* odd mode */
                *name = 0;
            return (0);
        }
        name++;
    }
    return (-1);                    /* too long or EOF or other error */
}

static int
tcp_write(tcp_work_t *w, char *results)
{
    int len = strlen(results);
    int written = 0;
    int wc;

    while (written < len) {
        if ((wc = write(w->fd, results, len-written)) <= 0) {
            tcp_error(w);
            return (-1);
        }
        results += wc;
        written += wc;
    }
    if (write(fd_write_return, &w->fd, 4) != 4) {
        printf("can't write 4 bytes!\n");
        exit(0);
    }
    free(w);
}
```

```
static int
tcp_error(tcp_work_t *w)
{
    close(w->fd);
    pfds[w->fd].fd = -1;
    free(w);
    return (0);
}

void
accept_thread(int listen_fd)
{
    struct sockaddr addr;
    int len;
    int fd;

    for (;;) {
        if ((fd = accept(listen_fd, &addr, &len)) < 0) {
            if (errno != EINTR)
                perror("accept");
        } else {
            if (fd >= MAXCONS) {
                printf("fd too big!\n", fd);
                shutdown(fd, 0);
            } else {
                if (write(fd_write_return, &fd, 4) != 4) {
                    printf("can't write 4 bytes!\n");
                    exit(1);
                }
            }
        }
    }
}
```

```
void
tcp_thread(void *arg)
{
    struct sockaddr_in server;
    int i;
    int listen_fd;
    int fdr[2];
    pthread_t thread;
    int optval;

    if (pipe(fdr) < 0) {
        perror("pipe");
        exit(1);
    }
    fd_write_return = fdr[1];
    fd_read_return = fdr[0];

    /* set up listening fd */
    if ((listen_fd = socket(PF_INET, SOCK_STREAM, 0)) < 0) {
        perror("socket:");
        exit(1);
    }
    server.sin_family = AF_INET;
    server.sin_addr.s_addr = htonl(INADDR_ANY);
    server.sin_port = htons(PORT_NUM);
    optval = 1;
    if (setsockopt(listen_fd, SOL_SOCKET,
             SO_REUSEADDR, (char *)&optval, 4) < 0) {
        perror("setsocketopt:");
    }
    if (bind(listen_fd,(struct sockaddr *)&server,sizeof(server)) < 0) {
        perror("server bind:");
        exit(2);
    }
    listen(listen_fd, 10);
    pthread_create(&thread, NULL,
          (void *(*)(void *)) accept_thread, (void*)listen_fd);
    for (i = 0; i < MAXCONS; i++) {
        pfds[i].fd = -1;            /* ignore value */
        pfds[i].events = POLLIN;
    }
    pfds[fd_read_return].fd = fd_read_return;
    pfds[fd_read_return].events = POLLIN;
```

```
    for (;;) {
        if (poll(pfds, MAXCONS, -1) < 0) {
            if (errno != EINTR)
                perror("Poll");
        }
        for (i = 0; i < MAXCONS; i++) {
            int events = pfds[i].revents;

            if (events == 0)
                continue;
            if (events & POLLIN) {
                if (pfds[i].fd == fd_read_return) {
                    int buffer;

                    if (read(fd_read_return, &buffer, 4) != 4) {
                        printf("read return != 4\n");
                        exit(1);
                    }
                    pfds[buffer].fd = buffer;
                } else {                /* work to dispatch */
                    tcp_work_t *wptr = (tcp_work_t *) malloc(sizeof (*wptr));

                    wptr->work.todo = WORK_LOOKUP;
                    wptr->work.rfunc =
                          (int (*)(struct work *, char *))tcp_read;
                    wptr->work.wfunc =
                          (int (*)(struct work *, char *))tcp_write;
                    wptr->work.efunc =
                          (int (*)(struct work *))tcp_error;
                    wptr->fd = pfds[i].fd;
                    pfds[i].fd = -1;
                    dataq_enqueue(q, (void *) wptr);
                }
            }
        }
    }
}
```

Now we come to the UDP thread. With UDP, all messages are datagrams received on a single file descriptor. Here the easiest mechanism is to have the UDP threads read the message and prepare a work request that actually contains the already read data. Since we send all responses on the same port, we also need to keep track of the originating machine so we can send the data back to the correct requestor. As a reminder, this is all hidden from the service thread by the use of function pointers.

```
/*
 * Code to implement the udp thread. Note that no attempt is made
 * to make the the protocol reliable; we assume a local connection.
 */
static int udp_read(udp_work_t *, char *);
static int udp_write(udp_work_t *, char *);
static int udp_error(udp_work_t *);
static int udp_fd;

static int
udp_read(udp_work_t *w, char *name)
{
    memcpy(name, w->name, w->len);
    return (0);
}

static int
udp_write(udp_work_t *w, char *results)
{
    int n = strlen(results);

    if (sendto(udp_fd, results, n+1, 0, &w->addr, w->addrlen) != n + 1)
        printf("error in writing in udp_write\n");
    free(w);
    return (0);
}

static int
udp_error(udp_work_t *w)
{
    free(w);
    return (0);
}
```

```
void
udp_thread(void *arg)
{
    struct sockaddr_in server;
    int i;

    /* set up udp socket */
    if ((udp_fd = socket(PF_INET, SOCK_DGRAM, 0)) < 0) {
        perror("socket:");
        exit(1);
    }
    memset(&server, 0, sizeof (server));
    server.sin_family = AF_INET;
    server.sin_addr.s_addr = htonl(INADDR_ANY);
    server.sin_port = htons(PORT_NUM);
    if (bind(udp_fd, (struct sockaddr *) &server,
        sizeof (server)) < 0) {
        perror("server bind:");
        exit(2);
    }
    for (;;) {
        udp_work_t *w = (udp_work_t *) malloc(sizeof (*w));

        memset(&w->addr, 0, sizeof (w->addr));
        w->addrlen = sizeof (w->addr);
        if ((w->len = recvfrom(udp_fd, w->name, NAMESIZE, 0, &w->addr,
                &w->addrlen)) < 0) {
            perror("recvfrom");
            exit(1);
        }
        w->work.todo = WORK_LOOKUP;
        w->work.rfunc = (int (*)(struct work *, char *))udp_read;
        w->work.wfunc = (int (*)(struct work *, char *))udp_write;
        w->work.efunc = (int (*)(struct work *))udp_error;
        dataq_enqueue(q, (void *)w);
    }
}
```

The update thread is a little different than the other threads in that it doesn't handle externally generated requests; it scans the hash table periodically to refresh the most commonly used data items and discards any whose time to live has expired. We end up doing this in two passes; the first pass through the hash table finds the most popular cache entries; the subsequent pass constructs update or delete requests for those entries that are either popular or out of date. Entries that fit in neither case are ignored.

```
/* code to implement the update thread */
static int
update_read(update_work_t *w, char *name)
{
    strcpy(name, w->name);
    return (0);
}

static int
update_write(update_work_t *w, char *results)
{
    free(w);
    return (0);
}

static int
update_error(update_work_t *w)
{
    free(w);
    return (0);
}

struct sort {
    int hits;
    char *name;
};

/* this function produces a list of top 20 hits */
static void
billboard(nsdata_t *data, int *list, char *name)
{
    int i;
    if (data->hits) {
        for (i = 0; i < 20; i++) {
            if (list[i] < data->hits) {
                memmove(list+i+1, list+i, (20-i-1)*sizeof (i));
                list[i] = data->hits;
                break;
            }
        }
    }
}
```

```
struct bwork {
    time_t now;
    int min;
    int count;
};

static void
build_work(nsdata_t *data, struct bwork *ptr, char *name)
{
    update_work_t *w = NULL;

    if (data->hits < ptr->min) {
        if (data->time + ttl < ptr->now) {    /* delete */
            w = (update_work_t *) malloc(sizeof (*w));
            w->work.todo = WORK_DELETE;
        }
    } else if (data->hits == ptr->min && ptr->count > 0) {
        ptr->count--;
        w = (update_work_t *) malloc(sizeof (*w));
        w->work.todo = WORK_UPDATE;
    } else if (data->hits > ptr->min) {
        w = (update_work_t *) malloc(sizeof (*w));
        w->work.todo = WORK_UPDATE;
    }
    if (w) {
        strcpy(w->name, name);
        w->work.rfunc = (int (*)(struct work *, char *)) update_read;
        w->work.wfunc = (int (*)(struct work *, char *)) update_write;
        w->work.efunc = (int (*)(struct work *)) update_error;
        dataq_enqueue(q, (void *) w);
    }
}
```

```
void
update_thread(void *a)
{
    int i;
    int top20[20];
    for (;;) {
        struct bwork bwork;

        sleep(ttl/2);
        memset(top20, 0, sizeof (top20));
        hash_operate(h,
              (void (*)(void *, void*, void*)) billboard,
              (void *) top20);
        bwork.min = bwork.count = 0;
        for (i = 19; i >= 0; i--) {
            if (top20[i]) {
                if (!bwork.min)
                    bwork.min = top20[i];
                if (top20[i] == bwork.min)
                    bwork.count++;
                else
                    break;
            }
        }
        bwork.now = time(NULL);
        hash_operate(h,
              (void (*)(void *, void*, void*))build_work,
              (void *) &bwork);
    }
}
```

Code Example 7-5 Host Name Cache Daemon

One interesting aspect of the host name cache daemon is the use of a pipe to inform the TCP thread that the service thread has exhausted all pending data on the socket. The pipe provides asynchronous queueing and notification (since the TCP thread is parked in a `select()` or `poll()` system call), which is otherwise difficult to integrate with the structure of the TCP thread. This technique will be familiar to experienced X window system programmers; many common window system tool kits lack any effective signal handling mechanism, and pipes provide a ready technique for implementing one without race conditions (see "Multithreading a Graphical User Interface" on page 333).

There are several important techniques used in this program:

- Isolate the locking functionality from the guts of the application. Note that there are *no* calls to any of the locking functions in the source for the cache daemon. All the locking issues are handled in the `dataq` and `hash` routines, where they are readily debugged.
- Provide extensive checking to verify that the data structures are in the expected state. This *checking the invariant* is a critical part of the debugging process. Attempting to debug a large-scale threaded application without such checks enabled is difficult at best and often impossible.
- Design your data structures and their locking strategies after reviewing the access patterns of the application. In our cache daemon example, the need to scan the entire table to implement the update thread drove much of the design in the hash table code. While this makes reusable code more difficult, it is an important part of achieving good performance without excessive complexity.

Summary

In this chapter we've discussed reasons to both use and avoid threads. When using threads is appropriate, many applications can make use of one or more common patterns of thread usage or paradigms. Similarly, applications can use operations on data structures, like lists and queues, to connect or coordinate threads. These ideas are applicable to both uniprocessors and multiprocessors. We've avoided many of the issues in effectively using more than one processor, as a whole new set of design trade-offs and considerations become important. These are covered in Chapter 16, "Parallel Computation."

Thread-Specific Data 8

This chapter discusses a facility, called thread-specific data, that allows data to be associated with each thread. Thread-specific data is useful in adapting older interfaces that return pointers to static data for thread-safe operation.

This chapter should be read by more advanced readers, in particular readers who are adapting older, non-multithreaded libraries to a multithreaded environment.

Thread-Specific Data

Thread-specific data (TSD) is a set of pointers `(void *)` that are maintained for each thread[1]. Each pointer in a thread is associated with a value called a *key*. Keys are shared by all the thread in the process. When a thread accesses a pointer, it uses the associated key to get or set the value of the pointer for the calling thread. In other words, the same key will get or set a unique pointer value when used by different threads.

Allocating TSD keys

A new key is allocated by calling:

```
int
pthread_key_create(pthread_key_t *keyp, void (*destructor)(void *));
```

Once a key is allocated, all threads can access the associated thread-specific pointer, including the threads that exist at the time the key was created. The new key is returned in the location pointed to by *keyp*. The initial value of the pointer in each thread is `NULL`. A system can limit the number of keys a process can allocate. The minimum number a system supports is defined by the macro `PTHREAD_KEYS_MAX` in `<limits.h>`, which must be at least 128 (128 is also the value of the `_POSIX_THREADS_KEYS_MAX` macro). The run-time limit may be larger and is returned by `sysconf()` when passed the value of the

1. The actual storage used for the set of pointers is usually part of the process address space, so it is possible for other threads to accidentally overwrite these pointers. However, there is no explicit way to obtain their address, and the system maintains them on a per-thread basis.

_SC_THREAD_KEYS_MAX macro in <unistd.h>. pthread_key_create() returns an error if it cannot allocate any more keys or associated thread-specific data items.

When you call pthread_key_create() you can optionally specify a *destructor* function that is associated with the key. When a thread exits, the thread-specific data values for all the currently allocated keys are tested. If a TSD value is not NULL, then the destructor function associated with that key is called with the TSD value as an argument. The destructor typically frees memory pointed to by the bound value. Destructors are *not* executed if a thread in the process calls exit(), _exit() or abort().

Once TSD values for all the allocated keys are tested and destructors are called, the values are rechecked to ensure that calling the destructors did not set more TSD values. This process is repeated until all TSD values for the exiting thread are NULL or at least the number of times specified by the value of the PTHREAD_DESTRUCTOR_ITERATIONS macro in <limits.h>, which must be at least 4 (4 is also the value of the _POSIX_THREAD_DESTRUCTOR_ITERATIONS macro). The run-time limit may be larger and is returned by sysconf() when passed the value of the _SC_THREAD_DESTRUCTOR_ITERATIONS macro in <unistd.h>.

The repeated calling of destructors until the TSD values are NULL allows the destructor functions to be fairly relaxed about the routines they call. In particular, the destructors do not have to restrict themselves to interfaces that are guaranteed to not use TSD, since this can potentially reallocate TSD for keys that have already been destroyed. Instead, the destructors must not allocate TSD for keys that have a cyclic dependency on the key whose value is being destroyed. For example, allocating TSD associated with the key whose value is being destroyed or allocating TSD for a key whose destructor would eventually cause the allocation of TSD associated with the key whose value is being destroyed.

Accessing TSD Values

Thread-specific data values are accessed and modified by calling:

```
int
pthread_setspecific(pthread_key_t key, const void *value);

void *
pthread_getspecific(pthread_key_t key);
```

pthread_setspecific() sets the *value* of the TSD in the calling thread that is associated with *key*. It can return an error if the key is illegal (one that has not been previously allocated). pthread_getspecific() returns the value stored in the calling thread's TSD associated with the key.

The key passed to pthread_setspecific() or pthread_getspecific() must have been allocated by pthread_key_create(). For example, the following code won't work:

```
/* Warning: This won't work! */
static pthread_key_t key;

a()
{
    void *ptr;

    if ((ptr = pthread_getspecific(key)) == NULL &&  /* error! */
            pthread_setspecific(key, NULL) != 0) {   /* error! */
        pthread_key_create(&key, ...);
        ...
    }
    ...
}
```

In the above code, you cannot rely on pthread_setspecific() to return NULL or for pthread_getspecific() to return an error for an uninitialized key.

Using TSD

TSD is useful in situations where old code is being used by multiple threads. For example, consider a set of routines that implement a buffered reading of a database of fixed size records. The interface has two routines.

- my_getnextrec() returns a pointer to the next serial record. The record resides in an internal buffer that my_getnextrec() fills when required. It returns the first record the first time it is called.
- my_rewind() causes the next call to my_getnextrec() to get the first record.

There are two threading problems inherent in the interface if a common buffer is used. First, if two threads each call my_getnextrec(), the second call can cause the internal buffer to be filled with new data overwriting the record that the first thread may still be operating on. Secondly, if a thread calls my_rewind(), it affects all future calls to my_getnextrec() by all the other threads in the process.

A simple solution is to redefine the interface to avoid such problems (see "Considerations in Using TSD," below). However, in some cases maintaining the old interface can be of prime importance. Another solution is to reimplement my_getnextrec() so that the record it returns is stored in memory associated with the calling thread (i.e., TSD). In addition, my_rewind() is defined to affect only future calls to getnextrec() made by the thread calling my_rewind(). In effect, each separate thread will see the behavior of these two functions to be the same as the original single-threaded behavior.

Here's an example of this reimplementation using the TSD interfaces.

In file my.h:

```
struct my_rec {
    /* record data */
};

extern struct my_rec *my_getnextrec();
extern void my_rewind();
#define MY_BUFNREC 10
```

In file my.c:

```
/*
 * This is an example of an older interface that returns a pointer
 * to a statically allocated buffer. It has been reimplemented to
 * place the buffer in TSD. This preserves the interface but prevents
 * more than one thread from cooperating to share the buffer or
 * record offset.
 */

#include <stdlib.h>
#include <pthread.h>
#include <stdio.h>
#include <unistd.h>
#include "my.h"

static int database;    /* file descriptor for database file */
static pthread_once_t my_once = PTHREAD_ONCE_INIT;
static pthread_key_t my_key;
typedef struct {        /* per-thread data */
    int recno;
    int lastbuf;        /* terminating condition */
    struct my_rec recbuf[MY_BUFNREC]; /*I/O buffer */
    /* any other per thread data */
} my_tsd_t;
```

```
/* Internal functions */
/*
 * my_init() is called only once when any of the my_*() routines are
 * entered for the first time. This allows the data_base variable to
 * be initialized once here so it will not require locking to be read
 * in the other functions. See "Data Races" on page 30.
 */
static void
my_init(void)
{
    /*
     * Allocate the key for the my_*() routines' TSD.
     * Since malloc is used to allocate the per-thread data free()
     * is used to destroy it when a thread exits.
     */
    if (pthread_key_create(&my_key, free) != 0) {
        fprintf(stderr, "myinit: cannot create key");
        exit(1);
    };
    database = open(/*database file*/);
    ...
}

/*
 * my_gettsdp() returns the pointer to the data structure associated
 * with each thread. If there is no data structure because this is
 * the first time the current thread called one of the my_*()
 * routines, then a data structure is allocated and TSD is set to
 * point to it.
 */
static my_tsd_t *
my_gettsdp()
{
    my_tsd_t *my_tsdp;

    /* get the pointer to my_tsd for this thread */
    my_tsdp = (my_tsd_t *) pthread_getspecific(my_key);
    if (my_tsdp == NULL) {
        /* first time called in this thread, allocate my_tsd */
        my_tsdp = (my_tsd_t *)malloc(sizeof (my_tsd_t));
        my_tsdp->recno = 0;
        pthread_setspecific(my_key, (void *)my_tsdp);
    }
    return (my_tsdp);
}
```

```
/* External functions */
/*
 * Get the next serial record, starting at the first. Current record
 * number can be different in different threads.
 */
struct my_rec *
my_getnextrec()
{
    int bufrecno;
    int nbytes;
    my_tsd_t *my_tsdp;

    pthread_once(&my_once, my_init);  /* init first time thru */
    my_tsdp = my_gettsdp();/* get ptr to thread's data */
    bufrecno = my_tsdp->recno % MY_BUFNREC;
    /* If first record in buffer, fill the buffer */
    if (bufrecno == 0) {
        /*
         * Use positioned I/O (see "Positioned I/O" on page 59)
         * as seek ptr is shared by all threads.
         */
        nbytes = pread(database,
            (caddr_t)my_tsdp->recbuf, sizeof (my_tsdp->recbuf),
            sizeof (struct my_rec) * my_tsdp->recno);
        my_tsdp->lastbuf = (nbytes / REC_SIZE) + 1;/* last buffer */
        if (nbytes == 0)
            return (NULL);
    }
    if (bufrecno >= my_tsdp->lastbuf) {
        return (NULL);
    }
    my_tsdp->recno++;
    return (&my_tsdp->recbuf[bufrecno]);
}

/* Start again at first record. Will not affect other threads. */
void
my_rewind()
{
    pthread_once(&my_once, my_init);
    my_gettsdp()->recno = 0;
}
```

Code Example 8-1 Reimplementing an Interface Using TSD

Deleting TSD keys

Allocated TSD keys can be freed by calling:

```
int
pthread_key_delete(pthread_key_t key);
```

which removes the *key* and the associated values in all threads. If any of the associated values are not `NULL`, `pthread_key_delete()` will not call the associated destructor. Instead you must clean up any state, such as storage, associated with these values[2]. Normally, this is not a burden since `pthread_key_delete()` is used mostly when libraries are dynamically unloaded. Any active state should have already been cleaned up by the time this happens.

Considerations in Using TSD

Interfaces such as `my_getnextrec()` which return a pointer to data maintained by the routine in global storage can be made usable by more than one thread by replacing the global storage by TSD. The problem in this approach is that it prevents more than one thread from cooperating to use the buffer. For example, it may be desirable to use several threads to process the records retrieved by `my_getnextrec()`. This would allow the record processing to be concurrent. However, the TSD version in Code Example 8-1 maintains an individual next-record pointer for each thread so that the different threads will see the same records.

Redefining Interfaces for Threads

A better strategy would be to change the interface to operate on buffer "objects" in a manner similar to `FILE`s in `stdio` (see Chapter 4, "Using Libraries in Multithreaded Programs"). For example:

2. Having `pthread_key_delete()` call destructors would make its implementation unnecessarily complicated since it would have to look up values and call destructors in threads other than the one executing `pthread_key_delete()`.

```
typedef struct {
    pthread_mutex_t lock;
    int recno;
    int lastbuf;                        /* last buffer with some data */
    struct my_rec recbuf[MY_BUFNREC]; /* I/O buffer */
} *recbuf_t;


static pthread_once_t my_once = PTHREAD_ONCE_INIT;

static void
my_init(void)
{
    database = open(file, O_RDONLY);
}

/*
 * Allocate a new recbuf. Called before my_getnextrec().
 */
recbuf_t
my_open()
{
    recbuf_t rbp;

    rbp = (recbuf_t) malloc(sizeof (*rbp));
    pthread_mutex_init(&rbp->lock, NULL);
    rbp->recno = 0;
    return (rbp);
}
```

```
/*
 * Copy next record from buffer into record pointed to by recp.
 */
int
my_getnextrec(recbuf_t rbuf, struct my_rec *recp)
{
    int bufrecno;
    int nbytes;

    pthread_once(&my_once, my_init);
    pthread_mutex_lock(&rbuf->lock);
    bufrecno = rbuf->recno % MY_BUFNREC;
    /* If first record in buffer, fill the buffer */
    if (bufrecno == 0) {
        /* use positioned I/O as seek ptr is shared by all threads */
        nbytes = pread(database,
            (caddr_t)rbuf->recbuf, sizeof (rbuf->recbuf),
            sizeof (struct my_rec) * rbuf->recno);
        if (nbytes == 0) {
            pthread_mutex_unlock(&rbuf->lock);
            return (0);
        }
        rbuf->lastbuf = (nbytes / REC_SIZE) + 1;
    }
    if (bufrecno >= rbuf->lastbuf) {
        pthread_mutex_unlock(&rbuf->lock);
        return (0);
    }
    *recp = rbuf->recbuf[bufrecno];
    rbuf->recno++;
    pthread_mutex_unlock(&rbuf->lock);
    return (1);
}
```

Code Example 8-2 Redefining an Interface for Thread-Safe Operation

This allows multiple threads to either cooperate or to have independent record buffers. In the former case, `my_open()` is called once and the resulting record buffer object is subsequently used by the cooperating threads. In the latter case, each thread does an independent call to `my_open()` to get its own record buffer object.

Summary

Thread-specific data is useful for reimplementing libraries whose interfaces rely on some global state without changing library interfaces. However, doing so can make it impossible for multiple threads to cooperate in using an interface. Still, there are many libraries where backward compatibility is more important than potential concurrency.

Signals 9

This chapter describes signal handling in a multithreaded process and some of the differences between signal handling in a single-threaded process and in a multithreaded process. The chapter also explains how the nonlocal `goto` interface (e.g. `setjmp()` and `longjmp()`) can be used in a multithreaded program.

This chapter should be read by more advanced readers who require non-default response to signals received by a multithreaded process.

Signal Mask

Each thread has its own signal mask. This lets a thread block some signals while it uses memory or other state that is also used by a signal handler. A new thread inherits the signal mask of the thread that created it. The initial thread inherits the signal mask of the thread in the parent process that called `exec()`.

A thread's signal mask is modified by calling:

```
int
pthread_sigmask(int how, const sigset_t *set, sigset_t *oset);
```

The value of *how* defines the manner in which the set of signals pointed to by *set* affects the calling thread's signal mask.

- If *how* is `SIG_BLOCK`, the set of signals is added to the thread's signal mask.
- If *how* is `SIG_UNBLOCK`, the set of signals is deleted from the thread's signal mask.
- If *how* is `SIG_SETMASK`, the set of signals replaces the thread's signal mask.

The *set* argument is created using the `sigemptyset()`, `sigfillset()`, `sigaddset()`, and `sigdelset()` routines. If *oset* is not `NULL`, the signal set it points to is set to the value of the previous signal mask.

`pthread_sigmask()` has an interface that is similar to the older interface `sigprocmask()`. There is no single process signal mask when there is more than one thread in a process, so `sigprocmask()` must not be used in multithreaded processes[1]. For backward compatibility, `sigprocmask()` can still be used by processes with only one thread.

Signal Generation

Signals can be generated by several different types of events. Some of these events are directly caused by the execution of some code by a thread. For example, a reference to an unmapped, protected, or bad memory can generate `SIGSEGV` or `SIGBUS`, floating point exception can cause `SIGFPE`, and execution of illegal instructions can cause `SIGILL`. Such events are referred to as *traps*; signals generated by traps are said to be *synchronously generated*. While a particular signal may be generated by a trap, it may also be generated by an event other than a trap (e.g., a `SIGSEGV` can be generated by sending it via `kill()`).

Signals may also be generated by events outside the process (e.g., `SIGINT`, `SIGHUP`, `SIGQUIT`, `SIGIO`, etc.) or by calling `kill()` or `sigsend()`. Such events are referred to as *interrupts*; signals generated by interrupts are said to be *asynchronously generated*.

Sending Signals to Threads

Signals may be directed at a particular thread by other threads in the process via:

```
int
pthread_kill(pthread_t thread, int signal);
```

`pthread_kill()` sends the *`signal`* to *`thread`*. If the target thread has the signal masked it remains pending on the thread until the thread unmasks it. This can be done only within the process. There is no direct way for a thread in one process to send a signal to a specific thread in another process. If *`signal`* is `0`, no signal is sent; only error checking is performed. This can be used to find out whether a thread still exists.

---

1. The specific wording in POSIX is that the behavior of `sigprocmask()` in a multithreaded process is "unspecified." This means that an implementation is free to do anything, including making it equivalent to `pthread_sigmask()` or returning an error in multithreaded processes. UNIX International compliant systems do the former.

raise()

The ANSI C standard defines a function, raise() that sends a signal to the current process to signal some programmatically determined exception. In a multithreaded environment raise() sends a signal to the thread calling it. It is equivalent to the following code:

```
int
raise(int sig)
{
    return (pthread_kill(pthread_self(), sig));
}
```

Signal Delivery

All threads in a process share the set of signal actions set up by signal(), sigaction() and its variants, as usual. If a signal action is marked SIG_DFL or SIG_IGN, the action on delivery of the signal (i.e., exit, core dump, stop, continue, or ignore) is performed on the entire process including all of the process threads. For example, if the default action is to stop, all the threads in the process stop; if the default action is to exit, the entire process exits.

Signals may also be delivered to particular threads in the process. The choice of which thread receives the signal depends on how the signal is generated. Signals generated by traps are sent to the thread that caused the trap. Asynchronously generated signals are sent to the process as a whole where they may be serviced by any thread that has the signal unmasked. If more than one thread is able to receive a signal sent to the process, only one is chosen. This allows an application to handle several independently generated signals in different threads simultaneously. If all the threads in the process have the signal masked, it remains pending on the process until one of the threads unmasks the signal. For example, an application can enable several threads to handle a particular I/O interrupt. As each new interrupt comes in, another thread is chosen to handle the signal until all the enabled threads are active and have masked the signal. Any additional signals remain pending until one of the signal handling threads completes processing and re-enables the signal.

As in single-threaded processes, the number of signals received by a process (or a thread) is less than or equal to the number sent.

Signal Handlers

For multi-threaded processes, there are two different ways for handling signals delivered to a thread: signal handlers and waiting for signals. Signal handlers are similar to the historical POSIX signal model. Signal handlers are set up by setting the signal action to the address of a signal handling routine. This sets the handler for all threads in the process since the signal action is process-wide. When a thread receives a signal, it is interrupted and begins executing the signal handler.

In multithreaded programs, signal handlers are primarily used to process synchronously generated signals (i.e., traps such as floating-point exceptions). However, they may also be used to process asynchronously generated signals for compatibility with older code. As in single-threaded processes, both the code in asynchronous signal handlers and the code that runs while signals are unmasked must be carefully controlled to ensure that process state is not corrupted when a thread is interrupted. A better way to handle asynchronously generated signals is to wait for them in separate threads (see "Waiting for Signals" below). This avoids the problems associated with interrupted code and allows you to use normal synchronization primitives to control asynchrony.

Async-Safe Functions

Functions that may be called from signal handlers are said to be *async-safe*[2]. The complete list of async-safe functions can be found in Table 9-1. Sometimes making a function async-safe can be quite difficult and expensive. In particular, an async-safe function can be interrupted at any time by an asynchronous signal and can be re-entered by being called from the signal handler. They must either manipulate no memory that is common between invocations (i.e., global memory), be atomic with respect to user programs (e.g., system calls), or they must protect themselves from being re-entered by masking signals while they are manipulating global data. Async-safe functions are also fork-safe (see "Process Creation and Destruction" on page 64). For this reason the list of async-safe functions is small. In general, applications should do only the minimum possible in the handlers for asynchronous signals, such as setting a flag or posting a semaphore.

Sometimes an application can guarantee that a signal handler is not entered "asynchronously." In other words, the signal can be delivered only at specific points in the code where it is known which routines can be interrupted by the signal. Examples of this are traps that can happen only at certain points, or when an application leaves signals masked except when executing certain known

2. To be precise: the behavior of the system is undefined when an async-unsafe function is called from a signal handler that interrupts an async-unsafe function.

Table 9-1 POSIX.1 Async-Safe Functions

`_exit()`	`fdatasync()`	`read()`	`tcflow()`
`access()`	`fork()`	`rename()`	`tcflush()`
`aio_error()`	`fstat()`	`rmdir()`	`tcgetattr()`
`aio_return()`	`fsync()`	`sem_post()`	`tcgetpgrp()`
`aio_suspend()`	`getegid()`	`setgid()`	`tcsendbreak()`
`alarm()`	`geteuid()`	`setpgid()`	`tcsetattr()`
`cfgetispeed()`	`getgid()`	`setsid()`	`tcsetpgrp()`
`cfgetospeed()`	`getgroups()`	`setuid()`	`time()`
`cfsetispeed()`	`getpgrp()`	`sigaction()`	`timer_getoverrun()`
`cfsetospeed()`	`getpid()`	`sigaddset()`	`timer_gettime()`
`chdir()`	`getppid()`	`sigdelset()`	`timer_settime()`
`chmod()`	`getuid()`	`sigemptyset()`	`times()`
`chown()`	`kill()`	`sigfillset()`	`umask()`
`clock_gettime()`	`link()`	`sigismember()`	`uname()`
`close()`	`lseek()`	`sigpending()`	`unlink()`
`creat()`	`mkdir()`	`sigprocmask()`	`utime()`
`dup2()`	`mkfifo()`	`sigsuspend()`	`wait()`
`dup()`	`open()`	`sleep()`	`waitpid()`
`execle()`	`pathconf()`	`stat()`	`write()`
`execve()`	`pause()`	`sysconf()`	
`fcntl()`	`pipe()`	`tcdrain()`	

sections of code. In such situations async-unsafe functions may be called from a signal handler if it is known that the signal did not interrupt any async-unsafe function.

Nonlocal `goto`

The scope of `setjmp()`, `sigsetjmp()`, `longjmp()`, and `siglongjmp()` is limited to one thread. In other words, the thread that initialized the `jmp_buf`, using `setjmp()` or `sigsetjmp()`, must be the thread that calls `longjmp()` or `siglongjmp()` using the same `jmp_buf`. This also means that a thread that handles a signal can only perform a `longjmp()` if the associated `setjmp()` was performed in the same thread. `sigsetjmp()` and `siglongjmp()` save and restore the calling thread's signal mask, respectively.

As with single-threaded programming, using `longjmp()` in an asynchronous signal handler must be carefully controlled. Consider what would happen if a routine such as `malloc()` were interrupted by an asynchronous signal whose handler used `longjmp()`. This would not only jump out of the signal handler, but it would also jump out of the middle of `malloc()`, perhaps while its internal state was inconsistent. In this case `malloc()` (or `free()` since it shares the same state) would no longer be usable! This situation can occur when any function that is not async-safe is interrupted. In general, you must only allow async-safe functions to be interrupted if the signal handlers use `longjmp()`. Calls to async-unsafe functions must be protected by blocking signals.

Waiting for Signals

We've seen that handlers for asynchronous signals must be very carefully crafted. A much easier and safer way to handle asynchronous signals is to block signals in all threads and to explicitly wait for them in one or more separate threads. The advantage of this is that the "handler" thread is not restricted to async-safe functions and can use normal thread primitives to coordinate with other threads when a signal occurs.

```
#include <signal.h>

int
sigwait(const sigset_t *set, int *signalp);
```

`sigwait()` waits for a pending signal that is in *set*. While waiting, the signals in *set* are unblocked. When a signal is received, `sigwait()` clears the pending signal, restores the signal mask to the value at the time `sigwait()` was called and returns the received signal number into the location pointed to by *signalp*. If more than one thread has called `sigwait()` and is waiting for the same signal, then one thread is chosen and it returns from `sigwait()`, while the others continue to wait.

```
#include <signal.h>

int
sigwaitinfo(const sigset_t *set, siginfo_t *info);

int
sigtimedwait(const sigset_t *set, siginfo_t *info,
    const struct timespec *timeout);
```

`sigwaitinfo()` waits for a pending signal in the same way as `sigwait()` except that it can return additional signal information if *info* is not `NULL`. `sigtimedwait()` is similar to `sigwaitinfo()` except that it will return `-1` and set `errno` to `EAGAIN` if the signal is not delivered within the time interval specified by *timeout*.

`sigwait()` is typically used by creating one or more threads to wait for signals. The signals of interest are usually masked in all threads so they are not accidentally delivered. This restricts delivery to the calls to `sigwait()`. In particular, signals must be masked when a thread calls `sigwait()`. An easy way to do this to block asynchronous signals in the initial thread. Then subsequently created threads will inherit its signal mask.

When a signal arrives, one of the threads waiting for the signal returns from `sigwait()`, handles the signal and waits for more signals. The signal handling thread is not restricted to using async-safe functions and can synchronize with other threads in the usual way instead of setting and restoring signal masks.

```
#include <pthread.h>
#include <signal.h>
#include <stdlib.h>
#include <stdio.h>
#include <string.h>

pthread_mutex_t m = PTHREAD_MUTEX_INITIALIZER;
int hup = 0;
sigset_t hupset;

int
main()
{
    pthread_t t;
    extern void *handle_hup(void *);

    sigemptyset(&hupset);           /* initialize set to empty */
    sigaddset(&hupset, SIGHUP);     /* add SIGHUP */
    /*
     * Block signals in initial thread. New threads will inherit this
     * signal mask.
     */
    pthread_sigmask(SIG_BLOCK, &hupset, NULL);
    pthread_create(&t, NULL, handle_hup, NULL);
    for (;;) {
        ... do stuff
        pthread_mutex_lock(&m);
        if (hup) {
            ... cleanup
            break;                  /* got SIGHUP. we're done. */
        }
        pthread_mutex_unlock(&m);
    }
    return (0);
}
```

```
/*
 * Signal handler thread. We're not restricted to async-safe
 * functions since we're in a thread context.
 */
void *
handle_hup(void *arg)
{
    int sig;
    int err;

    err = sigwait(&hupset, &sig);
    if (err || sig != SIGHUP)
        abort();
    pthread_mutex_lock(&m);
    hup = 1;
    pthread_mutex_unlock(&m);
    return (NULL);
}
```

Code Example 9-1 Waiting for Signals with `sigwait()`

An application cannot set up handlers and use `sigwait()` on the same signal[3]. Code Example 9-1 sets a flag, `hup`, to indicate that `SIGHUP` was received and that the computation should terminate. For another, more structured, way to terminate a computation, see Chapter 11, "Thread Cancellation."

Keep in mind that signals that are ignored (i.e., whose action is set to `SIG_IGN` or are ignored by default) are discarded immediately, whether blocked or not, and cannot be waited for. In some cases, it may be necessary to set up a dummy signal handler routine as the signal action to allow the signal to be blocked instead of being discarded.

sigsuspend()

There is another historical mechanism for waiting for signals:

```
int
sigsuspend(sigset_t *set);
```

`sigsuspend()` also waits until a signal in *`set`* arrives. Like `sigwait()`, the signals in *`set`* are unblocked while waiting. However, `sigsuspend()` allows the normal signal handler to be run, and it restores the signal mask and returns when the signal handler returns. Like `pause()`, it will return with an `EINTR` error. If

3. This restriction allows systems to implement `sigwait()` by setting up internal handlers.

more than one thread has called `sigsuspend()` and is waiting for the same signal, one thread is chosen to run the handler and its call to `sigsuspend()` will return when the handler returns.

`sigsuspend()` allows the points at which signals are taken to be controlled. However, these points have to carefully considered as explained above. In general, using a separate thread and `sigwait()` is easier and less error prone.

Pending Signals

When a signal is generated and cannot be delivered due to masking, it is said to be pending. Signals directed to a particular thread via `pthread_kill()` become pending on the thread, while signals directed at the process (normally signals like `SIGINT` or `SIGHUP`, or signals generated using `kill()`) become pending on the process. The function:

```
int
sigpending(sigset_t *set);
```

returns the set of signals pending on either the process or the thread calling `sigpending()`. This is typically used to poll for the presence of asynchronous signals while these signals are masked. `sigpending()` returning an indication that a signal is pending does not guarantee that the signal is associated with the thread that called `sigpending()`. If the signal is pending on a process, other threads may service the signal. For example, if two threads execute the following code:

```
sigset_t sigintset;

sigemptyset(&sigintset);
sigaddset(&sigintset, SIGINT);
...
/* signals are masked */
sigpending(&set);
if (siginset(&set, &sigintset))
    sigwait(&sigintset);
```

Then both may see the same `SIGINT` pending and therefore both will execute `sigwait()`. One thread will then process the `SIGINT` while the other waits until the next `SIGINT` arrives.

Per-Thread Signal Handlers

An application can have per-thread signal handlers based on the per-process signal handlers. The following code sets up a per-thread handler for `SIGFPE`.

```
static pthread_key_t handler_key;/* key for per-thread handler */
static pthread_once_t fpe_once = PTHREAD_ONCE_INIT;

static void
fpe_init(void)
{
    struct sigaction sa;
    static void process_fpehandler();

    pthread_key_create(&handler_key, NULL);
    sa.sa_handler = process_fpehandler;
    sigemptyset(&sa.sa_mask);
    sa.sa_flags = 0;
    sigaction(SIGFPE, &sa, NULL);
}

static void
process_fpehandler(int sig)
{
    void (*handler)(int);

    handler = (void (*)(int))pthread_getspecific(handler_key);
    /* if sig is not SIGFPE or if no handler set, then abort() */
    if (sig != SIGFPE || handler == NULL)
        abort();
    (*handler)(sig);        /* call the per-thread handler */
}

int
set_thread_fpehandler(void (*fpehandler)(int))
{
    static int once = 0;
    struct sigaction *actp;

    /* can't do per-thread SIG_IGN or SIG_DFL */
    if (fpehandler == SIG_DFL || fpehandler == SIG_IGN)
        return (EINVAL);
    pthread_once(&fpe_once, fpe_init);/* init first time thru */
    pthread_setspecific(handler_key, (void *)fpehandler);
}
```

Code Example 9-2 Setting Up Per-Thread SIGFPE *Handlers*

Here's a simple use of the per-thread handler:

```
pthread_key_t fpe_buf_key;
pthread_once_t buf_once = PTHREAD_ONCE_INIT;

void
thread_fpehandler(int sig)
{
    siglongjmp(*(jmp_buf *) pthread_getspecific(fpe_buf_key), 1);
}

void
buf_key_init(void)
{
    pthread_key_create(&fpe_buf_key, NULL);
}

void *
thread(void *arg)
{
    jmp_buf fpe_buf;
    float a = *(float *)arg;

    pthread_once(&buf_once, buf_key_init);
    set_thread_fpehandler(thread_fpehandler);
    pthread_setspecific(fpe_buf_key, (void *)&fpe_buf);
    if (sigsetjmp(fpe_buf, 1) == 0) {
        /* do calculation */
        a = a/0;                    /* cause SIGFPE */
    } else {
        /* exception */
        printf("got SIGFPE\n");
    }
    return (NULL);
}
```

Code Example 9-3   Using Per-Thread Signal Handlers

Note that in this case `siglongjmp()` from the handler is safe because the signal is synchronously generated.

Summary

Signal handling, particularly asynchronously generated signal handling, is complex even in single-threaded programs. We've explained a mechanism using `sigwait()` that can substantially reduce this complexity for asynchronously generated signals.

Advanced Synchronization 10

This chapter explains how synchronization primitives can be used between processes and can be placed in mapped files. The chapter also introduces semaphores.

This chapter should be read by programmers who require interprocess synchronization or who require a synchronization primitive suitable for signal handlers.

Interprocess Synchronization

Threads in two or more processes can use a single synchronization variable jointly. Such a synchronization variable is called process-shared. Process-shared synchronization variables must be allocated in memory that is shared and is writable by the processes involved through mapping files or System V shared memory. Refer to `mmap()` (and `shmop()` for UI). Once the synchronization variable is allocated, it must be initialized with the `process-shared` attribute set to `PTHREAD_PROCESS_SHARED`. By default, this attribute is `PTHREAD_PROCESS_PRIVATE`. Process-private synchronization variables can be used only by the threads in the process in which it was initialized. The `process-shared` attribute in a mutex attributes structure is manipulated by calling:

```
int
pthread_mutexattr_setpshared(pthread_mutexattr_t *attr,
    int pshared);

int
pthread_mutexattr_getpshared(const pthread_mutexattr_t *attr,
    int *psharedp);
```

`pthread_mutexattr_setpshared()` sets the value of the `process-shared` attribute in a mutex attributes structure and `pthread_mutexattr_getpshared()` fetches it. The corresponding operations on a condition variable attributes structure are:

```
int
pthread_condattr_setpshared(pthread_condattr_t *attr,
    int pshared);

int
pthread_condattr_getpshared(const pthread_condattr_t *attr,
    int *psharedp);
```

Once the `process-shared` attribute is set up, the attributes structure can be used repeatedly to initialize synchronization variables of the corresponding type for interprocess or intraprocess synchronization.

Synchronization Variables in Files

Process-shared synchronization variables can also be placed in files. Once initialized, subsequent processes can then map the file in and use the synchronization variable. For example, an initialized process-shared mutex can be stored in a file (see Code Example 10-1). Processes can map the file into their address space, acquire the mutex when they need to access it, access the file, release the lock, and unmap the file. The interprocess mutex ensures that other processes doing the same thing concurrently do not access or modify the data in the file while another process holds the mutex.

Note – Process-shared synchronization is an optional feature in POSIX. A system supports process-shared synchronization if the `_POSIX_THREAD_PROCESS_SHARED` macro is defined in `<unistd.h>`. This can be tested dynamically by calling `sysconf()` using the `_SC_THREAD_PROCESS_SHARED` macro from `<unistd.h>` as an argument. `sysconf()` returns `-1` if the feature is not supported.

As an example suppose we're trying to independently access a record in a file that contains 1000 records[1].

```
#ifndef _POSIX_THREAD_PROCESS_SHARED
#error implementation does not support pshared
#endif
```

1. We restrict the code to a fixed size file to avoid the complexity of coordinating the file size for this simple example.

```
/* layout of a file */
struct file {
    struct data_record {
        pthread_mutex_t lock;/* pshared lock on record data */
        int value;
    } rec[1000];
};

/* per-process global variables */
struct file *filep;             /* pointer to where file is mapped */
int opencnt = 0;                /* # threads that have file open */
/* mutex that protects opencnt and filep */
pthread_mutex_t file_lock = PTHREAD_MUTEX_INITIALIZER;

/*
 * Initialize the database file. This should be called only once. The
 * caller must ensure it cannot overlap with a call to set_value().
 */
void
create_db()
{
    int fd;
    struct data_record *recp;
    pthread_mutexattr_t pshared;

    fd = creat("my_file", 0777);
    ftruncate(fd, sizeof (struct file));
    (void) pthread_mutexattr_init(&pshared);
    (void) pthread_mutexattr_setpshared(&pshared,
        PTHREAD_PROCESS_SHARED);
    filep = (struct file *) mmap(NULL, sizeof (struct file),
        PROT_READ | PROT_WRITE, MAP_SHARED, fd, 0);
    close(fd);
    for (recp = &filep->rec[0]; recp < &filep->rec[1000]; recp++) {
        (void) pthread_mutex_init(&recp->lock, &pshared);
        recp->value = 0;
    }
    opencnt++;
}
```

```
/*
 * open_db() must be called before set_value() if this process did
 * not create the file. The file_lock prevents the file from being
 * opened twice in the same process, if called simultaneously.
 */
void
open_db()
{
    int fd;

    pthread_mutex_lock(&file_lock);/* ensure only 1 owner */
    if (opencnt == 0) {
        fd = open("my_file", O_RDWR);
        filep = (struct file *) mmap(NULL, sizeof (struct file),
            PROT_READ | PROT_WRITE, MAP_SHARED, fd, 0);
        close(fd);
    }
    opencnt++;
    pthread_mutex_unlock(&file_lock);
}

/*
 * The thread that called open_db() or create_db() must call
 * close_db() when it is done calling set_value().
 */
void
close_db()
{
    pthread_mutex_lock(&file_lock);
    if (--opencnt == 0)
        munmap((void *)filep, sizeof (struct file));
    pthread_mutex_unlock(&file_lock);
}

/*
 * Set the value for a record number.
 */
void
set_value(int recno, int value)
{
    pthread_mutex_lock(&filep->rec[recno].lock);
    filep->rec[recno].value = value;
    pthread_mutex_unlock(&filep->rec[recno].lock);
}
```

Code Example 10-1 Interprocess Synchronization Example

The ability to synchronize threads in different processes does not come without cost. In particular, waking up threads in a different process usually requires operating system intervention while waking up threads in the same address space can be faster (see "Contention Scope and Process-Shared Synchronization Variables" on page 226). In general, it is best to specify `PTHREAD_PROCESS_SHARED` only when interprocess synchronization is explicitly required.

Interprocess Synchronization and Process Death

Interprocess synchronization variables represent a compromise between performance and reliability. While they require operating system support to wake up threads in other processes they need not enter the operating system each time they are used. For example, locking a process-shared mutex may not enter the operating system if the mutex is available. Similarly, unlocking a process-shared mutex may not enter the operating system if there are no other threads waiting for the mutex. This performance boost comes at a cost in reliability. Consider what would happen if a process died while holding a process-shared mutex for a record in Code Example 10-1. Threads in other processes may wait forever to acquire the lock on a record.

Semaphores

A semaphore is a synchronization variable that contains a non-negative integer value. There are two basic operations on a semaphore: increment and decrement. A semaphore starts out with some initial value, which is zero by default. If a thread attempts to decrement the value when it is zero, the thread blocks until some thread increments it. The increment and decrement operations are called post and wait, respectively. These names serve to remind the programmer that decrementing the semaphore may block, while incrementing it never will.

Note – Semaphores are an optional feature in POSIX. A system supports semaphores if the `_POSIX_SEMAPHORES` macro is defined in `<unistd.h>`. This can be tested dynamically by calling `sysconf()` using the `_SC_SEMAPHORES` macro from `<unistd.h>` as an argument. `sysconf()` returns `-1` if the feature is not supported.

POSIX semaphores have a slightly different style of interface than the other synchronization variables. Some of this difference is due to semaphores being part of the earlier POSIX realtime standard (P1003.1b) instead of the Pthreads standard (P1003.1c). In the realtime standard, semaphores are primarily interprocess synchronization variables, since threads were not part of the POSIX standard at the time the realtime extension was added. Hence the definition of semaphores in POSIX represents somewhat of a compromise between pure threads-based semaphores and pure process-based semaphores, such as is found in the UNIX International threads interfaces [Novell 95]. A process-based implementation would typically store the semaphore state in the kernel and have a mechanism to control which processes can access the semaphore. A threads-based implementation would normally store the semaphore state in process or shared memory in a mapped file and only contact the kernel when necessary for interprocess synchronization.

Due to the potential of a limited kernel implementation, POSIX semaphores may have several restrictions. The total number of semaphores that a process may open can be limited. For example, connections to named semaphores can be implemented using file descriptors. The minimum number a system supports is defined by the macro `_POSIX_SEM_NSEMS_MAX` in `<limits.h>`, which must be at least 256. The run-time limit may be larger and is returned by `sysconf()` when passed the value of the `_SC_SEM_NSEMS_MAX` macro in `<unistd.h>`. In addition, the system may limit the maximum value that can be counted on a semaphore. The system will support at least the value of the `_POSIX_SEM_VALUE_MAX` macro in `<limits.h>`, which must be greater than or equal to 32,767. The run-time limit may be larger and is returned by `sysconf()` when passed the value of the `_SC_SEM_VALUE_MAX` macro in `<unistd.h>`.

Named and Unnamed Semaphores

POSIX semaphores come in two types: named and unnamed. Named semaphores are associated with a global string of the same form as a pathname[2]. Unnamed semaphores are similar to the Pthreads synchronization variables; they are allocated in process memory and initialized. Like the Pthreads synchronization variables unnamed semaphore may or may not be usable by more than one process, depending on how it is allocated and initialized. Named semaphores, however, can always be shared by several processes. Named semaphores also have an owner user-id, group-id, and a protection mode. These authorize access to the named semaphore in the same manner as regular files. Unnamed semaphores are either private, inherited through `fork()`, or are protected by access permissions of the regular file they are allocated and mapped in.

The implementation may or may not associate the named semaphore with a real file that is visible in the file system, or it may simply use the string as internal semaphore name inside the kernel. To be strictly portable, the name must begin

2. A portable POSIX pathname consists of components separated by "/" (slash) with each component composed of the letters a-z and A-Z, the numbers 0-9 and the symbols ".", "_", and "-" (period, underscore, and hyphen). The system can limit the size of each component and the entire pathname.

with a slash (/) character and must not contain any other slash characters. This name space is shared by all processes in the system, so if a set of processes use the same name, they will get the same semaphore.

Both named and unnamed semaphore are represented by the type `sem_t` when a process is operating on them. `sem_t` and all of the semaphore routines are defined in the file `<semaphore.h>`.

Creating and Opening Named Semaphores

Named semaphores are created or opened by:

```
sem_t *
sem_open(const char *name, int oflag, ...);
```

`sem_open()` returns a connection to a named semaphore. The *oflag* argument is similar to the second argument to `open()`. Like `open()`, *oflag* contains a number of independent bits. If *oflag* contains `O_CREATE`, a new semaphore is created if no semaphore associated with *name* exists. When `O_CREATE` is set, the third argument must contain an access *mode* of type `mode_t` and the fourth argument contains a *value* of type `unsigned int`. If the semaphore is created, the access mode is set to *mode* and the initial value is set to *value*. If `O_CREATE` and `O_EXCL` are set, then `sem_open()` will fail if the semaphore `name` already exists.

Named semaphores are closed by calling:

```
int
sem_close(sem_t *sem);
```

This destroys the connection to the named semaphore. `sem_close()` must not be used on unnamed semaphores.

Unlinking Named Semaphores

Like regular file names, the names associated with named semaphores are removed from semaphore name space by unlinking them. When the name for a named semaphore is unlinked, the semaphore itself is not destroyed until all processes using the semaphore close it.

Initializing and Destroying Unnamed Semaphores

Unnamed semaphores are explicitly initialized by:

```
int
sem_init(sem_t *sem, int pshared, unsigned int count);
```

The initial value of the semaphore is set to *count*. If *pshared* is non-zero, the semaphore may be used by more than one process.

```
int
sem_destroy(sem_t *sem);
```

The unnamed semaphore that is destroyed must have been explicitly initialized by `sem_init()`. `sem_destroy()` must not be used on named semaphores. `sem_destroy()` can return an error if the implementation detects that the semaphore is being waited for.

Waiting For and Posting Semaphores

The primary semaphore operations are:

```
int
sem_wait(sem_t *sem);

int
sem_post(sem_t *sem);
```

`sem_wait()` decrements the semaphore. If the semaphore is zero when `sem_wait()` is called, `sem_wait()` blocks until some other thread increments it. `sem_post()` increments the semaphore. If the semaphore value was incremented from zero and if there are any threads blocked in `sem_wait()` for the semaphore, one of them is awakened. By default, the implementation can choose any of the waiting threads. For example, it is legal for the implementation to increment the semaphore before checking for waiting threads. Another running thread may then decrement the semaphore before any awakened thread can. The awakened thread may then have to block again. Both these functions can return errors if the semaphore has been improperly initialized.

The simple definition of semaphores can be easily written in terms of mutexes and condition variables. For example:

```
typedef struct {
    pthread_mutex_t lock;
    pthread_cond_t nonzero;
    unsigned int count;
    unsigned int waiters;
} sem_t;
```

```
int
sem_wait(sem_t *sp)
{
    pthread_mutex_lock(&sp->lock);
    while (sp->count == 0) {
        sp->waiters++;
        pthread_cond_wait(&sp->nonzero, &sp->lock);
        sp->waiters--;
    }
    sp->count--;
    pthread_mutex_unlock(&sp->lock);
    return (0);
}

int
sem_post(sem_t *sp)
{
    pthread_mutex_lock(&sp->lock);
    if (sp->waiters)
        pthread_cond_signal(&sp->nonzero);
    sp->count++;
    pthread_mutex_unlock(&sp->lock);
    return (0);
}
```

Code Example 10-2 A Non-async-safe Implementation of Semaphores

The difference between this implementation and semaphores is that `sem_post()` is async-safe. That is, it can be called from an asynchronous signal handler. The code shown cannot be. For example, if a signal interrupts `sem_wait()` while the mutex is held, a call to `sem_post()` will deadlock (block forever) waiting for a mutex the thread already owns.

Sometimes it is convenient to attempt to avoid blocking:

```
int
sem_trywait(sem_t *sem);
```

`sem_trywait()` decrements the semaphore only if it greater than zero. Otherwise it returns an error.

Getting a Semaphore's Value

The current value of a semaphore can be interrogated by calling:

```
int
sem_getvalue(sem_t *sem, int *valuep);
```

which stores the current value into the location pointed to by *valuep*.

Using Semaphores

Some operating systems use semaphores as the only synchronization primitive. They can have the same effect as mutexes when used to protect critical sections. Here's Code Example 3-2 on page 25 rewritten with semaphores:

```
#include <semaphore.h>

int checking;
int savings;
sem_t lock;

void
savings_to_checking(int amount)
{
    sem_wait(&lock);
    savings -= amount;
    checking += amount;
    sem_post(&lock);
}

int
total_balance()
{
    int balance;

    sem_wait(&lock);
    balance = checking + savings;
    sem_post(&lock);
    return (balance);
}
```

Code Example 10-3 Using Semaphores to Protect a Critical Section

Semaphores can also have similar functionality to condition variables, since they can be used between threads. There are several reasons to have separate mutexes and condition variables. First, the implementation of mutexes can take advantage of the fact that mutexes must be released by the thread that acquired them. In particular, the implementation can use efficient hardware primitives, such as test-and-set instructions to provide the necessary atomicity without having more complicated functions. In addition, realtime implementations can forward the priority of the waiting threads to the owners to avoid priority inversions (See Chapter 12, "Threads Scheduling"). Likewise, condition variables have advantages over semaphores. Condition variables have a broadcast capability, and they can be very lightweight since they have no state.

The state in a semaphore can be used in a number of ways. The most obvious is to use the atomic count within the semaphore directly. Shown below is a program that copies the standard input to the standard output using threads:

```
/*
 * Program to copy standard input to standard output. The program
 * uses two threads. One reads the input and puts the data in a double
 * buffer. The other reads the buffer contents and writes it to
 * standard output.
 */
#include <semaphore.h>

sem_t empty_bufs;               /* number of empty buffers */
sem_t full_bufs;                /* number of buffers that are full */
struct {
    char data[BSIZE];
    int nbytes;                 /* number of bytes in this buffer */
} buf[2];                       /* double buffer */

main()
{
    pthread_t t_reader;
    extern void reader(), writer();
    int err;

    sem_init(&empty_bufs,0, 2);    /* two empty bufs */
    sem_init(&full_bufs,0, 0);     /* zero full bufs */
    /* Create reader */
    err = pthread_create(&t_reader,NULL,(void *(*)(void *))reader,NULL);
    if (err)
        exit (1);
    /* Do the writer operation in this thread */
    writer();
    return (0);
}
```

```
void
reader()
{
    int i = 0;
    size_t nbytes;

    do {
        sem_wait(&empty_bufs);
        nbytes = read(0, buf[i].data, BSIZE);
        buf[i].nbytes = nbytes;
        sem_post(&full_bufs);
        i = (i + 1) % 2;
    } while (nbytes > 0);
}

void
writer()
{
    int i = 0;
    size_t nbytes;

    do {
        sem_wait(&full_bufs);
        nbytes = buf[i].nbytes;
        if (nbytes > 0) {
            write(1, buf[i].data, nbytes);
            sem_post(&empty_bufs);
            i = (i + 1) % 2;
        }
    } while (nbytes > 0);
}
```

Code Example 10-4 File Copy Using Semaphores

Programming note

This program is unlikely to improve performance very much if both the input file and the output file are on the same disk drive. There is only one disk arm and parallel access can't actually happen, though there might be some secondary grouping of I/Os. Performance will also probably not improve even if the files are regular files on separate disk drives. The file system would ordinarily recognize the serial input and output pattern and generate asynchronous read-ahead and write-behind requests. In other words, the system provides some degree of multithreading automatically for regular files. However, if the two files were separate raw devices, there could be much performance gain as there would be a lot of I/O overlap.

Semaphores and Signal Handlers

Another typical use of semaphores is to record asynchronous signals. As noted above, it is difficult to use a mutex to both synchronize threads and signal handlers. A semaphore can solve this problem by atomically recording that a signal happened:

```
sigint_handler(int sig)
{
    sem_post(&sigint_sem);
}
```

The occurrence of the signal can either be waited for using `sem_wait()` or polled for using `sem_trywait()`.

Semaphores and the Memory Model

It's worth exploring how semaphores are used to ensure that code is data race free. The file copy implemented with semaphores in Code Example 10-3 is a good example to analyze. For each buffer, the reader modified the data and updated `nbytes` before incrementing the `full_bufs` semaphore. The write would not look at the buffer until this semaphore was incremented. Similarly, the reader would not touch a buffer until it knew that the write was done with it via the `empty_bufs` semaphore. Therefore, no individual buffer would be accessed simultaneously by both threads.

This is a different paradigm than protecting memory with mutexes. With mutexes the acquisition and release of the mutex brackets the access to the memory it protects. With semaphores, a thread must "own" the memory (i.e., be the only one to access it) then hand off control of the memory with `sem_post()`. The receiver must explicitly receive control using `sem_wait()` before accessing the memory. This tends to be more difficult to reason with than the equivalent structured locking technique.

Summary

Interprocess synchronization can be used synchronize threads in different processes that share memory or other resources. This can allow extremely fast interprocess communication while providing the protection of having some non-shared address space.

Counting semaphores are a "classic" synchronization primitive. While they can be used as (heavyweight) mutexes, they are more typically used in producer-consumer problems, such as the file copy in Code Example 10-4. However, the structured locking techniques using mutexes tend to be easier to reason about. One of the real values of the Pthreads definition of semaphores is that posting is async-safe, allowing them to synchronize threads with signals.

Thread Cancellation 11

This chapter describes a mechanism that allows the programmer to request that a particular thread in the process terminate in a structured manner. This chapter should be read by application programmers who need to be able to terminate threads and by library programmers who need to anticipate the cancellation of a thread it is executing inside the library.

Destroying Other Threads

Sometimes it is desirable to have particular threads in a process stop what they are doing and terminate. A typical situation is where a user wants to stop a particular operation that was in progress or where an application is no longer interested in the results of operations being executed by a set of threads. One example is a program with a graphic user interface where the user had requested some long operation like simulating airflow over a wing. Such operations are best done in separate threads as this allows the user interface to remain responsive to further requests, including cancelling previous operations (see "User Interface Responsiveness" on page 4). If an operation that is in progress is cancelled, the threads that were executing the operation must be notified and terminated. Another example is where an application uses several threads to search a large data base for a record meeting some criteria. Once the record is found, the other threads participating in the search should be notified and terminated.

An obvious technique to destroy a thread is for the application to associate a termination flag with each thread and then have each thread periodically test its flag. Unfortunately, this requires the application programmer to sprinkle the code with periodic tests of the threads termination flag. This can be impossible if the code for operation to be terminated is in a library supplied by someone else. Another problem is that the code can be waiting for some external event (e.g., waiting for a response packet from a remote machine) and therefore cannot test its termination flag for some indeterminate period. Another technique is to send a signal to the thread to be terminated. The signal handler in the target thread then executes a nonlocal goto[1] to a place that skips the computation and either calls

---

1. It is not safe to call `pthread_exit()` from an asynchronous signal handler. See "Async-Safe Functions" on page 164.

`pthread_exit()` or returns from the thread start function. The code in Code Example 11-1 demonstrates this technique along with its pitfalls. The example is similar to the situation in Code Example 2-1 on page 14 in which a separate thread is used to decompress pictures that are about to be displayed while the user is still looking at previously decompressed pictures. The difference here is that the thread can continue decompressing several pictures beyond the picture currently being displayed. This is implemented by putting pictures on a circular buffer FIFO queue after each one is decompressed. The display thread then gets the pictures off the list. The decompression thread waits if it gets too far ahead, to limit the amount of memory used.

```
/* WARNING: This code has bugs! */
/*
 * Code to decompress a list of files. Decompress up to PIC_MAX
 * pictures ahead of the display thread. Start by calling
 * pic_decomp() in a newthread. Call get_next_pic() to get
 * decompressed pictures. Send SIGUSR1 to thread to cause termination.
 * NOTE: only one decompression thread at a time is allowed.
 */
jmp_buf cancel;                  /* jmp buf for termination */
pthread_mutex_t pic_lock;        /* locks pic_{buf,inbuf,rd,wr} */
pic_t *pic_buf[PIC_MAX];         /* holds decompressed pictures */
unsigned int pic_inbuf = 0;      /* num pictures in circ. buffer */
unsigned int pic_rd = 0;         /* read pointer in circ buf */
unsigned int pic_wr = 0;         /* write pointer in circ buf */
pthread_cond_t pic_notempty = PTHREAD_COND_INITIALIZER;
pthread_cond_t pic_full = PTHREAD_COND_INITIALIZER;
static pthread_once_t once = PTHREAD_ONCE_INIT;

/* signal handler to terminate thread */
static void
handle_usr1(int sig)
{
    longjmp(cancel, 1);
}
```

```
/* once function to initialize some variables */
static void
pic_init()
{
    struct sigaction sa;

    sa.sa_handler = handle_usr1;
    sigemptyset(&sa.sa_mask);
    sa.sa_flags = 0;
    sigaction(SIGUSR1, &sa, NULL);/* init SIGUSR1 handler */
}

/* add a decompressed picture to the list */
static void
add_pic(pic_t *picp)
{
    pthread_mutex_lock(&pic_lock);
    while (pic_inbuf == PIC_MAX)
        pthread_cond_wait(&pic_full, &pic_lock);
    if (pic_inbuf == 0)
        pthread_cond_signal(&pic_notempty);
    pic_buf[pic_wr] = picp;
    pic_inbuf++;
    pic_wr = (pic_wr + 1) % PIC_MAX;
    pthread_mutex_unlock(&pic_lock);
}

/* call this to get decompressed pictures */
pic_t *
get_next_pic()
{
    pic_t *picp;

    pthread_mutex_lock(&pic_lock);
    while (pic_inbuf == 0)
        pthread_cond_wait(&pic_notempty, &pic_lock);
    if (pic_inbuf == PIC_MAX)
        pthread_cond_signal(&pic_full);
    picp = pic_buf[pic_rd];
    pic_inbuf--;
    pic_rd = (pic_rd + 1) % PIC_MAX;
    pthread_mutex_unlock(&pic_lock);
    return (picp);
}
```

```
/*
 * Thread start function to decompress a list of file names.
 * SIGUSR1 should be masked.
 */
void *
pic_decomp(char **namesp)
{
    int fd;
    pic_t *picp;
    sigset_t nset;

    pthread_once(&once, pic_init);
    sigemptyset(&nset);
    sigaddset(&nset, SIGUSR1);
    if (setjmp(cancel) == 0) {
        pthread_sigmask(SIG_UNBLOCK, &nset, NULL);
        while (*namesp != NULL) {
            fd = open(*namesp, ...);
            picp = (pic_t *) malloc(sizeof(pic_t));
            ... decompress file into picp
            close(fd);
            add_pic(picp);
            namesp++;
        }
        add_pic(NULL);      /* signal end of list */
    } else {
        /* Cleanup from signal. */
        /* Warning! Many bugs here */
        pthread_mutex_lock(&pic_lock);
        while (pic_inbuf > 0) {
            picp = pic_buf[pic_rd];
            if (picp != NULL)
                free(picp);
            pic_inbuf--;
            pic_rd = (pic_rd + 1) % PIC_MAX;
        }
        pthread_mutex_unlock(&pic_lock);
    }
    return (NULL);
}
```

Code Example 11-1 Terminating Threads Using Signals

The thread that is displaying pictures and responding to user input starts the process by creating a thread that calls `pic_decomp()` with a `NULL`-terminated array of pointers to names of files. The thread continues decompressing pictures (and waiting if it gets too far ahead) until the last picture. It will then put a `NULL` pointer on the picture list to mark the end and exit. When the last picture is removed from the list the display thread must `pthread_join()` with the decompression thread at which point the process can start over. If the user chooses to stop displaying the current series of pictures the display thread must send the decompression thread a `SIGUSR1` signal and then wait for it to exit. The decompression thread cleans out the already decompressed pictures when it receives the signal. When the decompression thread exits, the display thread restarts the decompression with a new list.

If the signal arrives while the thread is executing between lines 27 and 35 in `add_pic()` (called from line 69), the `pic_lock` mutex will already be held when the signal cleanup code (lines 74 through 82) is executed and line 74 will deadlock. Worse yet, the functions `malloc()`, `pthread_mutex_lock()`, and `pthread_mutex_unlock()` are not async-safe, and they may be interrupted in the midst of execution (they may also be holding internal locks) potentially disabling the allocator and threads package. Another problem is that if the program is interrupted while the thread is executing between lines 65 and 70,the memory allocated in line 66 and/or the file descriptor allocated in line 65 will never be freed. It is not sufficient to test for non-`NULL` values in `picp` or `fd` in the cleanup code since the allocation may have already occurred before the result is stored in the result variable[2].

The asynchronous termination problem can be partially controlled by unblocking the interrupts only around sections of code that are safe to be interrupted. However this is laborious and error-prone to program, can be very inefficient and still suffers from the problem that code supplied by other parties must understand that asynchronous interruption is possible by certain signals (e.g., `SIGUSR1` in Code Example 11-1) and there must be an additional agreement to ensure that all `SIGUSR1` signal handlers set by the various parties are called. This still leaves the problem of cleaning up internal resources (such as allocated memory) when a thread is terminated.

In order to avoid these problems, Pthreads provides a mechanism called *thread cancellation* that allows a thread that can be terminated by others (i.e., cancelled) to control when the thread is interrupted and to provide a uniform mechanism for cleaning up the state of the cancelled thread.

2. The values of automatic or register variables are undefined when returning after a `longjmp()`. However, there is still a potential resource leak even if the results are assigned to static variables.

Cancelling Threads

A thread can request that another thread in the same process terminate execution by calling:

```
int
pthread_cancel(pthread_t thread);
```

where *thread* is the identifier for the target thread. This is called *cancelling* the target thread. `pthread_cancel()` only marks the cancellation request in the target thread; it does not wait until the thread actually terminates.

Cancellation Points

By default, the thread that is the target of a cancellation request does not act on it immediately. Instead it keeps executing normally until it calls a routine that is a *cancellation point*. When a thread reaches a cancellation point it may check to see whether a cancellation request is pending and then act on it. This type of cancellation is called *deferred cancellability*. This prevents the problems associated with asynchronous thread termination. However, the programmer must ensure that routines that are cancellation points are called regularly or else cancellation will be deferred for too long.

Suppose a thread calls a routine such as `read()` or `scanf()` that may block for a long time waiting for user input. If the thread is cancelled while blocked in these routines, the thread may ignore the cancellation request for a long time. Fortunately, all the basic POSIX interfaces that may block for unbounded periods are also cancellation points, as shown in Table 11-1.

Table 11-1 Required POSIX Cancellation Point Routines

`aio_suspend()`	`open()`	`sigtimedwait()`
`close()`	`pause()`	`sigwait()`
`creat()`	`pthread_cond_timedwait()`	`sigwaitinfo()`
`fcntl(,F_SETLKW,)`	`pthread_cond_wait()`	`sleep()`
`fsync()`	`pthread_join()`	`system()`
`mq_receive()`	`pthread_testcancel()`	`tcdrain()`
`mq_send()`	`read()`	`wait()`
`msync()`	`sem_wait()`	`waitpid()`
`nanosleep()`	`sigsuspend()`	`write()`

POSIX leaves it up to the particular implementation as to whether the additional routines shown in Table 11-2 are cancellation points. This allows an implementation to take advantage of situations where the routines never block for long periods.

Table 11-2 Optional POSIX Cancellation Point Routines

closedir()	fseek()	getpwnam()	readdir()
ctermid()	ftell()	getpwnam_r()	remove()
fclose()	fwrite()	getpwuid()	rename()
fcntl()	getc()	getpwuid_r()	rewind()
fflush()	getc_unlocked()	gets()	rewinddir()
fgetc()	getchar()	lseek()	scanf()
fgets()	getchar_unlocked()	opendir()	tmpfile()
fopen()	getcwd()	perror()	tmpname()
fprintf()	getgrgid()	printf()	ttyname()
fputc()	getgrgid_r()	putc()	ttyname_r()
fputs()	getgrnam()	putc_unlocked()	ungetc()
fread()	getgrnam_r()	putchar()	unlink()
freopen()	getlogin()	putchar_unlocked()	
fscanf()	getlogin_r()	puts()	

When a thread is cancelled at a cancellation point, there may be side effects. For example, if a thread was cancelled while calling `read()` some of the data may have already been transferred. Subsequent reading of the same file descriptor will not see the transferred data. In general, the side effects are the same as if the routine had been interrupted by a signal and would have returned `EINTR`.

> **Warning –** The routines listed in Table 11-1 and Table 11-2 are not required to test that the calling thread has been cancelled every time they are called. They are required to test for cancellation only when the routine blocks.

This allows cancellation to be implemented without additional overhead when there is no blocking. Note that even though `pthread_mutex_lock()` might block, it is not a cancellation point. The reasoning here is that mutexes should be used only for short critical sections. Hence, a wait for a mutex should never be too long and certainly not unbounded.

Table 11-1 and Table 11-2 only refer to routines defined by POSIX. Other popular system interface routines that are not (currently) defined by POSIX, such as networking interfaces, may also be cancellation points. A good rule of thumb is that if a function can return with an `EINTR` error, it is likely to be a cancellation point.

Cancellation Cleanup Handlers

Deferred cancellation solves many of the problems of asynchronous cancellation. However the problem of cleaning up intermediate state after a cancellation request is recognized still remains. POSIX provides a method by which cleanup code can be executed if a cancellation occurs within a code segment.

```
void
pthread_cleanup_push(void (*cleanup_handler)(void *), void *arg);

void
pthread_cleanup_pop(int execute);
```

`pthread_cleanup_push()` pushes a descriptor containing a pointer to a function, *cleanup_handler*, and an argument, *arg*, onto a LIFO[3] cleanup handler stack associated with each thread. When a thread calls `pthread_exit()` or accepts a pending cancellation request, the descriptors on its cleanup stack are popped one by one and the cleanup handler is called with the stored argument. This means that the cleanup handlers are executed starting at the one most recently pushed onto the cleanup stack towards the least recently pushed. When the last cleanup handler returns, the thread-specific data destructors, if any, are called (see Chapter 8, "Thread-Specific Data"). When the last TSD destructor returns, the thread exits with a completion status of `PTHREAD_CANCELED`. The cleanup handlers and TSD destructors are *not* executed if a thread in the process calls `exit()`, `_exit()` or `abort()`.

`pthread_cleanup_pop()` removes the most recent descriptor pushed onto the cleanup stack. If *execute* is non-zero, `pthread_cleanup_pop()` executes the popped descriptor's cleanup handler using the associated argument.

The two routines, `pthread_cleanup_push()` and `pthread_cleanup_pop()` must be in the same lexical scope. In C, you can consider them to bracket a lexical scope much like '{' and '}' respectively. This restriction allows them to be efficiently implemented as macros using only automatic storage[4]. It also is similar to language supported exception facilities. In fact, this facility can be replaced by a language supported exception facility for some language bindings other than C. Because of this scoping restriction, a program must not jump or return out of the scope between `pthread_cleanup_push()` and `pthread_cleanup_pop()`.

---

3. Last In First Out

4. Failure to properly bracket these routines may cause a syntax error on systems where these routines are implemented as macros.

For example, the scoping restriction disallows code like the following:

```
/* This is disallowed! */
pthread_cleanup_push(cleanup1, NULL);
while (...) {
    ...
    pthread_cleanup_pop(0);
    pthread_cleanup_push(cleanup2, NULL);
    ...
}
pthread_cleanup_pop(0);
```

The `execute` argument to `pthread_cleanup_pop()` allows you to have code in the cleanup handler that is executed whether the protected section of code is cancelled or not.

```
void
cleanup(void *bufp)
{
    free(bufp);
}

int
checksum(int fd)
{
    char *bufp;
    int nbytes, i;
    int sum = 0;

    bufp = (char *) malloc(4096);
    pthread_cleanup_push(cleanup, bufp);
    while ((nbytes = read(fd, bufp, 4096)) > 0) {
        for (i = 0; i < nbytes; i++)
            sum += (int) bufp[i];
    }
    pthread_cleanup_pop(1);
    return (sum);
}
```

Code Example 11-2 Finalization Using `pthread_cleanup_pop()`

The cleanup handlers are not restricted in what routine they may call except that they may not execute a nonlocal goto out of the handler. Once a thread is cancelled, it cannot be cancelled again, so further calls are not interrupted.

Cleanup Handlers and Condition Variables

Deferred cancellation while waiting for a condition variable is treated somewhat specially. When a call `pthread_cond_wait()` or `pthread_cond_timedwait()` is cancelled, the mutex is reacquired before calling any cleanup handlers. Consider the following code:

```
cleanup()
{
    ... cleanup assuming lock is held
}

void
a()
{
    pthread_mutex_lock(&lock);
    pthread_cleanup_push(cleanup, ...);
    ...
    while (!condition)
        pthread_cond_wait(&cond, &lock);  /* cancellation point */
    ...
    read(...);                            /* cancellation point */
    ...
    pthread_cleanup_pop(0);
    pthread_mutex_unlock(&lock);
}
```

Code Example 11-3 Cleanup of Critical Sections

The cleanup handler can assume that the mutex is held for the whole critical section, even though the thread may be cancelled at other points besides the condition wait.

Code Example 11-1 can now be rewritten, using deferred cancellation and cleanup handlers as follows:

```
/* cleanup handler for add_pic() */
void
add_pic_cleanup(void *picp)
{
    if (picp != NULL)                 /* free buf in progress */
        free(picp);
    pthread_mutex_unlock(&pic_lock);
}
```

```
/* add a decompressed picture to the list */
static void
add_pic(pic_t *picp)
{
    pthread_mutex_lock(&pic_lock);
    pthread_cleanup_push(add_pic_cleanup, picp);
    while (pic_inbuf == PIC_MAX)
        pthread_cond_wait(&pic_full, &pic_lock);/* cancel pt */
    if (pic_inbuf == 0)
        pthread_cond_signal(&pic_notempty);
    pic_buf[pic_wr] = picp;
    pic_inbuf++;
    pic_wr = (pic_wr + 1) % PIC_MAX;
    pthread_cleanup_pop(0);
    pthread_mutex_unlock(&pic_lock);
}

/* cleanup handler for pic_decomp() */
void
pic_cleanup(void *arg)
{
    pic_t *picp;

    /* No other thread should be using buffer during cancellation
*/
    while (pic_inbuf > 0) {
        picp = pic_buf[pic_rd];
        if (picp != NULL)
            free(picp);
        pic_inbuf--;
        pic_rd = (pic_rd + 1) % PIC_MAX;
    }
}
```

```
   /* Thread start function to decompress a list of file names */
35 void *
36 pic_decomp(char **namesp)
37 {
38     int fd;
39     pic_t *picp;

40     pthread_cleanup_push(pic_cleanup, NULL);
41     while (*namesp != NULL) {
42         fd = open(*namesp, ...);    /* cancellation point */
43         picp = (pic_t *) malloc(sizeof(pic_t));
44         decompress file into picp
45         close(fd);                  /* cancellation point */
46         add_pic(picp);              /* cancellation point */
47         namesp++;
48     }
49     add_pic(NULL);                  /* cancellation point */
50     pthread_cleanup_pop(0);
51     return (NULL);
52 }
```

Code Example 11-4 Terminating Threads Using Deferred Cancellation

When the display thread wants to cancel decompression, it must execute:

```
pthread_cancel(decomp_thread);
pthread_join(decomp_thread, NULL);
```

Code Example 11-4 relies on knowing exactly where cancellation can occur. If cancellation occurs at line 42, `pic_cleanup()` will free all the pictures in the queue. The queue mutex is not required since it is unlocked, and the display thread is not using it since it is calling `pthread_join()`. If the cancellation occurs at line 14, `add_pic_cleanup()` will free any pending picture and unlock `pic_lock`. `pic_cleanup()` will be called next to free the pictures in the buffer. The file descriptor, `fd`, need not be cleaned up since it will either fail to be allocated by a cancellation at line 42 or it will be closed by the time the other cancellation points at lines 46 or 49 are reached.

Code Example 11-4 also illustrates that a routine containing a call to a cancellation point is also a cancellation point as far as the calling code is concerned.

Detaching Threads During Cancellation

`pthread_join()` is a cancellation point. If thread A is cancelled while waiting for thread B it is sometime desirable to detach thread B by calling `pthread_detach()` in Thread A's cancellation handler rather than holding up the cancellation by waiting for thread B.

Testing for Cancellation

Programmers may force testing for cancellation by calling:

```
void
pthread_testcancel(void);
```

This is useful where the thread is compute bound and may not call a cancellation point (or at least one that may block) for a long time. For example, suppose the decompression code in the `pic_decomp()` function in Code Example 11-4 maps in the file to decompressed as follows:

```
len = lseek(fd, 0, SEEK_END);
addr = mmap(...,fd, 0);         /* map in file (don't use read()) */
for (i = 0; i < len; i++) {
    ... decompress next byte into picp
    if ((i % 512) == 0)         /* test cancellation every 512 bytes */
        pthread_testcancel();
}
```

Code Example 11-5 Using `pthread_testcancel()`

This code would have no cancellation points during the entire time that the file is being decompressed if it were not for the calls to `pthread_testcancel()` after each 512 bytes are processed.

Asynchronous Cancellation

Code Example 11-1 at the beginning of this chapter illustrated some of the pitfalls of terminating a thread asynchronously. However, there are times when this is useful. Calling:

```
int
pthread_setcanceltype(int type, int *oldtypep);
```

with a *type* argument of `PTHREAD_CANCEL_ASYNCHRONOUS` turns on asynchronous cancellation for the calling thread, and sets its `canceltype` cancellation attribute. The previous `canceltype` is stored in the location pointed to by *oldtypep*. When asynchronous cancellation is enabled, the thread will be asynchronously interrupted when a cancellation request is received, execute any cleanup handlers and then exit. If the *type* argument is `PTHREAD_CANCEL_DEFERRED`, thread cancellation is deferred until a cancellation point is reached. Cancellation is always deferred for any newly created threads regardless of the cancellation type of the creating thread. Similarly, the initial thread (the one that calls `main()`) also starts out with deferred cancellation.

Consider the section of the pic_decomp() function that uses pthread_testcancel() shown in Code Example 11-5. Note that inserting the call to pthread_testcancel() is somewhat disruptive to the readability of the code and the number of bytes between checking is arbitrary. An alternative is to allow asynchronous cancellation. In order to avoid the problems of asynchronous cancellation, we will only allow asynchronous cancellation during the decompression phase, where it is safe to interrupt as shown in Code Example 11-6.

```
len = lseek(fd, 0, SEEK_END);
addr = mmap(...,fd, 0);          /* map in file */
pthread_setcanceltype(PTHREAD_CANCEL_ASYNCHRONOUS, &old);
for (i = 0; i < len; i++) {
    decompress next byte into picp
}
pthread_setcanceltype(old, &old);

 ...

struct mfile {
    int fd;
    void *addr;
    size_t len;
};

 /* cleanup handler for pic_decomp() */
void
pic_cleanup(void *arg)
{
    struct mfile *mfp = arg;
    pic_t *picp;

    if (mfp->fd != -1)
        close (fd);
    if (mfp->len != 0)
        munmap(mfp->addr, len);
    while (pic_inbuf > 0) {
        picp = pic_buf[pic_rd];
        if (picp != NULL)
            free(picp);
        pic_inbuf--;
        pic_rd = (pic_rd + 1) % PIC_MAX;
    }
}
```

```
30 void *
31 pic_decomp(char **namesp)
   {
32     struct mfile mf;
33     pic_t *picp;

34     mf.fd = -1; mf.len = 0; mf.addr = NULL;
35     pthread_cleanup_push(pic_cleanup, &mf);
36     while (*namesp != NULL) {
37         mf.fd = open(*namesp, ...);/* cancellation point */
38         len = lseek(fd, 0, SEEK_END); /* cancellation point */
39         mf.addr = mmap(NULL, len, PROT_READ, MAP_PRIVATE, fd, 0);
40         mf.len = len;
41         close(mf.fd); mf.fd = -1;
42         picp = (pic_t *) malloc(sizeof(pic_t));
43         pthread_setcanceltype(PTHREAD_CANCEL_ASYNCHRONOUS, &old);
44         for (i = 0; i < len; i++) {
45             decompress next byte into picp
46         }
47         pthread_setcanceltype(old, &old);
48         munmap(mf.addr, mf.len); mf.len = 0;
49         add_pic(picp);              /* cancellation point */
50         namesp++;
51     }
52     add_pic(NULL);                  /* cancellation point */
53     pthread_cleanup_pop(0);
54     return (NULL);
55 }
```

Code Example 11-6 Using Asynchronous Cancellation

The code between lines 3 and 7 essentially becomes one cancellation point as far as the remainder of the code is concerned. This code cannot allocate addition resources or use synchronization, or do anything else that is not async-safe. Such code is said to be *async-cancel safe*.

Disabling Cancellation

A thread can also disable cancellation completely by calling:

```
int
pthread_setcancelstate(int state, int *oldstatep);
```

with a `state` argument of `PTHREAD_CANCEL_DISABLE`. This sets the thread's `cancelstate` cancellation attribute. The previous `cancelstate` is stored in the location pointed to by *oldstatep*. When cancellation is disabled, the thread will not act on pending cancellation requests. Calls to cancellation point routines are not interrupted and calls to `pthread_testcancel()` have no effect. A pending cancellation request will remain pending until cancellation is reenabled. If the *state* argument is `PTHREAD_CANCEL_ENABLE`, thread cancellation is enabled. Cancellation is always enabled for any newly created threads regardless of the cancellation state of the creating thread. Similarly, the initial thread (the one that calls `main()`) also starts out with cancellation enabled.

Disabling cancellation is useful where acting on a cancellation point is undesirable even though a cancellation request is pending. An example of such a situation would be a function that would be unlikely to take a long time or block for long at a cancellation point and that would require a complicated cleanup. Keep in mind that any routine that may block for a long time with cancellation disabled prevents timely cancellation.

Normally, you shouldn't explicitly enable cancellation in a library routine as this might violate the caller's wishes that the routine operate with cancellation disabled. Disabling cancellation over a scope should be paired with a call to restore the old state value and not a call that enables it.

The cancellation state (enabled or disabled) and the cancellation type (deferred or asynchronous) are independent of each other. For example, disabling cancellation does not affect the type; it will be the same when cancellation is reenabled.

Using Cancellation

Cancellation provides a standard and relatively efficient mechanism for cleanly terminating threads. Unfortunately, programmers don't necessarily use the mechanism even though it exists. For example, routines in a library that contains calls to cancellation point routines must usually install cleanup handlers to behave properly when a cancellation occurs. In general, it is not safe to assume that complex library routines are safe with respect to cancellation (even if they are thread-safe) unless explicitly labeled as such in the documentation. It is probably best to disable cancellation around calls to suspect routines in cancellable threads even though that may delay cancellation substantially.

The above warnings also applies to application routines. As we've seen, routines that call cancellation points are themselves cancellation points with respect to their callers. Many of the routines in an application can become cancellation points through this indirection. In most cases, applications should uniformly apply safety with respect to deferred cancellation so that unsuspecting future program maintainers don't accidentally call a routine that is not safe with respect to cancellation from a cancellable thread.

Similarly, routines that are safe with respect to deferred cancellation are not necessarily safe with respect to asynchronous cancellation. Again, it is best to not assume this property unless it is explicitly stated in the documentation. Safety with respect to asynchronous cancellation is only required in special circumstances (as is async-safety in general) and can be expensive[5]. If the routine is not trivially async-safe because it has no global state, then the typical techniques to make a routine async-cancel safe are to either disable cancellation on entry to a routine and restore the old state on exit or to set up the deferred cancellation type on entry to a routine and restore the old type on exit.

As a general rule, cancellation safety with respect to deferred cancellation is relatively efficient and most general purpose libraries should attempt this level of safety wherever possible.

Summary

Cancellation provides a standard, structured mechanism for handling thread destruction. However, you must still be careful to understand the possible cancellation points whenever you expect to cancel a thread. You should be particularly careful to determine whether the external routines called by cancellable threads are safe with respect to cancellation.

5. Setting the cancellation state and type can be roughly equivalent to setting signal masks in many implementations.

Threads Scheduling 12

This chapter discusses the general POSIX model of how threads are scheduled. It describes the POSIX threads scheduling interfaces and gives examples of the Solaris implementation. It explains some of the POSIX realtime scheduling models. This chapter also explains how some of the scheduling models affect performance.

Thread Scheduling Models

Threads require resources such as processor time, memory, and file descriptors in order to execute properly. Some of these resources, such as file descriptors, are separately allocated to each process. A thread in a process competes for these resources only with other threads inside the process. Other resources, such as real memory, are allocated globally across the system. The threads in all the processes in the system directly compete for these resources. So threads contend for resources within two different *contention scopes*: the *process scope* and the *system scope*.

The purpose of contention scope takes some explanation. The original POSIX and UNIX specifications supported only a single thread of control in a process. Various coroutine libraries were used to simulate threads. These were mainly used for program structure; the classic example is discrete event simulation where each thread represents an independent, asynchronous service that is being modeled. When using these coroutine libraries, the underlying kernel has no knowledge of the threads that are being created. The kernel schedules the single process thread and the library in turns allocates this processing time to the threads, as illustrated in Figure 12-1. In other words, multiple threads are scheduled onto the single kernel-supported thread of control. We'll refer to this as the "N to 1" scheduling model.

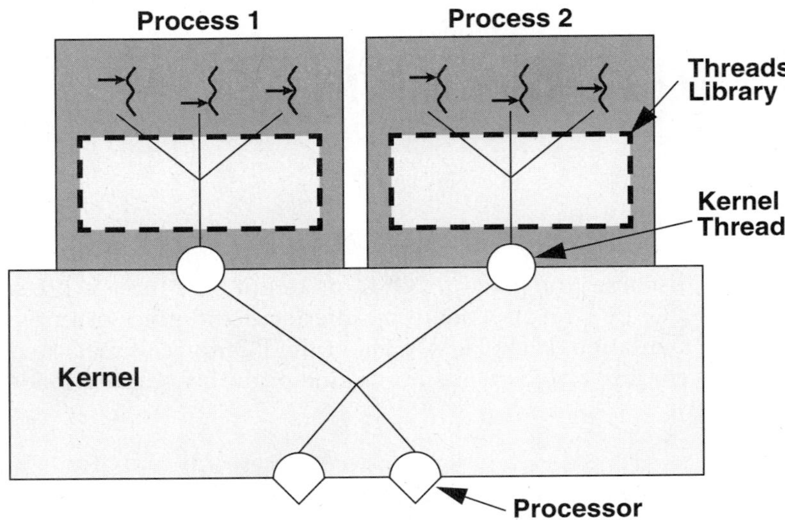

Figure 12-1 N to 1 Thread Scheduling

The disadvantage of this model is that there is really only one kernel-supported thread of control. When one thread blocks in the kernel waiting for, say, an I/O operation to complete, all the other threads in the process are also blocked. For the same reason, threads cannot simultaneously run on different processors. The advantage of the "N to 1" scheduling model is that threads can be created, destroyed and switched quickly, since there is no direct kernel involvement[1]. In addition, threads occupy only process resources, in particular virtual memory. It is easy to have many threads without occupying kernel-based resources. An example of using a library like this would be in discrete event simulation, as shown in Figure 1-9 on page 9, where there may be hundreds of threads.

Direct operating system support of multiple threads of control in a process solves many of the deficiencies of the "N to 1" model. The threads library can directly map threads onto operating system supported threads (kernel threads), as shown in Figure 12-3. We'll refer to this as the "1 to 1" scheduling model. In this model, when one threads blocks, other threads continue to run and threads within a process can run simultaneously on different processors. However, creating, destroying and scheduling operations are usually significantly slower[2] than in the "N to 1" model.

1. One of the reasons for this improvement is that the thread switcher does not have to cross a protection boundary into the kernel. In addition, the scheduler can make purely local decisions. It does not have to prioritize all the threads in the system, only those in the process.

2. The operations can be anywhere from two to ten times slower than equivalent user operations on Solaris 2. Other implementations have measured similar results [Anderson 89].

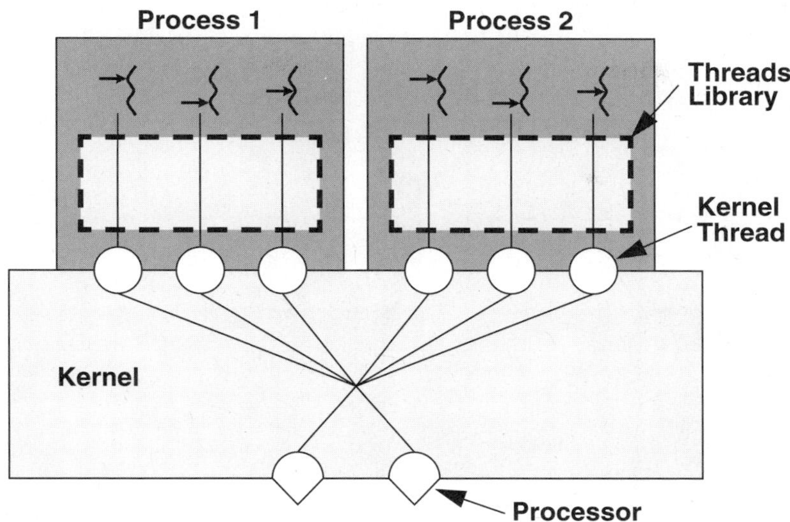

Figure 12-2 1 to 1 Thread Scheduling

A third technique, which is the one used by Solaris 2, combines the scheduling models in a way that preserves the advantages of each. In the "M to N" scheduling model, the operating system directly supports multiple threads of control in a single process; however, the thread library does not necessarily directly assign a user thread to a kernel thread[3]. Instead the library multiplexes user threads on a pool of kernel threads that it maintains, as shown in Figure 12-3. In the "M to N" scheduling model, there are two levels of scheduling: the threads library schedules threads on kernel threads that are in turn scheduled onto the available processors by the operating system. In this sense, the operating system threads of control can be looked at as virtual processors, and the threads library as a microcosm of an multiprocessor operating system.

This scheduling model allows the threads library to quickly create, destroy and switch between threads while also supporting real concurrency. For example, an application can create many threads, yet the threads library need create only as many kernel threads as there are user threads that are simultaneously running. The remaining threads are not visible to the operating system.

There are some cases in which it is not desirable for a thread to be scheduled purely local to a process. In particular, threads that must be scheduled on a realtime basis must be prioritized and scheduled with respect to all the other threads in the system; in other words, they must have a system-wide contention

3. In Solaris 2, kernel threads are called *lightweight processes* or LWPs.

scope. Process 2 in Figure 12-3 shows how the threads library can bind a realtime user thread to a kernel thread to make it globally visible while keeping some threads local to the process.

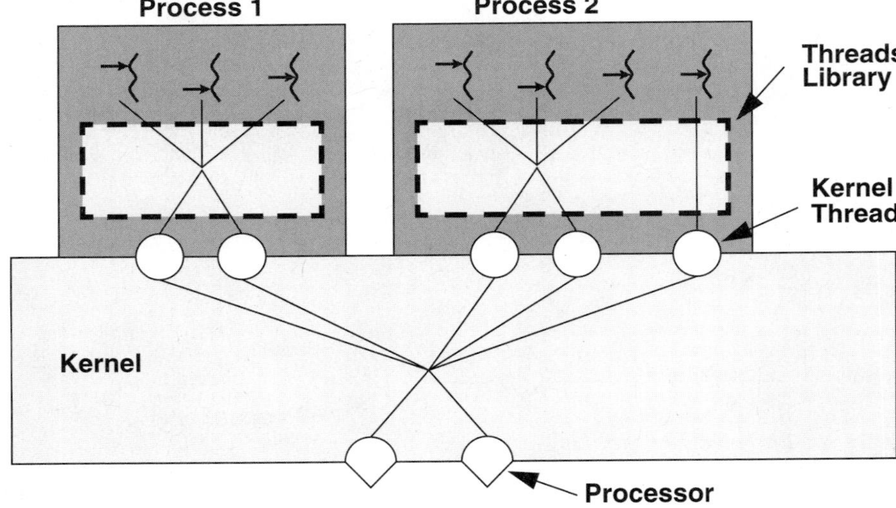

Figure 12-3 M to N Thread Scheduling

An example that exploits this feature is a window system server that creates a thread per window (or widget) for program structure. Such a server would have dozens of threads, yet only a small number would be active at any one time. The number of kernel threads required is proportional to the number of simultaneously active threads, not the number of existing threads. The window server may also have a single thread that updates the cursor to track the mouse. Such a thread has important realtime requirements with respect to the system, and can be added to the system contention scope while the other threads remain in the process contention scope.

Using Contention Scope

The scheduling models above represent real implementations, though there are other possible implementation strategies. The key point is that process contention scope allows threads libraries to do local optimizations, while system contention scope tends to remove the possibility of these optimizations in favor of exact scheduling characteristics with respect to all the threads in the system. In general, use the implementation-defined default contention scope (usually process contention scope, if it is available). System contention scope should be explicitly used only when true realtime behavior is desired.

Note – Some systems may not implement both process and system contention scopes.

It is up to the system implementation to determine how process contention scope threads are in turn scheduled by the system and, therefore, how they relate to system contention scope threads. In Solaris 2, the system-wide scheduling parameters of the underlying kernel threads are inherited from the thread that executed `fork()` in the creating process.

The POSIX P1003.1b (realtime) standard defines scheduling mechanisms for single-threaded processes. This includes:

```
#include <sched.h>

int
sched_setparam(pid_t pid, const struct sched_param *param);

int
sched_setscheduler(pid_t pid, int policy,
    const struct sched_param *param);

int
sched_getparam(pid_t pid, struct sched_param *param);

int
sched_getscheduler(pid_t pid);
```

These function can set and get the scheduling parameters and policies (see below) of either the calling process or of other processes. If the target process contains threads, then `sched_setparam()` and `sched_setscheduler()` affects only threads within the process that have process contention scope. Threads with system contention scope are ignored.

Thread Scheduling Attributes

Each thread executes independently. However, there are typically more threads than there are processors to run them. This means that the system must choose which threads to run on the available processors. The policies used to assign processors to run threads can have a dramatic impact on the system. It would be unfortunate if the thread chosen to run is doing a long calculation that is not time-critical while delaying a thread that is directly responsible for some time-critical action, such as updating the cursor in response to mouse movement or opening a valve. For this reason, POSIX threads each have a scheduling policy that is used to determine when the thread is to be scheduled to run. Each thread also has a set of scheduling parameters that can be used to affect the thread's scheduling policy. The information contained in the parameters can vary between different scheduling policies.

Note – Scheduling policies are an optional feature in Pthreads. The threads implementation supports this feature if the macro `_POSIX_THREAD_PRIORITY_SCHEDULING` is defined in `<unistd.h>`. This can be tested dynamically by calling `sysconf()` using the `_SC_THREAD_PRIORITY_SCHEDULING` macro from `<unistd.h>` as an argument. `sysconf()` returns `-1` if the feature is not supported. The definitions for macros, functions, and names beginning with `SCHED_` or `sched_` are found in the `#include` file `<sched.h>`.

A threads scheduling policy can be set when it is created via the `schedpolicy` attribute in the thread creation attributes (see "Thread Attributes" on page 19). The `schedpolicy` attribute is set by calling:

```
int
pthread_attr_setschedpolicy(pthread_attr_t *attr, int policy);

int
pthread_attr_getschedpolicy(const pthread_attr_t *attr,
    int *policyp);
```

POSIX defines three thread scheduling policies: `SCHED_FIFO`, `SCHED_RR`, and `SCHED_OTHER`, which will be explained later. POSIX implementations need not implement all three defined policies, though they must at least implement `SCHED_OTHER`.

The parameters used by the scheduling policy are set via the `schedparam` attribute in the threads attribute structure. The `schedparam` attribute consists of a `sched_param` structure with at least one defined member:

```
struct sched_param {
    ...
    int sched_priority;
    ...
};
```

The `schedparam` attribute is set by calling:

```
int
pthread_attr_setschedparam(pthread_attr_t *attr,
    const struct sched_param *paramp);

int
pthread_attr_getschedparam(const pthread_attr_t *attr,
    struct sched_param *paramp);
```

The contentionscope attribute allows each thread to specify the contention scope in which the thread's scheduling policy applies. In the process scope, the scheduling policy applies only to threads in the process; in the system scope, the scheduling policy applies to all the threads on the system. The contentionscope attribute is set or retrieved by calling:

```
int
pthread_attr_setscope(pthread_attr_t *attr, int contentionscope);

int
pthread_attr_getscope(const pthread_attr_t *attr,
    int *contentionscopep);
```

The contentionscope attribute may be set to PTHREAD_SCOPE_PROCESS or PTHREAD_SCOPE_SYSTEM.

Scheduling policies and parameters can also be interrogated and changed after a thread has been created by calling:

```
int
pthread_setschedparam(pthread_t thread,
    const int policy, const struct sched_param *param);

int
pthread_getschedparam(pthread_t thread,
    int *policyp, struct sched_param *param);
```

Inheriting Scheduling Attributes

The thread scheduling policy does not always have to be explicitly set. The thread can also use the same scheduling policy and parameters as the creating thread via the inheritsched attribute which is set by calling:

```
int
pthread_attr_setinheritsched(pthread_attr_t *attr,
    int inheritsched);

int
pthread_attr_getinheritsched(const pthread_attr_t *attr,
    int *inheritschedp);
```

If the inheritsched attribute is set to PTHREAD_INHERIT_SCHED, the new thread scheduling policy and parameters is set to be the same as the creating thread and the schedpolicy and schedparam attributes in the thread creation attributes structure are ignored. If the inheritsched attribute is set to PTHREAD_EXPLICIT_SCHED, the new threads scheduling policy and parameters are set from the schedpolicy and schedparam attributes in the thread creation attributes structure.

Thread Scheduling Policies

Threads go through several states as they are created, execute, and are destroyed, as shown in Figure 12-4[4]. In the diagram, the *destroyed* state is a pseudo-state in which the thread does not exist. When a thread is created it is immediately *runnable*. At some point, it is chosen to be executed on a processor at which point it becomes *active*. While it is executing, it can *block*, for example, on a synchronization variable and then be woken up when the synchronization variable releases it. While it is running, another, higher priority thread may become runnable, at which point the scheduling policy may decide to preempt the active thread, making it runnable again. The thread may also exit and either be immediately destroyed if the thread was detached or become a zombie until another thread joins with it.

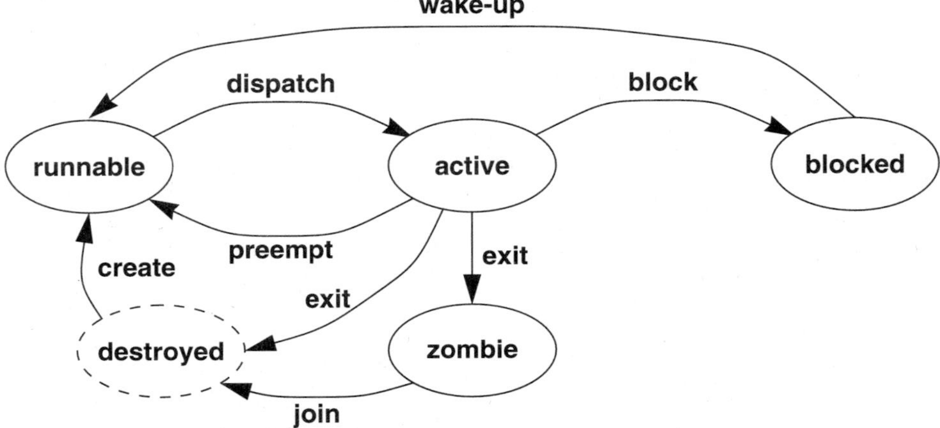

Figure 12-4 POSIX Thread States

Scheduling policies come into play when threads enter and leave the *runnable*, *blocked*, and *active* states. The POSIX scheduling policies are defined in terms of a conceptual implementation model. This may or may not reflect an actual implementation, though there should not be a way by which the program can tell the difference from the implementation model.

4. UNIX International threads have a slightly more complicated state diagram. See Appendix B, "UNIX International Threads."

Priorities

In the implementation model, each thread has a integer priority (sched_priority in the sched_param structure) that can range between an implementation defined minimum and maximum. The implementation's minimum and maximum priority for each scheduling policy can be retrieved by calling:

```
#include <sched.h>

int
sched_get_priority_min(int policy);

int
sched_get_priority_max(int policy);
```

Where *policy* is one of the supported scheduling policies (SCHED_FIFO, SCHED_RR, or SCHED_OTHER). The difference between the minimum and maximum priorities (i.e., the number of implemented priorities) must be at least 32.

The implementation model is based on a structured queue of runnable threads called a *run queue*. The run queue consists of an ordered list with an element for each implemented priority level. Each element in the list consists of a queue of runnable threads, as shown in Figure 12-5. The thread that will be chosen to run next will be the thread at the head of the highest priority non-empty queue. A scheduling policy determines how and when the threads that are scheduled under that policy are placed on the queue associated with each thread's priority.

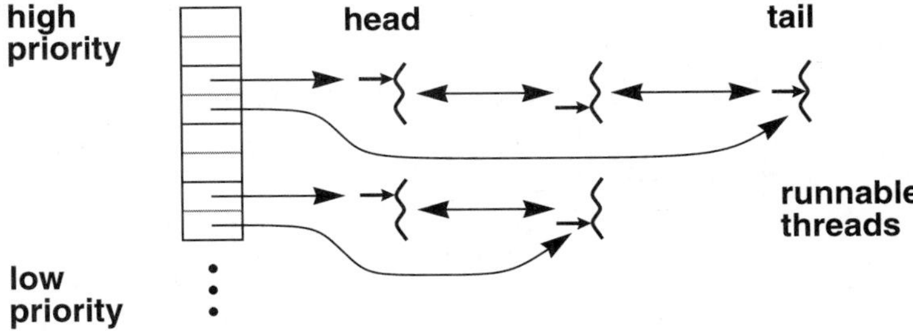

Figure 12-5 Scheduling Policy Implementation Model

Yielding

A running thread can also choose to defer its execution to other threads of equal priority by calling:

```
#include <sched.h>

int
sched_yield();
```

This relinquishes the processor and puts the thread at the tail of its priority queue, allowing the other threads with equal priority to run.

Scheduling Policies

The different scheduling policies specify exactly how and when a thread is moved on and off the run queue when scheduling events occur.

First in, first out

The first in, first out scheduling policy, `SCHED_FIFO`, places its threads on the run queue in the following manner:

- When an active thread is preempted, it is placed on the head of the queue associated with its priority.
- When a blocked thread becomes runnable, it is placed on the tail of the queue associated with its priority.
- When an active thread is the target of `pthread_setschedparam()`, it is placed on the tail of the queue associated with its new priority.
- When an active thread calls `sched_yield()`, it is placed on the tail of the queue associated with its priority.

`SCHED_FIFO` also determines the order in which the threads that are blocked on synchronization variables are awakened: the highest priority thread that has been blocked the longest will be unblocked first.

`SCHED_FIFO` is a simple, fixed priority scheduling algorithm. However, it can also be abused since there is nothing to prevent the thread from running continuously without giving up the processor. For this reason, using this scheduling policy will usually require privilege on time-sharing systems.

Round robin

The round robin policy, SCHED_RR, is identical to SCHED_FIFO except that an active SCHED_RR thread is automatically preempted after is has been running continuously for a *time quantum* associated with the entire process. The value of the time quantum can be retrieved by calling:

```
#include <sched.h>

int
sched_rr_get_interval(pid_t pid, struct timespec *quantump);
```

sched_rr_get_interval() sets the timespec structure pointed to by *quantump* to the time quantum for process *pid*. The time quantum for the current process is retrieved if *pid* is zero. sched_rr_get_interval() will return an error if *pid* does not refer to the current process and the calling process does not have sufficient privilege to access the target process. Like SCHED_FIFO, using SCHED_RR will usually require privilege on time-sharing systems even though the thread is forced to give up the processor after its time quantum has expired. This is done because the priority is fixed and a high priority thread will prevent lower priority threads from running. The main difference from SCHED_FIFO is that time is shared between runnable threads of equal priority.

Other

The SCHED_OTHER policy is defined by each implementation. Typically it will be what is most effective for general use. The SCHED_OTHER policy can, in fact, be identical to SCHED_FIFO or SCHED_RR. For example, they will likely be the same in embedded realtime systems. However, SCHED_OTHER can also be quite different in other cases. For example, on time-sharing systems the actual priority can float while the sched_priority value can assign a relative scheduling bias as nice() does in UNIX systems.

The SCHED_OTHER policy also allows optimizations that are forbidden by the strict priority scheduling policies. For example, the requirement that the highest priority thread that has been blocked the longest will be unblocked first prevents the implementation of a simple spin blocking policy (see "Spin Blocking" on page 271) which may produce random unblocking orders. In general, SCHED_OTHER should be used unless there are specific requirements for strict priority scheduling.

Scheduling Allocation Domain

A multiprocessor system sometimes restricts the set of processors a thread may run on. One reason for this is by running a consistent set of threads on the same set of processors the processor caches will contain the data and code for the set of threads without this data being flushed from the cache by the execution of other threads that require different code and data. In other words, the caches stay "warmer" (see Chapter 15, "Multiprocessor Issues"). The set of processors that a thread may run on is called the *scheduling allocation domain* of the thread. Clearly, scheduling allocation domains can affect the relative order in which threads executed.

The Pthreads standard does not contain any interfaces that manipulate scheduling allocation domains, as this can be very implementation specific. However, it requires implementations of Pthreads to define how the various scheduling policies interact with whatever restrictions on scheduling allocation domain the system supports.

Priority Inversion

Threads in either of the two fixed priority scheduling policies can run into a common problem called *priority inversion,* where lower priority threads block the execution of higher priority threads. Priority inversions can occur whenever threads of different priorities compete for resources. However, this problem frequently occurs with synchronization variables because they are almost always used by different threads. One way this occurs is when a lower priority thread owns a mutex that a higher priority thread attempts to acquire. The higher priority thread must wait until the lower priority thread releases the lock. This situation is called a *bounded priority inversion* because the duration of the priority inversion is limited by the duration of the critical section. This type of priority inversion can be controlled by limiting the duration of critical sections. An example of a bounded priority inversion on a single processor system is shown in Figure 12-6.

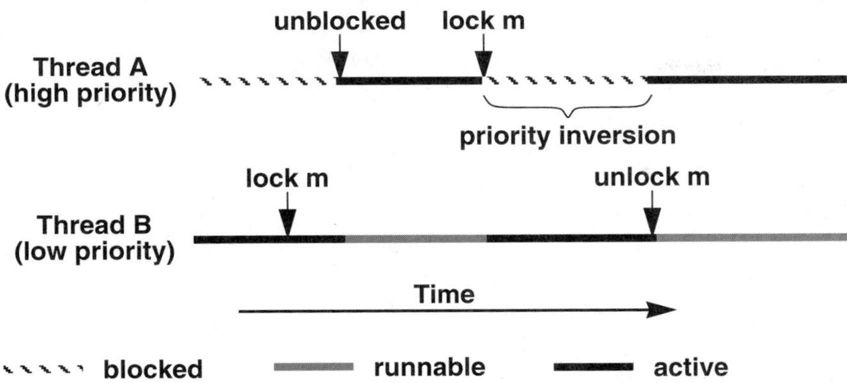

Figure 12-6 Bounded Priority Inversion on a Single Processor System

Another, more insidious, type of priority inversion is an *unbounded priority inversion*. For example, suppose a high priority thread attempts to acquire a mutex owned by a lower priority thread. In this case the high priority thread may be blocked indefinitely by a medium priority thread that prevents the low priority thread from releasing the lock, as illustrated in Figure 12-7. The higher priority thread will be blocked as long as any medium priority thread is runnable, regardless of the length of any critical sections.

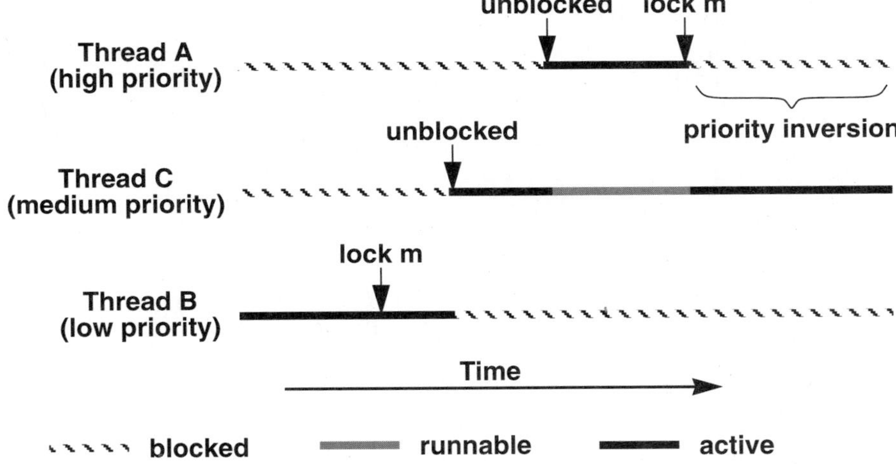

Figure 12-7 Unbounded Priority Inversion on a Single Processor System

POSIX provides two solutions for the unbounded priority inversion problems caused by owning mutexes: the priority ceiling and priority inheritance protocols. Each mutex that is used by threads of differing priorities must be set up to use the desired protocol when the mutex is initialized. This is done by setting the `protocol` attribute in the mutex initialization attributes. The protocol attribute is set or retrieved by calling:

```
int
pthread_mutexattr_setprotocol(pthread_mutexattr_t *attr,
    int protocol);

int
pthread_mutexattr_getprotocol(const pthread_mutexattr_t *attr,
    int *protocolp);
```

The valid *protocol* values are: PTHREAD_PRIO_NONE, PTHREAD_PRIO_PROTECT, and PTHREAD_PRIO_INHERIT. The latter two values refer to the priority ceiling and priority inheritance protocols respectively. The value PTHREAD_PRIO_NONE specifies that neither the priority ceiling or priority inheritance protocols are to be used. Both these protocols can temporarily raise the thread's priority over the priority set by the program or inherited from the creating thread (the base priority).

Note – The priority inheritance and priority ceiling protocols are optional features in POSIX threads. The threads implementation supports the priority ceiling protocol feature if the _POSIX_THREAD_PRIO_PROTECT macro is defined in <unistd.h>. It supports the priority inheritance protocol feature if the _POSIX_THREAD_PRIO_INHERIT macro is defined. This can be tested dynamically by calling sysconf() using the _SC_THREAD_PRIO_PROTECT or the _SC_THREAD_PRIO_INHERIT macros from <unistd.h> as an argument. sysconf() returns -1 if the feature is not supported. If either _POSIX_THREAD_PRIO_PROTECT or _POSIX_THREAD_PRIO_INHERIT is defined then _POSIX_THREAD_PRIORITY_SCHEDULING must also be defined.

Priority Ceiling Protocol

A mutex initialized to use the priority ceiling protocol must also be initialized with a value called the *priority ceiling*. The priority ceiling for a mutex is contained in the `prioceiling` mutex attribute, which may be set or retrieved by calling:

```
int
pthread_mutexattr_setprioceiling(pthread_mutexattr_t *attr,
    int prioceiling);

int
pthread_mutexattr_getprioceiling(const pthread_mutexattr_t *attr,
    int *prioceilingp);
```

The priority ceiling must be a valid thread priority. Whenever a thread acquires this mutex, its priority is raised to the priority ceiling of the mutex, if its priority is not higher already. When the mutex is released, the thread's priority is set to the maximum of the base priority, inherited priority (see below) and the priority ceilings of all the mutexes the thread still owns. Figure 12-8 shows an example in which thread *B*, that has base priority *p*, locks mutex `m`, that has priority ceiling *p+x*. While thread *B* holds `m`, its priority is raised to *p+x*. This prevents any thread below priority *p+x* from preempting thread *B* and causing an unbounded priority inversion.

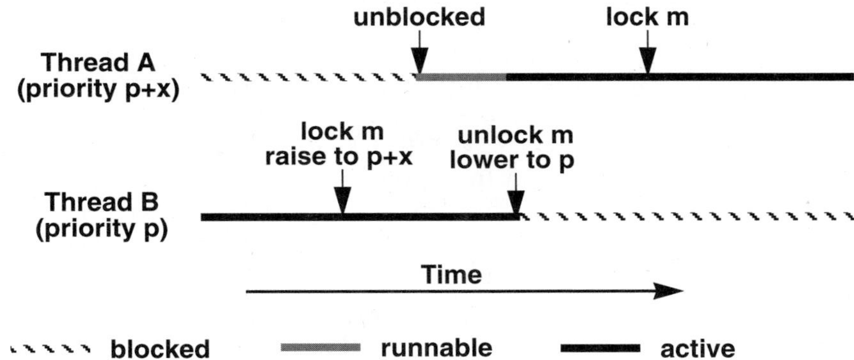

Figure 12-8 Priority Ceiling Protocol

This protocol guarantees that the critical section a mutex protects will be executed by a thread running with a priority that is at least equal to the priority ceiling for the mutex. The priority ceiling value must be greater than or equal to the highest priority of all the threads that may lock the mutex, otherwise this protocol will not prevent priority inversions. This can make the priority ceiling protocol somewhat difficult to use as it requires a priori knowledge of the threads that may use a particular mutex and their priorities. On the other hand, it is relatively simple to implement.

A mutex's priority ceiling can also be retrieved or changed after the mutex has been initialized by calling:

```
int
pthread_mutex_setprioceiling(pthread_mutex_t *mp,
    int prioceiling, int *old_ceiling);

int
pthread_mutexattr_getprioceiling(const pthread_mutex_t *mp,
    int *prioceilingp);
```

Priority Inheritance

The priority inheritance protocol simplifies the programmer's job by not requiring a priori knowledge of the priorities of the threads that will use a mutex. When a thread acquires a mutex that is initialized to use the priority inheritance protocol, its priority is not changed. The action happens when a thread attempts to acquire a mutex that is already owned by another thread. In this case, the priority of the owning thread is raised to the priority of the thread that has been blocked, if the new priority would be higher. In other words, the owning thread *inherits* the priority of any blocked threads. When the thread releases a mutex it loses the inherited priority of those threads blocked on the released mutex, though it retains the priority of threads blocked on other mutexes it may own. Figure 12-9 shows an example in which thread *B*, which has base priority *p*, locks mutex `m`, which has priority ceiling *p+x*. When thread *A* attempts to acquire `m`, it blocks, and thread *B*'s priority is raised to that of thread *A*. This prevents threads that have priority lower than *p+x* from prevent thread *B* from completing the critical section.

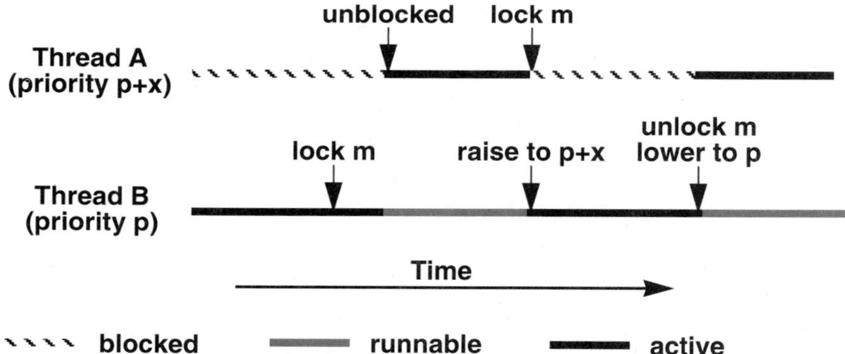

Figure 12-9 Priority Inheritance Protocol

Scheduling Strategies

The precise scheduling control of the `SCHED_FIFO` and `SCHED_RR` scheduling policies are most useful for realtime systems that have tight bounds on response time. In such systems a thread's priorities directly reflect the priority of the event that it is responding to. Programmers must understand exactly how much time each thread takes to compute a response to an event. The worst-case response time for a particular event is computed by first computing the worst case response time for the thread responding to the event and then adding the worst case response times for all the higher priority threads that may run concurrently in response to other events (see Figure 12-10). Such systems must avoid unbounded priority inversions as they add unbounded intervals to the response time.

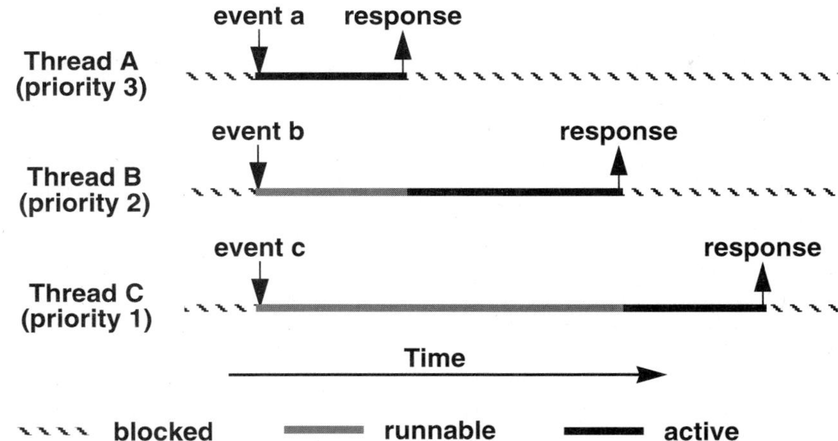

Figure 12-10 Priority and Response Time

The SCHED_FIFO and SCHED_RR scheduling policies can also be used to control the wake-up order in synchronization variables. Threads scheduled by SCHED_OTHER do not have to be unblocked in any particular order. In particular, certain blocking algorithms can cause some threads to remain blocked for long periods while others are allowed to continue (see "Starvation" on page 273). Specifying SCHED_FIFO or SCHED_RR causes threads to wait in FIFO order.

Even though SCHED_OTHER is not exactly specified it can still be used to bias scheduling. A typical example is when a thread is used to defer work. The thread doing the deferred work can be run at a lower priority to avoid interfering with the parts of the program that must be more responsive. In Code Example 12-1 the code first shown in Code Example 2-1 on page 14, which displays a series of compressed pictures by decompressing the next one while the current one is being displayed, has been modified to lower the priority of the decompressing thread.

```
int
main(int argc, char *argv[])
{
    pthread_t pic_thread;
    int fileno;
    pic_buf_t *buf;
    extern void *get_next_picture(void *);
    extern void display_buf(pic_buf_t *);
    struct sched_param sparam;
    pthread_attr_t low_attr;
    int policy;

    pthread_getschedparam(pthread_self(), &policy, &sparam);
    sparam.sched_priority--;
    pthread_attr_init(&low_attr);
    pthread_attr_setschedparam(&low_attr, &sparam);
    for (fileno = 1; fileno < argc; fileno++) {
        if (fileno == 1)    /* do the first file w/o a thread */
            buf = get_next_picture((void *)argv[fileno]);
        else                /* wait for decompression to finish */
            pthread_join(pic_thread, (void **)&buf);
        if (fileno < argc-1)/* launch thread to do next, if any */
            pthread_create(&pic_thread, NULL,
                get_next_picture, (void *)argv[fileno+1]);
        display_buf(buf);       /* display current picture */
        free(buf);              /* free picture*/
        if (getchar() == EOF )/* wait for user to finish looking */
            break;
    }
    return (0);
}
```

Code Example 12-1 Deferring Low Priority Work

Thread Scheduling in Solaris 2

Solaris implements both the process and system contention scopes using the "M to N" scheduling model, as mentioned previously (see [Powell 91]). The kernel-supported threads of control are called *lightweight processes* (LWPs). Threads in the system contention scope are permanently associated with an LWP and are called *bound threads*. Binding a thread to an LWP makes it directly visible to the operating system. They are scheduled by the operating system and contend for processing time with all the other LWPs in the system. Threads in process contention scope are scheduling by the Pthreads library onto a pool of LWPs managed by the library. These are called *unbound threads*. The user threads are not directly visible to the operating system. They contend for execution resources (LWPs) only with other unbound threads in the process. The LWPs are in turn scheduled by the operating system.

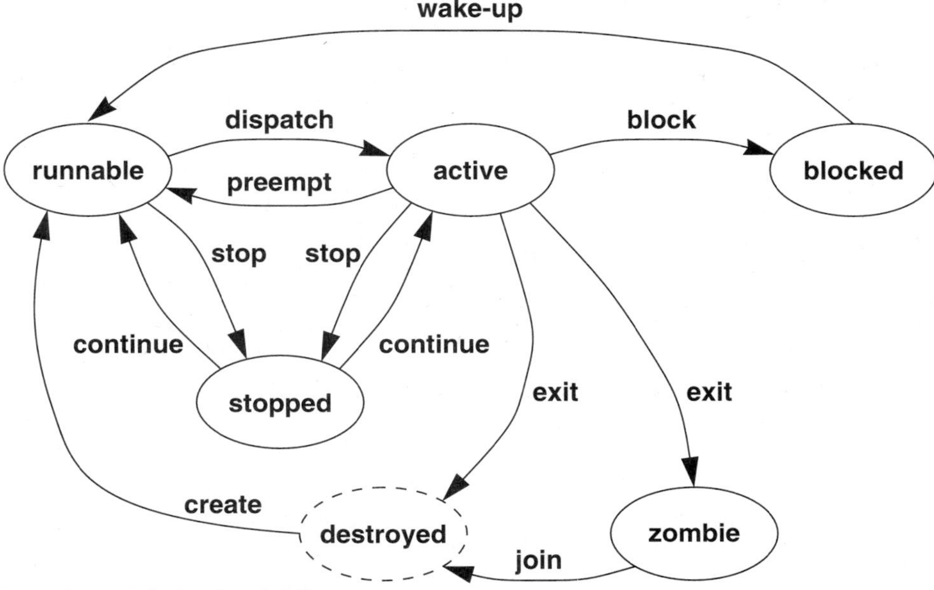

Figure 12-11 Solaris Thread States

Threads in Solaris 2 have an additional state, *stopped*, beyond the states required by POSIX. This state supports the UNIX International interfaces that stop threads from running and then start them again. This state also allows debuggers to stop individual threads. Threads in the *active* state are being run by an LWP. While a thread is *active*, its underlying LWP can in turn be in one of four different states itself with respect to the kernel, as shown in Figure 12-12. A thread in the *active* state is running on a processor only when its underlying LWP is in the *running* state. If an *active* thread on a *running* LWP makes a blocking system call, say `read()`, its underlying LWP will enter the *blocked* state. If the running LWP's time quantum expires it enters the *runnable* state. In either case the thread remains in the *active* state since, as far as the threads library is concerned, the LWP is still executing the thread.

Concurrency and Process Contention Scope Threads

How large should the pool of LWPs (i.e., running threads and on the idle list) that can run unbound threads be? If there were one LWP for every thread, there wouldn't be much resource savings over a "1 to 1" scheduling model, though

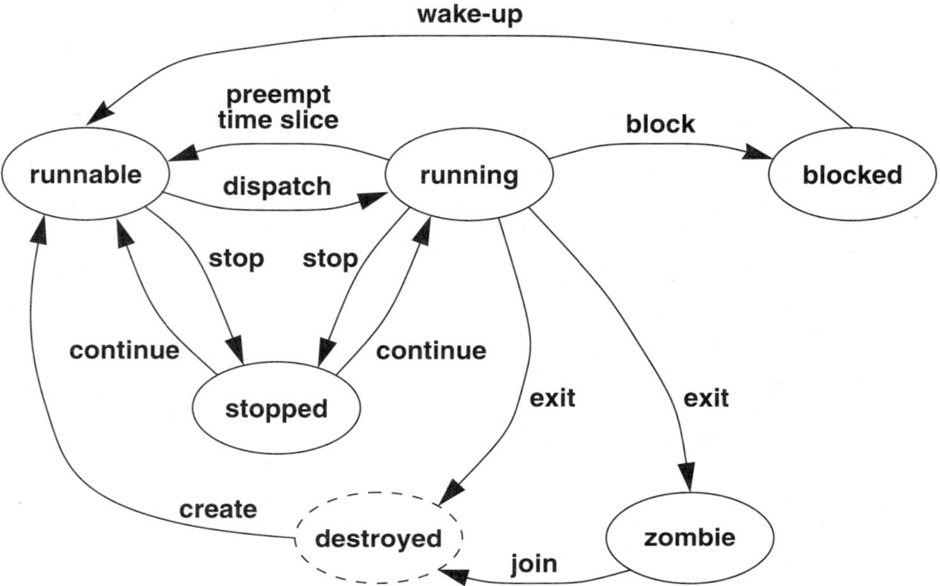

Figure 12-12 Solaris LWP States

context switching can still be done without operating system intervention. On the other hand, if there is only one LWP in the pool, the library is reduced to the "N to 1" scheduling model. In particular, if there are too few LWPs, then if the active threads executes a system call that blocks on some long term event (e.g., wait for the user to type a character or for a packet to come in on the network), other runnable threads will wait indefinitely for an available LWP. At the very least the library should have enough LWPs to prevent such indefinite waits.

The Solaris threads library and the operating system cooperate to ensure that there are at least enough LWPs to prevent indefinite waiting[5]. However, this minimal number may not be enough to ensure reasonable performance. A better situation is where the number of LWPs exactly tracks the number of runnable threads. However, the number of runnable threads can change very quickly (e.g., `pthread_cond_broadcast()` can wake up many threads) so the Solaris threads library does not create LWPs too aggressively nor does it destroy idle LWPs

5. This requires special cooperation between the operating system and threads library: the operating system sends the process a special signal when all the LWPs in the process are blocked in indefinite waits. The threads library catches the signal and creates more LWPs.

immediately. Instead, LWPs are destroyed only after the library notices that they have been idle for some time. The threads library smooths out the LWP requirement as shown in Figure 12-13.

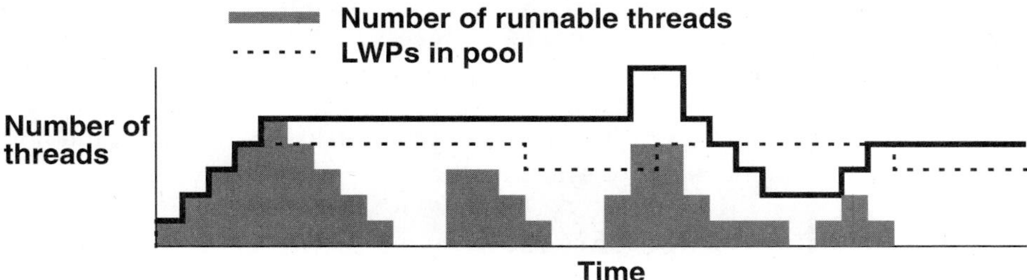

Figure 12-13 LWP Pool Size

The threads library cannot always anticipate the needs of the application. The UNIX International standard allows the program to give the library a hint for the number of threads it expects to run concurrently (see `thr_setconcurrency()` in "Concurrency Level" on page 379).

Scheduling unbound threads

While Solaris currently[6] does not implement `SCHED_FIFO` or `SCHED_RR`, the default scheduling policy, `SCHED_OTHER`, has much in common with `SCHED_FIFO` in process contention scope. Process contention scope threads in Solaris are scheduled onto LWPs strictly according to thread priority which can range from 0 to 127. The LWPs, in turn, are scheduled according to the policy of the LWP (running a thread) that created the process. In most cases this is the classic time-sharing policy typical of many UNIX systems.

The time-sharing policy's goal is to provide reasonably fair service and good interactive response in a multi-user system. The policy limits the amount of time that an LWP can continuously run on a processor to a time quantum. The policy continuously adjusts the priority of the runnable LWPs based on their recent behavior and the amount of time they have been waiting for the processor. LWPs that tend to block on I/O get larger priorities and shorter time quantums. LWPs that are compute bound get lower priority and longer time quantums. Roughly, the reasoning behind this is interactive or I/O bound LWPs tend to wake up when an I/O has returned, run for a short amount of time while they compute the next action, then block. They get high priority so that they can quickly respond. It is less important that compute bound LWPs immediately run and they are most effective when they have the processor for longer periods.

6. As of December 1995.

The time-sharing behavior of LWPs can cause some surprising results. LWP priority and thread priority are not tied together[7]. So sometimes lower priority threads get scheduled on LWPs that have higher system priority. This effect is usually not noticeable as threads switching tends to average out LWP behavior except in certain situations. For example, a process that has some threads that are compute bound that occasionally synchronize with non-compute bound threads using process-private synchronization variables. In this case non-compute bound threads can be scheduled on LWPs that were previously used by compute bound threads and therefore have lower system priority.

System Contention Scope Threads

Solaris also does not implement `SCHED_FIFO` or `SCHED_RR` for system contention scope threads. The default `SCHED_OTHER` policy is the default time-sharing policy described above. However, system scope threads may also use the scheduling policies defined by UNIX International. This includes a realtime (i.e., fixed priority) policy as well as a time-sharing policy. System scope threads can switch to a particular scheduling policy by calling `priocntl()` (see "Thread Priorities" on page 381).

Contention Scope and Process-Shared Synchronization Variables

The combination of contention scope and the setting of the process-shared attribute of synchronization variables can affect performance. Synchronization variables that are initialized with their `process-shared` attribute set to `PTHREAD_PROCESS_SHARED` block by calling the operating system[8] (see "Interprocess Synchronization" on page 173). Like other system calls, the calling thread remains *active* as far as the threads library is concerned. If the synchronization variables were instead initialized with `PTHREAD_PROCESS_PRIVATE`, the calling threads block in the threads library without directly calling the operating system. Instead, the thread is placed on the sleep queue associated with the synchronization variable and it enters the *blocked* state. Threads in the process contention scope give up their LWP which can then run other *runnable* threads. The LWP for threads in the system contention scope waits by calling the operating system until the threads library wakes it up when the thread unblocks. This technique allows process-private synchronization for

---

7. Setting the underlying LWP's priority whenever a different thread was switched to it would slow down thread switching and throw away many of the advantages of the "M to N" scheduling model.

8. If process-shared synchronization variables don't block (i.e., an unlocked mutex), then the calling thread can proceed without involving the operating system. However, if the calling thread is using either of the `SCHED_FIFO` or `SCHED_RR` scheduling protocols, then it must call the operating system if there are other waiting threads, since they must be awakened first.

process contention scope threads to happen quickly without operating system intervention. Process-shared synchronization or synchronization with system contention scope threads is significantly slower.

Summary

Programs that use threads to overlap I/O may be relatively immune from thread scheduling issues as they are mostly blocked. However, thread scheduling can have a profound effect on the performance of programs that synchronize frequently or have realtime requirements. POSIX thread scheduling has several mechanisms to provide strict realtime priority scheduling. It also allows programs to specify exactly their scheduling requirements, allowing threads implementations to improve performance where programs need only local scheduling or do not require strict scheduling behavior.

Threads and Processes: Advanced Topics 13

This chapter describes the limitations imposed by any default stack manager, why certain applications might need to circumvent these limitations and how a programmer could go about doing so. The chapter also discusses the interfaces to allow you make a routine safe with respect to calls to `fork()` by other threads in the process — in other words, how to make routines *fork-safe*.

You should read this chapter if you require threads with larger stacks, create a large number of threads or must exactly manage the placement of thread stacks in the process address space; or if you are programming a routine that must function in the child process after a call to `fork()` (but before the child calls `exec()`).

Managing Thread Stacks

Thread stacks are usually automatically and transparently managed by the system. In general, a threads programmer should not be concerned with the details of stack management such as thread stack sizes or thread stack allocation. However, threads programmers should be aware of the system specific limitations imposed by the default stack management system. For certain applications, these limitations might prove too restrictive. In such cases, programmers will have to bypass the default stack manager and manage stacks on their own.

A multithreaded process's available address space is split between process text, static data, heap, and thread stacks. Thread stacks are allocated in portions of the address space of a multithreaded UNIX process. Therefore, the number of threads limits the amount of address space available for a process's text/data and vice versa.

Default Stack Management

Unless the `pthread_attr_t` threads attributes structure is explicitly set to specify stack attributes, the threads implementation manages the stack itself. The default stack size for a thread, which varies from system to system, is usually large enough for most threads programs. The default size chosen represents a trade-off between the maximum number of threads, available program address space and system resource usage. The stacks are allocated in an area that is unlikely to interfere with other growable data segments. The layout shown in Figure 13-1 is one example.

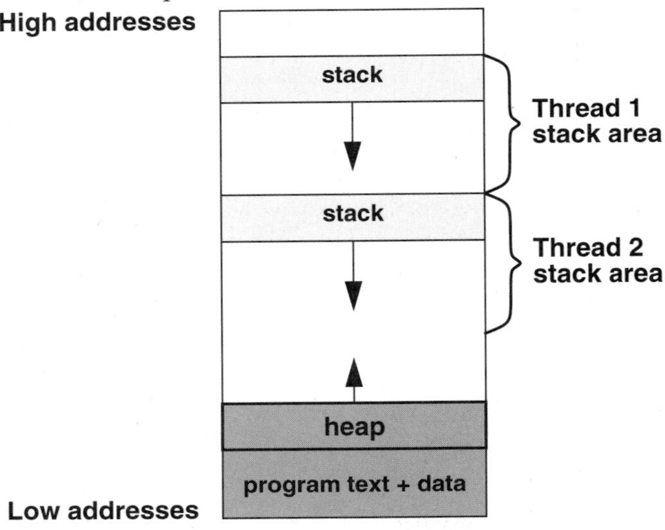

Figure 13-1 Typical Stack Layout in a Multithreaded Process

Default stack management in Solaris 2

Since the properties of the default stack management are system dependent, it is useful to show the trade-offs made by one implementation as a design example. In Solaris 2 the default stack size of one megabyte[1] which is considered more than sufficient for most code paths. When a thread is created the stack is memory mapped (using `mmap()`) from anonymous, zeroed memory (`/dev/zero`). This is similar to the algorithm used to allocate additional heap space or the stack in a single-threaded UNIX process. The allocated stack includes space for per-thread implementation information, such as the save area for register state, flags, and queue linkage.

The relatively large stack size is possible for several reasons. First, most Solaris machines have one to four gigabytes of virtual address space available. This allows hundreds of default thread stacks without seriously impacting the available virtual address space. Secondly, real memory is not allocated to each

1. As of Solaris 2.4. Including red zone and per-thread overhead.

thread stack area until is actually used because Solaris has a full virtual memory system. Typically, each thread uses several kilobytes of real memory. Lastly, the Solaris implementation maps anonymous memory for thread stacks using a special flag (`MAP_NORESERVE`) that prevents the reservation of virtual memory swap space for the mapped region until pages are actually used. This prevents a large number of threads from reserving the entire available swap space. This is identical to the behavior of the single-threaded UNIX process stack. The downside of this technique is that, like the single-threaded process stack, sometimes a thread will attempt to allocate an additional page within the mapped region and fail due to lack of swap space.

Red zones

If thread stacks are allocated next to each other or next to other data structures, this data will be corrupted if a neighboring thread overflows its stack. This will cause random, hard to debug failure that depends on the nature of the corruption. In order to mitigate this problem, Solaris 2 reserves an inaccessible page at the end of the area in which the stack is allowed to grow, as shown in Figure 13-1. This inaccessible region is called a *red zone*. When a thread uses up its stack it causes a segmentation fault along with a core dump at the time the overflow occurs.

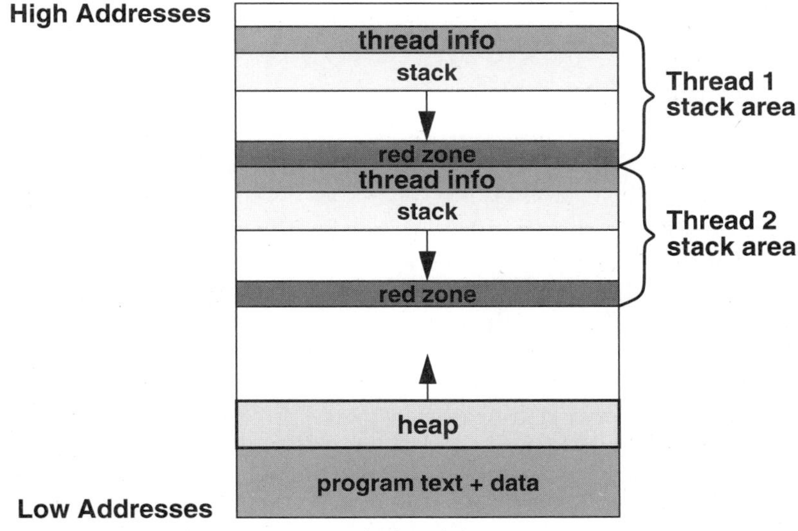

Figure 13-2 Solaris 2 Stack Layout in a Multithreaded Process

Red zones are not foolproof. For example, a procedure that has an automatic variable allocation that is larger than the size of the red zone may simply overshoot the red zone if the automatic variables are sometimes not fully used. In addition, when thread hits a red zone it causes a segmentation violation (SIGSEGV) that cannot be handled as there is no more stack for that thread. Typically this results in core dump that must be analyzed to determine that the cause was a stack overflow. However, this is better than the more random errors or failures caused by clobbering the surrounding data.

Thread Stack Size Limits

In general, a thread's stack must be large enough to handle the code that the thread executes. A typical system's default stack manager ensures that threads have sufficiently large stacks so the programmer usually does not have to worry about this problem. However, a thread may execute code which needs a significantly larger stack size. For example, functions that allocate large amounts of data on the stack as automatic variables: A thread which calls `giant()` in Code Example 13-1 needs to have a stack which is at least 10MB in addition to minimum stack space required for any procedure[2]. Other examples are highly recursive functions, or layered programs in which procedure calls nest 40 or 50 procedures deep. In these cases the stack requirements are large not because any one procedure requires a large stack frame but simply because there are many stack frames on the stack at the same time.

```
giant()
{
    char big_array[10*1024*1024];
    /*
     * big_array[] has 10MB
     */
}
```

Code Example 13-1 Function Requiring a Large Stack

In the traditional single-threaded UNIX process, the single thread had a large stack[3]. In a multithreaded process, the space available for stack allocation has to be shared among multiple threads. Hence each thread typically has a smaller stack than the one available to the only thread in the traditional UNIX process. The threads programmer should be aware of a thread's stack space limitation with respect to the code it may execute, especially when a single-threaded application is being redesigned or ported to use threads. Mysterious failures might occur in old code which used to work fine in the single-threaded process but now starts failing in the multithreaded process because it is being executed by threads with smaller stacks.

---

2. The minimum stack space for a procedure is typically in the range of 4 to 100 bytes depending on the architecture and the type of procedure.

3. Several megabytes on most UNIX systems with virtual memory capability.

One way to reduce the stack requirement is to modify the code. Recursion can be turned into loops or large automatic storage allocations can be turned into heap allocations. However, this is not desirable in many cases. The alternative is to bypass the default stack management and manage your own stacks.

Managing Your Own Thread Stacks

There are some reasons why a multithreaded program might have to customize thread stack management for its own special needs:

Applications with a large number of threads

If an application needs a number of threads that is more than the upper limit established by the default stack size, threads can be created with smaller stack sizes.

Applications requiring large stacks

If an application contains code paths such as the ones described in "Thread Stack Size Limits" and the default stack size is not enough to execute these code paths, the programmer would have to use larger stack sizes for those threads which may execute these code paths. Of course, increasing the stack sizes reduces the maximum possible number of threads a process can contain.

Application storage management

Some applications require exact control over the process address space. An example of this an application with a garbage collector that must keep track of all memory allocations. One way it can keep track of thread stack memory is to interpose on the thread creation primitive and allocate/manage thread stacks underneath the exported thread creation interface.

Note – The ability to manage stacks is an optional feature in POSIX threads. The threads implementation supports customized stack management if the `_POSIX_THREAD_ATTR_STACKSIZE` and `_POSIX_THREAD_ATTR_STACKADDR` macros are defined in `<unistd.h>`. They enable stack size and stack address management respectively. This can be tested dynamically by calling `sysconf()` using the `_SC_THREAD_ATTR_STACKSIZE` or `_SC_THREAD_ATTR_STACKADDR` macro from `<unistd.h>` as an argument. `sysconf()` returns `-1` if the feature is not supported.

Managing thread stack sizes

The bare minimum stack size a thread needs is the amount of stack required by the machine architecture (e.g., procedure overhead for the thread start routine) and thread implementation (e.g., per-thread information). The system may provide this number as the value of the PTHREAD_STACK_MIN in <limits.h> if the value is fixed. If the value is indeterminate at compile-time, it can be retrieved when the program is run by calling sysconf() using the _SC_THREAD_STACK_MIN macro from <unistd.h> as an argument, as follows:

```
size_t ts_min;

ts_min = (size_t) sysconf(_SC_THREAD_STACK_MIN);
```

The value returned does not include any space for procedures other than the start routine or for any additional automatic storage allocation in the start routine, except for the required single argument and return value. However, the typical thread does make procedure calls and does allocate automatic variables. For such threads, it is your responsibility to estimate the stack requirement of the code the thread must execute and add this to the minimum.

One of the most difficult problems in determining additional stack space the thread requires is that a thread might execute code not owned by the programmer, e.g., library code. In addition, other parts of a program's run-time environment might be executed by a thread at instances which are not obvious to the programmer. For example, the dynamic linker may be invoked to resolve a symbol when the thread first references a symbol[4]. The dynamic linker executes using the thread's stack, which must have enough space left on it to let the linker run to completion. Another example is when a thread's memory allocation invokes a garbage collector. The thread stack size must include an allowance for these functions if they may be invoked. Be as liberal as possible with the extra allowance; a stack that is too small will cause somewhat mysterious failures when the program is run whenever an extra long stack is required.

Once the size is decided upon, it must be recorded in a pthread_attr_t structure that is then used to create one or more threads with the required stack size. The interface for setting up the stack size thread attribute is:

4. In Solaris 2, the lazy resolution of symbols can be disabled by setting the LD_BIND_NOW environment variable to 1 before running the program. Similarly, explicitly loading a library at run-time using dl_open() with RTLD_NOW mode will prevent the invocation of the dynamic linker for that library. Preventing lazy resolution eliminates the need to account for the dynamic linker's stack requirements. Since this is expensive, it should be done only for debugging purposes, such as isolating causes of thread stack overflows.

```
int
pthread_attr_setstacksize(pthread_attr_t *attr, size_t stacksize);

int
pthread_attr_getstacksize(const pthread_attr_t *attr,
    size_t *stacksizep);
```

`pthread_attr_set_stacksize()` will return an error if the proposed stack size is too small. Here's an example of setting up a new stack size:

```
    pthread_attr_t my_stack_attr;

    (void) pthread_attr_init(&my_stack_attr);
    (void) pthread_attr_setstacksize(&my_stack_attr,
        (size_t)sysconf(_SC_THREAD_STACK_MIN) + MY_REQUIREMENTS);
    create one or more threads
```

The Solaris 2 implementation places a red zone after all stacks that it allocates (i.e., those not allocated by the application), even those with application specified sizes, to enhance stack overflow detection.

Managing thread stack addresses

Applications that must control where thread stacks are allocated can set up the address in a `pthread_attr_t` structure using:

```
int
pthread_attr_setstackaddr(pthread_attr_t *attr, void *stackaddr);

int
pthread_attr_getstackaddr(const pthread_attr_t *attr,
    void **stackaddrp);
```

The application can allocate stack any way it chooses; however, it is a good idea to include a red zone at the end of the region the stack grows toward[5]. This adds some complexity to the stack allocation, but not having a red zone makes failure due to stack overflow notoriously difficult to detect. A reasonable alternative or supplement to red zones is to use a debugging tool that carries out checks at run-time to detect stack overflow along with extensive testing.

Stack growth

A thread stack has a fixed size. Apparently, it would seem that one has to trade off the probability of stack overflows with the cost of stack memory, i.e., a larger stack would mean a lower probability of a stack overflow but more expense in terms of swap space and real memory for the stack. This trade-off may or may

---

5. In most popular processor architectures the stack grows from higher address toward lower addresses. Therefore, the red zone should be below the stack area. However, there are machines in which stacks grow in the opposite direction.

not be an issue depending on how stacks are allocated (either by the threads implementation or the application). A good design is to have large thread stacks that are extremely cheap. This may be achieved on systems with virtual memory capability by allocating a sufficiently large amount of stack as some reserved space in virtual memory without allocating real memory. The real memory usage grows within the stack's fixed slot of virtual memory as necessary during the thread's execution. This is almost identical to the traditional UNIX stack growth; the only difference is that the traditional single-threaded UNIX process's single stack grew within a (typically) much larger fixed virtual memory slot, giving the perception of real growth.

Example

On Solaris 2, large but cheap thread stacks may be created using `mmap()` and its `MAP_NORESERVE` option. This is the technique used by the default stack manager in the threads library. The application may also create such stacks as shown in Code Example 13-2.

```
/*
 * Set up extra large stacks with extra large red zones.
 */
#include <sys/types.h>
#include <sys/mman.h>
#include <pthread.h>

#define ROUNDUP(x, y)  ((((x)+((y)-1))/(y))*(y))
#define MY_STACKSIZE   (2*1024*1024)
#define MY_REDZONE_SIZE(16*1024)
#define NTHREADS       10

int
main()
{
    size_t page, stacksize, redzonesize;
    int zerofd, i;
    void *stacks_start;
    char *addr;
    pthread_attr_t stack_attr;
    int pagesize;
    extern void *func(void *);

    pagesize = (size_t) sysconf(_SC_PAGESIZE);
    stacksize = (size_t) ROUNDUP(
        sysconf(_SC_THREAD_STACK_MIN) + MY_STACKSIZE,
        pagesize);
    redzonesize = (size_t) ROUNDUP(MY_REDZONE_SIZE, pagesize);
```

```
    /* create stacks using /dev/zero for unnamed zero-filled memory. */
    zerofd = open("/dev/zero", O_RDWR);
    stacks_start = mmap(NULL, NTHREADS * (stacksize + redzonesize),
        PROT_READ | PROT_WRITE, MAP_PRIVATE | MAP_NORESERVE,
        zerofd, 0);
    /*
     * We assume we're on a machine in which the stack grows down.
     * The red zone goes below the allocated stack. The red zone page
     * is made inaccessible by turning off read and write permission.
     * We don't simply skip or unmap the red zone as other mmap()
     * calls might then use the skipped addresses.
     */
    addr = (char *) stacks_start;
    for (i = 0; i < NTHREADS; i++) {
        mprotect(addr, redzonesize, PROT_NONE);
        addr += stacksize + redzonesize;
    }

    /* set up thread attributes */
    (void) pthread_attr_init(&stack_attr);
    (void) pthread_attr_setstacksize(&stack_attr, stacksize);
    (void) pthread_attr_setdetachstate(&stack_attr,
            PTHREAD_CREATE_DETACHED);
    addr = (char *) stacks_start + redzonesize;/*skip over red zone */

    /* create the threads each with a stack */
    for (i = 0; i < NTHREADS; i++) {
        (void) pthread_attr_setstackaddr(&stack_attr, addr);
        pthread_create(NULL, &stack_attr, func, NULL);
        addr += stacksize + redzonesize;
    }
    pthread_exit(0);        /* only kill main thread */
    /* NOTREACHED */
    return (0);
}

void *
func(void *arg)
{
    /*
     * thread which needs a non-default stack size.
     */
    ...
}
```

Code Example 13-2 Creating Your Own Stacks on Solaris 2.

Stack caching

A significant portion of the cost of creating/destroying a thread is the cost of allocating and reclaiming its stack. Caching a stack instead of freeing it usually speeds up both thread creation and destruction. Caching involves some care as the thread using the stack must be waited for (using `pthread_join()`) to ensure that it is no longer using the stack before the stack can be reallocated to a new thread.

Strategies for Using `fork()`

"Using fork()" on page 64 detailed the problems that may be encountered when using `fork()` in an multithreaded process and a simple strategy to deal with these problems. In most cases, the simple strategy of calling `exec()` immediately in the child of the `fork()` should be sufficient. However, sometimes you need to design code that is called in the child process before it calls `exec()`. In other words, you must make some code safe with respect to calls to `fork()`, or *fork-safe*.

Code Example 13-3 below shows the fork-safety problem. The child may need to call `incr_count()` to increment the global counter, `count`. If, at the time of calling `fork()`, thread1 owns `cnt_lock`, because it is in the process of calling `incr_count()`, the child will inherit an address space that indicates that `cnt_lock` is held. Now when the child calls into `incr_count()`, it will deadlock on the call to acquire `cnt_lock` inside `incr_count()`. This is because `thread1` is not cloned in the child and no thread will unlock this lock in the child.

```
pthread_mutex_t cnt_lock;
int count;

void
incr_count()
{
    pthread_mutex_lock(&cnt_lock);
    count++;
    pthread_mutex_unlock(&cnt_lock);
}

void *
thread1()
{
    ...
    incr_count();
    ...
}
```

```
void *
thread2()
{
    ...
    if (fork() != NULL) {
        /* parent */
        ...
    } else {
        /* child */
        incr_count();
        ...
    }
}
```

Code Example 13-3 The `fork()` *Problem*

Strategies that may be used to deal with these problems are:

1. Keep track of the routines that may have been in progress at the time `fork()` was called and the routines that rely on other threads to function, and only call the ones where there is no possible conflict. This requires great care since a change in some unrelated part of the program that calls new routines can now cause problems when a `fork()` happens.
2. Restrict the thread in the child process to only call the functions that are fork-safe. See Table 5-1 on page 65 for a list of such functions.
3. Have the thread that calls `fork()` first acquire all the locks that may be used by routines called by the thread in the child process. Then, after the call to `fork()`, the thread can release the locks in both the parent and the child. The thread in the child must also recreate any helper threads and put them in a usable state. This strategy prevents other threads in the parent from acquiring these locks at the time `fork()` is called. For example, in Code Example 13-3 the call to `fork()` can be preceded by a call to acquire `cnt_lock`. The lock can be released in both the parent and the child after the call to `fork()` returns. One problem with this strategy is that locks and helper threads hidden in libraries must be known to the routine calling `fork()` (see "Fork Handlers," below).
4. Using one of the above strategies, call `exec()` (which is always safe to call) as soon as possible in the child. This reinitializes the address space, destroying all previously locked locks.

Remember, synchronization variables that are allocated in memory shared between the parent and the child usually don't have fork-safety problems, as the parent can still manipulate them.

Fork Handlers

In strategy 3 above, the programmer has to acquire all the locks in the program at the point where `fork()` is called. In a large program with a lot of locks distributed across several modules, it would be a tedious task to collect all the locks across all modules and lock/release them at one spot. Also, when a new lock is added in a module, it would be necessary to add it to the list of locks to be acquired and released when calling `fork()`. This leads to problems in code maintenance. A better approach would be to use fork handlers established via calling:

```
int
pthread_atfork(void (*prepare)(void), void (*parent)(void),
    void (*child)(void));
```

`pthread_atfork()` takes three function pointers. The first one, *`prepare`*, is executed in the parent just before the call to `fork()` is made. The second one, *`parent`*, is a routine executed by the parent after returning from `fork()`. The third routine, *`child`*, is executed by the child after returning from the call to `fork()`. The call to `pthread_atfork()` establishes these routines as fork handlers which are executed whenever fork is called. You can pass `NULL` instead of a function pointer when you don't want the corresponding handler. Multiple calls to `pthread_atfork()` simply add the handlers to the existing list of handlers.

In the usual case, the *`prepare`* function would acquire all the locks in the module. The *`parent`* and *`child`* functions would release all the locks in the module. Let's use fork handlers to solve the fork-safety problem in a variation of the previous code example shown in Code Example 13-4.

```
pthread_mutex_t cnt_lock;
pthread_mutex_t flg_lock;
int count;
int flag;

void
prepare()
{
    pthread_mutex_lock(&cnt_lock);
    pthread_mutex_lock(&flg_lock);
}

void
parent()
{
    pthread_mutex_unlock(&cnt_lock);
    pthread_mutex_unlock(&flg_lock);
}
```

```
void
child()
{
    pthread_mutex_unlock(&cnt_lock);
    pthread_mutex_unlock(&flg_lock);
}

int
main()
{
    ...
    pthread_atfork(prepare, parent, child);
    ... create thread1 and thread2
}

void
incr_count()
{
    pthread_mutex_lock(&cnt_lock);
    count++;
    pthread_mutex_unlock(&cnt_lock);
}

void
set_flag(int arg)
{
    pthread_mutex_lock(&flg_lock);
    flag = arg;
    pthread_mutex_unlock(&flg_lock);
}

void *
thread1()
{
    incr_count();
    set_flag(1);
    return (NULL);
}
```

```
51 void *
52 thread2()
53 {
54     ...
55     if (fork() != 0) {
56         /* parent */
57         ...
58     } else {
59         /* child */
60         incr_count();
61         set_flag(2);
62         ...
63     }
64     return (NULL);
65 }
```

Code Example 13-4 Using Fork Handlers to Solve the `fork()` *Problem*

The call to `pthread_atfork()` on line 27 establishes the fork handlers: `prepare()`, `parent()` and `child()`. When `thread2()` calls `fork()`, `prepare()` is automatically called, acquiring both locks, `cnt_lock` and `flg_lock`. This guarantees that `thread1()` cannot be holding either of the two locks. Then, after the call to `fork()` returns in the child process, `child()` is called automatically before going on to line 59. This releases the locks so the two calls to `incr_count()` and `set_flag()` in the child can execute successfully. The locks are released in the parent after the call to `fork()` returns by the calling of `parent()` before line 56 is executed.

Note that if the two locks are nested (i.e., one is requested while holding the other), the order in which the locks are acquired in the `prepare()` routine should follow the same hierarchy of lock acquisition as in the rest of the program. Otherwise, a lock ordering deadlock (see "Lock Ordering" on page 91) could occur.

The obvious advantage of using `pthread_atfork()` is that you don't have to collect all the locks from all modules at every place `fork()` is called. The calls to `pthread_atfork()` occur at the same place where the locks are used in the program. So, each module would have an initialization routine with a call to `pthread_atfork()` (called by `main()` or `pthread_once()`) establishing handlers for the locks in that module.

Fork handlers can also do more than acquire and release locks. For example, modules that create "helper" threads can recreate these threads in the child, after a process fork happens.

Intermodule dependencies

In some programs a higher level module calls a lower level module from within its monitor lock (see Figure 13-3). This situation establishes a lock hierarchy in that the higher level monitor lock must never be acquired after the lower level monitor lock. If the two modules establish independent fork handlers, as would be expected, the order in which the fork handlers are called must reflect this lock hierarchy.

Module A

```
a()
{
    pthread_mutex_lock(&a_lock);
    ...

    b();

    ...
    pthread_mutex_unlock(&a_lock);
}
```

Module B

```
b()
{
    pthread_mutex_lock(&b_lock);
    ...
    pthread_mutex_unlock(&b_lock);
}
```

Figure 13-3 Module Hierarchy

The *parent* and *child* fork handlers (which typically release module locks) are called in the order they were established by calls to `pthread_atfork()`. The *prepare* fork handlers (which typically acquire module locks) are called in the opposite order. This ordering allows a simple rule for establishing fork handlers in hierarchical modules: a higher level module must ensure that all the modules it depends on are initialized (and therefore should have registered any fork handlers) *before* calling `pthread_atfork()` to register its own handlers.

Summary

You will probably have to manage thread stacks relatively rarely. In most cases, the system provides adequate default stacks, though you may have to be particularly aware of stack issues on embedded or small-memory systems. On all systems keep thread stack issues in mind if you have threads that allocate large arrays on their stack or are particularly recursive.

Similarly, you should only have to deal with fork-safety when you use `fork()` to "clone" a process. Most cases where the new child process calls `exec()` without calling application or library routines that require locks don't have fork-safety issues.

Advanced Synchronization Strategies

14

This chapter explains synchronization strategies to use where structured code locking (monitor-style) or structured data locking (object monitor-style) provide insufficient concurrency. The chapter also describes results from queuing theory to help understand when simple monitors are insufficient. Finally, we give some guidelines for when to apply the techniques described in this chapter.

Critical Section Concurrency

Suppose the set of functions in a monitor each executes about 100 instructions in their critical sections which would take about 10 μsec on a 10 Mip machine[1]. If the module functions are called 300 times a second, the probability that an independent call to a module function will find the monitor locked is 0.3 percent. In this case, there is very low probability that any given call will see interference from other calls. In general, if the time the monitor is held is small compared to the average time between requests to hold the monitor and the requests are independent (e.g., they are not all synchronized to the same external event), usually there will be little interference. There is little cause to do any further optimization; simply follow the monitor discipline.

Lessons from Queuing Theory

The preceding analysis was very simplistic. It is worth analyzing what happens as a monitor is held more often. A monitor can be modeled as a simple queue with a single server:

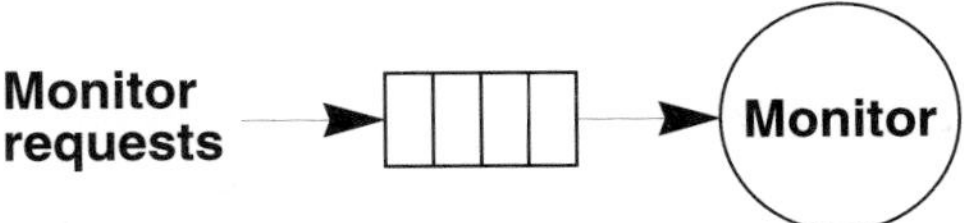

Figure 14-1 Queuing Model of Monitor

1. This kind of arithmetic is somewhat invalid. Machines seem to always run the Spec benchmark (i.e., the benchmark used to measure Mips) better than most real programs or the event driven codes typical of threads programming. In addition, the benchmark is not intended to measure actual machine instructions per second. However, we indulge the fantasy and assume this is close enough.

A call on a monitor function tries to acquire the monitor lock. The lock request is queued if the monitor is occupied when the request arrives. When the monitor releases the monitor lock after processing the current request, a queued request may now acquire the monitor lock and begin processing. In the following analysis, requests are assumed to occur randomly with the time between requests following a Poisson (exponential) probability distribution[2].

A more important measure than the probability of interference is the increase in perceived time to do a monitor function (the time spent waiting in the queue plus the time spent executing the function). For this type of queue having a Poisson arrival distribution (an M/G/1 queue[3]), queuing theory provides the following formula (see [Kleinrock 75] or [Ferrari 78]):

$$\frac{\text{Time in queue}}{\text{Average service time}} = \frac{\rho\,(1 + C^2)}{2\,(1 - \rho)}$$

$$\rho = \frac{\lambda}{\mu} = \frac{\text{Average arrival rate}}{\text{Average service rate}}$$

$$C = \frac{\text{Std. deviation of service distribution}}{\text{Average service time}}$$

Figure 14-2 Pollaczek-Kintchine Formula for M/G/1 Queues

A monitor with a single function that has no conditional branches in the critical section will execute the critical section in almost the same amount of time every time it is called[4]. In this case C, the coefficient of variation, is zero and the average service time is simply the time to execute the single critical section. The traffic intensity, ρ, is the average request rate (calls per second) multiplied by the service time. This case corresponds to an M/D/1 queue (D for deterministic). The increase in service time as perceived by the requestor as the traffic intensity increases is shown in Figure 14-3. The figure shows that it takes a substantial request rate to show an even modest increase in the service time. For example, it takes approximately 15,000 calls per second to see a 10 percent increase in a 10 microsecond critical section.

When the monitor has several functions that take differing amounts of time, or a function with execution time that varies depending on the arguments, the coefficient of variation is not zero. Figure 14-3 shows the graph for C=1. As an

2. Interarrival Time $= a(t) = \lambda e^{-\lambda t}$ where λ is the average arrival rate. The Poisson distribution is a good model for interactive user events.

3. *M* stands for Markov arrival model (the Poisson distribution), *G* stands for a general (any) service distribution, and the numeric entry stands for the number of servers.

4. There is usually some variation in execution time due to the effects of cache misses, page faults, and interrupts.

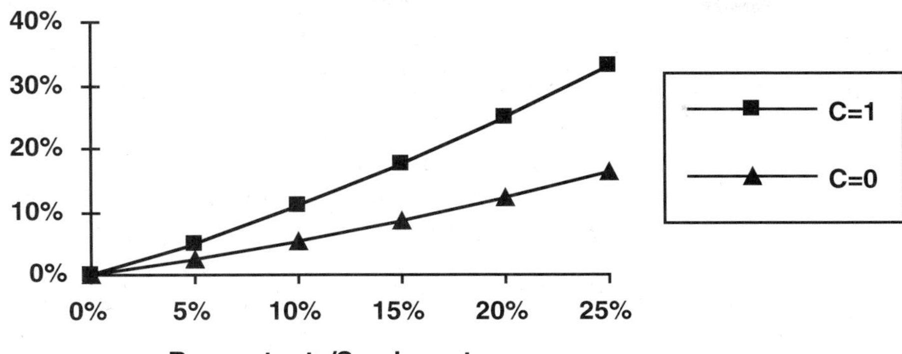

Figure 14-3 Increase in Service Time for M/G/1 Monitor

example, Figure 14-4 shows that a monitor that has two functions with fixed execution times of 10 µsec and 60 µsec has a maximum coefficient of variation of about 1 when the probability of executing the longer function is about 10-20 percent. The coefficient of variation is still about 0.5 even when there is 1 percent probability of executing the longer function. Figure 14-3 shows that variance in execution times can cause the service time to increase more rapidly with traffic intensity. However, it still takes a large request rate to produce a noticeable effect: approximately 6,000 calls per second to produce a 10 percent increase for C=1 in the two function example.

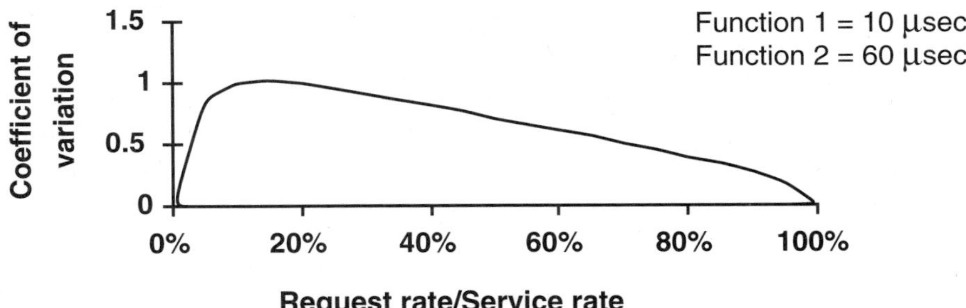

Figure 14-4 Coefficient of Variation for Two Function Monitor

Lessons learned

There are several lessons obtained from this analysis. First, it takes a large request rate compared to the monitor service time for independent requests to back up on the monitor lock. The monitor discipline is adequate for a wide range of situations. Second, the variance in service time can cause a significant effect. A conservative approach would be to always base service times on the time to execute the longest critical section in the monitor. Lastly, variance in service time is yet another reason why the monitor lock should not be held across long operations like I/O, even if they only occur occasionally.

If the monitor lock is not held across I/O operation, there is little to be gained by increasing concurrency inside the monitor on a uniprocessor. The critical section will be compute bound and there are no other processors available. However, on a multiprocessor or in situations where the monitor lock must be held across I/O operations, large request rates may cause threads to wait on the monitor lock and not make use of the available parallelism.

Read/Write Locks

For those cases where neither a monitor or object monitor will suffice, there are a variety of techniques to use to increase concurrency. Perhaps the simplest is the multiple-reader, single-writer lock (or read/write lock, for short). It is useful in situations where the data in a monitor is read more often than it is modified. A read/write lock allows read access to proceed concurrently while allowing only one thread to modify the data. It is acquired for either reading or writing and then it is released. Code Example 14-1 shows an implementation of read/write locks using mutexes and condition variables.

```
typedef struct {
    pthread_mutex_t m;              /* read/write monitor lock */
    int rwlock;                     /* >0=# rdrs, <0=wrtr, 0=none */
    pthread_cond_t readers_ok;      /* start waiting readers */
    unsigned int waiting_writers; /* # of waiting writers */
    pthread_cond_t writer_ok;       /* start a waiting writer */
} rwl_t;

void
rwl_init(rwl_t *rwlp)
{
    pthread_mutex_init(&rwlp->m, NULL);
    pthread_cond_init(&rwlp->readers_ok, NULL);
    pthread_cond_init(&rwlp->writer_ok, NULL);
    rwlp->rwlock = 0;
    rwlp->waiting_writers = 0;
}
```

```
/*
 * Acquire a read lock. Multiple readers can go if there are no
 * writers.
 */
void
rwl_rdlock(rwl_t *rwlp)
{
    pthread_mutex_lock(&rwlp->m);
    while (rwlp->rwlock < 0 || rwlp->waiting_writers)
        pthread_cond_wait(&rwlp->readers_ok, &rwlp->m);
    rwlp->rwlock++;
    pthread_mutex_unlock(&rwlp->m);
}

/*
 * Acquire a write lock. Only a single writer can proceed.
 */
void
rwl_wrlock(rwl_t *rwlp)
{
    pthread_mutex_lock(&rwlp->m);
    while (rwlp->rwlock != 0) {
        rwlp->waiting_writers++;
        pthread_cond_wait(&rwlp->writer_ok, &rwlp->m);
        rwlp->waiting_writers--;
    }
    rwlp->rwlock = -1;
    pthread_mutex_unlock(&rwlp->m);
}
```

```
/*
 * Unlock the read/write lock.
 */
void
rwl_unlock(rwl_t *rwlp)
{
    int ww, wr;

    pthread_mutex_lock(&rwlp->m);
    if (rwlp->rwlock < 0)      /* rwlock < 0 if locked for writing */
        rwlp->rwlock = 0;
    else
        rwlp->rwlock--;
    /*
     * Keep flags that show if there are waiting readers or writers so
     * that we can wake them up outside the monitor lock.
     */
    ww = (rwlp->waiting_writers && rwlp->rwlock == 0);
    wr = (rwlp->waiting_writers == 0);
    pthread_mutex_unlock(&rwlp->m);
    /* wakeup a waiting writer first. Otherwise wakeup all readers */
    if (ww)
        pthread_cond_signal(&rwlp->writer_ok);
    else if (wr)
        pthread_cond_broadcast(&rwlp->readers_ok);
}
```

Code Example 14-1 An Implementation of Multiple Readers, Single Writer Locks

Technical Notes

The implementation shown in Code Example 14-1 gives priority to waking up waiting writers when a lock is released. Otherwise a continuous stream of read requests could prevent any writer from making progress. In addition, the implementation of `rwl_unlock()` takes care to signal the condition variables after the object monitor lock is released to avoid having awakened waiters immediately block on the held mutex.

On a multiprocessor, the `cond_broadcast()` in `rwl_unlock()` may cause several threads to contend for the mutex. The degree to which this is either a problem or an advantage depends on the implementation of mutexes. If this is a problem on a particular implementation, an alternate strategy would be to use `cond_signal()` and have each awakened reader wake up another.

The implementation shows that read/write locks can have substantial overhead when compared to using simple mutexes. The critical sections protected by such locks should be relatively large, so that the extra available concurrency is not dominated by the locking overhead.

Note that the implementation n Code Example 14-1 is unsafe with respect to `fork()` (see "Strategies for Using fork()" on page 238). These functions will need fork handlers if fork-safety is required (see "Fork Handlers" on page 240).

The following example is of a bank account. The code allows multiple threads to have concurrent read-only access to the account balance, while only a single writer is allowed. Note that the `get_balance()` function needs the lock to ensure that the addition of the checking and saving balances occurs atomically:

```
rwl_t account_lock;
float checking_balance = 100.0;
float savings_balance = 100.0;
...
rwl_init(&account_lock);
...

float
get_balance() {
    float bal;

    rwl_rdlock(&account_lock);
    bal = checking_balance + savings_balance;
    rwl_unlock(&account_lock);
    return(bal);
}

void
transfer_checking_to_savings(float amount) {
    rwl_wrlock(&account_lock);
    checking_balance = checking_balance - amount;
    savings_balance = savings_balance + amount;
    rwl_unlock(&account_lock);
}
```

Code Example 14-2 Bank Account Using Read/Write Lock

Read/Write Lock Conditions

As with mutexes, users of read/write locks must sometimes wait for events. Code Example 14-3 shows an implementation of `rwl_condwait()`, a function similar to `cond_wait()`, that atomically releases a read/write lock and blocks on a condition and then reacquires the proper lock when awakened. The caller of `rwl_condwait()` must retest the condition in the same manner as with condition variable wait.

```
void
rwl_condwait(pthread_cond_t *cvp, rwl_t *rwlp)
{
    int writer = 0;

    pthread_mutex_lock(&rwlp->m);
    if (rwlp->rwlock < 0) {     /* rwlock < 0 if locked for writing */
        rwlp->rwlock = 0;
        writer = 1;             /* remember this is a write lock */
    } else {
        rwlp->rwlock--;
    }
    /* Signal waiting writer first. Otherwise wakeup all readers. */
    if (rwlp->waiting_writers && rwlp->rwlock == 0)
        pthread_cond_signal(&rwlp->writer_ok);
    else if (rwlp->waiting_writers == 0)
        pthread_cond_broadcast(&rwlp->readers_ok);
    /* Release monitor, wait for wakeup. Caller must retest condition. */
    pthread_cond_wait(cvp, &rwlp->m);
    pthread_mutex_unlock(&rwlp->m);
    /* reacquire read or write lock */
    if (writer)
        rwl_wrlock(rwlp);
    else
        rwl_rdlock(rwlp);
}
```

Code Example 14-3 Waiting for a Condition with a Read/Write Lock

This can be used as follows, to wait for events that can be protected by a read/write lock:

```
extern float checking_balance;
extern float savings_balance;
extern rwl_t account_lock;

pthread_cond_t account_added; /* account has been added to */
```

```
/* Delete an amount from checking */
void
delete_checking(float amt)
{
    rwl_wrlock(&account_lock);
    /* wait until checking balance is sufficient */
    while (checking_balance < amt)
        rwl_condwait(&account_added, &account_lock);
    checking_balance -= amt;
    rwl_unlock(&account_lock);
}

/* Add an amount to checking */
void
add_checking(float amt)
{
    rwl_wrlock(&account_lock);
    checking_balance += amt;
    rwl_unlock(&account_lock);
    pthread_cond_broadcast(&account_added);
}
```

Code Example 14-4 Using Read/Write Conditions

This use of read/write locks preserves the structured locking style while allowing increased concurrency, in some cases.

Breaking Up Locks

Read/write locks are good for situations where there are many, lengthy read-only operations. Other techniques must be used where the proportion of modifications may be higher. A relatively simple technique is to break up a single monitor lock into several locks that protect portions of the data. Code Example 14-5 shows an implementation of a hashed list that uses a separate mutex for each hash bucket. This allows operations on records that hash to different buckets to proceed concurrently. This situation should occur often if the hash is effective and the bucket lists are relatively small.

```
/*
 * Simple example of a single, fixed hashed record list. Each element
 * contains a string, "name", that is the hash key and a data record.
 *
 * The hashed list consists of NBUCKETS hash buckets each containing
 * the list of elements that hash to the bucket. Each bucket also
 * has a mutex that protects the bucket list. This allows concurrent
 * searches on different buckets. The hash key "name" is a string.
 */
extern int hash(char *);
typedef void *rec_t;

struct list_elt {
    struct list_elt *forw;      /* next element */
    struct list_elt *back;      /* previous element */
    char busy;                  /* element is being used */
    pthread_cond_t notbusy;     /* element has stopped being used */
    char name[256];             /* hash key */
    rec_t rec;                  /* data record */
};
typedef struct list_elt *helt_t;

struct hlist {
    struct bucket {
        pthread_mutex_t bucket_lock;
        struct list_elt head;
    } bucket[NBUCKETS];
};
typedef struct hlist *hlist_t;

/* Internal functions */

/* Find an element in the hash bucket given the name */
static
struct list_elt *
find_elt(struct list_elt *headp, char *name)
{
    struct list_elt *eltp;

    for (eltp = headp->forw; eltp != headp; eltp = eltp->forw) {
        if (strcmp(name, eltp->name) == 0)
            return (eltp);      /* found it */
    }
    return (NULL);
}
```

```
/* Create and destroy elements */
static
struct list_elt *
new_elt(char *name, rec_t rec)
{
    struct list_elt *eltp;

    eltp = (struct list_elt *) malloc(sizeof (struct list_elt));
    if (eltp != NULL) {
        pthread_cond_init(&eltp->notbusy, NULL);
        strcpy(eltp->name, name);
        eltp->rec = rec;
        eltp->busy = 0;
    }
    return(eltp);
}

static
void
delete_elt(struct list_elt *eltp)
{
    pthread_cond_destroy(&eltp->notbusy);
    free(eltp);
}

/* External functions */

/* Create a new hash_list */
hlist_t
new_hashlist()
{
    hlist_t hlp;
    int i;

    hlp = (hlist_t) malloc(sizeof (struct hlist));
    if (hlp == NULL)
        return (NULL);
    for (i = 0; i < NBUCKETS; i++) {
        pthread_mutex_init(&hlp->bucket[i].bucket_lock, NULL);
        hlp->bucket[i].head.forw = &hlp->bucket[i].head;
        hlp->bucket[i].head.back = &hlp->bucket[i].head;
    }
    return(hlp);
}
```

```
/*
 * Find the list element associated with "name". If found, the data
 * pointer is returned "busy" so that the caller can manipulate it.
 */
helt_t
hlist_find(hlist_t hlp, char *name)
{
    struct list_elt *eltp;
    struct bucket *bp;

    bp = &hlp->bucket[hash(name)];     /* compute hash */
    pthread_mutex_lock(&bp->bucket_lock);
    while ((eltp = find_elt(&bp->head, name)) != NULL && eltp->busy) {
        pthread_cond_wait(&eltp->notbusy, &bp->bucket_lock);
        /* re-search list; elt may have been deleted during wait */
    }
    if (eltp != NULL)
        eltp->busy = 1;
    pthread_mutex_unlock(&bp->bucket_lock);
    return (eltp);
}

/*
 * Give up ownership of data
 */
void
hlist_done(hlist_t hlp, helt_t eltp)
{
    struct bucket *bp;

    bp = &hlp->bucket[hash(eltp->name)];/* compute hash */
    pthread_mutex_lock(&bp->bucket_lock);
    assert(eltp->busy);    /* check user is following protocol */
    eltp->busy = 0;
    pthread_cond_signal(&eltp->notbusy);
    pthread_mutex_unlock(&bp->bucket_lock);
}
```

```
/*
 * Add a list element. Duplicates are not allowed.
 */
int
hlist_add(hlist_t hlp, char *name, void *datap)
{
    struct list_elt *eltp, *headp;
    struct bucket *bp;
    int err = 0;

    bp = &hlp->bucket[hash(name)];    /* compute hash */
    pthread_mutex_lock(&bp->bucket_lock);
    headp = &bp->head;
    if ((eltp = find_elt(&bp->head, name)) == NULL) {
        if ((eltp = new_elt(name, datap)) != NULL) {
            eltp->forw = headp->forw;
            eltp->back = headp;
            headp->forw->back = eltp;
            headp->forw = eltp;
        } else
            err = ENOMEM;
    } else
        err = EEXIST;
    pthread_mutex_unlock(&bp->bucket_lock);
    return (err);
}
```

```
/*
 * delete an element from the list. If not present return error.
 */
hlist_delete(hlist_t hlp, char *name)
{

    struct list_elt *eltp;
    struct bucket *bp;
    int err = 0;

    bp = &hlp->bucket[hash(name)];     /* compute hash */
    pthread_mutex_lock(&bp->bucket_lock);
    while ((eltp = find_elt(&bp->head, name)) != NULL && eltp->busy)
        pthread_cond_wait(&eltp->notbusy, &bp->bucket_lock);
    if (eltp != NULL) {
        eltp->forw->back = eltp->back;
        eltp->back->forw = eltp->forw;
    } else {
        err = ENOENT;
    }
    pthread_mutex_unlock(&bp->bucket_lock);
    /* do final deletion outside monitor to reduce hold time */
    if (eltp != NULL)
        delete_elt(eltp);
    return (err);
}
```

Code Example 14-5 Hashed List with Hashed Locks

Breaking up locks can sometimes introduce new issues other than concurrency. For example, Code Example 6-5 on page 82 used a global lock and two condition variables to implement a read-only record cache. The single lock can become a bottleneck that seriously impacts performance, especially on a multiprocessor. The main issue in breaking this global lock into per-bucket locks is lock ordering. The problem stems from the sharing of data buffers between all buckets. When one bucket runs out of data blocks, it steals a non-busy buffer from some other bucket (in `alloc_rec()`). In this case, another bucket lock will have to be acquired while the current bucket lock is held. A lock ordering deadlock may occur unless an order in which bucket locks are to be acquired is established (see"Lock Ordering" on page 91). Once an order is established, you can attempt to defy the order by using a non-blocking lock operation (e.g., `pthread_mutex_trylock()`). If this fails then you must give up the first buffer and reacquire both locks in the correct order.

Explicitly Locked Functions

Certain functions are called extremely often, usually by inner loops in an application. For such functions, the overhead of acquiring and releasing locks can be significant. A technique to reduce the locking overhead is to hold the monitor lock across a series of calls to monitor functions. This makes the locking more explicit to the caller of the interface. A good example of this technique is the `flockfile()` and `funlockfile()` functions that are used to protect calls to `putc_unlocked()`, `putchar_unlocked()`, `getc_unlocked()`, and `getchar_unlocked()` in `stdio` (see "stdio" on page 51).

The `flockfile()` and `funlockfile()` functions can also be used to bracket a series of calls to ordinary `stdio` functions (e.g., `printf()`) to make the series atomic. In other words, successive calls to `stdio` functions protected by `flockfile()` will not be interleaved with calls made by other threads. The problem is that the `flockfile()` lock must be the same one used by the ordinary `stdio` functions in order to ensure atomicity. So if `printf()` is called after `flockfile()` the calling thread will self-deadlock if ordinary locking protocols are used.

Recursive Locks

A solution to this problem is to construct a locking protocol that allows the thread that already owns the lock to proceed. This is known as a *recursive lock*. An implementation and application of `flockfile()` and `funlockfile()` using this technique is shown in Code Example 14-6.

```
typedef struct {
    struct rlock {
        pthread_mutex_t mon;    /* monitor for recursive lock */
        pthread_t owner;        /* recursive lock owner */
        unsigned int busy;      /* busy count */
        pthread_cond_t notbusy;/* indicates not busy */
    } rl;
    ... the rest of the FILE structure
} FILE;
```

```
void
flockfile(FILE *fp)
{
    pthread_mutex_lock(&fp->rl.mon);
    if (fp->rl.busy != 0) {
        /* lock is busy, is this thread the owner? */
        if (fp->rl.owner != pthread_self()) {
            /* not owner, wait until lock is not busy */
            do {
                pthread_cond_wait(&fp->rl.notbusy, &fp->rl.mon);
            } while (fp->rl.busy != 0);
        }
    }
    fp->rl.owner = pthread_self();/* not locked, set owner */
    fp->rl.busy++;
    pthread_mutex_unlock(&fp->rl.mon);
}

void
funlockfile(FILE *fp)
{
    unsigned int ownershipcnt;

    pthread_mutex_lock(&fp->rl.mon);
    ownershipcnt = --fp->rl.busy;
    pthread_mutex_unlock(&fp->rl.mon);
    if (ownershipcnt == 0)
        pthread_cond_signal(&fp->rl.notbusy);
}

int
printf()
{

    flockfile(stdout);
    ...
    funlockfile(stdout);
}
```

Code Example 14-6   Recursive Lock Implementation of Explicitly Locked Files

As with read/write locks, recursive locks incur some overhead over simple mutexes. They should be used only in situations where the recursive semantic is required.

Object-Unsafe Functions

Modules that operate on objects (either literally in C++, or using a C equivalent) can avoid locking overhead by restricting the concurrent use of object instances. Such modules or classes need only protect the global data (and static members, in C++). The caller of a member function must ensure that more than one thread cannot operate on the same instance of an object at any one time. The caller is free to operate on different instances of the same class simultaneously. The module or class with this restriction is said to be *object-unsafe*. Object implementations that have no global data or do not operate on other global state are object-unsafe.

This technique is useful for highly used classes whose objects tend to be used by only one thread or, alternately, when the threads in an application tend to operate on distinct classes of objects. However, this technique is somewhat prone to errors, as the caller must take care to never pass references to object-unsafe objects between threads unless special synchronization is done. It is usually a good idea to provide an alternate class or subclass that is thread-safe in case the caller cannot guarantee the restrictions.

Object-unsafe objects can record the thread ID of the thread that created them and check it when member functions are called:

```
class X {
#ifndef NDEBUG
    pthread_t owner;
#endif
//...
    X();
    void f();
};

X::X()                  // constructor
{
#ifndef NDEBUG
    owner = pthread_self();
#endif
    //...
}

X::f()
{
    assert(owner == pthread_self());
}
```

Code Example 14-7 Checking Object-Unsafe Member Functions

Locking Guidelines II

This section presents some techniques to use when you find that the simple structure locking strategies presented in Chapter 6, "Synchronization Strategies" don't provide sufficient performance. However, it is not a good idea to use a more complicated procedure where a simple one will do, so:

- Try structured code locking (monitor-style) first.
- If that yields insufficient concurrency, try structured data locking (object monitor style).

Follow the guidelines in "Locking Guidelines" on page 98. One of these two techniques should be sufficient in most cases. When a function is called relatively often (see "Critical Section Concurrency" on page 245) such that contention on the monitor lock is a performance bottleneck (usually on multiprocessors or in cases where I/O must be done under the monitor lock), then try the following alternate techniques:

- Try breaking the monitor lock into smaller units or try read/write locks (if data is read more than modified).
- If a set of functions are called frequently in an inner loop, try defining an explicit locking function that protects calls to unlocked functions. This technique is used in `stdio` which provides `flockfile()` and `funlockfile()` along with the unlocked I/O functions like `putc_unlocked()`.
- If the object operated on by a set of functions tends to be used by only one thread or the threads operate on distinct sets of objects, then implement object-unsafe functions. If you do this, then it is a good idea to also implement an alternate thread-safe class or subclass because of the tricky restrictions that must be obeyed by callers of object-unsafe functions.

Multiprocessor Issues 15

This chapter describes the modern tightly coupled shared memory multiprocessor environment. It also describes common pitfalls that occur when attempting to take advantage of such machines.

Shared Memory Multiprocessors

The classic shared memory multiprocessor model, shown in Figure 15-1, has a number of processors sharing a common memory. When a processor attempts a memory operation (load or store) it contends with other processors for the memory and then carries out the operation.

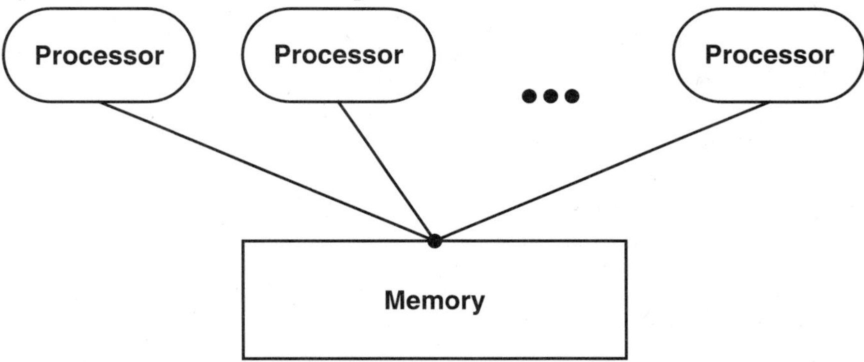

Figure 15-1 Classic Shared Memory Multiprocessor

Unfortunately, implementing exactly this model in hardware means that all memory operations must not only go to a slow system memory, but they must also contend with traffic from other processors. An alternative strategy, shown in Figure 15-1, is to give each processor a small *cache* composed of fast memory. Cache sizes from 64K bytes to more than 2M bytes are popular. This alleviates both the slow access problem and the contention problem as most memory accesses are to the local processor cache. Unfortunately, this architecture leaves the problem of keeping the values in the caches *consistent* with the model in

Figure 15-1[1]. That is, if Processor 1 has the value of location *X* in its cache and Processor 2 stores a new value in that location, then Processor 1 must see the new value the next time it loads location X. The system uses a *cache consistency protocol* to keep consistent values in the cache.

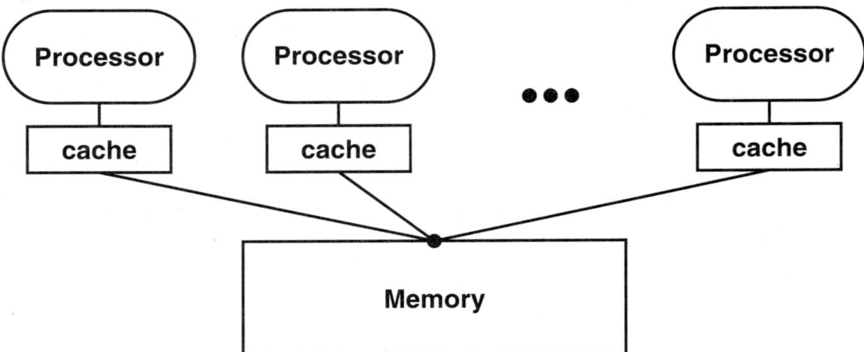

Figure 15-2 Shared Memory Multiprocessor with Cache

Caches and Cache Consistency Protocols

The presence of caches and cache consistency protocols in a multiprocessor can have profound effects on the performance of parallel programs. It is important to understand the cause of these effects in order to avoid them, if possible.

Caches store the values of memory locations in groups called *cache lines*. Typical line sizes are 4, 8, 16, 32 or 64 bytes. The address of the first location is always aligned to a multiple of the cache line size. When a location is accessed that is not in some cache line resident in the cache, the contents of the entire cache line are fetched from memory and placed in the cache, displacing some other cache line. This operation is called a *cache miss*. Cache misses are usually 10 to 100 times slower than when the location is found to be resident in the cache (called a *cache hit*).

The most popular protocol for keeping the values in the processor caches consistent is the *write-invalidate protocol*. This protocol allows the values in a cache line to reside in more than one cache in the system if the processors are only reading the values. If a processor tries to modify a value in a cache line, it must first *invalidate* (delete) copies of the cache line in any other cache in the system. Therefore, when a cache line is modifiable, there can be only one copy of it in the system; when the cache line is not modifiable, there can be many copies.

1. Many modern multiprocessors don't actually enforce this strict a consistency model. See "Weaker memory models" in this chapter and "Data Races" on page 30.

An alternative, the *write-broadcast protocol*, allows multiple copies of cache lines even if the values are being modified. When a modification is made to a cache line that has more than one copy the new values are broadcast to the other copies in the system so that they can keep consistent contents.

In either of these protocols cache lines may be grouped into blocks for the purposes of keeping track of consistency. In this case, the smaller cache line unit is the amount that is fetched from memory when the cache line is not resident, while the larger grouping is the amount that is invalidated or shared and updated as required by the protocol. Typically two or four cache lines are grouped in a block. This can raise the system block size to 16, 32, 64, 128, or even 256 bytes.

Write sharing

Consider what happens when more than one processor in the system repetitively writes to the same location. In the write-invalidate protocol, the valid copy of the cache line containing the location is moved between the writing processor caches on demand. This causes a (slow) cache miss whenever the processor writing the location was not the last processor to have accessed it. The write broadcast protocol is somewhat better in that such sharing does not cause a full cache miss. However, modification causes the updated values to be broadcast across the processor interconnection network. This can use up a significant portion of the processor interconnection network's available bandwidth.

The same situation occurs when more than one processor in the system repetitively writes different locations in the same cache block. This happens because the cache block is the unit by which the system keeps track of consistency. This situation is called *false sharing* because the block is shared between processors even though they are accessing independent locations. Recall that on some multiprocessors the block size can be as large as 256 bytes. This means, for example, that a program that modifies two independent 128 byte structures that reside in the same cache line simultaneously in two different threads can incur the costs associated with write sharing.

Memory model

Up to this point we've described the consistency protocol as implementing the classic model of Figure 15-1 as far as the programmer is concerned. In this model each processor executes read or write operations on memory one at a time in the order specified by the program, and the memory operations of all processors in the system appear to happen in some global order, though the operation histories of different processors are interleaved arbitrarily. The memory model as viewed by the programmer of such machines is a *sequentially consistent* memory model. In this environment, threads can synchronize using ordinary memory operations even though this would be a data race (see "Definition of a data race" on page 32). For example, two threads can do mutual exclusion using a procedure called Dekker's algorithm[2]:

```
volatile char A = 0;    /* "volatile" prevents movement of */
volatile char B = 0;    /*   memory accesses by optimizer */
volatile char turn = 1;
```

Thread 1

```
A = 1;
while (B == 1) {
    if (turn == 2) {
        A = 0;
        while (turn == 2)
            ;
        A = 1;
    }
}
/* critical section */
turn = 2;
A = 0;
```

Thread 2

```
B = 1;
while (A == 1) {
    if (turn == 1) {
        B = 0;
        while (turn == 1)
            ;
        B = 1;
    }
}
/* critical section */
turn = 1;
B = 0;
```

Code Example 15-1 Dekker's Algorithm for Sequentially Consistent Machines

The variables `A`, `B` and `turn` in Code Example 15-1 use the type-qualifier `volatile` to prevent the compilation system from changing the number or order accesses to these variables. For example, the compiler may decide to optimize by removing the code for "`A = 0;`" before the `while()` loop in thread 1, since the final value of `A` in the block is 1 and nothing else references it.

Access atomicity

Even with a memory model that is sequentially consistent, there can be some surprises. On Complex Instruction Set Computers (CISC) there may be instructions that will add a value to a memory location. This must be implemented as a fetch of the location contents from memory, then adding the value and storing the result back to memory. On a uniprocessor this operation is usually atomic with respect to interrupts (and therefore signals). On a multiprocessor this operation is rarely atomic with respect to other processors. A more subtle point is that even primitive loads and stores may not be atomic. For example, some CISC processors allow 32-bit integers to be aligned on 16-bit or even 8-bit boundaries. A single instruction access to a misaligned integer may

2. From [Ben-Ari 82].

cause two separate memory fetches. If another processor is writing the integer at the time, the load instruction may return part old and part new data for the integer.

Processor consistency

Some higher performance multiprocessors use a memory model called *processor consistency*[3]. In this model, the new value of a location is not immediately visible when the store instruction completes. Load instructions will interrogate memory before the values set by previous store instructions issued by the same processor are visible to other processors; though a processor can see the results of previous stores issued by itself. However, the new values are stored in memory in the order in which the store instructions are issued when the location is finally updated.

In most cases, processor consistency is implemented by each processor having a fast FIFO buffer local to the processor (typically before the cache) that holds the values set by store instructions called a *store buffer.* An example is shown in Figure 15-3. Store instructions put the new value and the address of the location to be modified in the store buffer and then complete. Store instructions don't have to wait until the cache coherency protocol is run and subsequent load instructions to locations not in the store buffer don't have to wait until the new values are set. The store buffer is emptied serially sometime later, which then sets the values in memory.

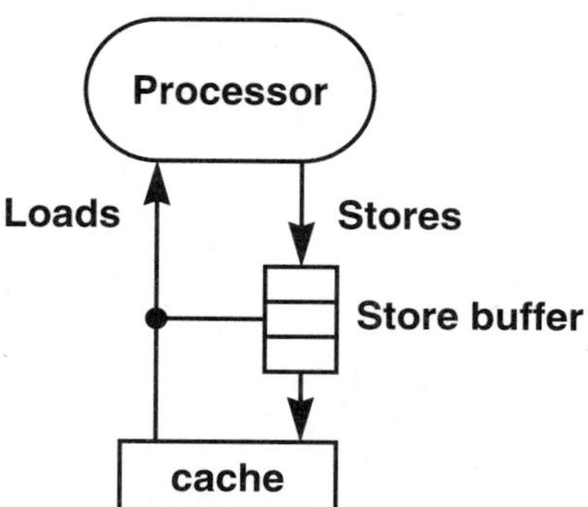

Figure 15-3 Processor with Store Buffer

Dekker's algorithm will not work on machines with processor consistency. To see this, consider the first two statements in the algorithm. The first statement sets a value "owned" by the thread to 1 and then looks at the other thread's value to see if it has done the same. If two threads do this simultaneously on two different

3. Or a close relative called Total Store Ordering.

processors they will each set their values, but they will be unable to see the value set by the other thread if it is still in the store buffer. This will allow both threads to execute the critical section.

Still, many non-synchronization algorithms that contain data races and work on sequentially consistent machines, such as the circular buffer code in Code Example 3-5 on page 30, continue to work with processor consistency. This makes processor consistency a popular memory model because it improves performance quite a bit (see [Gharachorloo 91]) without requiring a weaker memory model and breaking more algorithms.

Weaker memory models

More recent high-performance or large scale multiprocessors use weaker memory models that relax the requirements on the ordering of memory operations so that several operations can overlap. In multiprocessors with weak memory models the results of stores can become visible in an order different from the order in which they were issued, loads can interrogate memory in an order different from the issuing order, and there are no ordering constraints between loads and stores. The circular buffer code in Code Example 3-5 on page 30 will *not* work on such machines. It fails because the consumer may see the new value of `wrptr` but the old value of the data in the buffer.

Some multiprocessors with weak memory models are also non-causal. That is, the ordering of memory operations may be different when viewed by different processors. Suppose the variables `A`, `B` and `C` are initially zero and that three processors in the system run the code shown in Code Example 15-2.

Processor 1	Processor 2	Processor 3
`A = 1`	`if (A == 1)` `    B = 1;`	`if (B == 1)` `    C = A;`

Code Example 15-2 Testing Causality

On non-causal systems it is possible for processor 2 to see `A==1` and then set `B=1` and for processor 3 to see `B==1` and yet still see `A==0` if the new value of `A` has not propagated to processor 3 yet.

Systems with weak memory models must provide some means of reestablishing the order of memory operations where required. Usually this is done either by restricting the ordering of ordinary memory operations with respect to the special synchronization instructions or with respect to *memory barrier* instructions (also called fence or sync instructions). The simplest case is where all ordinary memory operations that are issued prior to the issuing of a special instruction must complete (and be visible to all other processors) before any memory operations that follow the special instruction are issued. It is also possible to have semipermeable barriers. For example, stores issued under the mutex must complete before another processor can see that the mutex is released. This is shown in Code Example 15-3.

```
int
pthread_mutex_lock(pthread_mutex_t *mp)
{
    for (;;) {
        int r;

        /*
         * test first so that we don't write (and invalidate cache line)
         * during spin. This helps prevent excessive coherence traffic.
         */
        if (mp->lock == UNLOCKED) {
            r = LOCKED;
            /*
             * swap inst is also a barrier. No subsequent memory
             * operations will be performed before swap completes.
             */
            SWAP(&mp->lock, r);    /* atomically swaps r and mem loc */
            if (r == UNLOCKED)
                break;
        }
    }
    return (0);
}

int
pthread_mutex_unlock(pthread_mutex_t *mp)
{
    /*
     * The store-barrier ensures that all previous stores issued
     * under the mutex complete before the mutex is released.
     */
    STORE_BARRIER;
    mp->lock = UNLOCKED;
    return (0);
}
```

Code Example 15-3 Spin Mutex with Semipermeable Barrier Instructions

It is important to note that the differences in machine memory models can be detected only when there is more than one thread active; a single thread cannot discern any differences.

Note – The above discussion of the multiprocessor memory model affects mostly implementors of threads libraries and multiprocessor run-time environments. The underlying machine memory model does not affect multithreaded programs that are data race free. Such programs use Pthreads functions that contain the appropriate barrier and synchronization instructions to ensure that program memory access is consistent.

Synchronization Instructions

The synchronization primitives supplied by the system vendor can take advantage of particular hardware synchronization instructions. There are several typical kinds of instructions.

Swap

A *swap* instruction typically exchanges the contents of a register with the contents of a memory location atomically with respect to other processors.

```
/* done atomically */
temp = *mem_addr;
*mem_addr = reg;
reg = temp;
```

A variant of swap, called *test-and-set*, always stores a fixed value to memory and atomically returns the old contents of the location (like swap with a fixed value in the register).

Compare-and-swap

The *compare-and-swap* (CAS) instruction atomically exchanges the contents of a register with the contents of a memory location only if the contents of the location matches a particular value held in another register. Otherwise, the new contents are returned.

```
/* done atomically */
temp = *mem_addr;
if (temp == old_value_reg)
    *mem_addr = new_value_reg;
old_value_reg = temp;
```

The compare-and-swap instruction is more powerful then the swap instruction as it can be used to implement wait-free synchronization (see "Wait-Free Synchronization" on page 273).

Load-reserved, store-conditional

This synchronization mechanism consists of a pair of instructions, a load and a store. The *load-reserved* instruction fetches the contents of a memory location and "reserves" the location by recording its address in an internal processor register, overwriting any previous reservation. If another processor writes to the reserved location, the reservation is cleared. The *store-conditional* instruction stores a new value in a memory location only if there is an existing reservation that matches the address to be modified. If there is no reservation or if the store address does not match the current reservation, the memory is not modified and a flag is set to indicate the failure.

The mechanism used to detect that a location has been modified by another processor is typically associated with the cache consistency protocol (e.g., invalidate and write-broadcast events). This usually means that a reservation will be cleared whenever any location in the cache line is changed by another processor, so you must be aware of potential false sharing problems when using this pair of instructions. Like compare-and-swap, the load-reserved/store-conditional instruction pair can be used to implement wait-free synchronization.

Synchronization on Multiprocessors

Multiprocessors bring a number of new issues to the implementation and use of synchronization variables. In particular, there are several performance issues that arise. This should not be surprising since one of the main reasons to apply threads on multiprocessors is to gain performance.

Spin Blocking

The implementation of synchronization variables can block by putting the thread on a queue of blocked threads and descheduling the blocking thread. This is called *sleeping*. The processor that was running the blocked thread then runs another runnable thread, if there are any. Otherwise, the processor is given back to the system. The sleep queue that records the list of blocked threads is usually ordered according to the required unblocking protocol (e.g., `SCHED_FIFO` or `SCHED_RR`; see Chapter 12, "Threads Scheduling"). For example, the highest priority thread that has been waiting the longest would be at the head of the queue. If the order of wake-up is not constrained (e.g., `SCHED_OTHER`), the implementation may let a new thread lock the mutex before a sleeping thread can be awakened. In other words, the order of wake-up may not be FIFO.

The overhead of switching threads when they are put to sleep can range from hundreds to thousands of instructions. On uniprocessors, sleeping is appropriate so that the processor can go on to execute a thread that will unblock the waiter.

On multiprocessors, the overhead of switching threads can be avoided by repetitively testing the synchronization variable to see if blocking is still required. This is called *spin blocking*. This type of blocking can be particularly appropriate for mutexes where the hold time for the mutex may be less than the time it takes to block and wake up a thread.

Implementations that use instructions similar to swap usually test for the lock being held using a load instruction before attempting to modify the location.

```
pthread_mutex_lock(mutex_t *mp)
{
    ...
    r = LOCKED;
    do {                        /* swap instr is barrier. No loads */
        while (&mp->lock == LOCKED)
            ;
        SWAP(&mp->lock, r);     /* following swap will be performed */
    } while (r == LOCKED);      /* before swap completes */
    ...
}
```

This prevents some write sharing problems. However, there is still a write sharing collision when the lock is released and there are many waiting threads spinning on the lock. In some cases the additional bus traffic can adversely affect the time in which the processor that obtained the lock can execute the critical section. In such cases it may be effective for each thread to delay some variable period before retrying the lock acquisition or to spin on separate locations. See [Anderson 90] for a comparison of algorithms.

The blocking behavior of a synchronization primitive varies from vendor to vendor. Most often condition variables and semaphores put the blocking thread to sleep. Mutexes have variety of blocking implementations such as always sleep, always spin, spin for awhile then sleep (see [Karlin 91]), or spin until the owner goes to sleep (see [Eykholt 92]). Implementations that spin usually do so only when the order of wake-up is not constrained (for example, by thread priority).

If the vendor does not provide a spinning mutex, the spin blocking characteristic can be simulated by:

```
int
spin_lock(pthread_mutex_t *mp)
{
    int err;

    while ((err = pthread_mutex_trylock(mp)) == EBUSY)
        ;
    return (err);
}
```

Code Example 15-4 Spin Mutex Using Pthreads Primitives

However, this can have severe performance repercussions if the owner of the mutex itself is descheduled or blocked. A better strategy is to limit spinning to some reasonable amount:

```
int
spin_lock(pthread_mutex_t *mp)
{
    int err;
    int i;

    i = SPINLIMIT;
    while (--i && (err = pthread_mutex_trylock(mp)) == EBUSY)
        ;
    if (i == 0)
        return (pthread_mutex_lock(mp));
    return (err);
}
```

Code Example 15-5 Spin Mutex with Spin Limit

Where SPINLIMIT should be adjusted according to the system[4]. Portable software should probably rely on the system vendor's implementation.

One problem with this simple version of spin blocking is that it can cause an enormous amount of bus traffic and delay when there are many threads blocking on the same lock. A queuing technique can be used to alleviate this problem; see [Anderson 90] for more details.

Starvation

If a spin blocking synchronization variable is heavily used it is possible that one of the spin blocking threads may fail to acquire the lock for a long period even though the lock is regularly released. For example, the thread that released the lock may be the most likely to reacquire it since the lock is already in the cache of its processor. This is called *starvation*. One technique to avoid starvation is to refrain from using spin blocking and use one of the scheduling policies that specify the wake up order (SCHED_FIFO or SCHED_RR). Another technique is to use spin blocking with queuing; see [Anderson 90] for more details.

Wait-Free Synchronization

Sometimes low level operations can be done without a traditional critical section. Consider the traditional implementation of incrementing a counter.

4. For example, adjusting SPINLIMIT so the spin time is 50–100% of thread context switch time is usually effective. See [Anderson 90] and [Karlin 91].

```
mutex_t m;
int counter = 0;

inc_cnt()
{
    (void) pthread_mutex_lock(&m);
    counter++;
    (void) pthread_mutex_unlock(&m);
}
```

If a thread was in the critical section when it gets descheduled due to timeslice expiration or if it takes a page fault while accessing its stack, then the mutex will prevent other threads from accessing the counter. On some architectures this can be avoided by incrementing the counter using wait-free synchronization. For example, on architectures with the compare-and-swap primitive, we could write the following:

```
extern int CAS(int *mem_addr, int old_value, int new_value);
int counter = 0;

inc_cnt()
{
    int old, last;

    old = counter;
    while ((last = CAS(&counter, old, old + 1)) != old)
        old = last;
}
```

Code Example 15-6 Wait-Free Increment

A thread being descheduled for any reason anywhere in `inc_cnt()` cannot prevent another thread from incrementing the counter using the wait-free technique. Depending on the machine architecture it is possible for other primitives to be implemented in a wait-free manner, including arithmetic and logical operations on a memory location and certain list manipulations. It is also possible to do operations on more complex data structures by doing the operation on a copy of the data structure and then updating a single data structure pointer to point to the new one while ensuring that the original data structure has not changed using wait-free techniques (see [Herlihy 90] and [Herlihy 91]).

Convoys

A convoy is a persistent situation where a group of threads that repetitively use a monitor always block on the monitor lock and then follow each other through the monitor (hence the name "convoy") even though the lock hold time is short and lock contention is relatively rare. A convoy can be created when one of the using threads is descheduled while holding the monitor lock causing the other threads in the group to quickly block. If sleep blocking is used, then by the time the original thread wakes up, releases the lock, iterates, and attempts to reacquire the lock, there may still be sleeping threads waiting for the lock. If the unlocking algorithm is strictly ordered, this situation will persist for the group of threads. It is caused by the iteration time being small compared to the sleep/wake-up time and a strict ordered wake-up.

Convoys are usually noticed when a program suddenly slows down dramatically when the load reached a certain point. Convoys can usually be prevented by using spin waiting. Another method is to "break up" the hot mutex into several mutexes, if possible.

Livelock

Sometimes programs back out the acquisition of locks or other resources and then retry in order to prevent deadlock. If more than one thread does this simultaneously it can lead to a situation where the threads are continually backing out and retrying. This is called *livelock*. Livelock can be prevented by using a lock or resource acquisition hierarchy (see "Lock Ordering" on page 91) to prevent deadlock instead of backing out.

Summary

The cache consistency protocols on modern multiprocessors can cause surprising effects if a multithreaded program manipulates memory without using the thread synchronization routines. Proper use of these routines restores a consistent view of memory to all the threads sharing a memory area. In general, attempting to manipulate memory without using synchronization routines is both difficult and non-portable.

You can also encounter some new types of performance degrading effects when running multithreaded programs on a multiprocessor. These effects, such as convoys or livelock, are encountered relatively rarely when compared to the usual lock contention bottlenecks, but you should keep them in mind when performance tuning.

Parallel Computation 16

One of the most powerful uses of threads is to speed up the execution of computationally intensive programs on shared memory multiprocessors. Unfortunately, effectively applying threads in this environment usually requires a deep understanding of the structure of the algorithm and how a proposed parallelized version of the algorithm is affected by the overheads of threads and the shared memory multiprocessor environment. Fortunately, many different algorithms have similar structures. This chapter covers in more detail a number of the thread paradigms introduced in Chapter 7, "Using Threads," that are useful in many parallel computation situations. Detailed templates and examples are presented.

Using Threads to Parallelize Algorithms

Threads running on separate processors in a shared-memory multiprocessor allow you to use "parallel processing algorithms" in your program. Unlike the other uses of threads described in this book, using threads to implement parallel algorithms can be frustrating:

- There are lots of techniques for "parallelizing" your program. How do you choose one that's not too hard to program and that offers substantial speedups compared to uniprocessor execution? Does the performance of the technique scale up in proportion to the number of processors you use?
- The overheads involved in synchronizing threads and sharing data among multiple processors may actually reduce the performance of your program. How can you anticipate and mitigate these problems?
- Like many performance improvements, parallelizing increases the complexity of your program. How can you be sure it's still correct?

These are all tough problems: we do not yet know how to solve an arbitrary problem efficiently on a multiprocessor of arbitrary size. This section does not offer universal solutions, but tries to demonstrate some simple ways to get started. By sticking with some common "paradigms" for parallel algorithms and threads, you can avoid a lot of errors and aggravation.

Though it may seem simplistic, the most important step in writing a parallel program is to think carefully about the global structure of your program and the computing structures that threads offer. To speed up the program, we're looking for a way to divide the work into a set of *tasks* so that:

- The tasks interact little with each other;
- The data shared by separate tasks is contained in a minimum of simple data structures that can be protected by locking mechanisms to prevent unsynchronized access;
- The number of tasks can be varied so as to match the number of processors;
- All tasks have equal computing requirements, or, instead, are configured in such a way that the set of tasks can keep all the processors fairly busy.

As we've seen, Amdahl's Law (Figure 7-3 on page 103) sets limits on the scalability of parallelized computations. Scalability is limited due to three kinds of overheads: synchronization overhead, contention, and balance. The synchronization operations required for correct multithreaded operation take time to execute, even when there is no contention. When two or more threads share data or locks, the system slows down due to contention for shared resources. And finally, balance refers to the ability of the algorithm to divide work evenly among the available processors. In the "serial" sections of your program, where only a single processor is used, balance is worst. Poor balance is often the result of dividing the work into large, unequal chunks: when the smaller chunks finish, they leave processors idle. If there are always at least as many runnable threads as available processors, the thread scheduler can keep the processors busy. While balance can be improved by dividing work into many small chunks that can be easily scheduled onto idle processors, making the *grain size* of the processing chunks small is usually accompanied by an increase in synchronization overhead, which hurts scalability.

Thread Paradigms

There are many ways to make your program parallel. Some techniques are very complex, depend on complicated data structures and locking strategies, depend on clever non-obvious algorithms, or require compiler support. We present a different approach in this section: three simple control structures, or paradigms, that can be applied to a wide range of applications.

Each paradigm can be characterized by:

- How the work is divided among parallel threads, and whether each thread executes the same code;
- How the threads are synchronized;

- What data is shared among the threads and how it is protected by locks or other means to avoid data races.

The simplest paradigm is the *master-slave*. The main master thread launches a set of slave threads and allocates to each slave a portion of the work to be done; the amount of work is known in advance by the master and divided evenly among the slaves. The master starts the slaves and waits for all of them to reach a synchronization point, or *barrier*. The master may then compute and release the slaves again if needed. This pattern is repeated until the work is done. Example: a loop requiring 1,000 iterations is divided among four threads, each of which does 250 iterations.

Another versatile paradigm is the *workpile*, in which a set of worker threads request chunks of work to do from a "workpile," usually some form of queue. As part of the work, a worker may cause additional entries to be added to the workpile. The pattern terminates when the workpile is finally emptied; alternatively, a worker thread may choose to terminate the process. Example: a search algorithm uses a workpile of promising paths that are extended by worker threads.

The final paradigm is the *pipeline*, in which a task is passed to a succession of threads, each of which performs part of the overall work required; the threads are much like workers on an assembly line. In most cases, the processing in each pipeline stage is different, but there are applications for *homogeneous pipelines* in which the code executed in each stage is the same. Example: a graphics rendering pipeline in which stages successively transform, clip, and render geometry to form an image.

Each of these three paradigms is explained in more detail in the following sections, and each is illustrated with one or more examples.

Master-Slave Paradigm

The simplest paradigm for parallel algorithms is the "master-slave" arrangement. A single master thread, usually the main thread of your program, partitions work evenly among a set of slave threads. The slave threads are launched together, and each one is assigned to a separate partition of work. The master thread waits for all slave threads to complete their work and then continues.

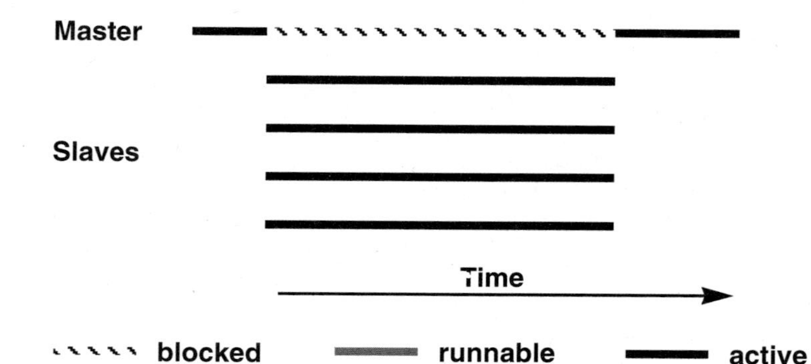

Figure 16-1 Master-Slave Thread Execution

This pattern is illustrated by the following template:

Master	**Slave**

Initialization
`for (i = 0; i < n; i++)`
`   pthread_create(...,slave,...);`
`/* slaves are now running */`
 	
Master processing if any
 	
`for (i = 0; i < n; i++)`
`   pthread_join(...);`
Finalization if any
	`slave(void *params);`
	Slave processing: index i (in params) tells each slave what work to do. Put results into global memory or params
	`pthread_exit();`

This simple kind of master-slave paradigm is used when the amount of work to be done is known in advance and when it's easy to partition the work into *n* roughly equal parts that don't depend on each other. The most common application is to a loop, where *m* iterations of the loop are partitioned among the *n* threads. Usually *m* is much greater than *n*, so each thread invocation executes quite a few iterations of the loop. A key requirement is that each iteration of the loop must be independent of every other iteration of the loop; thus no synchronization is required among the slaves. Here are some examples where this method applies:

- Multiplying two matrices. Each row in the product matrix can be computed by a separate slave. The result for each row depends only on the values in the matrices being multiplied, and not on the results of other rows.

- Transform-coding an image, for example in computing the discrete cosine transform (DCT) of every 8x8 pixel block in an image that is 640 by 480 pixels. There are m = 4,800 blocks to be done, and the blocks are independent of each other.
- Computing the cross-correlation of two signals, e.g., two images, by iterating over all samples in the signal, computing the mean-square distance between the sample and its correlate, and summing the distances. This example computes a running sum over the iterations of the loop. In the master-slave paradigm, each slave will compute a sum for the iterations it is handling, and store the sum in the thread's parameter record. After all slave threads have finished, the master thread computes the final sum by summing the entries in the parameter records of all threads.

Master-Slave Example: Matrix Multiply

To illustrate the master-slave paradigm, we present an example of a matrix multiply routine that also computes the trace of the resulting matrix. The trace is the sum of the diagonal elements. The outermost loop, which iterates over rows in the result matrix, is partitioned among the slave threads.

```
#define MAX_PARALLEL   20  /* maximum number of threads to use */
#define SCHED_FUDGE    1.2 /* Threads/processor ratio (see text) */

#define MREF(mt, row, col)mt->m[(row) * mt->n_cols + (col)]

typedef struct {         /* Matrix of variable size */
    int n_rows;          /* # rows in matrix: 0 <= row < n_rows */
    int n_cols;          /* # columns in matrix: 0 <= col < n_cols */
    float m[1];          /* MREF(m,row,col) elt in row-major order */
} matrix_t;

typedef struct {         /* parameter record for slave procedure */
    int i;               /* index of slave thread 0 <= i < n */
    int n;               /* number of slave threads */
    matrix_t *a,*b,*c;   /* compute c = a*b */
    float trace_ans;     /* trace contribution for this part of matrix */
} mm_params;
```

```
/*
 * This is the "slave procedure" that each slave thread will execute.
 * Each thread is passed a structure of type mm_params; these parameter
 * records differ only in the value of index i for each slave.
 */
void *
matrix_multiply_slave(void *param)
{
    mm_params *p = (mm_params *)param;
    matrix_t *a = p->a;
    matrix_t *b = p->b;
    matrix_t *c = p->c;
    int row, col, j;        /* c[row,col] is what is being computed */
    float trace = 0.0;

    /*
     * Calculate which rows the p->i th thread will process. Since
     * the number of threads may not divide m = c->n_rows exactly, we
     * adopt the convention that for index 0 <= i < m%n, the thread
     * will process floor(m/n)+1 rows, while all others will process
     * floor(m/n) rows.
     */
    int quot = c->n_rows / p->n;
    int rem = c->n_rows % p->n;
    int do_rows = quot + ((p->i < rem)? 1 : 0);
    int first_row = quot * p->i + ((p->i < rem)? p->i : rem);

    for (row = first_row; row < first_row + do_rows; row++) {
        for (col = 0; col < c->n_cols; col++) {
            /* Compute c[row,col] */
            float sum = 0.0;
            for (j = 0; j < a->n_cols; j++)
               sum += MREF(a, row, j) * MREF(b, j, col);
            MREF(c, row, col) = sum;
            if (row == col) trace += sum;
        }
    }
    /* Record partial trace answer in parameter record */
    p->trace_ans = trace;
    return (NULL);
}
```

```
/* Compute c = a * b, return trace of c */
float
matrix_multiply_trace(matrix_t *a, matrix_t *b, matrix_t *c)
{
    mm_params params[MAX_PARALLEL];
    pthread_t thread[MAX_PARALLEL];
    int thread_present[MAX_PARALLEL];
    int n_threads = min(MAX_PARALLEL,
            (int)(sysconf(_SC_NPROCESSORS_ONLN) * SCHED_FUDGE));
    int i, res;
    float trace = 0.0;

    for (i = 0; i < n_threads; i++) {
        thread_present[i] = TRUE;
        params[i].i = i;
        params[i].n = n_threads;
        params[i].a = a;
        params[i].b = b;
        params[i].c = c;
        res = pthread_create(&thread[i],
                NULL, matrix_multiply_slave, (void *)&params[i]);
        if (res != 0) {
            thread_present[i] = FALSE;     /* flag no thread created */
            matrix_multiply_slave(&params[i]);/* just do it */
        }
    }
    for (i = 0; i < n_threads; i++) {
        if (thread_present[i] != FALSE)
            pthread_join(thread[i], NULL);/* wait for thread to exit */
        trace += params[i].trace_ans;
    }
    return (trace);
}
```

Code Example 16-1 Master-Slave Matrix Multiply

The `matrix_multiply_trace()` routine shown above correctly computes the product of the two matrices (provided no arithmetic exceptions occur). Although the code does not show the reasoning, it has been constructed carefully to avoid data races. Let's categorize the data that is shared among the threads, and argue in each case that there are no data races.

1. **Master->slave.**
   The matrices *a* and *b*, and the parameter records, are all written by the master thread and read by the slave threads. In the absence of synchronization, this would cause a data race. But all writing by the master

is separated from reading by a slave with a call to `pthread_create()`, a function that ensures all writes have propagated to main memory (see "Data Races" on page 30). So all slaves will see the values written by the master.

2. **Slave->slave.**
   In this example, no slave writes a memory location that another slave reads. Each slave is writing a separate region of the result matrix, *c*, and the partial results of the trace computation are stored by each slave in a separate memory location. Thus there is no need for locks or any other mechanism for synchronizing the slaves to each other; they are independent of one another.

3. **Slave->master.**
   The slaves write the result matrix, *c*, and the `trace_ans` entry in the parameter record corresponding to each slave. The master refrains from reading this data until after executing `pthread_join()`, a function that ensures that all writes initiated by the exiting thread have propagated to main memory (see "Data Races" on page 30). So the master will correctly see the values written by the slaves.

Note one other feature of the program: we have been careful to deal with the case when a thread cannot be created. There's a simple way to insure a correct result when this happens: the master thread calls the slave procedure directly. Performance will suffer, but the result will be correct. Note too that the main thread is idle while the slaves work; an alternative would be to use the main thread to do part of the work as well as the slaves.

The program is modular about its use of threads: every thread that is created is also explicitly destroyed by waiting at `pthread_join()`. The routine is thus reentrant, i.e., several separate threads could call `matrix_multiply_trace()`, and each call would create a set of slave threads that would be correctly managed by their respective master.

Note the use of stack allocation for the slave parameter records used by the slave threads. The example is careful to ensure that all of the threads that reference the parameter records exit before the procedure that allocated the stack storage (`matrix_multiply_trace()`) exits.

How many slave threads should `matrix_multiply_trace()` create? To exploit parallelism to the maximum extent, we should use at least as many threads as there are processors available. But if we use exactly one thread per processor a balance problem may reduce performance. To see why, consider what happens on a four-processor system running four matrix multiply threads when the kernel scheduler decides to run another job on one of the processors, as shown in Figure 16-2. One thread now becomes delayed relative to the other three, causing the entire parallel section, when all slaves are expected to be running, to be delayed. During some of this time, several processors may be idle. So the ideal balance, in which all processors are busy, is not achieved.

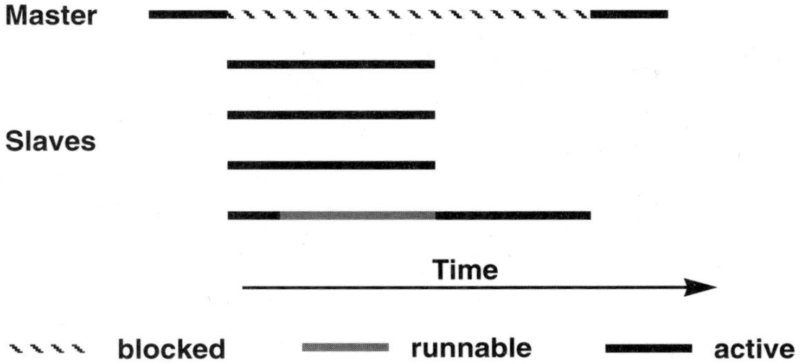

Figure 16-2   Master-Slave with Scheduling Delay

If the computation is broken up into a larger number of smaller parts, the scheduler is better able to achieve good balance, as shown in Figure 16-2. Too many threads, however, incur overheads in creating and destroying them, in memory for stack space, and in other system resources. You may wish to experiment with different strategies for choosing the right number of threads; your experiments need to consider both the number of processors available and the amount of work required for each thread (sometimes called the *grain size*). Allocating a few more threads than the number of processors is a good starting point. The thread scheduler will time-slice runnable threads, which helps avoid this problem — in effect, replacing the grain size of the computation with that of a scheduling quantum.

How does our algorithm scale? That is, does the program speed up in proportion to the number of processors available to share the work? Of course, if the matrices to be multiplied are small, the overheads of creating and joining threads will exceed the computational work. Indeed, a general-purpose routine would test the matrix size and use a conventional serial implementation for small matrices. But for large matrices, we should expect the program to scale well, in part because there is no slave-to-slave synchronization required and because the data sharing is modest.

Consider the effects of caching parts of the result matrix, *c*, which is shared among all the slaves. The program above allocates to each slave responsibility for computing a certain number of rows of the result matrix. The matrix is in row-major order which would tend to put nearby elements in the same row in the same cache line, and therefore keeps the chances of false sharing to a minimum.

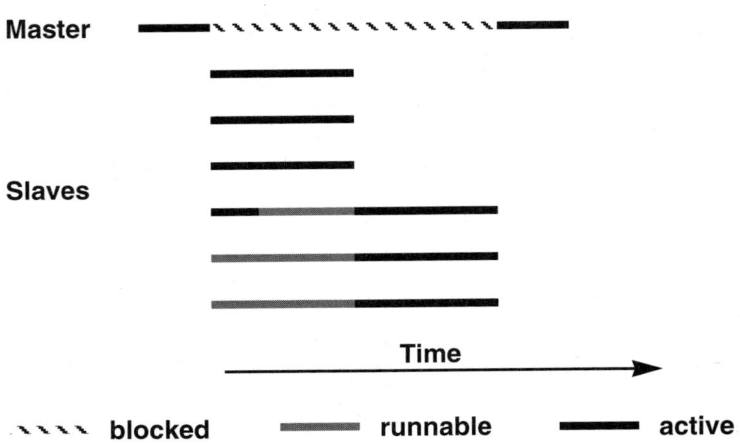

Figure 16-3 Master-Slave with Scheduling Delay and Extra Threads

Compilers sometime use the master-slave paradigm to automatically parallelize loops within a program. Typically a parallelizing compiler will generate code such that the main flow of the computation is controlled by the master. When the master encounters a parallelizable loop, it divides up the loop's work and gives it to a set of slaves. When the slaves finish, the master continues with the main computation. These techniques are illustrated more fully in "Parallelizing Using Compiler Techniques" on page 311.

Barrier Synchronization

The key element of the master-slave paradigm is that every slave thread must complete its task before the computation can proceed. Rather than requiring each thread to exit in order to synchronize we can allow a pool of threads to remain ready to work on subsequent computations, as shown in Figure 16-4. Note that each thread must synchronize to start the computation and to end it. When each thread resumes execution, it can retain its state and local variables, which is not possible when threads exit and are recreated.

A synchronization structure that conveniently implements this pattern is called a *barrier.* A barrier is initialized by specifying how many threads share the barrier; in the master-slave paradigm, this number is the number of slaves plus one for the master. In the example of Figure 16-4, five threads share the barrier, one master and four slaves. The main operation on a barrier is `barrier_wait()`

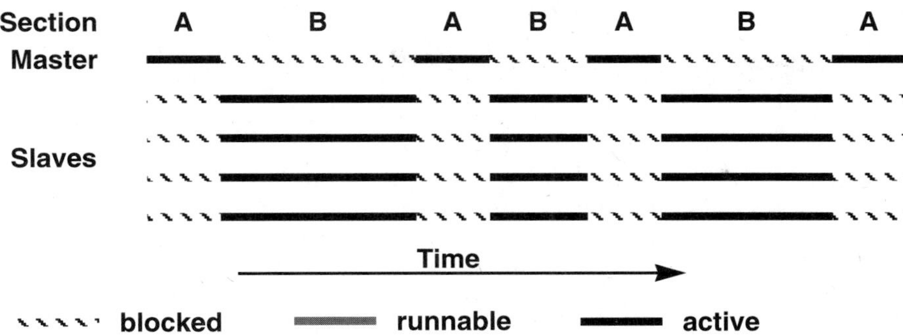

Figure 16-4 Master-Slave with Slave Pool

which will block until the number of threads specified in the initialization are waiting at the barrier. When the last thread arrives at the barrier, all the threads are released. The master-slave paradigm then becomes:

Master

```
Initialization
bar = barrier_init(n+1);
for (i = 0; i < n; i++)
    pthread_create(...,slave,...);
/* Slaves are now running */
while (not done) {
    A: Fill in work for slave to do
    barrier_wait(bar);
    /* Slaves are now working */
    B: Master processing if any



    /* Wait for slaves to finish */
    barrier_wait(bar);
    A: Process results
}
for (i = 0; i < n; i++)
    pthread_join(...);
Finalization if any
```

Slave

```
slave(void *params);
while (not done) {
    /* A: wait for work */
    barrier_wait(bar);
    B: Slave processing: data in
     global memory or params tells
     what to do. Put results
     into global memory or params
    /* Wait till all are done */
    barrier_wait(bar);
}

pthread_exit();
```

This paradigm is structured so that the slaves are in a loop in which two calls to `barrier_wait()` divide the loop into two sections we have labeled *A* and *B*. During section *A*, the master is running and sets up work for the slaves to do; this section corresponds to the region where the master thread is active in Figure 16-4. When the master and all *n* slaves have entered the barrier by calling `barrier_wait()`, the barrier releases all the threads and all return from the call. Now both master and slaves are in section *B*, where the slaves perform work, and the master may be idle. (However, this structure makes it easy for the master thread to assume a share of the work during section *B*, in effect participating as another slave.) At the end of section *B*, the master and slaves call `barrier_wait()` again; now all threads are in section *A* and the process repeats.

The barriers provide the synchronization necessary to avoid data races between the master and the slaves. Data written by the master or slaves during one section can be safely read by the master and all slaves in any subsequent section, because `barrier_wait()` not only contains the necessary synchronization function that forces data writes to memory, but also sequences all of the threads so that a reader of shared data can know that the data was written during a previous section. The template shown above uses this synchronization so that the master can safely pass work parameters to the slaves and the slaves can safely pass results back to the master. For example, the master could specify a different matrix multiplication task each time, or could use a more general parameter record to specify different slave tasks with each invocation. This design allows a pool of slave threads, waiting in the barrier, to be used by the master in a wide variety of ways at different times during the execution of the program.

An implementation of a *symmetric summing barrier* is shown below. The design is symmetric in that master and slave threads are not distinguished. An asymmetric barrier, in which master and slaves are treated differently, is more appropriate in the special case where the master and slaves truly alternate processing (i.e., the master does no work in section B and the slaves do no work in section A). In this case, you will notice that both master and slaves make two immediately adjacent calls to `barrier_wait()` with no intervening computation; these can be collapsed into a single call that requires less synchronization overhead.

The *summing* nature of the barrier allows all the threads to exchange an important piece of information as part of the synchronization at the barrier. Each caller of `barrier_wait()` specifies an integer. When `barrier_wait()` returns, it provides a result that is the sum of all the values specified in the calls to `barrier_wait()` by threads entering the barrier. This feature is not used in the template shown above, but will be important in a more complex example that follows. It's obvious how to remove the code used for summing if you don't need it.

```
typedef struct barrier_struct {
    pthread_mutex_t lock; /*Mutex lock for the entire structure*/
    int n_clients;        /*Number of threads to wait for at barrier*/
    int n_waiting;        /*Number of threads have called barrier_wait*/
    int phase;            /*Flag to separate waiters from fast workers*/
    int sum;              /*Sum of arguments passed to barrier_wait*/
    int result;           /*Answer to be returned by barrier_wait*/
    pthread_cond_t wait_cv; /*Clients wait on condition var. to proceed*/
} *barrier_t;

/*Create & initialize a barrier with the given number of client threads*/
barrier_t
barrier_init(int n_clients)
{
    barrier_t barrier =
        (barrier_t) malloc(sizeof (struct barrier_struct));
    if (barrier != NULL) {
        barrier->n_clients = n_clients;
        barrier->n_waiting = 0; barrier->phase = 0; barrier->sum = 0;
        pthread_mutex_init(&barrier->lock, NULL);
        pthread_cond_init(&barrier->wait_cv, NULL);
    }
    return (barrier);
}

/* Destroy a barrier */
void
barrier_destroy(barrier_t barrier)
{
    pthread_mutex_destroy(&barrier->lock);
    pthread_cond_destroy(&barrier->wait_cv);
    free(barrier);
}
```

```
/* Wait until the required number of threads enter the barrier */
int
barrier_wait(barrier_t barrier, int increment)
{
    int my_phase;
    pthread_mutex_lock(&barrier->lock);
    my_phase = barrier->phase;
    barrier->sum += increment;
    barrier->n_waiting++;
    if (barrier->n_waiting == barrier->n_clients) {
        barrier->result = barrier->sum;
        barrier->sum = 0;
        barrier->n_waiting = 0;
        barrier->phase = 1 - my_phase;
        pthread_cond_broadcast(&barrier->wait_cv);
    }
    /* Wait for the end of this synchronization phase */
    while (barrier->phase == my_phase) {
        pthread_cond_wait(&barrier->wait_cv, &barrier->lock);
    }
    pthread_mutex_unlock(&barrier->lock);
    return (barrier->result);
}
```

Code Example 16-2 Symmetric Summing Barrier

There is a subtle point in the design of the barrier in the use of the `phase` element which can have two values, 0 or 1. When the final thread arrives at the barrier it flips the value of `phase`. This tells the other threads waiting at the barrier that the current phase of waiting has ended and the next has begun. A fast thread may wake up, and hit the *next* use of the barrier before a slower thread wakes up and tests the condition. A slow thread can never see the value of `phase` flip twice while it is waiting since only the final thread arriving at the barrier will change the value of `phase`.

Master-Slave Example: Relaxation

Barrier synchronization can be used to enforce sequencing among slaves to avoid data races when one slave must write data that another slave must read. The matrix multiplication example does not show this form of data dependency: the work of each thread is independent of that of the other threads. This section presents a more general example that uses the symmetric summing barrier to coordinate slave dependencies.

The example is a relaxation algorithm or "Jacobi iteration" of the form often used to solve Laplace's equation to determine, for example, the steady-state temperature over a strangely shaped body when the temperature of its boundaries is held fixed. The algorithm approaches a solution iteratively; in each iteration, the temperature of a point is computed to be the average of the temperatures of its four neighbors, except that temperatures at the boundary are not changed. If $T_i(x, y)$ is the temperature at location (x,y) after the ith iteration of the algorithm assuming that space has been quantized into a two-dimensional grid, then the algorithm computes the temperature values for the next iteration as follows:

$$T_{i+1}(x,y) = (T_i(x-1,y) + T_i(x+1,y) + T_i(x,y-1) + T_i(x,y+1)) / 4$$

The algorithm below uses a matrix `t` (the `matrix_t` type introduced in the matrix multiplication example) to represent the solution matrix. It identifies boundary points using another matrix, `boundary`. On each iteration, it computes a new solution matrix and tests for convergence.

```
void
relax(matrix_t *boundary, matrix_t *t)
{
    matrix_t *t_old = t;
    matrix_t *t_new = matrix_alloc(t->n_rows, t->n_cols);
    matrix_t *temp;
    int row, col, converged;

    do {
        converged = TRUE;
        for (row = 0; row < boundary->n_rows; row++)
            for (col = 0; col < boundary->n_cols; col++) {
                if (MREF(boundary, row, col) == 0) {
                    /* Not on boundary */
                    float v = (MREF(t_old, row-1, col) +
                        MREF(t_old, row+1, col) +
                        MREF(t_old, row, col-1) +
                        MREF(t_old, row, col+1)) / 4.0;
                    if (abs(v - MREF(t_old, row, col)) > 0.000001)
                        converged = FALSE;
                    MREF(t_new, row, col) = v;
                } else {
                    MREF(t_new, row, col) = MREF(t_old, row, col);
                }
            }
        if (converged == TRUE && t_new == t) break;
        /* Swap old and new arrays for next iteration */
        temp = t_new; t_new = t_old; t_old = temp;
    } while (TRUE);
    matrix_free(t_old);
    /* Result is in t */
}
```

Code Example 16-3 Single-Threaded Solution to Laplace's Equation

Unlike the matrix multiplication problem, we cannot parallelize this algorithm by partitioning the outer loop (the do loop) because each iteration depends on the previous iteration. But we can partition the next inner loop so that each slave will work on a different group of rows of the grid. After each slave has computed values for t_new for its assigned rows, all slaves will synchronize at a summing barrier. This barrier will serve to separate the iterations of the outer loop, i.e., computing a new value for the entire solution matrix. The summing feature of the barrier is used to detect completion: when every slave thread signals that the solution has converged in the region for which it is responsible, the computation of all slaves can stop. In this example, the master need not join the barrier to synchronize with each iteration; it merely waits for all slave threads to exit. Code Example 16-4 shows the entire program.

```
#define MAX_PARALLEL 20/* maximum number of threads to use */

typedef struct {        /* parameter record for slave procedure */
    int i;              /* index of thread 0 <= i < n */
    int n;              /* number of threads */
    matrix_t *boundary, *t, *t_temp;
    barrier_t barrier;/* barrier to use for synchronization */
} relax_slave_params;

/*
 *The procedure  each slave thread will execute. Slaves will be passed
 *the same parameters, except that param->i will differ for each one.
 */
void *
relax_slave(void *param)
{
    relax_slave_params *p = (relax_slave_params *)param;
    matrix_t *boundary = p->boundary;
    matrix_t *t_old = p->t;
    matrix_t *t_new = p->t_temp;
    matrix_t *temp;
    int row, col;
    int converged, n_done;

    /*
     * Calculate which rows the p->i th thread will process. Since
     * the number of threads may not divide m = boundary->n_rows
     * exactly, we adopt the convention that for index 0 <= i < m % n,
     * the thread will process floor(m/n)+1 rows, while all others
     * will process floor(m/n) rows.
     */
    int quot = boundary->n_rows / p->n;
    int rem = boundary->n_rows % p->n;
    int do_rows = quot + ((p->i < rem)? 1 : 0);
    int first_row = quot * p->i + ((p->i < rem)? p->i : rem);
```

```
  do {
    converged = TRUE;
    for (row = first_row; row < first_row + do_rows; row++) {
        for (col = 0; col < boundary->n_cols; col++) {
            if (MREF(boundary, row, col) == 0) {
                /* Not on boundary */
                float v = (MREF(t_old, row-1, col) +
                    MREF(t_old, row+1, col) +
                    MREF(t_old, row, col-1) +
                    MREF(t_old, row, col+1)) / 4.0;
                if (abs(v - MREF(t_old, row, col)) > 0.000001)
                    converged = FALSE;
                MREF(t_new, row, col) = v;
            } else {
                MREF(t_new, row, col) = MREF(t_old, row, col);
            }
        }
    }
    /*
     * Synchronize at barrier, declaring done only if
     * result is in p->t
     */
    n_done = barrier_wait(p->barrier,
        ((converged == TRUE && t_new == p->t)? 1 : 0));

    /* Swap old and new arrays for next iteration */
    temp = t_new; t_new = t_old; t_old = temp;

  } while (n_done != p->n);  /* wait for all p->n slaves to be done */
  return (NULL);
}
```

```
void
relax(matrix_t *boundary, matrix_t *t)
{
    relax_slave_params params[MAX_PARALLEL];
    pthread_t thread[MAX_PARALLEL];
    int n_threads = min(MAX_PARALLEL, sysconf(_SC_NPROCESSORS_ONLN));
    barrier_t barrier = barrier_init(n_threads);
    matrix_t *t_temp = matrix_alloc(t->n_rows, t->n_cols);
    int i, res;

    assert(barrier != NULL && t_temp != NULL);
    for (i = 0; i < n_threads; i++) {
      params[i].i = i;
      params[i].n = n_threads;
      params[i].boundary = boundary;
      params[i].t = t;
      params[i].t_temp = t_temp;
      params[i].barrier = barrier;
      res = pthread_create(&thread[i], NULL,
              relax_slave, (void *)&params[i]);
      assert (res == 0); /* Relax must be able to allocate threads */
    }

    /* Wait for all threads to terminate */
    for (i = 0; i < n_threads; i++)
      pthread_join(thread[i], NULL);

    matrix_free(t_temp);
    barrier_destroy(barrier);
}
```

Code Example 16-4 Master-Slave Solution to Laplace's Equation

Note the logic used to terminate the computation. Each slave adds zero or one to the quantity summed at the barrier: zero if it is not ready to terminate, and one if it is. All slaves can then detect when the entire computation is finished, and exit.

Spin Barriers

On multiprocessors, the overhead of sleep-waiting on a barrier can sometimes dominate the computation costs of the loop. For this reason, barriers are sometimes implemented with spin waiting.

```
/* (Non-summing) spin barrier */
typedef struct spin_barrier {
    int n_clients;       /* Number of threads to wait for at barrier */
    pthread_mutex_t lock; /* Mutex for elements below*/
    int n_waiting;       /* Number of threads waiting at the barrier */
    int phase;           /* Separate waiters from fast workers */
} *spin_barrier_t;

/* create and init a barrier with the number of client threads */
spin_barrier_t
spin_barrier_init(int n_clients)
{
    spin_barrier_t barrier =
        (spin_barrier_t)malloc(sizeof (struct spin_barrier));
    if (barrier != NULL) {
        barrier->n_clients = n_clients;
        barrier->n_waiting = 0;
        barrier->phase = 0;
        pthread_mutex_init(&barrier->lock, NULL);
    }
    return (barrier);
}

/* destroy a barrier */
void
spin_barrier_destroy(spin_barrier_t barrier)
{
    pthread_mutex_destroy(&barrier->lock);
    free(barrier);
}
```

```
/* wait until the required number of threads has reached the barrier */
void
spin_barrier_wait(spin_barrier_t barrier)
{
    int my_phase;

    while (pthread_mutex_trylock(&barrier->lock) == EBUSY)
        ;               /* spin for mutex */
    my_phase = barrier->phase;
    barrier->n_waiting++;
    if (barrier->n_waiting == barrier->n_clients) {
        barrier->n_waiting = 0;
        barrier->phase = 1 - my_phase;
    }
    pthread_mutex_unlock(&barrier->lock);
    /* Wait for end of this synchronization phase */
    while (barrier->phase == my_phase)    /* WARNING! Data race */
        ;               /* spin block */
}
```

Code Example 16-5 Barrier Synchronization with Spin-Blocking

Notice that the implementation has a data race (see "Data Races" on page 30) in that phase may be written by the last thread entering the barrier at the same time that it is being read by waiting threads. However, this will work on almost all machine architectures for the following reasons. First, only one bit of phase is changed so if different bits of phase are interrogated at different times (due to the alignment of phase in memory or to a small system bus size) it doesn't matter as the other bits will always be zero. Secondly, in most multiprocessors, when the value of phase is changed it will propagate to the other processors eventually. Lastly, the use of the actual Pthread mutexes inserts any required memory barriers (see "Weaker memory models" on page 268) so that any data written before the barrier is entered is visible to the other threads after the barrier unblocks.

The implementation can also waste time spinning if other threads are overly delayed due to scheduling. You might try modifying the implementation to add spinning limits as in Code Example 15-5 on page 273.

Workpile Paradigm

The workpile paradigm uses a number of worker threads, each of which requests an assignment of work from a central workpile, does some computation, and then asks for a new work assignment. This process repeats until there is no more work to do. In some applications, the workpile is fixed at the outset, while in others, the worker threads can add new entries to the workpile. The template for a worker thread is of the following form:

Worker

```
while (ptr = work_get(workpile) != NULL) {   -- get work from workpile
        compute on work assignment indicated by "ptr"
        can call work_put(workpile, ptr_new) to add work to the pile
}
```

In this template, the worker threads loop continuously, removing and processing work from the workpile. Work is represented by an application-dependent structure that tells the worker what to do. In the process of performing its assigned task a worker may add new work to the pile.

The workpile paradigm is widely applicable. Here are some examples:

- Parallelizing loops.
  Each work assignment corresponds to one iteration of the loop. The workpile method may achieve somewhat better balance than the master-slave paradigm, because work is assigned in smaller chunks: an individual iteration rather than a block of iterations allocated evenly among the slave threads. The workpile is especially effective when the amount of computation in each iteration is expected to vary widely.
- Ray tracing.
  A parallel ray-tracing algorithm creates a raster-scan image from a description of geometric objects in a scene by casting a ray corresponding to each pixel in the image and computing which objects are struck by the ray, and hence the brightness of the pixel. A workpile implementation might assign to each worker a separate pixel in the image, or it might assign an entire scan-line of pixels to each worker.
- Rendering multiple images.
  To print an n-page document, a workpile implementation might assign each page to a different worker. To create an animated video sequence of n frames, a workpile implementation might assign each frame to a different worker. Note, however, that balance may be a problem because each work assignment is quite large (large grain size).
- Tessellation.
  A set of n complex geometric objects must be tessellated into patches of triangles that approximate the surfaces of the objects. Different objects have different tessellation routines: parallelepipeds, spheres, ellipses, nonuniform

rational B-spline (NURB) surfaces, etc. Tessellation is often done as a precursor to rendering an image of complex objects, so that the rendering software or hardware can operate on simple triangles only.

- Shortest-path search.
  Consider searching for the shortest route from one spot to another over a network of roads, represented as a graph, where each vertex of the graph represents an intersection of roads and each edge of the graph represents a road, labeled with the travel time along the road. Each vertex records the minimum travel time from the start to that vertex; it is initialized to a very large number. The workpile is a queue of vertices, each of which must be explored. A worker is assigned a vertex to explore; it computes a travel time to any destination vertex that can be reached by one road from the assigned vertex. If this time represents a new minimum time, the destination vertex is added to the work queue.
- Game playing.
  This, too, is a search application. The workpile contains possible future positions in the game; a worker explores legal moves from a position and enters the resulting new positions in the workpile.
- Divide-and-conquer algorithms.
  Divide-and-conquer algorithms map to multiprocessors by assigning to each thread a separate division of the problem. This is one form of workpile: each subdivision of the problem is entered on the workpile. Quicksort, the example we explore more fully below, is such an algorithm.

Workpile Controllers

A workpile controller manages a queue of work assignments specified by pointers to structures. It can implement the `work_put()` and `work_get()` procedures suggested by the template above. Alternatively, the controller can manage a pool of worker threads and use a callback mechanism to call an application-dependent procedure whenever there is work to do. The initiating thread can wait until all the workers have finished and there is no more work to be done. Such a controller is shown below.

The workpile controller keeps the work pointers in a FIFO queue. While the correctness of a workpile algorithm cannot depend on the order in which entries are extracted from the workpile, the *performance* of the algorithm can vary. Generally, a LIFO scheme corresponds to a depth-first search of a work space, while a FIFO scheme corresponds to breadth-first search. A controller used in a search algorithm might maintain a priority queue of work, sorted so that the most promising path will be explored first.

```
/* Workpile controller */
typedef void (*work_proc_t)(void *);
typedef struct workpile_struct {
    pthread_mutex_t lock;        /*mutex for this structure*/
    pthread_cond_t work_wait;    /*workers waiting for work*/
    pthread_cond_t finish_wait;  /*to wait for workers to finish*/
    int max_pile;                /*length of workpile array*/
    work_proc_t worker_proc;     /*work procedure*/
    int n_working;               /*number of workers working*/
    int n_waiting;               /*number of workers waiting for work*/
    int n_pile;                  /*number of pointers in the workpile*/
    int inp;                     /*FIFO input pointer*/
    int outp;                    /*FIFO output pointer*/
    void *pile[1];               /*array of pointers - the workpile*/
} *workpile_t;

/*
 *Allocates and initializes a workpile that holds max_pile entries.
 *worker_proc is called to process each work item on the queue.
 */
workpile_t
work_init(int max_pile, work_proc_t worker_proc, int n_threads)
{
    int err;
    pthread_t t;
    workpile_t wp = (workpile_t)
        malloc(sizeof (struct workpile_struct) +
            (max_pile * sizeof (void *)));
    static void worker(workpile_t wp);

    if (wp != NULL) {
        pthread_mutex_init(&wp->lock, NULL);
        pthread_cond_init(&wp->work_wait, NULL);
        pthread_cond_init(&wp->finish_wait, NULL);
        wp->max_pile = max_pile;
        wp->worker_proc = worker_proc;
        wp->n_working = wp->n_waiting = wp->n_pile = 0;
        wp->inp = wp->outp = 0;
        while (n_threads--) {
            err = pthread_create(&t, NULL,
                (void *(*)(void *))worker, (void *)wp);
            assert(err == 0);
        }
    }
    return (wp);
}
```

```
/* Puts ptr in workpile. Called at the outset, or within a worker. */
void
work_put(workpile_t wp, void *ptr)
{
    pthread_mutex_lock(&wp->lock);
    if (wp->n_waiting) {
        /* idle workers to be awakened */
        pthread_cond_signal(&wp->work_wait);
    }
    assert(wp->n_pile != wp->max_pile);/* check for room */
    wp->n_pile++;
    wp->pile[wp->inp] = ptr;
    wp->inp = (wp->inp + 1) % wp->max_pile;
    pthread_mutex_unlock(&wp->lock);
}

/*
 * Worker thread routine. Continuously looks for work, calls the
 * worker_proc associated with the workpile to do work.
 */
static void
worker(workpile_t wp)
{
    void *ptr;

    pthread_mutex_lock(&wp->lock);
    wp->n_working++;
    for (;;) {
        while (wp->n_pile == 0) {     /* wait for new work */
            if (--wp->n_working == 0)
                pthread_cond_signal(&wp->finish_wait);
            wp->n_waiting++;
            pthread_cond_wait(&wp->work_wait, &wp->lock);
            wp->n_waiting--;
            wp->n_working++;
        }
        wp->n_pile--;
        ptr = wp->pile[wp->outp];
        wp->outp = (wp->outp + 1) % wp->max_pile;
        pthread_mutex_unlock(&wp->lock);
        /* Call application worker routine. */
        (*wp->worker_proc)(ptr);
        pthread_mutex_lock(&wp->lock);
    }
    /* NOTREACHED */
}
```

```
/* Wait until all work is done and workers quiesce. */
void
work_wait(workpile_t wp)
{
    pthread_mutex_lock(&wp->lock);
    while(wp->n_pile !=0 || wp->n_working != 0)
        pthread_cond_wait(&wp->finish_wait, &wp->lock);
    pthread_mutex_unlock(&wp->lock);
}
```

Code Example 16-6 Workpile Controller

Workpile Example: Quicksort

Quicksort is a good example of a divide-and-conquer algorithm that can be implemented nicely using the workpile paradigm. The algorithm is recursive: to sort an array, it moves those keys that lie below the median value of the array to the front of the array, and those that lie above the median value to the end of the array, and then makes recursive calls on the two subarrays thus formed [Knuth 73]. When asked to sort a sufficiently short array, the algorithm uses a conventional insertion sort rather than recursive calls.

This algorithm is easily adapted to the workpile paradigm by making the unit of work the sorting of an array. The recursive calls put additional work on the workpile. There's no point in putting a large number of work units on the workpile, because we'll want to use many fewer threads than there are recursive calls for sorting. So we adopt the simple expedient of queuing only those recursive calls at a sufficiently high level in the tree of recursive calls.

```
/* Fewer than SORT_DIRECT items are sorted with an insertion sort. */
#define SORT_DIRECT 20
/* Work at this depth or less generates a separate work item. */
#define DEFER_DEPTH 6

typedef struct {
    float *data;        /* Array to sort */
    int n;              /* Number of elements in the array */
    int depth;          /* Depth of recursion */
    workpile_t wp;      /* Workpile to use */
} quick_sort_args;
static workpile_t quick_sort_workpile = NULL;
```

```
void
quick_sort_aux(float *data, int n, int depth, workpile_t wp, int
deferrable)
{
    int i,j;

    /* If array small, use insertion sort */
    if (n <= SORT_DIRECT) {
        for (j = 1; j < n; j++) {
            /* data[0..j-1] in sort; find a spot for data[j] */
            float key = data[j];
            for (i = j - 1; i >= 0 && key < data[i]; i--)
                data[i+1] = data[i];
            data[i+1] = key;
        }
        return;
    }
    /* Defer this work to work queue if policy says so */
    if (deferrable && depth <= DEFER_DEPTH) {
        quick_sort_args *q = (quick_sort_args *)
                              malloc(sizeof (quick_sort_args));
        assert(q != NULL);
        q->data = data; q->n = n; q->depth = depth; q->wp = wp;
        work_put(wp, (void *)q);
        return;
    }
    /* Otherwise, partition data based on a median estimate */
#define swap(i,j) {float t = data[i]; data[i] = data[j]; data[j] = t;}
    i = 0;
    j = n - 1;
    for (;;) {
        while (data[i] < data[j]) j--;
        if (i >= j) break;
        swap(i, j); i++;
        while (data[i] < data[j]) i++;
        if (i >= j) { i = j; break; }
        swap(i, j); j--;
    }
    /* Median value is now at data[i] */
    /* Partitioned so that data[0..i-1] <= median <= data[i+1..n-1] */
    quick_sort_aux(data,       i,     depth+1, wp, TRUE);
    quick_sort_aux(&data[i+1], n-i-1, depth+1, wp, TRUE);
}
```

```
/* Called from workpile controller with argument pointing to work. */
void
quick_sort_worker(void *a)
{
    quick_sort_args *q = (quick_sort_args *)a;
    quick_sort_aux(q->data, q->n, q->depth, q->wp, FALSE);
    free(q);
}

/* Main routine, called by client to do a sort. */
void
quick_sort(float *data, int n)
{
    if (quick_sort_workpile == NULL) {
        int n_threads = sysconf(_SC_NPROCESSORS_ONLN) + 2;
        quick_sort_workpile = work_init(2 << DEFER_DEPTH,
            quick_sort_worker, n_threads);
        assert(quick_sort_workpile != NULL);
    }
    quick_sort_aux(data, n, 0, quick_sort_workpile, FALSE);
    /* Wait for all work to finish */
    work_wait(quick_sort_workpile);
}
```

Code Example 16-7 Workpile Example: Quicksort

Pipeline Paradigm

The pipeline is one of the simplest and most compelling paradigms for creating parallel applications. The simple producer-consumer idiom is an example of a two-stage pipeline: the producer creates or obtains a block of data and puts a pointer to the data on a queue; the consumer obtains entries from the queue, in the same order created by the producer, and does something with the data. The queue handles all of the synchronization needs of these two processes:

- When the producer tries to add an entry to a full queue, the producer will block until space in the queue is available.
- When the consumer tries to obtain an entry from an empty queue, the consumer will block until the producer puts at least one entry in the queue.

No locking is required beyond that within the queue functions. The producer has exclusive access to the data block until it is entered on the queue, after which the producer may not touch the data. When the consumer obtains an entry from the queue, it has exclusive access to the associated data block. A call to a synchronization primitive within the queue procedures (e.g., `pthread_mutex_lock()`) ensures that all the producer's writes to the data block are complete before the consumer references the block.

The key to the pipeline paradigm is a set of independent threads, linked into a pipeline by queues between each pair of stages. Each stage obtains work from an input queue, performs processing suitable for the stage, and places the work on the output queue that links to the next stage in the pipe.

This basic structure can be generalized to handle a number of applications. You are probably familiar with ways to use Unix pipes to couple the output of one process to the input of another to form a pipeline. The processes view the pipe as carrying variously streams of bytes, lines of text, blocks of data, or structured records. Using threads to implement the processes in a pipeline gives you higher performance and greater control over other aspects of the program, such as global parameters that do not flow through the pipeline.

Here are some examples of pipelines:

- Video decompression.
  A three-stage pipeline is organized to (1) read compressed data from a disk file, (2) decompress the data into a raster image format, and (3) copy the raster image to the display, perhaps re-formatting the pixel data to conform to the display hardware requirements. Some implementations might divide the decompression stage further into a stage (2a) that does the detailed bit-manipulation to decode the video stream and (2b) a stage to do image processing, such as the inverse discrete cosine transform (IDCT).

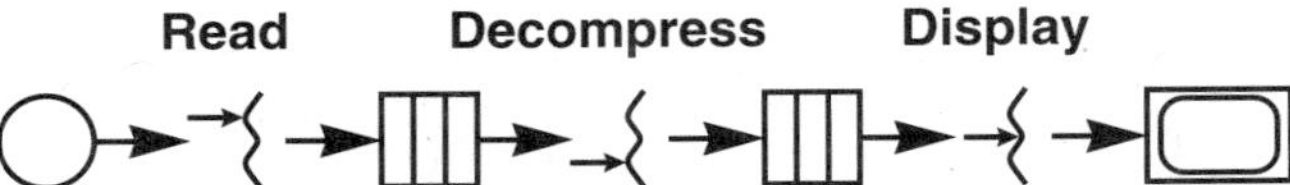

- Audio processing.
  A stream of digitized audio input might progress through a pipeline of processing to (1) read audio input, (2) cancel echoes from a room or phone line and adjust volume, (3) distinguish silence from spoken input, (4) invoke a speech recognizer to convert audio input to text, (5) send the text to a natural-language system to interpret and execute the spoken commands.

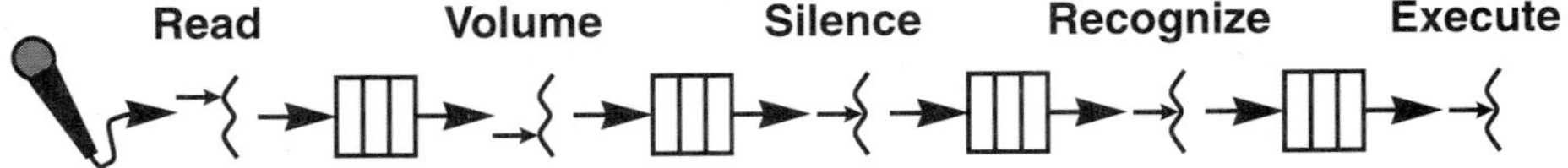

- Computer graphics rendering.
  Creating shaded renderings of three-dimensional geometric objects can be described as a pipeline of processes to: (1) enumerate the objects in the scene and generate geometric descriptions of each one, (2) apply a coordinate transformation to the geometry to account for the camera's viewing position, direction, and focal length, (3) clip the geometry so that elements outside the field of view of the camera are excluded, (4) apply a lighting model to compute

a shade for each face of the object, (5) scan-convert each face of the object, drawing the face in a *frame buffer* to obtain the final raster image. See [Newman 79] or [Foley 90] for more information on rendering.

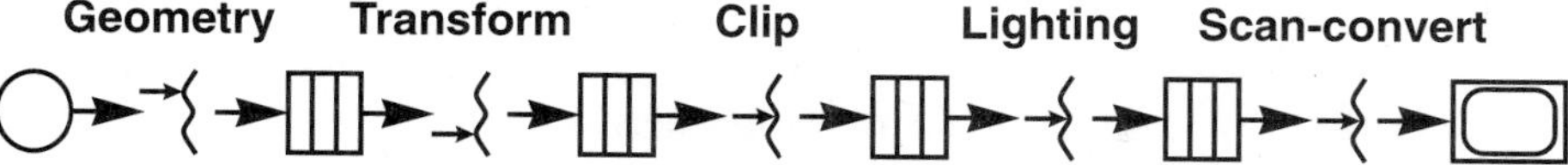

This last example is one that we will explore in some detail as our first example of the pipeline paradigm.

These examples are *inhomogeneous pipelines,* in which each stage performs a different kind of processing. Moreover, you can appreciate from the description of these pipelines that the number of stages may be fixed by the problem, and cannot necessarily be increased to exploit additional processors. To make matters still worse, the different stages are likely to require different amounts of processing, so that if we envision each stage being executed on a separate processor, the result will not be balanced: one processor will be the bottleneck, and others will be partially idle. It is very helpful to gauge, at the outset, the amount of work that each pipeline stage will do, and to try to design a pipeline that equalizes the work, or that can exploit more stages if more processors are available.

A contrasting approach is the *homogeneous pipeline,* in which each stage executes the same code. In effect, a pipe of *n* stages divides the work into *n* pieces much the way a master-slave arrangement with *n* slaves divides the work into *n* pieces. But the queue synchronization for the homogeneous pipeline is nothing like the barriers in the master-slave paradigm, as we shall see in the second example.

Pipeline Example: Graphics Rendering

The pipeline to compute a rendering of a scene from a geometric description can take several different forms, depending on many factors, including the choice of rendering algorithm. Our example uses five stages, outlined below. Typed *tokens* are passed down the pipeline. For example, a polygon is one kind of token passed down the entire length of the pipeline, with an attached data structure defining the geometry and color of the polygon. After outlining the pipeline stages, we'll see in detail how tokens flow down the pipe.

The stages are:

- *GEN*
  The first stage of the pipe is really the main thread, which determines the viewing parameters of the scene, generates geometric descriptions of objects, and so on. These functions call a few routines in a graphics package to

compute a rendering. This package is similar to the RenderMan language [Upstill 90]. In our example, the graphics package controls the pipeline structure, which is hidden from the client.

- `TRAN`
  The second stage of the pipe performs geometric transformations. For example, each vertex of a polygon is transformed first into a *camera coordinate system* to position the polygon relative to the camera and then into a *perspective coordinate system*, which accounts for the perspective projection of the camera.
- `CLIP`
  The third stage clips polygons to the limits of the viewing region of the camera. Polygons or portions of polygons that lie outside the field of view or behind the camera are rejected.
- `EDGE`
  The fourth stage computes a color, or shade, appropriate for each vertex of the polygon. This computation requires knowing the color and surface properties assigned to the polygon, the normal vector at the vertex, and details of lights specified for the scene. This stage also builds an edge data structure and attaches it to the polygon token.
- `PIXEL`
  The final stage executes a scan-line algorithm to enumerate the pixels covered by the polygon and to compute the depth and color of the polygon at each pixel. At each pixel, the depth is compared to the depth recorded in a *z-buffer*, to determine whether the polygon's pixel is closer to the camera than whatever other object has been previously recorded in the z-buffer, and if so, the polygon's color and depth replace those of the other polygon. In simplified form, the algorithm within the `PIXEL` stage is:

```
for (y = top of polygon; y >= bottom of polygon; y--) {
    for (each pair of polygon edges crossing scan-line y) {
        for (x = left edge; x <= right edge; x++) {
            if (z >= z_buffer[x, y]) {
                z_buffer[x, y] = z;
                image[x, y] = polygon_color;
            }
        }
    }
}
```

To maintain proper synchronization, state held in a pipeline stage is changed only as a consequence of processing a token in the stage. This strategy avoids any data locking, save for that embodied in the queues between stages: stages refer only to data that they "own." For example, the routine in the graphics package responsible for initialization sends a `begin` token down the pipe. This token specifies the width and height of the output image, in pixels. Each stage that needs to know this information copies these two parameters into static variables accessible only to that stage. Of course, the `begin` token also affords each stage the opportunity to do any initialization required. As another example, the `light` token is sent down the pipe with information about a light used to illuminate the scene; this information is captured in the *EDGE* stage.

Not all tokens flow down the full length of the pipeline. Of course, the `begin`, *end*, and `polygon` tokens proceed through all stages. Each stage that processes one of these tokens is responsible for forwarding the token onward by putting it on the stage's output queue. However, the `transformation` token, used to update the current transformation held in the *TRAN* stage, need flow only as far as the *TRAN* stage. After the token is processed, the stage simply returns the token to free storage rather than placing it on its output queue.

The token flow is also data-dependent. The `polygon` token is abandoned if a stage determines that the polygon described by the token need not be processed further. There are two cases:

- Back-face culling.
  If the *TRAN* stage determines that the polygon faces away from the camera, the polygon is not processed further. If the normal vectors at each vertex of the polygon point away from the camera (easy to determine in the camera coordinate system), the polygon is rejected. In complex scenes, it is common for roughly half the polygons to be rejected in this way.
- Clipping.
  If the `CLIP` stage determines that no part of the polygon falls within the viewing region, the polygon is not processed further.

The uneven processing duties of the different stages, coupled with the potential for early rejection of polygons, make it difficult to balance the pipeline. In most cases, the `PIXEL` stage will require the most computation. Indeed, to balance the processor utilization, it may be necessary to further parallelize the `PIXEL` stage, for example by splitting the main loop illustrated above so that several threads can compute in parallel. Such a hybrid approach that combines several algorithm paradigms is often found in parallel applications.

Pipeline Example: Relaxation

Some algorithms can be cast into a *homogeneous pipeline,* in which each stage executes the same algorithm, but on different data. This form of problem decomposition is similar to the master-slave or workpile, but the synchronization used in the pipeline form is quite different. And the reasoning behind the decomposition can be quite different, too.

For an example, let's return to the iterative solution of Laplace's equation illustrated in the master-slave paradigm (Code Example 16-3). Consider a pipeline in which we assign an iteration to each stage of the pipeline. The stage receives, from its input queue, the solution array for the previous iteration, computes a new iteration, and puts the new solution array on its output queue. This seems easy enough, but there are two problems:

1. Since we don't know in advance how many iterations will be required to reach convergence, we don't know how long to make the pipeline. Ideally, we'd like to use a number of pipe stages that is governed by the available parallelism (the number of processors) rather than a data-dependent quantity like the number of iterations required to achieve convergence.
2. More importantly, the scheme does not seem to allow parallel execution at all. Because each iteration depends on the results of the previous iteration, stage *i*+1 cannot begin execution until stage *i* has completed, and so on: it looks as if only a single stage will be runnable at a time.

The first problem is easily solved by connecting the pipeline into a *ring* of stages. We might choose four stages on a four-processor system. The solution will pass around the ring, each stage computing a new iteration, until convergence is achieved. When convergence is detected, the ring can be shut down and the solution array presented as the result.

The solution to the second problem is more subtle: it involves passing along the pipe not entire solution arrays, but partial results as they are computed. For example, suppose each stage were to queue separately the value of the solution at each point, $T_i(x, y)$, as soon as it is computed in a doubly nested loop over x and y. The next stage receives this value, and as soon as it has also received values for the neighbors at $(x+1,y)$, $(x-1,y)$, $(x,y-1)$, and $(x,y+1)$ it can compute a value for $T_{i+1}(x, y)$ and pass it along. So each stage is computing a new iteration, one solution element at a time.

Because a lot of overhead may be involved in passing each solution element separately, we will use a solution that passes each row of the solution matrix separately. Each pipe stage will need to buffer three rows, which we might call *previous, current*, and *next*. Together, these rows provide solution values from the previous iteration for all neighbors of the *current* row, and allow the stage to compute the values for the next iteration of the *current* row.

The final details we need to determine are how to initialize the computation and how to extract the answer. To initialize, we choose one of the pipe stages in the ring and cause it to send the initial solution array, row by row, to the next ring stage. After this stage finishes this task, it behaves just like any other stage in the ring. In order to avoid deadlock, the queues in the ring must have enough combined capacity to hold all the rows of the solution matrix. Otherwise, the initialization cannot complete before the queues fill up. The possibility of deadlock is a consequence of connecting the pipeline into a ring. A linear pipeline cannot deadlock because the last stage can always compute and thus remove items from its input queue, freeing up space for the next-to-last stage to put items in its output queue, and so on.

After a stage has finished computing an iteration, it knows whether the solution has converged. Unfortunately, at this point, the stage cannot copy the results into a result matrix, because it has already forwarded most of the rows of the solution on to the next stage. There are various ways to solve this problem. The solution we adopt is to find a specific stage that is guaranteed to have, as input, a converged solution, and copy this input into the solution array. One way to identify such a stage is: the iteration input to this stage did not converge, but the iteration computed in this stage converged, so the *next* iteration received as input to this stage will have converged. This scheme reports the results of iteration $i+n-1$, where i is the index of the first iteration that converges, and n is the number of stages in the pipeline. While this involves a little extra computation, the algorithm is such that the extra iterations do not impair the result.

Pseudo-code for the algorithm executed by each stage is shown in Code Example 16-8.

```
relax_pipe_proc(void *params)
{
    int stage = params->...    /* 0 <= stage < NSTAGES */
    if (stage == 0)
        for (all rows)
            queue_put(queue[1], a row of input matrix)
    for (;;) {      /* do an iteration */
        row_next = queue_get(queue[stage]);
        for (all rows) {
            /* shift down and get a new row */
            row_previous = row_current;
            row_current = row_next;
            if (!last_row) row_next = queue_get(queue[stage]);
            compute values for new iteration into new_row
            if (lastrow && solution has converged)
                mark new_row as converged
            queue_put(queue[(stage+1)%NSTAGES, new_row);
        }
        if (row_current is marked converged) {
            break;      /* input has already converged, we're done */
        } else if (solution has converged) {
            for (all rows) {
                row_current = queue_get(queue[stage]);
                copy row_current to output matrix
            }
            break;
        }
    }
}
```

Code Example 16-8 Pseudo-code for a Stage of the Pipelined Relaxation Algorithm

This algorithm uses an array of queues: `queue[i]` contains rows being passed from stage *i*–1 to stage *i*. The algorithm requires no locking beyond that provided within the `queue_put()` and `queue_add()` procedures, which add and remove entries from these queues. The rows flowing from stage to stage are accessed by only a single thread at a time and are passed from thread to thread via a queue operation that contains a call to a synchronization primitive (e.g., `pthread_mutex_lock()`) that ensures memory writes have completed.

Although the reasoning behind this algorithm is somewhat subtle, this version usually performs somewhat better than the master-slave version shown in Code Example 16-4. The reason is that the queues are much more resilient to small variations in execution history than a barrier. If one thread is slowed a bit due to an interrupt, the other threads continue to operate normally, and the buffering in the queues helps to smooth out variations. The overhead of queues is likely to be smaller, too, because the locks in the queues are shared by at most two processors, while the lock in a barrier is shared by all processors. The queues will perform much better than the barrier on a large machine.

Parallelizing Using Compiler Techniques

Modern compilers are able to analyze a program and determine whether portions of it can be transformed into an equivalent parallel variant. These techniques range from simple to intricate. The simplest class of transformations applies to loops, in effect determining automatically when separate iterations of a loop can be safely executed in parallel, using the master-slave technique demonstrated earlier in this chapter.

Sun's Fortran and C compilers are equipped to parallelize a loop if the iterations of the loop can be executed in any order. But determining whether the iterations of a loop can be executed in any order can be quite tricky. For simple examples, consider the following two Fortran loops:

```
do i = 1, 1001
    a(i) = b(i+1) * cos ((pi*(i-1)/1000)
end do
do i = 3, 100
    a(i) = a(i-2) + b(i)
end do
```

The first loop is parallelizable, because each iteration is independent of all other iterations; as long as the expression is evaluated for every value of *i* between 1 and 1001 inclusive, the order of evaluation does not matter. By contrast, the second loop cannot be parallelized easily, because iteration *j* must be executed after iteration *j*–2 in order to get the proper value for `a(i-2)` in the expression. The alert reader will also notice that the first loop is parallelizable only if the compiler is assured that arrays `a` and `b` are not *aliased*, i.e., that they do not share any common elements. For example, if `a` and `b` were equivalenced to the same array, then the first loop has an order dependency (you can see this by substituting "a" for "b" in the expression). If the loop appears inside a subroutine and `a` and `b` are arguments to the subroutine, the compiler cannot assume that the caller hasn't aliased the arrays, for example by passing the same array as the `a` argument and the `b` argument. When the compiler is trying to "automatically parallelize" a loop, it errs on the side of caution and will not parallelize if there is any possibility that the parallel form will be wrong.

Most loops are much more complicated than the simple examples above, and can prevent parallelization. For example, a scalar variable that is updated in some or all iterations would be sensitive to the order of execution, and would also require locking to avoid data races. A conditional jump outside the loop may terminate the loop before all iterations have executed, which will confound a parallelization scheme that executes iterations out of order. Most compilers have restrictions such as these that prevent automatic parallelization on many loops.

While some loops are so simple that they can be automatically parallelized, and others are so complicated that they cannot be parallelized with today's compilers, there is a middle ground where the compiler cannot determine whether it's safe to parallelize the loop, i.e., to generate code that will execute the iterations in arbitrary order. For example, consider the following loop:

```
do i = 1, lsearch
    call correl(corrs(i), sig1(1), sig2(1), 1, i, len-lsearch)
end do
```

This loop may or may not be safe to parallelize, depending on the details of the subroutine. For example, it might change the variable `i`, or it might store into the arrays `sig1` and `sig2` at indices computed from `i` so as to create an order dependency. On the other hand, if the subroutine creates no hidden order-dependencies, the programmer can indicate to the compiler that the loop is safe to parallelize using a *compiler directive*.

Code Example 16-9 is a complete program that illustrates several kinds of loops and parallelization techniques. The program matches two signals, stored in arrays `sig1` and `sig2`, to find the sample offset at which the correlation between the two signals is maximized. The subroutine `correl` does most of the work: it computes and returns the correlation between two arrays at a given offset position. The main loop inside this subroutine, labeled C-1 in the code, cannot be parallelized because the variable `sum`, which accumulates the correlation result, creates a dependency. This is unfortunate, because the obvious way to search for the maximum correlation, using the following loop, is itself unparallelizable because of dependencies on `mxcorr` and `imx`:

```
c LOOP M-1.
    mxcorr = 0.0
    do i = 1, lsearch
c           Subroutine 'correl' returns answer in 'curcorr'
        call correl(curcorr, sig1(1), sig2(1), 1, i, len-lsearch)
        if (curcorr .gt. mxcorr) then
            imx = i
            mxcorr = curcorr
        end if
    end do
```

There are two ways to adapt this program to obtain good parallel performance. The first is illustrated in the code example: recode the simple loop M-1 above into two loops M-2 and M-3 so that most of the work can be done in parallel. Loop M-2 just calls the `correl` subroutine and saves the computed correlation value in an array, `corrs`. Because the `correl` call does not create any order dependencies, the programmer has used the `c$par doall` directive to force the compiler to parallelize loop M-2. After all the correlations have been computed in parallel, loop M-3 finds the maximum. This loop cannot be parallelized because of variable dependencies, but it will be fast because it does very little work compared to the work done by M-2.

```
c correl.f -- A simple one-dimension correlation example
c f77 -O3 -autopar -explicitpar -loopinfo correl.f
c
      implicit real*8(a-h,o-z)
      parameter ( len = 30000, lsearch = 3000, period = 500d0 )
      dimension sig1(len), sig2(len), corrs(lsearch)
c Generate a test case
      center = len/2
      call sinc(sig1, len, 1.0d0, period, center)
      call sinc(sig2, len, 1.0d0, period, center+lsearch/3)
c
c Look for the offset 'imx' between sig1 and sig2 at which they are
c maximally correlated.
c
c LOOP M-2. Compute into corrs(i) the correlation between sig1 and sig2
c with sample offset i.  Note that these computations are all
c independent, and can be done in parallel.
c$par doall
      do i = 1, lsearch
          call correl(corrs(i), sig1(1), sig2(1), 1, i, len-lsearch)
      end do
c Find the maximum correlation by looking for max in corrs(i)
      mxcorr = 0
c LOOP M-3. This loop will not parallelize because of dependencies on
c variables mxcorr and imx, but it is a very fast loop.
      do i = 1, lsearch
          if (corrs(i) .gt. mxcorr) then
              imx = i
              mxcorr = corrs(i)
          end if
      end do
      print 10, imx-1
 10   format('The maximum offset is ', I5)
      end
```

```
c sinc -- fill array sig() with sin(x)/x
c   real*8 sig()    signal array                  out
c   integer n       number of samples             in
c   real*8 amp      amplitude                     in
c   real*8 period   number of samples             in
c   real*8 center   center of sync function       in
c
    subroutine sinc(sig, n, amp, period, center)
    implicit real*8(a-h,o-z)
    dimension sig(n)
    integer n
c LOOP S-1. This loop will automatically parallelize.
    do i = 1, n
       a = 2.0 * 3.14159 *(i-center)/period
c Avoid division by zero
       if (a .ne. 0) then
          sig(i) = amp * sin(a)/a
       else
          sig(i) = amp
       end if
    end do
    return
    end

c correl -- correlate two signals and return correlation
c   real*8 cor      correlation                       out
c   real*8 sig1()   first signal                      in
c   real*8 sig2()   second signal                     in
c   integer beg1    index of first sig1 sample        in
c   integer beg2    index of first sig2 sample        in
c   integer n       number of samples to look at      in
c
    subroutine correl(cor, sig1, sig2, beg1, beg2, n)
    implicit real*8(a-h,o-z)
    integer beg1, beg2, n
    dimension sig1(n), sig2(n)
       sum = 0.0
c LOOP C-1. This loop will not parallelize because of the dependency
c on variable sum from iteration to iteration.
       do i = 1, n
          sum = sum + sig1(i+beg1-1) * sig2(i+beg2-1)
       end do
       cor = sum
    return
    end
```

Code Example 16-9 Correlating Two Signals, Showing Automatic Parallelization

A second way to obtain good parallel performance is to adapt the `correl` subroutine itself so that it will parallelize. The idea is to break the single loop C-1 into two nested loops, arranged so that the outer loop contains no dependencies and will parallelize. This is the same technique we illustrated in the matrix multiply example: partition the loop into parts that can be executed on separate processors. The technique is much easier in this example because the compiler will handle the tiresome details of passing arguments and controlling threads. The loops C-2 and C-3 form partial sums and a final (small) loop C-4 collects the partial sums into a single answer. The parameter `ipar` specifies the number of partial sums to use.

Unless care is taken, this technique will exhibit severe performance problems because of false sharing: the partial sums accessed by separate processors in the C-3 loop will reside in the same cache line. To avoid this problem, we space out the partial sum array using the `icache` parameter, so the partial sum used by each iteration of C-2 will fall in a separate cache line. If you set `icache = 1`, corresponding to the simplest way to index the partial sums, performance will degrade noticeably!

```
      subroutine correl(cor, sig1, sig2, beg1, beg2, n)
      implicit real*8(a-h,o-z)
      integer beg1, beg2, n
      dimension sig1(n), sig2(n)
      parameter ( ipar = 20, icache = 4 )
      dimension sump(ipar * icache)
      ipn = n/ipar
c LOOP C-2.This loop should parallelize,but is not considered
c profitable, so we force it to parallelize.
c$par doall
      do ip = 1, ipar
          istart = 1 + (ip-1)*ipn
          iend = ip*ipn
          if (ip .eq. ipar) iend = n
          ipx = ip * icache
          sump(ipx) = 0.0
c LOOP C-3. Will not parallelize because of dependency.
          do i = istart, iend
              sump(ipx) = sump(ipx) + sig1(i+beg1-1) * sig2(i+beg2-1)
          end do
      end do
      cor = 0.0
c LOOP C-4. To collect partial sums. Will not parallelize.
      do ip = 1, ipar
          cor = cor + sump(ip * icache)
      end do
      return
      end
```

Code Example 16-10 Adapting the Correlation Routine for Parallel Computation

16

Performance

The whole point of writing a parallel algorithm is to obtain good performance on a multiprocessor. Often, understanding and improving the performance of a multithreaded program is quite difficult. There are four important performance problem areas: imbalance, synchronization overhead, lock contention, and data sharing overhead.

Imbalance

If there are ever fewer runnable threads than processors to run them, the parallel program is imbalanced, and the ideal speedup factor cannot be achieved. Usually this means that the grain size is too large; if the problem can be partitioned into more parts, they can be spread more evenly over the processors by the thread scheduler. Some experimentation may be required to find the best policy for each application to use in determining how many threads for a given number of available processors. Of course, the biggest threat to balance is sequential, unparallelized sections of your program.

Synchronization Overhead

Synchronization functions that manipulate locks, condition variables, and threads take time to execute. Even if they complete without delay, these calls add overhead. The obvious technique for reducing synchronization overhead is to do less of it. Sometimes this means increasing the amount of work each thread does between synchronizations (i.e., increasing the grain size). In other cases synchronization can be eliminated altogether, for example, by realizing that certain data cannot change and therefore need not be locked.

Lock Contention

When a thread tries to seize a lock and finds it already held by another thread, the first thread is delayed. This delay is an overhead of parallel processing. It is important to realize that lock contention cannot be eliminated. There are many techniques that can be applied to reduce contention, but contention will never be reduced to zero; it's an inevitable consequence of sharing. It can be reduced by several techniques, including shortening the execution time of the critical section that holds the lock, using read/write locks, and breaking up locks, as we've seen in Chapter 14, "Advanced Synchronization Strategies." In parallel programming you can also use spin blocking techniques (see "Spin Blocking" on page 271) to reduce the cost of contention when it happens. Since the critical sections for the barrier, workpile, and queue structures used in the paradigms shown in this chapter are all very short, spin blocking is likely to help improve performance.

Keep in mind that long-term continuous spin blocking is wasteful, and you should normally block after spinning for a while. Usually a spin time that is 50–100% of normal thread context switch time is effective (see [Anderson 90] and [Karlin 91]).

Data Sharing and False Sharing Overhead

When a processor writes data that is shared with another processor, traffic on the system bus linking the processors will be required in order to effect sharing. False sharing occurs when data values themselves are not shared, but because several data values fall within a single cache line, the cache lines must be shared between processors (see "Shared Memory Multiprocessors" on page 263).

To prevent false sharing, use a memory allocator that allocates memory in units of cache blocks and is aligned to cache block boundaries. Pad statically allocated memory sufficiently to avoid false sharing. For example, a static vector of `pthread_mutex_t` locks probably leads to false sharing between the locks; avoid sharing by making the elements of the vector at least a cache-block in size (see Code Example 16-10).

Performance and Problem Size

It is instructive to study how overheads change with the size of the problem being solved. In most cases, the overhead should remain fixed or increase more slowly than the computation required to solve the problem. Thus big problems show better speedup than small problems.

In one class of algorithm, overhead increases with the number of processors rather than with the size of the problem. For example, the master-slave matrix multiply synchronization overhead is fixed by the number of threads, hence the number of processors. As the matrix dimension n grows, the computation grows as n^3, while the contention due to false sharing of the result matrix tends to grow only as n (the false sharing is in the cache lines that hold elements at the boundary of two rows). The imbalance problems, largely mitigated by the thread scheduler, will also be reduced as the amount of computation grows. Barrier synchronization is very sensitive to the number of processors in use: for small and medium-sized problems, the cost of barrier synchronization will come to dominate the performance as the number of processors increases.

In another class of algorithm, the number of synchronization operations grows as the problem size grows, but more slowly. The pipeline relaxation example passes each row down the pipeline, so we can expect the overheads associated with the pipeline synchronization to grow as the dimension of the solution matrix. It turns out that larger matrices will require more iterations to converge, so the pipeline overhead will be invoked more often for this reason as well.

Rao describes (in [Rao 91]) first-order models of the performance of applications using different paradigms for implementation. He demonstrates a good fit between modeled and observed performance. These models are less useful when your program departs from the simple paradigms.

Guidelines for Writing Parallel Programs

Here are some things to keep in mind when attempting to take advantage of multiprocessing to increase program performance:

Let the compiler do it

Parallelizing compilers allow you to write a conventional sequential program while the compiler generates code to spread loop execution across processors. These compilers save you from tedious details of thread management and data locking. However, to obtain good performance, you will often need to recode your algorithm slightly or make more aggressive adaptations so that the compiler can parallelize your loops (see "Parallelizing Using Compiler Techniques" on page 311).

Program for correctness

When writing a multithreaded program, correct locking and synchronization are essential. Correctness can be obtained only by careful thinking and analysis of the structure of the application. It's very hard to find correctness bugs in parallel algorithms because you cannot duplicate synchronization failures from one run to another. The best defense is choosing a simple enough locking and synchronization scheme that you can persuade yourself it is correct. Tools like `lock-lint` can help.

Use modularity to confine threads programming to a few modules. Note, for example, that the matrix multiply, relaxation, and graphics examples all shield the client from the threading: the user of a routine to multiply a matrix, solve Laplace's equation, or render a scene cannot tell that he/she is using a multithreaded implementation. Similarly, the barrier, workpile, and queue modules we've used in this chapter help confine difficult synchronization code with a few small modules.

Postpone optimization

Don't do too much optimization until you verify the performance of your program. Splitting locks, queues and other data structures in an effort to achieve better performance often introduces more overhead than it saves. And these complex schemes can be the source of bugs, too. Use simple schemes first, and if possible, keep them.

Know where your algorithm spends its time

If you're porting an existing program, first study the performance of the program carefully. Know where it is spending its time (see "The process/debugger interface" on page 348), for as many different operating conditions as you have the stamina to examine. If you're programming from scratch, make some careful and sober estimates of where the program will spend its time. Are there other programs or subroutine packages whose performance will offer a clue to the performance of the program you're writing?

The reason it's important to understand where the time goes is that it's remarkably easy to misplace your efforts when parallelizing your program. You've doubtless experienced this phenomenon when tuning a conventional single-threaded program. And appearances can be deceiving: in one numerical-integration code, the "initialization" consumed all the time, and the "solution" was trivial, but the programmer wasted time parallelizing both. It's common to find programs that have been "over-parallelized": great effort has brought little gain.

Figure out how to measure the performance of your program and to experiment with various policies. In many cases, standard tools will suffice, but in some cases you will prefer to provide your own instrumentation. If possible, confine the instrumentation to modules involved in threading and synchronization (e.g, barrier, workpile controller, queue) to reduce your work.

Plan for debugging

Most of your bugs won't have anything to do with threads, but if your program is multithreaded, you may not be able to deterministically reproduce the bugs, catch them with breakpoints, and so on. If possible, write your multithreaded program in such a way that it can run with exactly one thread (or one thread besides the main thread, if the main thread is always blocked while the other thread is running). This will ensure reproducible behavior when looking for bugs. In cases where this is not possible, you can often write your program to run in a deterministic mode for debugging and a multithreaded mode for production. For example, the graphics pipeline can be run single-threaded by calling the next stage of the pipe directly rather than queueing the token for processing in a separate thread. The difference between single and multithreaded execution is then confined to a single function, the queue for passing a token on down the pipe.

Summary

The three paradigms we have presented, master-slave, workpile, and pipeline, do not exhaust the ways to design parallel algorithms; you might wish to consider other models as well. The Linda distributed programming system [Carriero 89] offers a way to synchronize work on multiprocessors or multicomputers. (Multicomputers coordinate processes using message passing between processors rather than shared memory.) Packages such as PVM [Geist 94], MPI [Gropp 94], and Molecule [Xu 89] are tools for writing message-passing applications. Usually it is much more work to write and tune a parallel program when shared memory is not available.

Multithreading Existing Code 17

This chapter explains strategies for multithreading existing libraries and applications. The section on libraries mainly describes how to ensure that libraries are thread-safe both with respect to shared resources such as memory and files and with respect to exported interfaces. The section on applications describes how to multithread applications that fall into several classes representing good candidates for multithreading.

It may be worthwhile to review the taxonomy of thread-safety in Chapter 4, "Using Libraries in Multithreaded Programs."

Libraries

A library that is linked into a multithreaded application may be called by more than one thread concurrently. The library writer must design how the library will run in this environment. There are several common reasons why a library will fail to operate properly when used in a multithreaded process (see [Jones 91]). The main sources of problems can be classified into three areas:

- Failure to account for simultaneous entry by different threads (thread-safety)
- Failure to account for calling thread cancellation (cancel-safety)
- Failure to account for process `fork()` (fork-safety)

Libraries must be treated slightly differently than whole applications because a library has few options in controlling when its entry points are called. Imposing irregular and implementation-dependent restrictions on calling can make the library much harder to use and can make it more difficult to maintain backward compatibility when an implementation is upgraded.

Thread-Safety

All global resources within a process, such as globally allocated memory and files, are shared by all threads within the process. Access to these resources has to be regulated to guarantee that the resources are in a consistent state when routines in library are simultaneously entered by different threads. In most cases, this protection is implemented using mutexes. As we've seen in Chapter 4,

"Using Libraries in Multithreaded Programs," you can hide the required synchronization within the library implementation where the library interfaces permit.

By now you are familiar with the ways in which access to variables that are referenced by more than one thread must be coordinated (see Chapter 3, "Synchronization"). When you are upgrading a non-multithreaded library you must first identify which memory will be shared and writable and which memory is only used by one thread at a time or is statically initialized and only read. As an example, Code Example 17-1 shows an thread-safe implementation of `malloc()` (with some irrelevant portions of the code deleted).

```
/* Thread-safe implementation of malloc() */
#define NBUCKETS 30
static union overhead *nextf[NBUCKETS];
static int pagesz;      /* page size */
static int pagebucket; /* page size bucket */
pthread_mutex_t ma_lock = PTHREAD_MUTEX_INITIALIZER;

void *
malloc(nbytes)
    size_t nbytes;
{
    register union overhead *op;
    register int bucket, n;
    register unsigned amt;

    pthread_mutex_lock(&ma_lock);
    if (pagesz == 0) {
        /* First time malloc is called, set up page size */
        pagesz = sysconf(_SC_PAGESIZE);
        op = allocate system memory for buckets;
        pagebucket = log2(pagesize);
    }
    /* Convert request into closest block size that satisfies request */
    n = pagesz - sizeof (*op) - RSLOP;
    if (nbytes <= n) {
        amt = 8;        /* size of first bucket */
        bucket = 0;
        n = -(sizeof (*op) + RSLOP);
    } else {
        amt = pagesz;
        bucket = pagebucket;
    }
```

```
    while (nbytes > amt + n) {
        amt <<= 1;
        if (amt == 0) {
            pthread_mutex_unlock(&ma_lock);
            return (NULL);
        }
        bucket++;
    }
    /* If nothing in hash bucket,request more memory from system */
    if ((op = nextf[bucket]) == NULL) {
        morecore(bucket);
        if ((op = nextf[bucket]) == NULL) {
            pthread_mutex_unlock(&ma_lock);
            return (NULL);
        }
    }
    /* remove from linked list */
    nextf[bucket] = op->ov_next;
    op->ov_magic = MAGIC;
    op->ov_index = bucket;
    pthread_mutex_unlock(&ma_lock);
    return ((char *)(op + 1));
}
```

```
   /* Allocate more memory to the indicated bucket */
50 static void
51 morecore(bucket)
52     int bucket;
53 {
54     register union overhead *op;
55     register int sz;          /* size of desired block */
56     int amt;                  /* amount to allocate */
57     int nblks;                /* how many blocks we get */

58     sz = 1 << (bucket + 3);
59     if (sz <= 0)
60         return;
61     if (sz < pagesz) {
62         amt = pagesz;
63         nblks = amt / sz;
64     } else {
65         amt = sz + pagesz;
66         nblks = 1;
67     }
68     op = (union overhead *) allocate amt more memory;
       /*Add allocated memory to that on free list for this hash bucket*/
69     nextf[bucket] = op;
70     while (--nblks > 0) {
71         op->ov_next = (union overhead *)((caddr_t)op + sz);
72         op = (union overhead *)((caddr_t)op + sz);
73     }
74 }
```

Code Example 17-1 Thread-Safe `malloc()`

In Code Example 17-1, the mutex, `ma_lock`, is used to protect all three global variables. The lock is acquired on entry to `malloc()` and is released on exit. The call to the internal routine `morecore()` on line 38 also needs to be protected, since it also uses the global variables `pagesz` and `nextf` on lines 61, 62, 65 and 69. Since `morecore()` is an internal routine and `malloc()` is the only routine that calls it, `ma_lock` is sufficient to protect calls to `morecore()`.

Memory is not the only shared resource that must be synchronized. Libraries that use external state, such as files, must also coordinate access. Similar techniques are used to protect memory with the added caveat that holding mutex locks across actual I/O operations can lock out other threads for unacceptably long times (see “Long Operations” on page 87). If the I/O is too long, one technique to use is to defer the work of doing the I/O to another thread (see “Deferring Work” on page 108).

Thread-unsafe interfaces

As we've seen in Chapter 4, "Using Libraries in Multithreaded Programs," a non-multithreaded library can present a thread-unsafe interface to the library user. There are three different types of interfaces that create problems in a multithreaded program: interfaces that return pointers to global data, interfaces that retain global state between invocations, and interfaces that use call-back routines.

Interfaces that return pointers to global data

Some non-multithreaded library interfaces return a pointer to structure allocated in a internal buffer maintained by the library. The caller of the interface directly manipulates the data in the structure. From the library's point of view, it can only assume that the caller is finished referencing the data when the caller sends new request or explicitly closes the interface. An example of this type of interface is `asctime()` which converts a data structure representing the current time and date (`struct tm`) into a printable string. It is declared as:

```
char*
asctime(const struct tm *tm);
```

`asctime()` returns a pointer to a 26-character string in a statically allocated buffer. When a new call to `asctime()` is issued, the library overwrites the contents of its internal buffer with the new string. This is not a problem in a single-threaded process since the single thread can take care not to issue a new call to `asctime()` until it is done with the string pointed to by the last call. However, in a multithreaded program, there may be multiple, concurrent calls to `asctime()` by different threads. Recomputing the string in the internal buffer in response to a new call will wipe out data that another thread may still be accessing.

One solution would be to use a separate internal buffer for each thread by using thread-specific data. This would seem to have the advantage of maintaining the `asctime()` interface. However, a user would have to be extremely careful if a pointer to a string is given to other threads; the thread that called `asctime()` must not issue another call until the other threads are done with the pointer.

A "cleaner" solution would be to redefine the interface to take a pointer to user-allocated memory in which the string representing the time would be stored. This is the approach Pthreads takes. It defines a new interface, `asctime_r()`, where the "`_r`" suffix indicates that the interface is re-entrant or thread-safe. The routine is defined as follows:

```
char*
asctime_r(const struct tm *tm, char *buf);
```

In this interface, the computed string is stored in the memory pointed to by *buf* which must be at least 26 characters long. For convenience, the value of *buf* is returned. If *tm* is invalid, `asctime_r()` returns NULL. The caller of `asctime_r()` has complete control over the buffer memory. For example, if only one thread ever calls `asctime_r()`, the caller is free to statically allocate the buffer.

Interfaces that retain state between invocations

Some non-multithreaded library interfaces result in a side effect: they mutate some hidden, global state that affects future calls to this interface. When such an interface is called from multiple threads, the concurrent changing of the global state could result in the state becoming garbled and inconsistent, breaking the interface. An example of this is the C library routine `strtok()` which parses a string into lexical token strings delimited by separator characters. It is defined as follows:

```
char *
strtok(char *s, char *sep);
```

`strtok()` is first called with a non-NULL input string, *s*, and a list of token separator characters in the string *sep*. It returns a pointer to a NULL-terminated token, which is inside *s* with a NULL substituted for the separator character. Subsequent calls to `strtok()` are made with *s* equal to NULL. `strtok()` remembers the previous position inside the original string and returns a pointer to the next sequential token. Clearly, multiple threads calling `strtok()` would have to carefully synchronize so that only one string at a time is parsed to completion. Otherwise the shared, hidden state (the end position of the last returned token) would be garbled. Worse still, simultaneous changes to the internal pointer may garble it, causing illegal accesses to memory.

A solution to this problem is again to change the interface so that the state is maintained by the caller and not in a global variable. Such an interface has been defined by POSIX and is called `strtok_r()`:

```
char *
strtok_r(char *s, const char *sep, char **lasts);
```

The new argument, *lasts*, points to a user-provided pointer which is used to save the current location in the original *s*. This lets each thread have its own parse string and next token pointer.

Interfaces that take call-back routines

Libraries whose interfaces allow user-supplied call-back functions provide their own unique difficulties when it comes to multithreading. Perhaps the most common example of this type of library are window system tool kits. Call-backs cause difficulties because they provide a natural way for the user to generate extremely complex and often recursive function call-graphs even in single-threaded programs. This complexity causes great difficulties for the developer attempting to design a locking scheme, since a thorough analysis of the possible state transitions in such a library is extremely difficult. One workable method to ensure that a library with a complex interface is made thread-safe is to design the locking scheme to maintain the following invariant:

> The set of possible function call-graphs involving the library must be the same for a multithreaded application as for a single-threaded application.

In other words, the locking scheme must ensure that any traversals through the library by a multithreaded application could also be done by a single-threaded application, albeit a rather complex one. Perhaps the easiest way of doing this is to implement a token scheme; no thread can enter the library unless it holds the token. Some libraries impose restrictions on which library routines may be called from a user call-back routine. This probably means that the library is maintaining some internal state while the call-back is in progress. If the token were released during the call-back, other threads may call the restricted routines and change the internal state. Alternatively, if the library allows any library function to be called during a call-back, you can safely release the token.

One simple technique of implementing such a token system is a single recursive mutex used to lock all entry points into the library. Note that this locking scheme does nothing to fix problems such as interfaces that export pointers to internal data, but it does ensure that the integrity of internal data structures are maintained. As an example, the following code implements such a token system:

```
typedef struct token {
    pthread_mutex_tc_lock;      /* lock to protect token */
    unsigned int    c_held;     /* recursion counter*/
    unsigned int    c_waiters;  /* number of threads waiting */
    pthread_t       c_tid;      /* id of thread holding token */
    pthread_cond_t  c_cv;       /* CV for acquisition wait */
} token_t;
```

```
void
token_lock(token_t *ptr)
{
    pthread_mutex_lock(&ptr->c_lock);
    if (ptr->c_held) {              /* someone has the token ?*/
        if (pthread_equal(ptr->c_tid, pthread_self())) {/* me? */
            ptr->c_held++;          /* increment recursion count */
            pthread_mutex_unlock(&ptr->c_lock);
            return;
        } else {                    /* someone else holds the token */
            ptr->c_waiters++;
            while (ptr->c_held)     /* wait for release */
                pthread_cond_wait(&ptr->c_cv, &ptr->c_lock);
            ptr->c_waiters--;
        }
    }   /* I've got it! */
    ptr->c_tid = pthread_self();
    ptr->c_held = 1;
    pthread_mutex_unlock(&ptr->c_lock);
}

void
token_unlock(token_t *ptr)
{
    pthread_mutex_lock(&ptr->c_lock);
    ptr->c_held--;
    if (ptr->c_held == 0) {
        /* original locker */
        if (ptr->c_waiters)            /* anyone else want this ? */
            pthread_cond_signal(&ptr->c_cv);
        ptr->c_tid = 0;
    }
    pthread_mutex_unlock(&ptr->c_lock);
}
```

Code Example 17-2 The Token System

Partial thread-safety

As we've seen in Chapter 4, "Using Libraries in Multithreaded Programs," libraries can have different variants of thread-safety. Some variants add library routines for explicit locking; others add routines that supply safe versions of unsafe interfaces. It is also possible to simply ask library callers to restrict when library routines may be used. Object-unsafe interfaces (see "Object-Unsafe Functions" on page 55) restrict a caller to only manipulate a discrete "object" with one thread at a time, though different threads may simultaneously manipulate different objects. Package-unsafe interfaces (see "Package-Unsafe Functions" on page 55) restrict the caller to entering any routine in the entire package or library with only one thread at a time. Thread-unsafe functions may only be called by the initial thread (the thread that called `main()`).

Calling unsafe functions

Libraries can usually call object-unsafe routines by providing the required object synchronization and ensuring that the objects implemented by the called library are not directly passed outside the calling library. Otherwise, external code might use different object synchronization than the calling library, which would allow multiple threads to access the same object simultaneously. The calling library can also declare itself to be object-unsafe and carefully associate objects implemented by the called library with objects it implements only on a one-to-one basis. This directly passes the access restrictions of the underlying library to the external caller.

Calling package-unsafe interfaces from within a library is also possible if the library can guarantee that it is the only code that calls the underlying library. In this case, the calling library can use an internal synchronization variable to regulate access to the package-unsafe library. Remember, all code that uses a package-unsafe library has to enforce single-thread access, and this usually requires a common synchronization variable.

Thread-unsafe functions must only be called from the initial thread, so routines that call thread-unsafe functions must themselves be declared thread-unsafe.

Cancellation-Safety

A major application of threads is to allow an application to keep responding to user input while previously requested actions are still taking place, including the cancellation of previous actions the user is no longer interested in. So it is desirable, in general, to allow threads that call into a library to be cancelled. However, there can be a problem when another thread in the process cancels a thread that is in the middle of a library function (see Chapter 11, "Thread Cancellation"): the cancelled thread may hold internal library synchronization variables and may have left internal library storage in an inconsistent state.

Recall that a thread can enable and disable the processing of cancellation requests and that cancellation requests can be processed in one of two ways, deferred and asynchronous. If the thread's cancellation type is set for deferred processing, a cancellation request will only be processed when the thread reaches a cancellation point (see "Cancellation Points" on page 192). Otherwise, it may happen anytime cancellation is enabled. By default, a thread uses deferred cancellation processing.

Clearly, library routines that don't maintain internal state between invocations and don't use synchronization are trivially safe with respect to cancellation. For other routines, one alternative is to document that the library is not safe with respect to cancellation. Another strategy is to disable the processing of cancellation requests (using `pthread_setcancelstate()`) for the duration of those library routines that need protection. However, this strategy can defeat the whole purpose in making the library safe with respect to cancellation. Cancellation point routines are typically ones that may block, so disabling the processing of cancellation requests may lock out the processing of cancellation requests for long periods of time. For example, even reading data from files can sometimes block for unacceptably long periods if the underlying file data resides on a remote file server that is congested or down. Even so, this may be the only viable strategy when using external libraries that are not cancellation-safe.

Note – Unfortunately, cancellation-safety, as with other exceptional conditions, is usually neglected by library implementors. If the library is not documented as cancellation-safe or is not obviously trivially safe (e.g., `sin()`[1]), then it is best to assume the library or routine is unsafe with respect to cancellation.

Assuming the default deferred cancellation processing policy, a better strategy is to have the library routines that need to be made cancellation-safe install one or more cancellation cleanup handlers (see "Cancellation Cleanup Handlers" on page 194) to make the library state consistent and unlock internal mutexes should the calling thread be cancelled at one of the cancellation points. Remember that library routines that call cancellation point routines are themselves cancellation points and library implementors should document this so that callers of library routines can also take precautions.

Library routines that include long-running computations without cancellation points can also block cancellation for a long period of time. One strategy to avoid this is to setup a cancellation handler in the library code, if required, and then simply insert regular calls to `pthread_testcancel()` in the long-running computation code.

Inserting calls to `pthread_testcancel()` may not be convenient or even possible in the case that the computation is contained in an external library. An alternative strategy is to turn on asynchronous cancellation for the duration of the computation.

Warning – Except in controlled cases where the state of the computation can be completely discarded if a cancellation occurs, it is usually difficult to recover from such unrestricted cancellation. It is roughly similar to recovering from an asynchronous signal that includes

1. Obviously, there are ways of coding `sin()` that would not be safe with respect to cancellation, but let's assume some common sense.

a longjmp() in single-threaded code. So, in general, few routines are safe with respect to asynchronous cancellation. If a routine is not asynchronous cancellation-safe, it is not safe for a thread with asynchronous cancellation enabled to call this routine.

Fork-Safety

Another potential source of failure within a library is due to the use of fork() in an MT application. This type of problem was discussed in "Using fork()" on page 64 and "Strategies for Using fork()" on page 238. To review, it is possible for a thread to be inside a library function that has acquired an internal lock when *another* thread in the process calls fork(). For example, in Code Example 17-3 there are two threads: thread1 and thread2. If thread1 is executing inside malloc() when thread2 executes fork(), thread1 may be holding the internal malloc() mutex, ma_lock (assuming malloc() is implemented as in Code Example 17-1). In this case, ma_lock will also be locked in the child process since it has a snapshot of the parent process's address space. However, only thread2 exists in the child process, so ma_lock will never be released in the child. If the child calls malloc(), it will block forever. Since the application has no knowledge of the locks internal to the library, it cannot protect itself against this possibility of deadlocking inside the library in the child of a fork().

```
void
thread1()
{
    ...
    ptr = malloc(20);
    ...
}

void
thread2()
{
    ...
    if (fork()) {
        /* parent */
        ...
    } else {
        /* child */
        ...
        ptr2 = malloc(100);
        ...
    }
    ...
}
```

Code Example 17-3 malloc() *and Fork-Safety*

In many cases, an application that calls fork() will call exec() soon after the return from fork() in the child. If there is little need to call a library function between fork() and exec(), one solution to this problem is to document the library as being fork-unsafe. Multithreaded applications using this library may never call into the library from the child of fork() before a call to exec().

There are certainly cases where a library must be called in the child between the return from fork() and a call to exec(), or where the child never calls exec(), in which cases libraries must be made safe with respect to fork(). The general mechanism used to make a library fork-safe is to establish a fork handler using pthread_atfork() (see "Fork Handlers" on page 240).

Note – Unfortunately, fork-safety, as with cancellation-safety, is usually neglected by library implementors. If the library is not documented as fork-safe or is not obviously trivially safe, it is best to assume the library or routine is unsafe with respect to fork().

Establishing Fork Handlers

If malloc() is required to be fork-safe (i.e., calls to malloc() as described in Code Example 17-3 are allowed), then the implementor can establish fork handlers as shown in Code Example 17-4. The handlers indicate actions to be performed in both the parent and child processes at the time of the fork(): in the parent before the fork() actually takes place and in both the parent and the child after the fork(). Typically, a library implementor will use fork handlers to acquire all of the library's internal locks before the fork() to ensure that the library's memory state is consistent and then release lock in both the parent and the child after the fork(). The fork handlers can also be used to clean up other state. For example, closing a file that should not be shared with a child process.

```
void
prepare()
{
    pthread_mutex_lock(&ma_lock);
}

void
parent()
{
    pthread_mutex_unlock(&ma_lock);
}
```

```
void
child()
{
    pthread_mutex_unlock(&ma_lock);
}

void
malloc_init()
{
    pthread_atfork(prepare, parent, child);
}
```

Code Example 17-4 Fork-Safe Library Exporting `malloc()`

A fork-safe library should have an initialization module that sets up the fork handlers (e.g., `malloc_init()` in Code Example 17-4) and is executed at program start-up or library loading[2], before the first usage of the library, or when the first library routine is called (e.g., using `pthread_once()`).

Applications

In many cases it is necessary to substantially alter the structure of a single-threaded application in order to make effective use of threads. However, there are some types of applications that may be at least partially multithreaded relatively easily[3]. These are typically of two general types: applications or utilities that fork multiple copies of themselves to achieve parallelism, and event-loop-style programs, as typified by graphical user interfaces. In both cases, careful design and execution are still required for successful multithreading, but in general these types of conversions are more successful than others, since the original designer needed to consider many of the same issues confronting the threads developer.

Multithreading a Graphical User Interface

As noted previously, a principle benefit of multithreading an existing graphical user interface is increased responsiveness to user requests. One of the more frustrating aspects of both programming and using applications with graphical user interfaces (GUIs) is dealing with operations that take an indeterminate amount of time. You are never sure when to give hints to the user (such as changing the cursor to an hourglass) that an long-running operation is underway, since the operation may also complete in milliseconds and the "waiting" symbols

2. For example, using the `.init` section for a library in Solaris 2 or UNIX International compliant systems.

3. Note that some applications may be effectively multithreaded transparently, such as a visualization application that uses a math package. The math package may suddenly use threads to increase performance tenfold; the application may not even need to be relinked.

cause needless flashing and repainting. On the other hand, if the operation does indeed take a long time the user may decide the button wasn't pressed after all and repeat the operation unless there are proper graphical hints. Using threads in such an application provides at a minimum a more responsive interface and perhaps one that permits more work to occur by allowing the user to enqueue multiple long-running requests. Since by far the most predominant framework for programming GUIs on UNIX systems is the X window system, the section will focus on supporting concurrency using X.

For a variety of reasons, there is very little support available for writing truly multithreaded applications using a high-level X tool kit. At present, no high level commercial tool kit is available that is thread-safe, although the recent release of thread-safe Xt gives one some hope that Motif will soon be given the same treatment. The lack of a thread-safe library forces the programmer converting an existing application into one of two courses: either wrap each call to the tool kit in a reentrant monitor, or confine all calls to the X tool kit to a single thread. The latter approach, while somewhat more confining for the programmer, is much simpler for porting a small number of applications and tends to introduce far fewer bugs, so we will cover it here in detail. If you want to explore issues involved in making a tool kit thread-safe, see [Smaalders 92] or study the Xt library that is part of X11R6 for a practical example.

If you are familiar with X-based programming you are well acquainted with the event loop model. In a nutshell, the application generally blocks in a `poll()` or `select()` system call, waiting for either X events or other data to arrive on a set of file descriptors, or for the blocking call to time-out and thus trigger the execution of a time-based operation such as blinking a cursor or animating an image. When a user event occurs (such as a mouse button push) the application receives X events from the server which causes the `poll()` or `select()` call to return. The tool kit code then processes the incoming events and determines which programmer-specified call-back functions (if any) are to be invoked as a result of the event. Those functions are then called and after they complete, the applications returns to the blocking system call. If the call-back functions take a long time to return, the GUI appears "frozen" in that it fails to respond to user input while X events are not being processed in the event loop. Various tool kits have implemented work-arounds to make it easier for the application writer to continue to process events and hence animate the interface, but these tend to require frequent calls to routines to check the event queue, a technique that is awkward at best and doesn't handle the problem of the call-back function blocking in another system call.

To see how you might use threads to prevent an existing GUI application from blocking, let's examine the (real) case of a meeting scheduling tool. In this tool, the user specifies a date, several attendees, and the machines on which their calendar databases may be found. The application then contacts each machine in turn, querying the resident database with a remote procedure call that retrieves the attendee's schedule for the day in question. As the schedule information is retrieved, each attendee's appointments and conflicts are displayed to the user in a graphical form. Once all the data has been retrieved the user can pick a time for the meeting that presents the fewest conflicts.

Soon after the release of this tool, users began to complain about its poor performance. Investigation soon revealed that the tool was blocking in the RPC calls when trying to connect to machines that were temporarily down. This would lead annoyed users to start pressing all the available buttons. After some specified number of seconds, the tool would time-out and report failure and continue processing the remainder of the list of attendees, whose machines might also be down and only then start reacting to all the earlier frenzied button pushing. It soon became clear to the developers that serializing the RPC calls and not processing user input immediately were the root cause of the problem. The developers examined the logic of the routine that was executed to retrieve and display the schedule data:

```
struct record {
    struct scheddata *sched;
    char *user;
    char *machine;
};

struct record *
get_records(char **users, char **machines, int count)
{
    int i;
    struct record *records;

    records = (struct record *) malloc(sizeof(*records) * count);
    for (i = 0; i  <count; i++) {
        records[i].sched = NULL;
        records[i].user = users[i];
        records[i].machine = machines[i];
        if (do_rpc_call(records + i) < 0) {
            display_rpc_failure(records + i);
        } else {
            display_schedule(records[i]);
        }
    }
    return(records);
}
```

Code Example 17-5 Meeting Scheduling Tool Logic

It was fairly clear to the developers that by placing each do_rpc_call() in a separate thread, they could perform all the RPC calls in parallel and wait at worst for one RPC time-out to occur regardless of the number of attendees. But since the tool kit routines called in display_schedule() were MT-unsafe, the developers knew they couldn't update the schedule display from the RPC thread; the thread running the GUI had to do the update to prevent all sorts of data corruption problems in the tool kit. However, the GUI thread had to be blocked on a poll() or select() call to handle user input, so it wasn't immediately obvious how to wake up the GUI thread when each RPC thread completed its tasks. After some thought the developers came up with the following solution: a UNIX pipe. The main thread creates a pipe and adds the output file descriptor to the list on which it waits for input. As each thread completes, it writes its index and exit status into the pipe, where it is retrieved by the call-back routine prior to the display update. The code for get_records() and helper routines ends up looking like this:

```
extern int pipe_descriptors[2];
struct record {
    struct scheddata *sched;
    char *user;
    char *machine;
};

void *
rpc_thread(struct record *arg)
{
    int data[2];

    data[0] = (int) arg;
    data[1] = do_rpc_call(arg);
    write(pipe_descriptors[1], data, sizeof(data));
    return (NULL);
}
```

```
struct record *
get_records(char **users, char **machines, int count)
{
    int i;
    pthread_t t;
    struct record * records;

    records = (struct record *) malloc(sizeof(*records) * count);
    for (i = 0; i < count; i++) {
        records[i].sched = NULL;
        records[i].user = users[i];
        records[i].machine = machines[i];
        pthread_create(&t, NULL,
            (void *(*)(void *))rpc_thread, (void *) (records + i));
    }
    return (records);
}

void
pipe_callback_routine(void)
{
    int data[2];

    read(pipe_descriptors[0], data, sizeof(data));
    if (data[1] < 0)
        display_rpc_failure((struct record *) data[0]);
    else
        display_schedule(data[0]);
}
```

Code Example 17-6 Meeting Scheduling Tool Logic

There are several additional issues with this type of conversion:

1. Once the user interface no longer blocks, the GUI often needs additional work. In this example, there didn't appear to be much need to schedule multiple meetings at the same time, so GUI changes could be limited to graying out (marking as busy and disabling) those controls and text fields that were not currently usable. In other types of applications, however, more significant changes might need to be made.
2. One of the key features most often missing on GUIs is a *STOP* key. For example, a user of the meeting scheduling tool might realize the machine name of one of the attendees was incorrect and press the *STOP* key so that he or she may correct the error. At this point the application needs to be able to cancel the threads, recover any memory they have allocated, and prepare for new input. In the example, the thread is likely to be executing various

RPC calls, so if the RPC library is not safe with respect to cancellation, this is likely to result in significant memory leaks. The easiest solution is to let them continue, but place their data structures, pipe descriptors, etc., on a cleanup list and then create a "janitor" thread to wait for the last one to complete before it does the cleanup.

3. The GUI thread needs to be very careful about modifying or freeing any data referenced by the threads until the threads have exited. In this example, the records data structure cannot be freed until the threads that were passed pointers to it have exited.
4. The protocols for freeing memory allocated by the RPC threads to transfer data back to the GUI thread need to be very clearly defined. In this example, the `sched` data structures (presumably allocated inside the `do_rpc_call()`) need to be cleaned up by the GI thread.

While the above enumeration of possible problems is not intended to dissuade you from multithreading a GUI application, the focus should remain on simplicity. Most experienced GUI programmers are well aware of the various interesting problems caused by the relatively asynchronous nature of X; adding threads to the mix does nothing to simplify those problems.

Summary

The issues faced by library programmers who wish to provide libraries for multithreaded programs are a bit different from those faced by multithreaded application programmers. Libraries typically cannot control when they are called. The obvious requirement for library writers is to prevent data races when accessing internal data structures, but there are some additional potential trouble spots library programmers must keep in mind:

- Access to external data
- Unsafe interfaces
- Call-back routines
- Cancellation-safety
- Fork-safety

Multithreaded application programmers must still cope with a world in which many externally provided libraries are not safe with respect to multiple threads. Applications that use non-thread-safe window libraries are frequently encountered. We've seen that careful programming can allow a multithreaded application to use unsafe window libraries.

Threads Development Environment 18

This final chapter describes the development environment for multithreaded applications, with examples from Solaris 2. The topics covered include: compiling and linking multithreaded programs, debugging, and performance tuning.

Compiling Multithreaded Programs

Multithreaded programs should set the `_POSIX_C_SOURCE` macro to specify that the program is a POSIX `1003.1c` compliant program. There are several levels of POSIX compliance which reflect the changes and additions to the standard, so `_POSIX_C_SOURCE` must be set to a value greater than `199506L`[1] to specify POSIX `1003.1c` compliance. In Solaris 2, the Pthreads library is `libpthread`, so an example compilation command would be:

```
cc -o file -D_POSIX_C_SOURCE=199506L file.c -lpthread
```

Defining `_POSIX_C_SOURCE` in this way turns on the thread-safe definitions of interfaces in (e.g., in `errno.h` and `stdio.h`)[2]. For example, the Solaris `stdio.h` file contains the following lines:

```
#if defined(_REENTRANT) || (_POSIX_C_SOURCE - 0 >= 199506L)
extern voidclearerr(FILE *);
extern int feof(FILE *);
extern int ferror(FILE *);
extern int getc(FILE *);
extern int getchar(void);
extern int putc(int, FILE *);
extern int putchar(int);
extern int fileno(FILE *);
#define getc_unlocked(p) \
    (--(p)->_cnt < 0 ?__filbuf(p) : (int)*(p)->_ptr++)
```

1. 1995 is the year and June (06) is the month that the POSIX 1003.1c threads standard was ratified. Future standards that are will have increasing numbers.

2. Similarly, users of the UNIX International interfaces must define `_REENTRANT`. See "Compiling and Linking UNIX International Programs" on page 382.

```
12 #define putc_unlocked(x, p) \
13     (--(p)->_cnt < 0 ?__flsbuf((unsigned char) (x), (p)) \
14                      : (int)(*(p)->_ptr++ = (x)))
15 #define getchar_unlocked()    getc_unlocked(stdin)
16 #define putchar_unlocked(x)   putc_unlocked((x), stdout)
17 #else /* !(defined(_REENTRANT) || (_POSIX_C_SOURCE - 0 >= 199506L))
*/
18 #define getc(p) \
19     (--(p)->_cnt < 0 ? __filbuf(p) :(int)*(p)->_ptr++)
20 #define putc(x, p) \
21     (--(p)->_cnt < 0 ? __flsbuf((unsigned char) (x), (p)) \
22                      : (int)(*(p)->_ptr++ = (x)))
23 #define getchar()  getc(stdin)
24 #define putchar(x) putc((x), stdout)
25 #wndif /* !(defined(_REENTRANT) || (_POSIX_C_SOURCE - 0 >=
199506L)) */
```

The thread-safe definition for `getc()` is a function declaration not a macro. The `getc()` function uses a lock to ensure safe reading from the file pointer. However, if `_POSIX_C_SOURCE` is not properly defined, the thread-unsafe version of `getc()` shown on line 18 is obtained. The proper definition of `_POSIX_C_SOURCE` also enables the definition of `getc_unlocked()` (see "Thread-Unsafe Functions" on page 54).

Other POSIX Libraries

Applications that use other POSIX functions such as the realtime extensions may have to link with additional libraries. For example, in Solaris 2, users of semaphores or other POSIX realtime extension functions would add `-lposix4` to the compilation line.

Header Files

The main header files programmers need to be concerned with for a multithreaded program are `errno.h`, `thread.h`, and `pthread.h`[3].

errno.h

As we've seen in "System Calls" on page 47, Pthreads gives each thread a copy of variable `errno` which is used to return the error code from many system calls. This is a bit tricky to do in C as `errno` is declared as a global variable. To get

3. `lock_lint` users should also include `<note.h>` and `<assert.h>` (if `lock_lint` assertions are used). See "Static Data Race Analysis" below for a description of `lock_lint`.

around this problem, the ANSI C and POSIX standards insist that C sources that rely on errno should include errno.h at the beginning of the file. In many implementations, this file will contain something like:

```
#define errno (*__errno())
extern int *__errno();
```

The function __errno() returns a pointer to an integer variable, located in per-thread memory. This would make all references to errno become references to a per-thread integer variable instead of a global variable.

Consider what happens when a multithreaded program has to link, dynamically or statically, with a thread-unsafe library (see "Thread-Unsafe Functions" on page 54). Typically, such a library is compiled with a reference to a fixed errno variable (i.e., it was not compiled using the above macro). In Solaris, the __errno() function returns a pointer to a common, fixed errno variable for the initial thread (i.e., the thread that initially called main()) which will also be shared with any thread-unsafe libraries. This allows thread-unsafe functions to be called from the main thread in a multithreaded program.

Programmers also want to generate single-threaded applications that have no need of the __errno() function. For this reason, the Solaris versions of errno.h include the following:

```
#if defined(_REENTRANT)) || (_POSIX_C_SOURCE - 0 >= 199506L)
extern int *__errno();
#define errno (*(__errno()))
#else
extern int errno;
#endif /* defined(_REENTRANT) || (_POSIX_C_SOURCE - 0 >= 199506L) */
```

A lot of existing code has files that do not include errno.h, but instead define errno as follows:

```
extern int errno;
```

Such references to errno have to be hunted down in old code that is being multithreaded.

pthread.h and semaphore.h

All programs using the POSIX threads interface must include the file pthread.h. This file declares all the function prototypes and type definitions in this interface. The POSIX P1003.1b semaphore interface is available via the semaphore.h file.

Static Data Race Analysis

The correctness of multithreaded programs requires a discipline of programming such as structured locking techniques explained in Chapter 6, "Synchronization Strategies," in order to avoid data races. Detecting violations of the multithreaded programming discipline can become difficult for large and complex systems. A simple example of such an error is the failure to acquire a protecting lock for a shared data variable. Bugs caused by such violations in the system are intermittent by nature in that only a particular sequence of thread execution will cause incorrect behavior. This make such bugs hard to detect during development. Even when the bug is detected (usually by a crash) it is difficult to determine the original cause of the error.

Static data race analysis can help detect potential data races before the program is run. In some sense it is similar to compiler type-checking and programs like `lint`. It has proved useful in detecting many bugs in multithreaded programs, especially complex ones like the Solaris kernel and device drivers.

`lock_lint`

A static data race analyzer program called `lock_lint` is available on Solaris. It is illustrative of static data race analysis in general. This tool detects[4] many instances of the following types of errors:

- Data races: e.g., missing locks for global data structures
- Inconsistent data locking
- Missing lock release
- Certain types of deadlock
- Incorrect use of locks with condition variables

`lock_lint` can operate in both interactive and non-interactive mode. In the interactive mode, you can ask for specific information about program locking; in the non-interactive mode, it behaves like `lint`.

Let's look first at a very simple, noninteractive use of `lock_lint`.

4. The features described here may not all be supported by the version of `lock_lint` available to readers currently. The original version of `lock_lint` was described in [Sterling 93].

```
 1 pthread_mutex_t lock;
 2 int global_var;

 3 func()
 4 {
 5     ...
 6     pthread_mutex_lock(&lock);
 7     global_var++;
 8     if (global_var > 10) {
 9         return;
10     pthread_mutex_unlock(&lock);
11     ...
12 }
```

Line 9 contains a bug where the function returns control without releasing the lock. This would lead to a deadlock if the function is called again or if the lock is requested again in some other parts of the program. Running `lock_lint` on this piece of code would produce an error message.

Once the program has been made clean with respect to `lock_lint`, the operation of running `lock_lint` can be made part of the regular process of building the product, as a quality assurance check and to trap errors that might creep in later.

`Lock_lint` annotations

When using the `lint` program checker you can insert annotations (`lint` comments) into the code to help `lint` in its analysis of the program. Similarly, you may need to annotate a program for `lock_lint`. The purpose of the annotation is primarily to help `lock_lint` understand the program better so it can do certain checking it would not be able to do otherwise, or to keep `lock_lint` quiet about intentional violations of the multithreaded programming discipline. These annotations are of two types: assertions and notes. Assertions establish invariants and notes impart information that helps `lock_lint` detect more types of errors. Code Example 18-1 shows an example.

```
 1 #include <pthread.h>
 2 #include <note.h>
 3 #include <assert.h>

 4 int sum = 0;
 5 pthread_mutex_t pmutex = PTHREAD_MUTEX_INITIALIZER;
 6 NOTE(MUTEX_PROTECTS_DATA(pmutex, sum))

 7 int
 8 main()
 9 {
10     pthread_t t1, t2;
11
12     /* Create threads to increment "sum" */
13     NOTE(COMPETING_THREADS_NOW);
14     pthread_create(&t1, NULL,
15         (void *(*)(void *)) t_increment, NULL);
16     pthread_create(&t2, NULL,
17         (void *(*)(void *)) t_increment, NULL);
18     pthread_join(t1, NULL);
19     pthread_join(t2, NULL);
20     /* print the answer */
21     NOTE(NO_COMPETING_THREADS_NOW);
22     printf("answer is %d\n", sum);
23     return (0);
24 }

25 void
26 t_increment()
27 {
28     pthread_mutex_lock(&pmutex);
29     incr();
30     pthread_mutex_unlock(&pmutex);
31 }

32 void
33 incr()
34 {
35     assert(MUTEX_HELD((pthread_mutex_t *)&pmutex));
36     sum += 1;
37 }
```

Code Example 18-1 `lock_lint` *Example*

Line 6 in Code Example 18-1 shows a `NOTE` to `lock_lint` that indicates that the global variable `sum` is protected by the lock `pmutex`, as shown in lines 28 and 30. However, at line 21 all threads but the initial thread are dead and it is no longer necessary to acquire the mutex before reading product. The NOTE at line 21 tells lock_lint that no other threads are active and prevents an error report from lock_lint at line 22 for not acquiring pmutex before accessing sum.

The assert() at line 35 causes lock_lint to check whether it believes pmutex is held. Assertions may also be checked when the program is run if it was compiled without NDEBUG defined. Table 18-1 lists some of the assertions that lock_lint supports[5].

Table 18-1 lock_lint *Assertions*

Assertion	**lock_lint Verification**
NO_LOCKS_HELD	No locks are held at this point. Useful before a thread makes a blocking call or exits.
NO_COMPETING_THREADS	There are no other threads that compete for variable access. You must use NOTE(NO_COMPETING_THREADS_NOW) somewhere earlier in the flow of control for lock_lint to verify this assertion.
MUTEX_HELD(lock_expr)	The mutex is held. Useful at function entry point if the function relies on the specified mutex being held when accessing global data.

The other type of annotation that lock_lint supports, is called a NOTE. A NOTE is a macro that contains a command as an argument, as shown in line 6 of the example. The NOTE macro is null when lock_lint is not running. Some of the more interesting uses of NOTEs are:

- Marking data which is read-only or readable without holding locks
- Establishing a locking order (i.e., a lock hierarchy) to help avoid deadlocks
- Marking functions as legitimately leaving locks or threads in a particular state which normally could result in errors
- Marking variables as being already protected
- Marking dynamic attribute changes such as the transitions in the visibility of shared state or unreachable code

Table 18-2 lists some of the NOTEs that lock_lint supports.

5. lock_lint also supports assertions and NOTEs related to the UNIX International reader/writer locks.

Table 18-2 lock_lint NOTEs

NOTE	Description
MUTEX_PROTECTS_DATA(mutex, data_list)	Associates a mutex lock with a list of variables.
SCHEME_PROTECTS_DATA("scheme", data_list)	Ignores access to the specified data.
READ_ONLY_DATA(data_list)	Marks data as read-only.
DATA_READABLE_WITHOUT_LOCK(data_list)	No locking required to read the data, only to write it.
LOCK_ORDER(list_of_locks)	Establishes an order on the acquisition of locks.
MUTEX_ACQUIRED_AS_SIDE_EFFECT(mutex_expr)	Enclosing function has the side effect of acquiring the mutex.
NO_COMPETING_THREADS_AS_SIDE_EFFECT	Enclosing function has the side effect of leaving the program single-threaded.
COMPETING_THREADS_AS_SIDE_EFFECT	Enclosing function has the side effect of creating threads.
ASSUMING_PROTECTED(data_expr, ...)	Assume data is protected.
COMPETING_THREADS_NOW	There may be concurrently executing threads.
NO_COMPETING_THREADS_NOW	There are no concurrently executing threads.
NOT_REACHED	This point in the code cannot be reached.
NOW_INVISIBLE_TO_OTHER_THREADS(data_expr, ...)	Data cannot be reached by other threads.
NOW_VISIBLE_TO_OTHER_THREADS(data_expr, ...)	Data can now be reached by other threads.

When used properly, static analyzers not only help avoid the difficulty of finding timing dependent data race bugs, but they also serve to help you maintain structured locking discipline. Where your program violates structured discipline the annotation can also serve to document the violations in a way that is understandable by both the analyzer and other programmers.

Debugging

Debuggers for single-threaded programs typically allow a user to set execution break-points, to examine register, stack and global data values, to display a program's call stack, and to step through instructions or language statements as the program executes. Debuggers that handle multiple threads must be a bit more complicated since there is not just one program thread.

The first additional capability is to allow a user to examine the call stacks, local data, and registers of particular threads in the process. It would be possible for debuggers with graphical user interfaces (GUIs) to simply have an individual window with separate display controls for each thread in the process, but there would be too many windows after several threads have been created. Instead, GUI-based debuggers usually allow the user to either focus on one thread or to designate which threads have separate windows. Command-line based debuggers simply provide a command that shifts the focus to a particular thread in the process after which the normal display commands are used that apply to the *current thread*.

When a thread hits a break point, it stops, and the debugger either shifts focus to it or ensures that there is a window to manipulate it. But what happens to the other threads? In some cases it is desirable that all the other threads stop, freezing the process state. This allows you to view the entire process state without dealing with other threads mutating it as you debug. This *synchronous* style of debugging is usually desirable in programs that share a lot of data.

Alternatively, there are situations in which it is desirable for the other threads to continue running. An example would be when debugging an application that has one thread that produces data and one that consumes data. Here it may be nice to let the producer thread run while debugging the consumer (or vice versa).

`debugger` on Solaris 2

Solaris 2 has a multithread aware debugger called `debugger`. It offers both graphical and command-line interfaces that are straightforward extensions of the previous, single-thread versions. `debugger` is restricted to synchronous debugging, i.e., all threads stop when any thread is stopped.

A sample view of the `debugger` is shown in Figure 18-1. The figure shows how `debugger` displays all the threads in the *Process Inspector* window. The program being debugged has 131 threads (bottom right of the *Process Inspector* panel). Clicking on any other thread from the *Process Inspector* panel will display that thread's stack in the *Stack Inspector* window. In the figure, thread 14 in the program has hit a breakpoint (at the entry to the function `_sched_lock()`). This event is highlighted by the arrow on the left of the thread id. The thread that hit the breakpoint automatically becomes the focus of the debugger and its stack is displayed by default in the *Stack Inspector* window. In addition, the *Process Inspector* also displays each thread's state (runnable, running, sleeping, etc.) at the time of the synchronous stop. The *Process Inspector* also shows whether a thread has process or system contention scope (i.e., whether a thread is *bound* or *unbound*; see Chapter 12, "Threads Scheduling"). For example, the "b" next to thread-id 2 means that thread 2 is a bound (system contention scope) thread.

The process/debugger interface

The extension of the process model for multithreading requires a compatible extension to the process/debugger interface. On SVR4 UNIX systems such as Solaris 2, the process/debugger interface is represented by the `/proc` file system. This lets a debugger have direct control over kernel-supported threads. In implementations, such as Solaris 2, that use the "M to N" or two-level scheduling model (see "Thread Scheduling Models" on page 205) `/proc` is insufficient because the threads abstraction seen by the programmer is implemented by a library on top of the kernel-supported threads. Solaris provides a support library, `libthread_db`, which the debugger may link with that allows the debugger to control the programmer visible threads without having to understand the internals of the threads library. Such an interface provides information such as the list and identity of all threads in the process, the state of each thread, the register set for each thread running on an kernel thread, information on signals, etc.

Performance Tuning

Debugging performance problems can be very difficult in multithreaded programming. With parallel execution of multiple threads running on multiprocessor machines, performance bottlenecks are usually not obvious. Even with sophisticated tools, you need to have a systematic approach that focuses on the right issues to find performance problems.

Critical Path Analysis

From the start of a multithreaded program's execution to its end, several different code paths are executed concurrently by the different threads. Each thread's execution consists of some compute activity separated by synchronization events where the thread either waits for an external event, such as an I/O completion, or waits for another thread to synchronize. A program's *critical path* is the path through the program that takes the longest time. Shortening the time taken by the critical path will shorten the time taken by the program (but not always by the same amount, as we'll see). Performance optimization of code that does not lie on the critical path will not improve overall program performance.

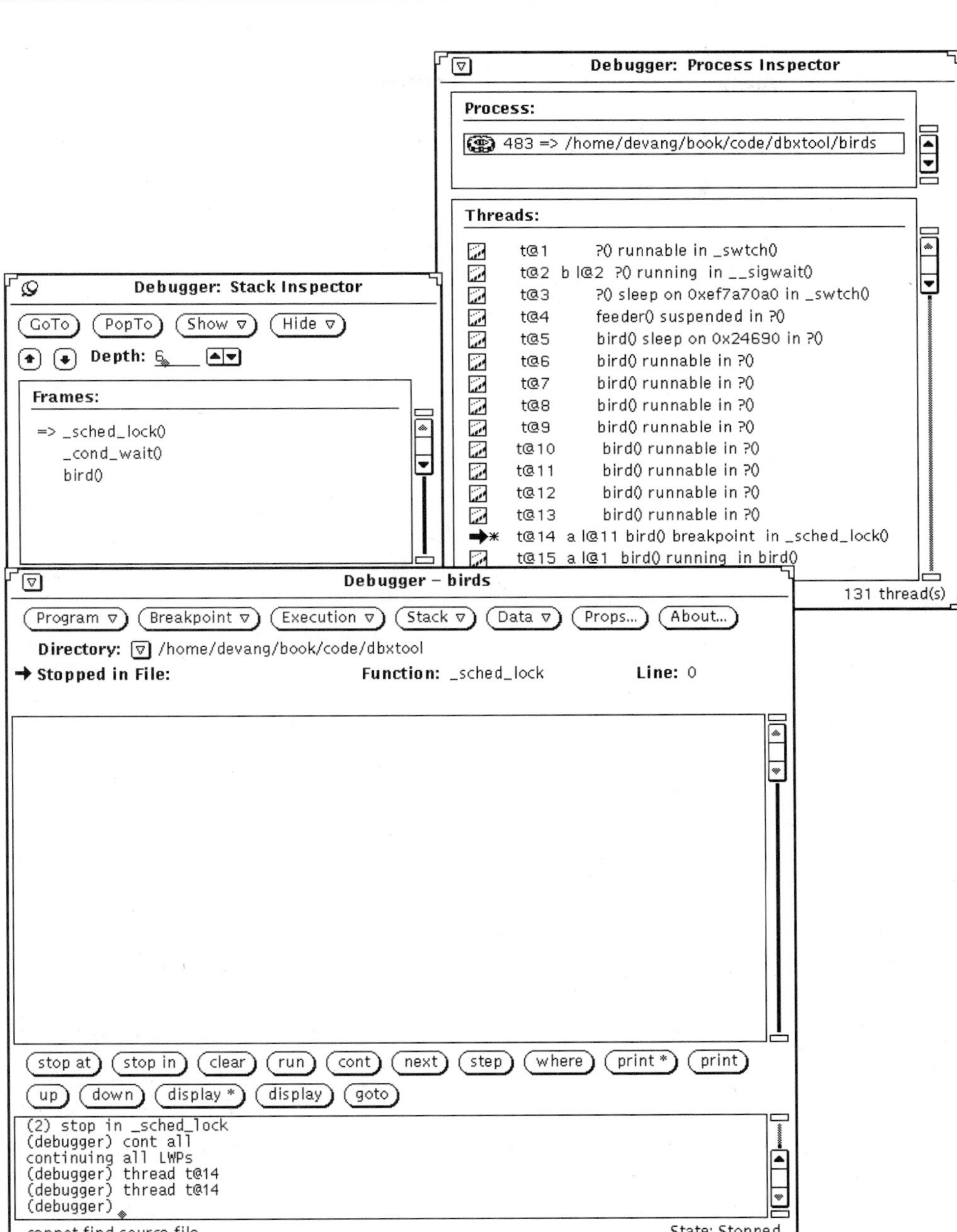

Figure 18-1 Multithreaded `debugger` *on Solaris with Threads Displayed and a Thread's Stack*

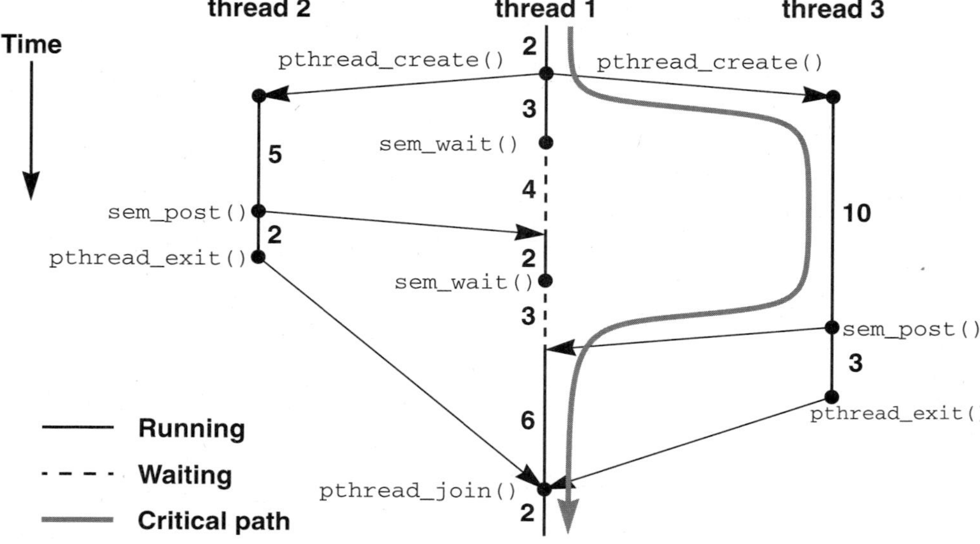

Figure 18-2 Critical Path in a Multithreaded Program

The critical path can, and often does, involve more than one thread. For example, Figure 18-2 shows the critical path in a measured run of a multithreaded program. In the figure, the main thread creates two additional threads. Each synchronization point (denoted by a dot) is a call to one of the routines that synchronize with other threads, such as `pthread_mutex_lock()/unlock()`, `pthread_cond_wait()/signal()`, `sem_wait()/post()`, or `pthread_exit()/join()`. The label on each arc is a weight which is proportional to the time taken by the associated activity. The critical path takes 22 units of time, including one unit each for the two interthread synchronizations along the path.

It is clear from the diagram that improving only the code executed by thread 2 will produce no performance gain. Similarly, improving the code executed by thread 1 that does not lie on the critical path will also not produce performance gain. Instead, suppose we improved the code executed by thread 3 so that it only took five units of time to issue the `sem_post()`. This would produce the event history illustrated in Figure 18-3. This produces a new critical path with a total of 19 units of time. This is not the expected five unit improvement since we have hit a new critical path.

How does one identify the critical path? Some tools, such as IPS-2[6] from the University of Wisconsin [Miller 90] [Yang 88], can do a critical path analysis based on trace data (see "Tracing" below). However, such tools are not widely available.

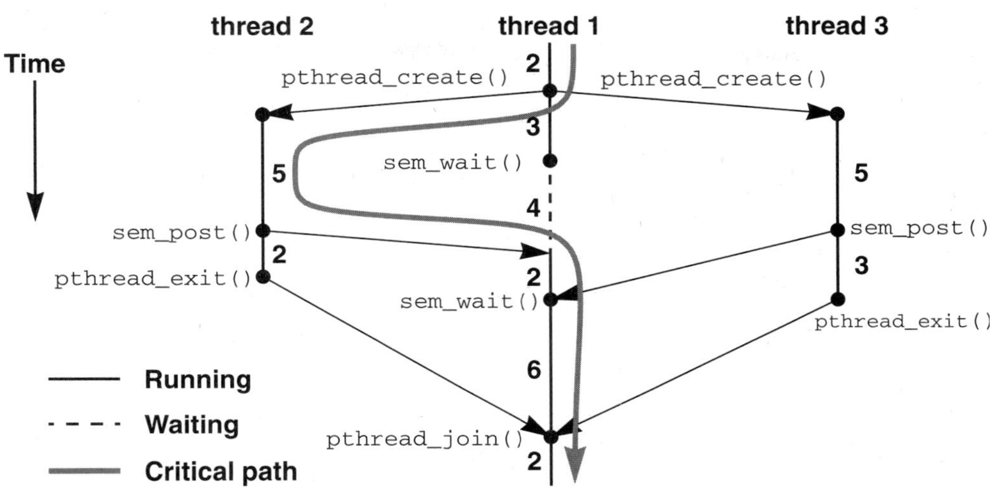

Figure 18-3 Critical Path After Improvement in Thread 3

In many applications that are coded with structured locking (see Chapter 6, "Synchronization Strategies") the critical path is dominated by a sequence of accesses to critical sections. An example of multiple threads accessing a single critical section is illustrated in Figure 18-4. In this situation, you can infer a lot about the critical path by analyzing the program's critical sections.

Critical Section Analysis

As you can see from Figure 18-4, critical sections along the critical path are likely to accumulate a lot of program time in both execution of the critical section itself and in program threads waiting to access the critical section. In general, a good heuristic procedure for finding critical sections that contribute significantly to the critical path is to find the critical sections that accumulate the most execution time and waiting time. There are two main reasons why a program might spend a lot of time accessing a critical section:

1. The code in the critical section is time-consuming.
2. Threads frequently access the critical section.

As we've seen in "Critical Section Concurrency" on page 245, these two reasons are not independent. The smaller the critical section's execution time, the less likely that a thread that wants to enter the critical section will find it locked by another thread. Critical sections that are time-consuming and do not have a lot of

6. IPS-2 is designed for multiprocess applications instead of multithreaded application, but the same principles apply.

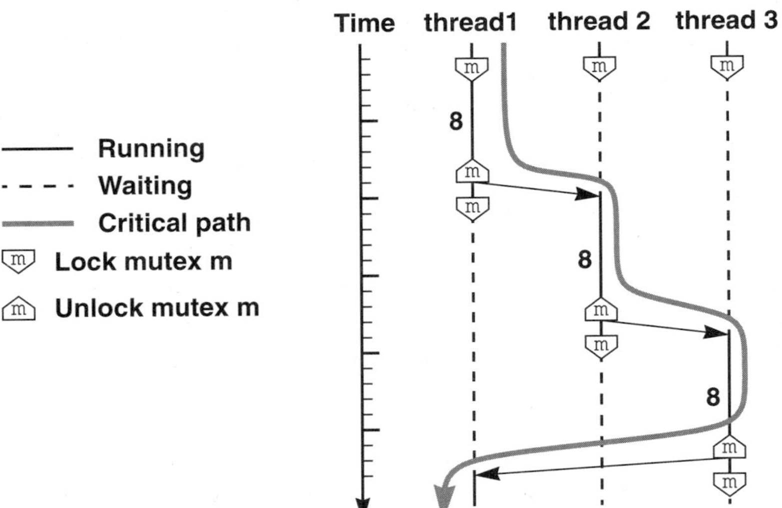

Figure 18-4 Critical Path Through a Single Critical Section

contention can be handled by normal code optimization techniques. You should also attempt to optimize the code in critical sections that have heavy contention, as this will reduce the chances of contention. In the example shown in Figure 18-4, an improvement of one time unit in the eight time unit critical section along the critical path is multiplied by the number of times the critical section is accessed along the critical path. This would improve the performance of the three traversals of the critical section along the critical path shown in the example from 26 times units to 23 time units (assuming a one time unit switching delay).

Alternatively, you can break up a single large critical section into several smaller critical sections. This can improve performance dramatically, especially on a multiprocessor, as it allows threads to overlap execution of a highly contended critical section. Figure 18-5 illustrates how splitting up the eight time unit critical section protected by a single mutex, `m`, in Figure 18-4 into two independent four time unit critical sections protected by two different mutexes, `a` and `b`, can improve performance of three traversals of the critical section from 26 time units to 18 time units. Of course, you must be careful that the overhead of the additional locking does not outweigh any performance gains due to increased parallelism.

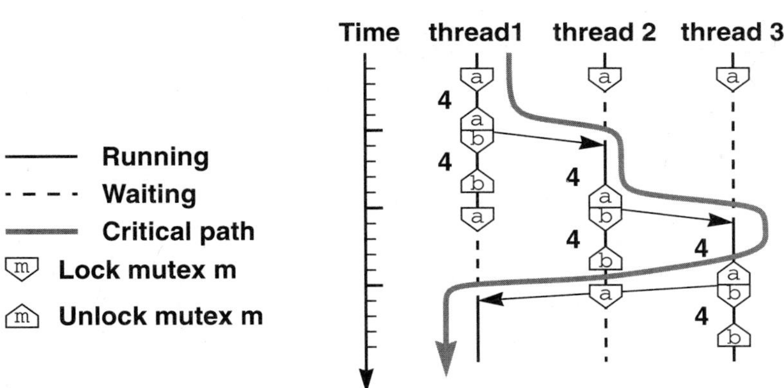

Figure 18-5 Splitting a Critical Section into Two Parts

Profiling

Profiling the execution of a multithread program can also be a straightforward extension of the traditional, profiling technique[7]. Profiling typically informs the user of time spent within functions of a particular program run. This can be used to measure the amount of time spent executing a critical section.

Profiling provides a macro-level view of a program's performance characteristics. It is usually the first step to be taken in determining why a program is performing as it does. Profiling tends to average the measurement of functions across some interval, usually the entire run. This averaging hides the exact distribution of program code, making it hard to understand trends and outliers in the performance of critical sections as the program runs. So profiling is great as a starting point for multithreaded programs, but needs to be supplemented by more sophisticated tools such as tracing, to gain a more refined understanding of performance problems.

Tracing

One of the oldest methods of debugging a program is to insert print statements in a program to trace the history of run-time values of key variables and other state. This technique is often necessary to determine how and why a particular scenario occurred. Unfortunately, print statements have to be inserted manually and once inserted cause noticeable effects on the program[8]. Program tracing tools build on this primitive concept using automation and lightweight techniques. These

7. For example, `prof`(1) and `gprof`(1) on Solaris 2.

8. Most programmers are familiar with the situation in which the program works with the print statements in, but fails when they are removed.

tracing tools also provide a means of carrying out sophisticated performance analysis of the traced program in addition to providing an event history for debugging purposes.

Tracing tools instrument programs by inserting *tracepoints* into the program's code. Each tracepoint is similar to a print statement which might be embedded in a program for debugging purposes. A variety of instrumentation code can be attached to these probes, but typically the output of a probe is a *trace record*. Trace records are usually collected into a trace file when the program is run, as shown in Figure 18-6. Some systems allow you to selectively enable tracepoints to allow some control over the amount of data generated and the overall load that generating the trace file has on the program. The major differences between a print statement and a tracepoint are:

- The implementation of a tracepoint is highly optimized to minimize intrusiveness, both in terms of time to execute and space to store the record.
- A high resolution[9] time stamp recording the time at which the probe was executed is automatically embedded in each trace record. The standard trace record can also include information such as the thread-id or the CPU-id.
- Some tracing tools automatically insert tracepoints at certain points such as procedure entry and exit.
- Some tracing systems instrument the libraries and operating system at interesting points such as context switches, page faults, or buffer flushing.
- The trace record has a standard format which is published to a host of post-processing trace tools used to interpret and analyze the data[10].

Each tracepoint is designed to record the appropriate probe-specific run-time state of the program. In this case, it records the start and finish of `func()`. If the standard trace format contains the thread-id and CPU-id, the trace file will have information on when the function was entered and exited, which thread executed it on which CPU, for each occurrence of the function call. The trace file is then fed into one of many possible trace analysis tools used to analyze the traced execution of the program. Such tools could provide information such as:

- A visual display of events along a timeline
- The number of times a procedure was called
- The average time spent inside a procedure or critical section
- The distribution of the time spent inside a procedure or critical section
- Do two or more threads execute a procedure or critical section simultaneously?

9. The resolution of time stamp is, of course, determined by the underlying hardware. For example, time stamps can have a resolution of one microsecond on a SPARCstation™ 1.

10. A trace format called Trace Normal Form (TNF) is available in Solaris 2.5.

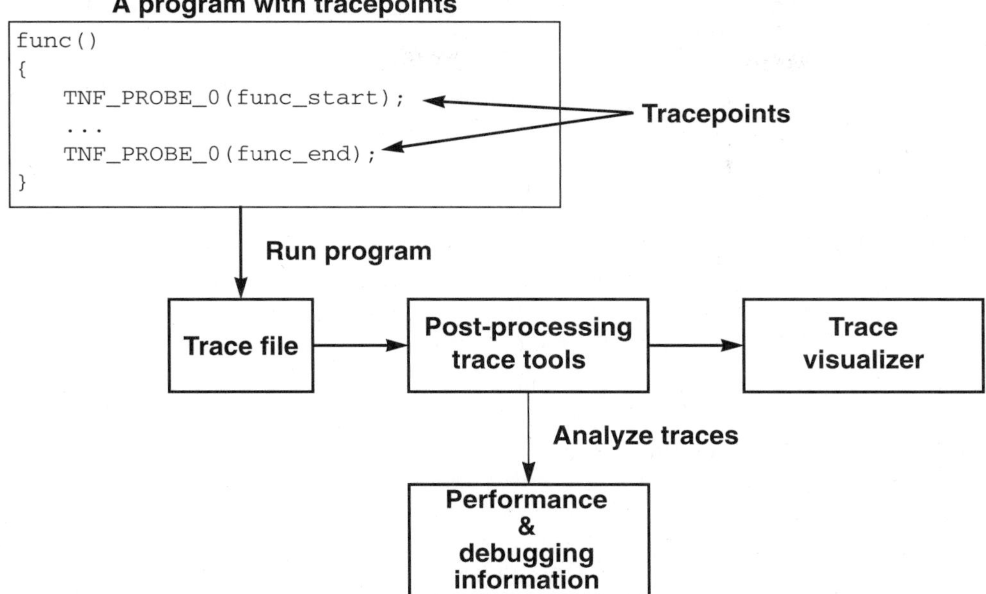

Figure 18-6 Program Tracing for Performance and Debugging Analysis

Tracing systems that have instrumented the libraries and operating systems can also provide information such as:

- When context switches occur and how long each one takes
- The distribution of the waiting time for a mutex or other synchronization variable
- When page faults or other I/O caused threads to wait

Many types of trace analysis look for pairs or patterns of events. For example, the entering and leaving of a function or a critical section form a pair of events that constitute an interval to be measured. In some cases the user must specify the pattern (e.g., display the time to execute a procedure only when called from a particular thread or procedure). Sophisticated tools can use this information to analyze a program run to find the critical path (See [Yang 88] and [Miller 90]).

Tracing for debugging

Debugging multithreaded programs has a dimension, concurrency, that is fundamentally different than single-threaded programs. Many single-threaded programs operate on static data, and running such programs twice over the same data will produce the same results. Many multithreaded programs are sensitive to the *timing* of input and to the relative scheduling of their internal threads. For these reasons, running the program twice on the same input may not give the same results. Traditional methods of debugging (e.g., single-stepping a program) can cause far too much disturbance in the execution history.

In many cases you must understand the exact history of events. Tracing allows you to instrument programs to extract the event histories in order to understand what went wrong in a particular run. It can be used to find both performance and correctness bugs. The fine granularity of the information provided makes tracing technology a microscope into the application and the system.

Tracing can also serve as an aid to understanding bugs in dynamic behavior of a program, such as deadlock, convoys, and livelock[11].

Tracing for performance analysis

Profiling performs a coarse, function-level and one-dimensional analysis of the performance characteristics of a program. It summarizes data over the entire run to get a quick overall picture of performance. It cannot distinguish individual events or determine, for example, the distribution of function running times. Tracing offers a finer grained analysis tool that is not restricted to measuring function run times. The availability of information on system activity such as page faults, context switching and state transitions interspersed with user traces can be invaluable in understanding performance characteristics of a program.

Tracing's flexibility comes at a cost: it can generate huge amounts of data (many megabytes[12]). The amount of data can not only affect the running of the program, but it can make it slow to perform analysis. You must place and/or enable tracepoints carefully to see enough detail without swamping the system.

Visualizing traces

Fortunately, many tracing systems offer a variety of tools to analyze the generated data. One of the most common tools is a trace visualizer. These tools generate a display of events in the trace file along a timeline in manner similar to an oscilloscope or logic analyzer. You have already seen similar displays in other parts of this book, such as Figure 1-2 on page 2. Using such displays, it is possible to visually relate concurrent thread activity. For example, a signalling of a condition variable can be related to the point at which another thread wakes up from waiting on the condition variable. The timeline would tell how long it took for the awakened thread to actually run.

11.See "Deadlock" on page 91, "Convoys" on page 274, and "Livelock" on page 275.

12.TNF also allows you to limit the amount of storage that a trace will occupy.

A trace visualization tool may also offer a variety of graphs that represent analysis of the data, such as the distribution of a critical section's execution time. The visual display of information offers an extremely high bandwidth information channel between humans and tools. It is difficult to see trends in rows upon rows of numbers, whereas when the same numbers are graphed trends, outliers or discontinuities quickly become apparent.

An example of a visual trace analyzer: `tnfview`

`tnfview` is a trace visualization tool being used internally at Sun Microsystems[13]. `tnfview` takes trace files written in a standard format called TNF or Trace Normal Format. Solaris 2 also generates standard trace records for interesting system activities such as thread state transitions, page faults, thread context switching, etc. `tnfview` uses these "known" system trace records, which are interspersed with the application's traces, to produce detailed displays of a program's execution both at the user level and the kernel level.

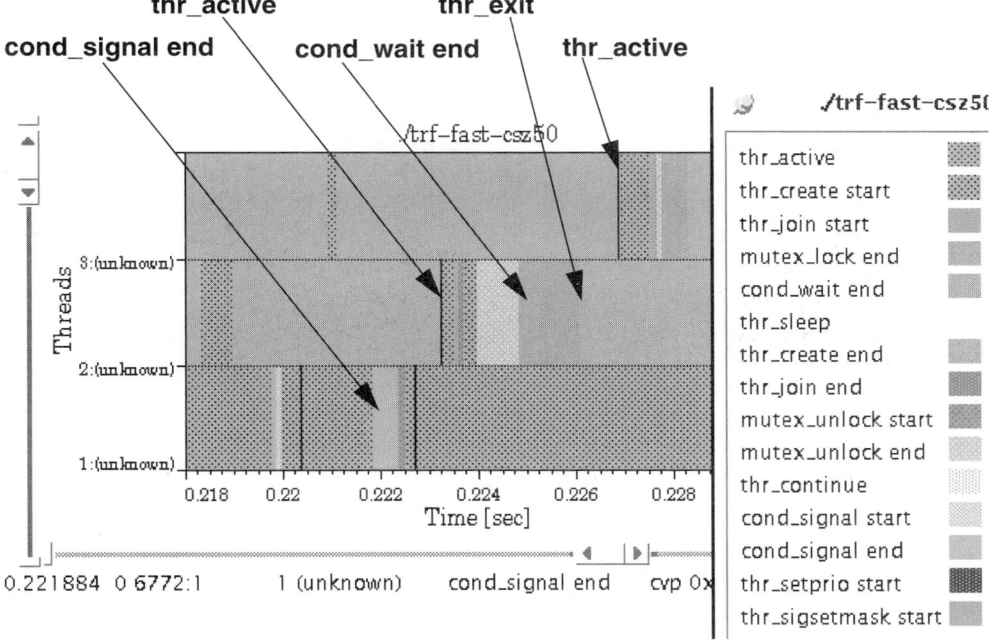

Figure 18-7 The Threads Display in the `tnfview` *Visualizer Tool*

13.Publicly available TNF tools can be found through: http://www.sun.com/smi/ssoftpress/threads/

`tnfview` employs various different types of views to display trace information. Figure 18-7 shows the *Threads* display of a trace file generated by a multithreaded program. The display represents a window in time of the program's execution. The vertical axis is a list of threads and the horizontal axis is the flow of time. Each thread's horizontal band contains the sequence of events that occurred for that thread. Each event is color coded; the legend in the pinned pop-up menu on the right-hand side lists some of the events and the color associated with each event.

There were three threads present during the time interval shown in Figure 18-7. At roughly 0.222 seconds of elapsed time into the program, thread 1 executed a `cond_signal end` event. Thread 2 was sleeping on this condition variable and it first generated a `thr_active` event indicating that it had started running. Then it generated a `cond_wait end` event, indicating that it had finished sleeping in `pthread_cond_wait()`. When thread 2 exits, thread 3, which had been in the runnable state all this time, could run, generating a `thr_active` event.

`tnfview` offers many other processing and display functions. Two of them are worth highlighting here:

- Latency Histogram
  This histogram analyzes pairs of events that represent a particular time interval. The x-axis represents increasing values of the time interval. It is evenly divided into a series of buckets that each represent a range of time intervals. The y-axis represents the number of times a time interval measurement times fell within the corresponding range. The display also contains overall statistics such as the mean and standard deviation.

  The latency histogram can reveal very useful insights into an activity's performance characteristics. It can show the distribution of the activity's performance, the existence of outliers, and can help in deducing the causes for the outliers. The case study below shows some of these advantages.

- Activity Analysis
  `tnfview` allows you to define an *activity* that consists of a collection of tracepoints. For example, suppose an execution path through a program encounters tracepoints T1, T2, and T3, while another encounters T4, T3, and T5. The paths call the same procedures and hence may encounter some of the same tracepoints such as T3. `tnfview` allows you to define two *activities*: one representing the T1, T2, T3 path and the other the T4, T3 and T5 path. You can then count the occurrences of both activities. Comparing the two numbers gives you an idea about how often one code path is taken as compared to the other code path. If one of them is very common, you can focus on optimizing that code path only.

An activity can also be plotted as a latency (y–axis) versus "sequence number of the activity's occurrence" (x–axis). `tnfview` calls this type of display a *real-latency scatter plot*. This plot helps to detect trends such as an increasing latency as the program executes or which subinterval is most expensive. `tnfview` allows you to select activity tracepoints based on pattern matching. This is a powerful means of analyzing paths in which the number of times a tracepoint may be generated is not predictable. The case study below shows how this is useful in performance debugging.

A performance visualization case study

Let's say we are trying to understand the performance characteristics of `mem_alloc()` on Solaris. To carry out performance analysis, we first insert trace probes at the start and end of `mem_alloc()` and run a test that calls the allocator 100 times. This run will generate 200 trace records, two for each allocation. The difference between each pair of trace records represents a time that is the cost of memory allocation.

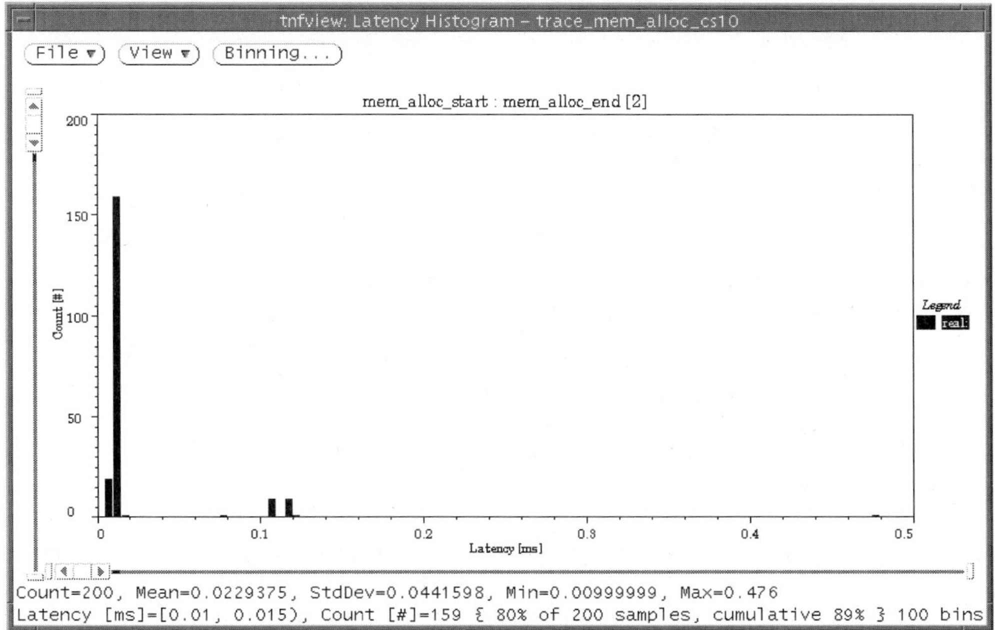

Figure 18-8 `tnfview` *Latency Histogram of Memory Allocation Times*

Plotting a latency histogram for the allocation numbers gives us the histogram shown in Figure 18-8. The bottom of the display shows that mean time for the memory allocation is about 23 microseconds. However, when we inspect the histogram data, we find two different concentrations of latency measurements: one centered around 5-15 microseconds and the other around 105-125 microseconds. We see that about 90% of the allocations take about 5-15 microseconds and the rest take about 105-125 microseconds.

The next step is to determine the pattern of change for these numbers: i.e., when do the fast allocations occur and when do the slow ones occur? Do they occur at random times, or in a more predictable and orderly fashion? To answer this, we go through the activity display of `tnfview`. We define the activity `START:mem_alloc:END` composed of `mem_alloc_start` as the first trace probe and `mem_alloc_end` as the other probe. The activity is then plotted using the real latency scatter plot as shown in Figure 18-9.

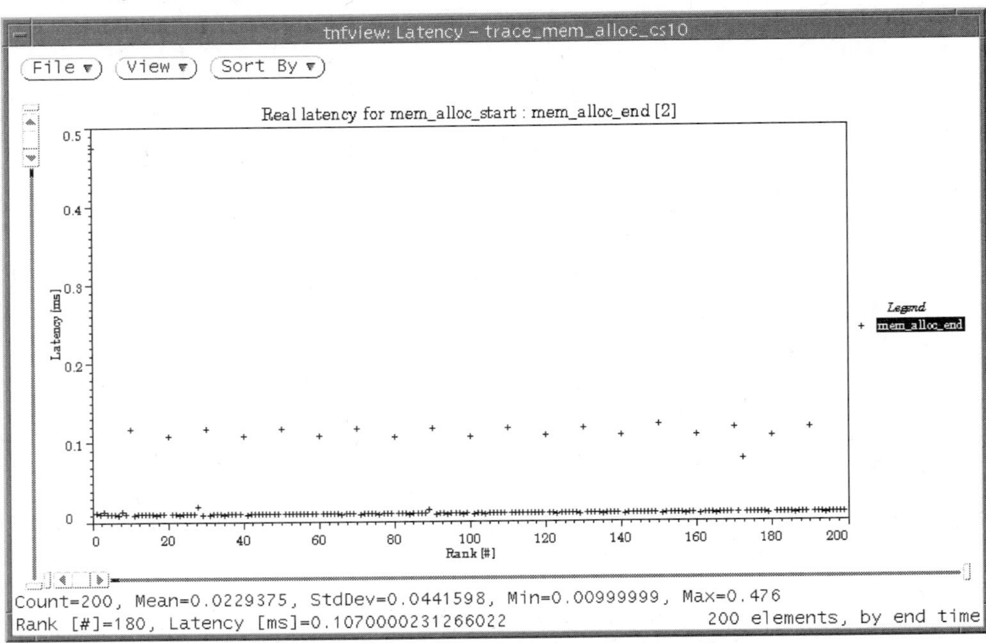

Figure 18-9 `tnfview` *Latency Scatter Plot of Memory Allocation Times*

Figure 18-9 shows the sequence of memory allocations versus the time taken by each allocation. Notice that *all* the fast allocations were punctuated at regular intervals by the slow allocations! In fact, the display shows that every tenth allocation is a slow one. One would guess that this might be some sort of cache effect; the first ten allocations could be hitting the cache and thus would be fast.

The next allocation would allocate real memory and fill the cache, taking a much longer time. Again, the next allocations, until a multiple of the cache size, would all be fast. The slow allocations were the times when the allocator did real allocation and filled the cache. On further checking we found that the size of the memory manager's cache was indeed ten times the amount allocated by the test program. To confirm this guess, the cache size was changed to forty and the experiment run again.

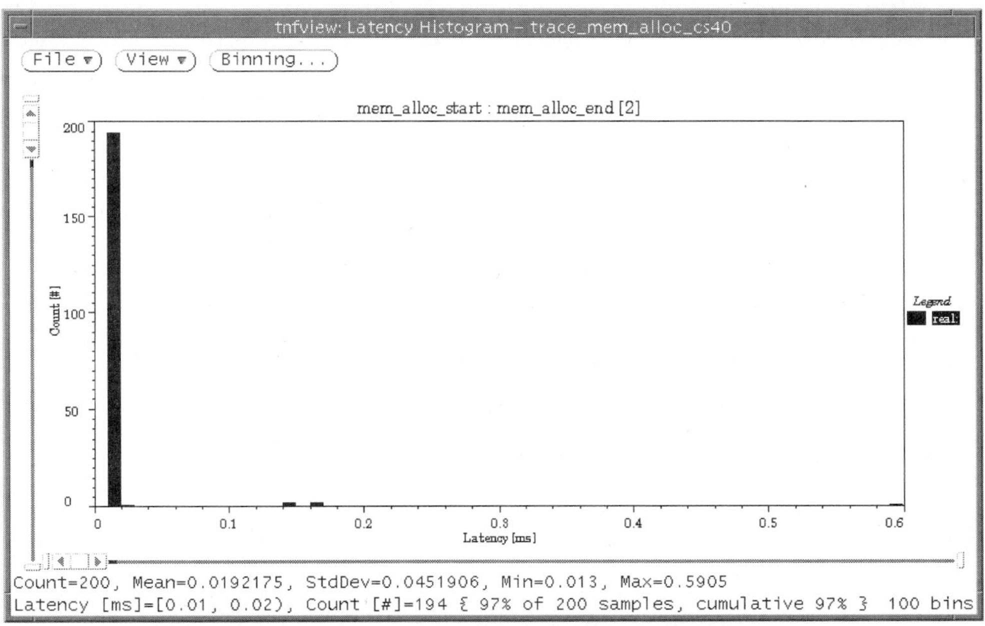

Figure 18-10 `tnfview` *Latency Histogram of Memory Allocation Times After Increasing Cache Size*

The histogram display for the new experiment is shown in Figure 18-10. The display shows that increasing the cache size did, in fact, work to decrease the number of slow memory allocations from 20 to approximately 4. This is confirmed by inspecting the activity display in Figure 18-11. Now the display shows that every 40th memory allocation is slow. Notice also that increasing the size of the cache from 10 to 40 reduced the overall mean from about 23 microseconds to about 19 microseconds, an ~18% improvement.

Using the histogram and activity displays, we were able to understand the performance characteristics of the memory manager: fast allocation depended on caching. Increasing the cache size was a way to reducing the overall cost of the allocator substantially.

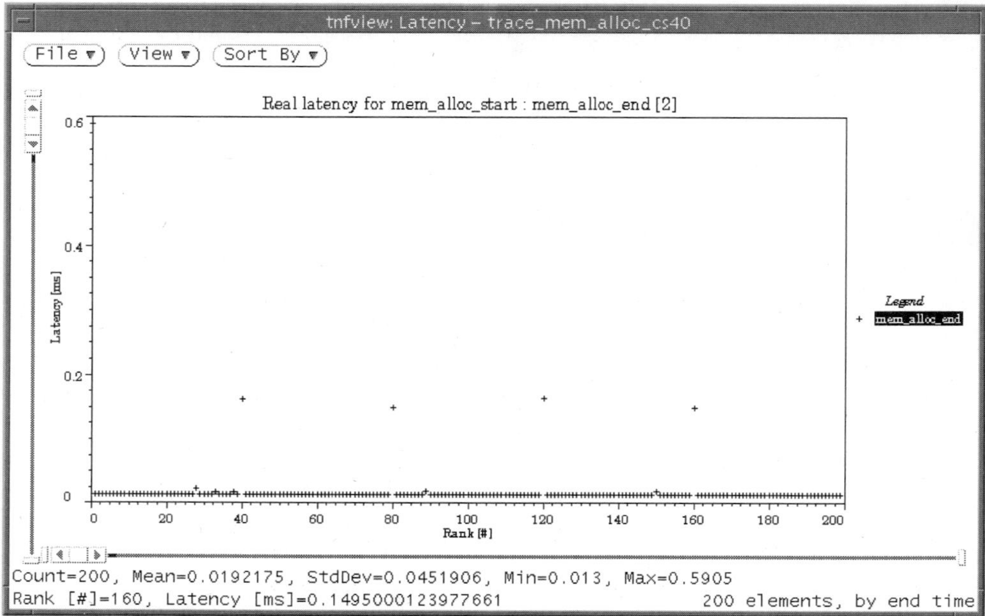

Figure 18-11 `tnfview` *Latency Scatter Plot of Memory Allocation Times After Increasing Cache Size*

Summary

Threads development environments can have a variety of tools to help you debug and tune multithreaded programs. Certain tools, such as debuggers and performance tools that profile and trace, are extensions of equivalent tools for single-threaded programs. Tools such as static data race analyzers are particular to multithreaded programs. The latter can help remove much of the difficulty of finding synchronization bugs by simply avoiding them in the first place. In addition, such tools can help document and maintain a structured locking discipline.

Example Programs

Complete, downloadable examples of multithreaded program are available on the Internet at:

http://www.sun.com/smi/ssoftpress/threads/

You will find several other examples to further demonstrate the techniques of multithreaded programming. Among the runnable programs are:

- `name_cache`
  A complete working version of the hostname cache daemon presented in Chapter 17, "Multithreading Existing Code."
- `mtperf`
  A Motif-based multithreaded perfmeter that uses threads to avoid blocking during RPC calls.
- `ms-mm`, `ms-relax`, `wp-mm`, `wp-sim`, `pl-relax`, and `pl-rend`
  A complete set of six running examples from Chapter 16, "Parallel Computation," including examples of simulation and matrix operations using the pipeline, workpile and master-slave paradigms. The rendering pipeline example produces a viewable 3D picture.

In addition, you will find an up-to-date list of errata in the same location.

UNIX International Threads

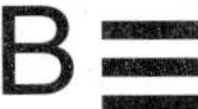

The UNIX International threads standard is an older UNIX threads standard adopted by a multicompany consortium, UNIX International, as part of the System V Interface Definition, Issue 4 [Novell 95]. This chapter describes the UNIX International threads standard (as implemented by Solaris 2) and its differences from POSIX threads.

Overview

The UNIX International (UI) threads standard is several years older than the POSIX Pthreads standard. It was designed with many of the same goals in mind as Pthreads. However, it also has features designed for application run-time environments rather than application programmers themselves. For example, it specifies how threads are mapped to kernel-supported threads.

Figure B-1 shows an overview comparison of the main features of POSIX and UNIX International threads interfaces. The box on the left shows the main features of the UI interface and the box on the right shows the main features of the POSIX interface. The intersection of the two boxes in the center of the figure shows the features that are supported in both interfaces. The main feature that POSIX adds is thread cancellation. The main features that the UI interface adds are daemon threads, read/write locks, thread suspension, concurrency control, and the ability to support both scheduling scopes (process and system) simultaneously within the same process.

The rest of this appendix is split into two sections:

- A description of the POSIX-UI mapping for the features common to both interfaces
- A discussion of the additional interfaces provided by UI, which are not provided by POSIX

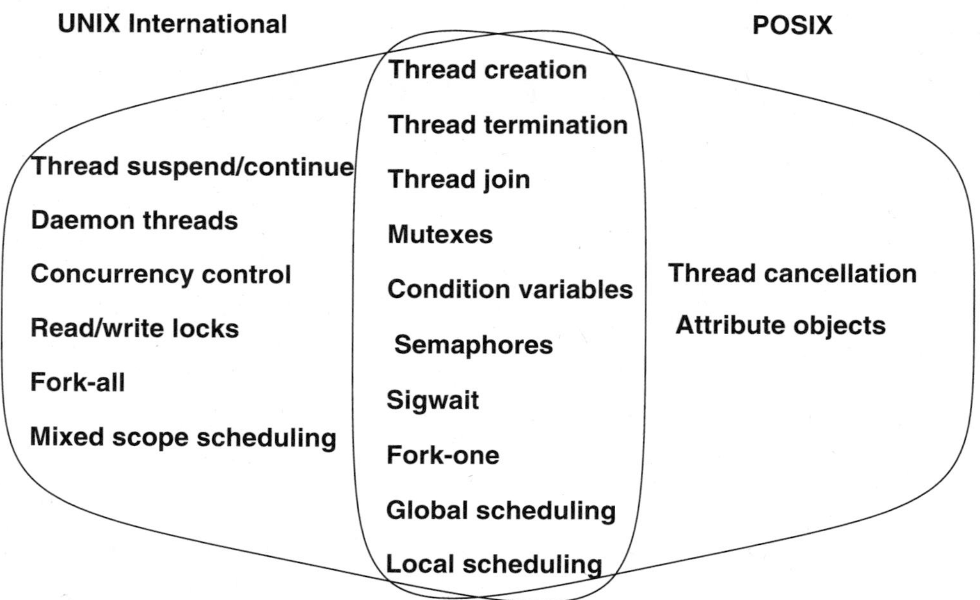

Figure B-1 Comparison of Thread Features in POSIX and UNIX International/Solaris Threads

POSIX/UI Common Features

Table B-1 shows the call-to-call mapping between the POSIX and UI application programming interfaces. Some of the features that are common to both POSIX and UI have minor, subtle differences which are nevertheless important to understand when porting from one interface to the other or using both interfaces within the same program[1].

Table B-1 POSIX-UI Application Programming Interface Comparison

POSIX	UNIX International
`pthread_create()`	`thr_create()`
`pthread_exit()`	`thr_exit()`
`pthread_join()`	`thr_join()`
`pthread_yield()`	`thr_yield()`
`pthread_self()`	`thr_self()`
`pthread_kill()`	`thr_kill()`
`pthread_sigmask()`	`thr_sigsetmask()`

1. In Solaris, on which both interfaces are available in release 2.5, a program can link with both `-lpthread` (POSIX threads) and `-lthread` (UI threads), i.e., use both the POSIX and UI interfaces within the same program.

Table B-1 POSIX-UI Application Programming Interface Comparison (Continued)

POSIX	UNIX International
pthread_setschedparam()	thr_setprio()
pthread_getschedparam()	thr_getprio()
-	thr_setconcurrency()
-	thr_getconcurrency()
-	thr_suspend()
-	thr_continue()
pthread_key_create()	thr_keycreate()
pthread_key_delete()	-
pthread_setspecific()	thr_setspecific()
pthread_getspecific()	thr_getspecific()
pthread_once()	-
pthread_equal()	-
pthread_cancel()	-
pthread_testcancel()	-
pthread_cleanup_push()	-
pthread_cleanup_pop()	-
pthread_setcanceltype()	-
pthread_setcancelstate()	-
pthread_mutex_lock()	mutex_lock()
pthread_mutex_unlock()	mutex_unlock()
pthread_mutex_trylock()	mutex_trylock()
pthread_mutex_init()	mutex_init()
pthread_mutex_destroy()	mutex_destroy()
pthread_cond_wait()	cond_wait()
pthread_cond_timedwait()	cond_timedwait()
pthread_cond_signal()	cond_signal()
pthread_cond_broadcast()	cond_broadcast()
pthread_cond_init()	cond_init()
pthread_cond_destroy()	cond_destroy()
-	rwlock_init()
-	rwlock_destroy()
-	rw_rdlock()
-	rw_wrlock()
-	rw_unlock()
-	rw_tryrdlock()
-	rw_trywrlock()
sem_init() POSIX 1003.1b	sema_init()
sem_destroy() POSIX 1003.1b	sema_destroy()
sem_wait() POSIX 1003.1b	sema_wait()

Table B-1 POSIX-UI Application Programming Interface Comparison (Continued)

POSIX	UNIX International
sem_post() POSIX 1003.1b	sema_post()
sem_trywait() POSIX 1003.1b	sema_trywait()
sem_getvalue() POSIX 1003.1b	-
pthread_mutex_setprioceiling()	-
pthread_mutex_getprioceiling()	-
pthread_mutexattr_init()	-
pthread_mutexattr_destroy()	-
pthread_mutexattr_setpshared()	*type* argument in mutex_init()
pthread_mutexattr_getpshared()	-
pthread_mutexattr_setprioceiling()	-
pthread_mutexattr_getprioceiling()	-
pthread_mutexattr_setprotocol()	-
pthread_mutexattr_getprotocol()	-
pthread_condattr_init()	-
pthread_condattr_destroy()	-
pthread_condattr_getpshared()	-
pthread_condattr_setpshared()	*type* argument in cond_init()
pthread_attr_init()	-
pthread_attr_destroy()	-
pthread_attr_getscope()	-
pthread_attr_setscope()	THR_BOUND flag in thr_create()
pthread_attr_getstacksize()	-
pthread_attr_setstacksize()	*stack_size* argument in thr_create()
pthread_attr_getstackaddr()	-
pthread_attr_setstackaddr()	*stack_addr* argument in thr_create()
pthread_attr_getdetachstate()	-
pthread_attr_setdetachstate()	THR_DETACHED flag in thr_create()
pthread_attr_getschedparam()	-
pthread_attr_setschedparam()	-
pthread_attr_getinheritsched()	-
pthread_attr_setinheritsched()	-
pthread_attr_getschedpolicy()	-
pthread_attr_setschedpolicy()	-

Process creation

There are potentially two different models of process creation for multithreaded programs: *fork-one* and *fork-all*. In the fork-one model only the thread requesting the fork is cloned in the child, whereas in the fork-all model, all threads in the parent are duplicated in the child process after the fork. POSIX supports only the fork-one model, but UI supports both models. The primitive that supports the fork-one model is `fork1()` in the UI interface, while `fork()` is used in POSIX. In UI, `fork()` supports the fork-all model of process creation. Note that the same name, `fork()`, means different things in the two standards. Table B-2 summarizes this issue.

Table B-2 Process Creation in the POSIX and UI Interfaces

Fork Model	POSIX Procedure	UI Procedure
Fork-one	`fork()`	`fork1()`
Fork-all	Not available	`fork()`

Scheduling: contention scopes

In UI, the equivalent of a thread in the POSIX *system contention scope* is the *bound thread* (created using the `THR_BOUND` flag to `thr_create()`). The UI equivalent of a thread in the POSIX *process contention scope* is called an *unbound thread*. POSIX does not require that a conforming platform support the ability to mix both scopes in the same process[2]. However, the UI model does require support for mixed scope scheduling, i.e., both *bound* and *unbound* threads can co-exist within the same process. This mapping is summarized in Table B-3.

Table B-3 Scheduling Scopes in the POSIX and UI Interfaces

POSIX	UNIX International
System scheduling scope	*Bound* threads. Created via the `THR_BOUND` flag passed to `thr_create()`.
Process scheduling scope	*Unbound* threads. These are the default threads.

Signals

The syntax of the call to `sigwait()` is different in the two interfaces. In POSIX, it takes two arguments, and in UI, just one. The additional argument in POSIX is a pointer to a location where the number of the signal received by `sigwait()` is returned. In UI, this signal number is the `sigwait()` return value:

```
int
sigwait(sigset_t *set);
```

Code Example B-1 UNIX International Syntax for `sigwait()`

2. The implementation of POSIX on Solaris supports such a mixed scope multithreaded program.

Semaphores

The POSIX semaphore interface is obtained via the POSIX 1003.1b realtime extension library. In Solaris 2, this library is obtained by linking with `-lposix4`[3]. See "Semaphores" on page 177.

Synchronization

All of the UI synchronization primitives other than read/write locks, such as mutexes, condition variables and semaphores, have interfaces that are almost identical to those in POSIX. The main difference is in the area of initialization of the synchronization objects. The UI synchronization variable initialization routines take three common arguments: a pointer to the synchronization variable to be initialized, a type argument that is used to specify one of several alternative behaviors, and an additional argument that passes data that depends on the specified behavior type. For example, the interface to initialize a mutex is:

```
int
mutex_init(mutex_t *mp, int type, void *arg);
```

Code Example B-2 UNIX International Syntax for `mutex_init()`

If the *`type`* argument is `USYNC_THREAD`, the synchronization variable can be used only by threads within the same process. This is equivalent to a POSIX synchronization variable initialized as `PTHREAD_PROCESS_PRIVATE`. If the *`type`* argument is `USYNC_PROCESS`, the synchronization variable can be used to synchronize threads in different processes (see "Interprocess Synchronization" on page 173). In the UI interface, synchronization variables that are statically allocated from zeroed memory behave as if they were initialized with `USYNC_THREAD`. In POSIX, the equivalent function is achieved by static initialization to a constant such as `PTHREAD_MUTEX_INITIALIZER` for mutexes. Table B-4 shows the mapping between the POSIX and UI interfaces for synchronization object behavior.

Table B-4 Synchronization Variable Initialization in the POSIX and UI Interfaces

POSIX	UNIX International
PTHREAD_PROCESS_SHARED	USYNC_PROCESS
PTHREAD_PROCESS_PRIVATE	USYNC_THREAD
PTHREAD_MUTEX_INITIALIZER PTHREAD_COND_INITIALIZER	Static allocation from zeroed memory

3. In the past, the realtime extensions were called P1003.4.

Additional Features of the UI Interface

The UNIX International application programming interface contains several features not included in Pthreads.

Read/Write Locks

There are many situations where data is read more often than it is modified. In these cases it is desirable to allow the reads to proceed concurrently while locking all but one thread when the data is to be modified. A multiple-reader, single-writer lock (or read/write lock, for short) does exactly this. A read/write lock is acquired either for reading or writing and then it is released. Like mutexes, read/write locks must bracket; that is, the thread that acquires the read or write lock must be the one that releases it.

Initializing and destroying read/write locks

Read/write locks are explicitly initialized by:

```
int
rwlock_init(rwlock_t *rwp, int type, void *arg);
```

If *type* is `USYNC_THREAD` or `USYNC_PROCESS`, *arg* is ignored. `rwlock_init()` can return an error if the implementation detects that an active read/write lock is being reinitialized. Read/write locks can also be initialized to the default type (with `USYNC_THREAD`) by allocating them in zeroed memory.

Read/write locks are destroyed by:

```
int
rwlock_destroy(rwlock_t *rwp);
```

The read/write lock that is destroyed must either have been explicitly initialized by `rwlock_init()` or it must have been implicitly initialized by use. This should be done whenever the memory associated with the mutex is freed or reused. `rwlock_destroy()` can return an error if the implementation detects that the read/write lock is being waited for.

Locking and unlocking read/write locks

```
int
rw_rdlock(rwlock_t *rwp);

int
rw_wrlock(rwlock_t *rwp);

int
rw_unlock(rwlock_t *rwp);
```

`rw_rdlock()` acquires a read lock. It blocks if a writer holds the lock. Otherwise the thread is allowed to proceed. `rw_wrlock()` acquires a write lock. It blocks if any readers or any writer hold the lock. `rw_unlock()` unlocks the read/write lock whether it was held for reading or writing. The thread that holds the lock must also release it. When a write lock is released, either one of the threads waiting for a write lock is awakened or some or all of the threads waiting for a read lock are awakened. However, implementations attempt to ensure, perhaps on a statistical basis, that writers are not locked out by continuous reading. These functions can return errors if the implementation detects that the read/write lock is improperly initialized.

When it's convenient to avoid blocking, use:

```
int
rw_tryrdlock(rwlock_t *rwp);

int
rw_trywrlock(rwlock_t *rwp);
```

These functions return an error if read or write lock could not be obtained without waiting.

Using read/write locks

The following example is of a bank account. While the program could allow multiple threads to have concurrent read-only access to the account balance, only a single writer is allowed. Note that the `get_balance()` function needs the lock to ensure that the addition of the checking and saving balances occurs atomically:

```
rwlock_t account_lock;
float checking_balance = 100.0;
float saving_balance = 100.0;
...
rwlock_init(&account_lock, 0, NULL);
...
```

```
float
get_balance() {
    float bal;

    rw_rdlock(&account_lock);
    bal = checking_balance + saving_balance;
    rw_unlock(&account_lock);
    return(bal);
}

void
transfer_checking_to_savings(float amount) {
    rw_wrlock(&account_lock);
    checking_balance = checking_balance - amount;
    savings_balance = savings_balance + amount;
    rw_unlock(&account_lock);
}
```

Code Example 18-2 Read/Write: Bank Account

Although read/write locks can provide more potential concurrency than mutexes, they should be used carefully since the read/write lock/unlock primitives are inherently more expensive. The decision of using a read/write lock versus a mutex lock should be made after experimenting with mutexes and determining that addition concurrency is required. For example, let's say that the frequency of read operations in an application is much greater than write operations. This might seem ideally suited for using read/write locks. However, if the number of threads that may concurrently enter the read critical section is low, and the critical section itself is small, it may be better to use mutexes to protect both the read and write critical sections. The increased concurrency in the read critical section may not be enough to offset the increased cost of locking/unlocking the read/write lock, making mutexes a faster and thus more appropriate alternative.

UI Resource Limits

The resource limits are set on the entire process, in other words, the sum of the resource use of all the threads in the process. For example, the CPU usage resource limit represents a limit on the sum of CPU usage by all the threads in the process. When a soft resource limit is exceeded, the offending thread is sent the appropriate signal. The sum of the resource usage for all threads in the process is available through `getrusage()`.

Suspend and Continue

The UI interface allows threads to be suspended and then continue operation where they left off. This is done by calling:

```
int
thr_suspend(thread_t target);

int
thr_continue(thread_t target);
```

This allows run-time environments to control thread execution. For example, an execution environment that contains a garbage collector can suspend certain threads while reclaiming memory.

The UI interfaces also allow a thread to be created in a suspended state. This allows the creating thread to set thread attributes that cannot be set using the simple `thr_create()` interface before the thread is started. This take the place of the Pthreads thread attributes interfaces. The following example shows how to create threads at different priority levels by creating a suspended thread, changing its priority and then letting it continue:

```
#include <thread.h>

main()
{
    thread_t t;
    extern void *t_func(void *);

    NOTE(COMPETING_THREADS_NOW);
    (void) thr_create(NULL, 0, t_func, NULL, THR_SUSPENDED, &t);
    (void) thr_setprio(t, 1);
    (void) thr_continue(t);
}
```

Code Example 18-3 Changing the Priority of a New Thread

The suspend/continue primitives have to be used carefully. For example, a thread can be stopped while holding a lock. If the continue operation requires the same lock for some reason, the program will deadlock. A programmer could run into such a deadlock unwittingly if the lock is within a library not owned by the application, as shown in the following example.

```
 1 #include <thread.h>
 2 #include <stdio.h>

 3 main()
 4 {
 5     int err;
 6     thread_t tid;
 7     extern void *T1(void *);

 8     (void) thr_create(NULL, 0, T1, NULL, 0, &tid)
 9     (void) thr_suspend(tid);
10     printf(“Suspended thread\n”);
11     /* ... do stuff ...*/
12     (void) thr_continue(tid);
13     printf(“Continued thread\n”);
14     (void) thr_join(tid, NULL, NULL);
15 }

16 void *
17 T1(void *foo)
18 {
19     printf(“Thread T1 running\n”);
20     /* ...do stuff ... */
21     printf(“Thread T1 done\n”);
22 }
```

Code Example 18-4 Example of Deadlock When Using `thr_suspend()/thr_continue()`

If thread `T1()` is inside the `printf()` (at line 19) and is holding the internal `stdio` mutex when it is suspended, then `main()` will deadlock when calls it `printf()` at line 10.

Daemon Threads

Sometimes a library or run-time environment must create threads intended to perform support roles during the life of a process, for example, a thread that does garbage collection, waits to receive RPC invocations, or flush I/O buffers. Such threads are analogs of system processes (daemons) which, in current systems, field service requests or do monitoring. The UNIX International interface allows an application to mark daemon threads by adding the `THR_DAEMON` flag when `thr_create()` is called. Thereafter, the application will exit when all non-daemon threads have exited.

Daemon threads are a convenience for implementors of run-time environments. In a strict Pthreads environment, which does not have daemon threads, applications that use run-time environment that creates hidden support threads must explicitly call `exit()` or call a library function that kills the support threads. Otherwise the process will be kept alive by the support threads.

Forking Multithreaded Processes

As mentioned in "POSIX/UI Common Features," the UI interface supports two models of forking multithreaded processes: the fork-one model and the fork-all model, provided by the calls `fork1()` and `fork()` respectively.

The fork-one model

Forking a process has two basic uses: to duplicate the entire process or to create a new process before calling `exec()`. For the latter purpose, the fork-one model is much more efficient than the fork-all model because only one thread is duplicated. However, there are several potential problems with the fork-one model of creating a process. These problems and the strategies that could be used in dealing with the problems were described "Process Creation and Destruction" on page 64 and in "Strategies for Using fork()" on page 238.

The fork-all model

Using the UI `fork()`, with the fork-all model of process creation, can also cause surprises:

- A general problem is shared state between the parent and child. For example, when a process forks, the duplicated file descriptors share the same underlying file description, which includes the file offset. If a thread was reading a file sequentially at the time that another thread called `fork()`, there would be two threads reading the file (one in the parent and the equivalent thread in the child) after the `fork()` completes. Since the file offset is shared, the threads would interleave requests with each getting different parts of the file.
- Another form of shared state that causes problems are process-shared locks in memory mapped with `MAP_SHARED`. If a thread was holding such a lock at the time another thread called `fork()`, then two threads would consider themselves the owner of the same lock after the `fork()` completes (the actual owning thread in the parent and the equivalent thread in the child). Note that this is desirable behavior for process-local synchronization variables, but is undesirable for process-shared synchronization variables.

- Threads that were in the process of executing interruptible system calls at the time `fork()` was called may see those system calls return with an error indicated and with `errno` set to `EINTR`, in both parent and child, if the implementation could not duplicate the system call state transparently or restart them.

Some strategies for coping with these situations are:

1. The thread calling `fork()` must coordinate with other threads operating on state that would be shared between parent and child so that the shared state is not being operated on at the time `fork()` is called.
2. Any shared locks that may be operated on by other threads at the time `fork()` is called are acquired by the thread calling `fork()` before the call to `fork()` and is released in the parent after the `fork()` completes.

Calling `vfork()` can also have problems in addition to the ones outlined for `fork1()` in that the thread in the child process must be careful not to change memory before it calls `exec()`. Remember that `vfork()` gives the parent's address space to the child. The parent gets its address space back after the child calls `exec()` or exits. It is important that the child not change the state of the parent. Locks acquired by the child and not released before the call to `exec()` will appear locked when the parent runs again.

Avoiding Data Races

Table B-5 shows the list of UNIX International functions (in addition to those listed in Table 3-1 on page 32) that ensure that the order of memory operations is preserved with respect to the execution of the function. The list contains all the synchronization primitives and several other system routines. Using the blocking, thread creation, or thread destruction characteristics of these functions, the programmer must ensure that it is not possible for a thread to write to a particular location at the same time that another thread is either reading or writing it. It is not an error to have unrestricted access to a location by more than one thread if they all are only reading from it.

Table B-5 Functions That Synchronize Memory with Respect to Threads

`fork1()`	`cond_wait()`	`rw_unlock()`
`fork()`	`cond_timedwait()`	`rw_wrlock()`
`thr_create()`	`cond_signal()`	`sema_post()`
`thr_join()`	`cond_broadcast()`	`sema_wait()`
`mutex_lock()`	`rw_rdlock()`	`sema_trywait()`
`mutex_trylock()`	`rw_tryrdlock()`	`waitid()`
`mutex_unlock()`	`rw_trywrlock()`	

Thread Scheduling

From a thread programmer's point of view, the UI thread scheduling model has many similarities to Pthreads. However, the UI model specifies much more detail on how threads and the underlying operating system interact.

UNIX International threads specifies an "M to N" or two-level thread scheduling model (see "Thread Scheduling Models" on page 205). In UI, threads are scheduled by a user threads package and are not known to the operating system. The threads package, in turn, uses kernel-supported threads called lightweight processes (LWPs) to schedule the user's threads, as shown in Figure B-2. An LWP is just like a thread in the sense that it represents an independent thread of control. This allows user level threads to be relatively lightweight in terms of system resources and have high performance while only using the heavier weight LWPs when real concurrency is required.

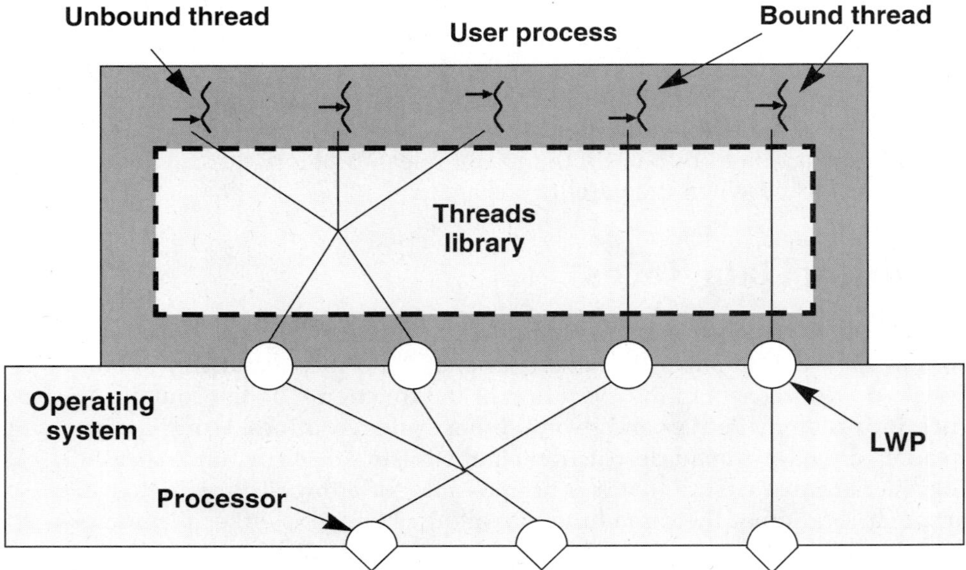

Figure B-2 UNIX International Thread Scheduling Model

In the UI interface, *unbound threads* are implemented by having the user-level threads library multiplex thread execution over a pool of LWPs. In other words, threads are scheduled over LWPs just as LWPs are scheduled over processors by the kernel. In a sense, LWPs can be looked at as virtual processors, and the threads library as a microcosm of an multiprocessing operating system. An *unbound thread* can be scheduled by the threads library to run on any LWP in the pool. It is not directly associated with any particular LWP, hence the term *unbound*. This is similar to the POSIX process contention scope for scheduling. The priority of unbound threads controls access to the underlying LWPs; it does not affect the priority of these LWPs as they compete for service with the LWPs of other processes in the system. By default these LWPs are scheduled using the normal time-sharing scheduling class (see "Scheduling Classes" below). However, this can be changed by starting the process under a different scheduling class.

Threads can also be *bound* to an LWP. Such threads will be forced to run on only one LWP for their entire lifetime. A *bound thread* is similar to a POSIX thread with system contention scope. A bound thread may be created by passing the `THR_BOUND` flag to `thr_create()`. Bound threads can directly set the priority or scheduling class of their underlying LWPs by using `priocntl()`. In essence, a *bound thread* is just like an LWP, except that it can interoperate and synchronize with other threads in the process, both *bound* and *unbound*, via the normal threads primitives such as `mutex_lock()`.

Typically, a *bound* thread is more expensive than the *unbound* thread in terms of memory and kernel resources and in creation and synchronization time. It is useful only in cases where a thread must have special scheduling behavior with respect to other system activities. For example, a thread that moves a cursor in response to mouse movement might be a bound thread that changes the scheduling of its LWP to belong to the fixed-priority scheduling class (also known as the realtime scheduling class). This would let the thread respond to mouse interrupt with high priority.

The UI interface also allows bound threads to be bound to a particular processor, as illustrated by the thread on the right-hand side of Figure B-2.

Concurrency Level

The threads library automatically adjusts the number of LWPs in the pool used to run unbound threads. Its objectives are:

- To prevent the program from being blocked by lack of unblocked LWPs. For example, if there are more runnable unbound threads than LWPs and all the active threads block in the kernel in indefinite waits (such as reading from a terminal), the process cannot progress until a waiting thread returns.
- To make efficient use of LWPs. For example, if the library creates one LWP for each thread, many LWPs will usually be idle and the operating system will be overloaded by the resource requirements of the unused LWPs.

The library usually ensures that there are enough LWPs in its pool for a program to proceed. If all of the LWPs in the process are blocked in indefinite waits (for example, blocked reading from a terminal or network), the operating system sends the new signal, `SIGWAITING`, to the process. This signal is handled by the threads library. If the process contains a thread that is waiting to run, a new LWP is created and the appropriate waiting thread is assigned to it for execution.

A contraction in the number of active threads can cause an excessive number of LWPs in the pool of a process. If LWPs in the pool remain idle for a certain period (that is, there are more LWPs than active threads) the threads library destroys the unneeded ones. The library "ages" LWPs. They are deleted if they are unused for a "long" time[4].

The `SIGWAITING` mechanism does not ensure that an additional LWP is created when one or more threads are compute bound and another thread becomes runnable. A compute-bound thread can prevent multiple runnable threads from being started because of a shortage of LWPs. The UI interface gives threads programmers direct control of the number of LWPs in the pool used to schedule unbound threads (see "Concurrency and Process Contention Scope Threads" on page 223) to prevent this situation. There are two mechanisms to control concurrency. First the programmer can directly set and get it using:

```
int
thr_setconcurrency(int new_level);

int
thr_getconcurrency(void);
```

`thr_setconcurrency()` sets the concurrency level to *`new_level`*. The new concurrency level is a hint; the library is free to increase or decrease it if it detects that the new level is inadequate or unjustified. If *`new_level`* is zero, the library uses its default mechanisms to set the concurrency level.

The second mechanism to adjust the concurrency level is to add the `THR_NEW_LWP` flag when a thread is created via `thr_create()`. This increments the concurrency level by one when the thread is created. In effect the application is telling the threads library that it expects the new thread to be continually using an LWP.

4. Currently five minutes in Solaris.

Thread Priorities

A thread's priority, set via `thr_setprio()` governs a thread's access to LWPs. This is mainly useful for *unbound* threads, since a *bound* thread does not need to compete for an LWP (it already has one dedicated to it). This priority is useful only in influencing the order in which a *bound* thread wakes up from a wait for a synchronization object which it shares with other *bound/unbound* threads in the process. For example, a mutex of type `USYNC_THREAD` (the default) may be shared by both a *bound* and *unbound* thread in the same process. If both threads are blocked on this mutex and the *bound* thread has a higher thread priority than the *unbound* thread, it will acquire the lock before the *unbound* thread, and vice versa.

A bound thread's useful priority is the priority of the LWP bound to the thread. The exact semantics of the LWP's priorities depend on the specific scheduling class that the *bound* thread's LWP lies in, e.g., in Solaris 2, a *bound* thread's LWP, by default, is in the time-sharing (TS) class. However, it can be put into the realtime (RT) class. In the RT class, its priority is always higher than all LWPs in the TS class. In the TS class, its priority changes dynamically according to typical UNIX TS scheduling to ensure fair scheduling with other *bound* threads' LWPs in the TS class. In the TS class, it is not guaranteed that the LWP with the higher priority will always run in preference to one with a smaller priority. The *bound* thread may change its LWP's scheduling class and priority by calling `priocntl()` on itself. The two main scheduling classes in which a *bound* thread's LWP might lie are described below.

Scheduling Classes

The UNIX International interfaces allow an implementation to support one or more *scheduling classes* which perform a function similar to the POSIX scheduling policies (see "Thread Scheduling Policies" on page 212). There are two defined classes: time-sharing and realtime. By default, the scheduling class on an LWP is inherited from the LWP that creates it. Subsequently created LWPs will inherit the scheduling class and priority of the initial LWP unless they change the LWP's parameters via `priocntl()`. This is especially important for bound threads, as their useful priority is the priority of their underlying LWP.

Time-sharing class

The time-sharing or TS scheduling class attempts to ensure fair access to CPU resources for LWPs in this class. The CPU resource allocation is proportionate to the LWPs' demand or consumption of CPU resources. While a time-shared LWP has a priority that can be changed by calling priocntl() this is only used as a scheduling bias; the operating system adjusts the LWPs dynamic priority to ensure overall system responsiveness. Typically, LWPs that run for a short amount of time before blocking are given increased priority while LWPs that are compute bound are penalized.

Realtime class

When an LWP is assigned to the realtime or RT scheduling class, its priority directly reflects the priority set by the user and is not varied by the operating system. For this reason, it is sometimes called the fixed-priority scheduling class. Typically, the system is configured so that LWPs in the realtime scheduling class always have higher priority than any time-sharing LWP. Bound threads attached to a realtime LWP are scheduled on a realtime basis with respect to all other LWPs in the system.

Compiling and Linking UNIX International Programs

Multithreaded programs that use the UNIX International interfaces must define the _REENTRANT macro to enable thread-safe definitions of interfaces (e.g., in errno.h and stdio.h). UNIX International threads library is in libthread, so an example compilation command would be:

```
cc -o file -_REENTRANT file.c -lthread
```

Header Files

In Solaris, both the UNIX International and POSIX interfaces can be used in the same program, though you should not mix them in the same source code file due to conflicting function signatures. To access the UNIX International threads interfaces, include the file thread.h. The UNIX International synchronization primitives can be accessed separately without the thread interfaces by including the file synch.h.

Manual Pages

This appendix contains the following manual pages for the thread interfaces. They are based on the Solaris 2.5 man pages.

man3T

man3R

man2

man3C

NAME

threads, pthreads, libpthread, libthread – thread libraries: libpthread and libthread

SYNOPSIS

POSIX

cc [*flag* **...]** *file* **... -lpthread [-lposix4** *library* **...]**

#include <pthread.h>

Solaris

cc [*flag* **...]** *file* **... -lthread [** *library* **...]**

#include <thread.h>
#include <sched.h>

MT-LEVEL

Fork1-Safe, MT-Safe

DESCRIPTION

Two threads libraries are available, POSIX and Solaris. Both implementations are interoperable, their functionality similar, and can be used within the same application. However, only POSIX threads are guaranteed to be fully portable to other POSIX-compliant environments. As indicated by the "Synopsis" section above, their use requires different source include files and different linking libraries.

Similarities

Most of the functions in both libraries, **libpthread** and **libthread**, have a counterpart in the other's library. POSIX functions and Solaris functions, whose names have similar endings, usually have similar functionality, number of arguments, and use of arguments, i.e.:

POSIX	Solaris
pthread_kill()	**thr_kill()**
pthread_sigmask()	**thr_sigsetmask()**
pthread_mutex_lock()	**mutex_lock()**
sem_wait()	**sema_wait()**

All POSIX threads function names begin with the prefix "**pthread**," with semaphore names being the exception.

Differences

POSIX

- is more portable,

- establishes characteristics for each thread according to configurable attribute objects,
- implements thread cancellation,
- enforces scheduling algorithms, and
- allows for cleanup handlers for **fork**(2) calls.

Solaris

- threads can be suspended and continued,
- implements an optimized mutex, reader/writer locking,
- may increase the concurrency, and
- implements daemon threads, for whose demise the process does not wait.

IMPLEMENTATION

POSIX	Solaris
Creation	
pthread_create()	thr_create()
pthread_attr_init()	---
pthread_attr_setdetachstate()	---
pthread_attr_getdetachstate()	---
pthread_attr_setinheritsched()	---
pthread_attr_getinheritsched()	---
pthread_attr_setschedparam()	---
pthread_attr_getschedparam()	---
pthread_attr_setschedpolicy()	---
pthread_attr_getschedpolicy()	---
pthread_attr_setscope()	---
pthread_attr_getscope()	---
pthread_attr_setstackaddr()	---
pthread_attr_getstackaddr()	---
pthread_attr_setstacksize()	---
pthread_attr_getstacksize()	---
pthread_attr_destroy()	---
---	thr_min_stack()
Exit	
pthread_exit()	thr_exit()
pthread_join()	thr_join()
pthread_detach()	---
Thread Specific Data	
pthread_key_create()	thr_keycreate()
pthread_setspecific()	thr_setspecific()
pthread_getspecific()	thr_getspecific()
pthread_key_delete()	---
Signal	
pthread_sigmask()	thr_sigsetmask()
pthread_kill()	thr_kill()

ID

pthread_self()	**thr_self()**
pthread_equal()	---
---	**thr_main()**

Scheduling

---	**thr_yield()**
---	**thr_suspend()**
---	**thr_continue()**
---	**thr_setconcurrency()**
---	**thr_getconcurrency()**
pthread_setschedparam()	**thr_setprio()**
pthread_getschedparam()	**thr_getprio()**

Cancellation

pthread_cancel()	---
pthread_setcancelstate()	---
pthread_setcanceltype()	---
pthread_testcancel()	---
pthread_cleanup_pop()	---
pthread_cleanup_push()	---

Mutex

pthread_mutex_init()	**mutex_init()**
pthread_mutexattr_init()	---
pthread_mutexattr_setpshared()	---
pthread_mutexattr_getpshared()	---
pthread_mutexattr_setprotocol()	---
pthread_mutexattr_getprotocol()	---
pthread_mutexattr_setprioceiling()	---
pthread_mutexattr_getprioceiling()	---
pthread_mutexattr_destroy()	---
pthread_mutex_setprioceiling()	---
pthread_mutex_getprioceiling()	---
pthread_mutex_lock()	**mutex_lock()**

pthread_mutex_trylock()	**mutex_trylock()**
pthread_mutex_unlock()	**mutex_unlock()**
pthread_mutex_destroy()	**mutex_destroy()**

Condition Variable

pthread_cond_init()	**cond_init()**
pthread_condattr_init()	---
pthread_condattr_setpshared()	---
pthread_condattr_getpshared()	---
pthread_condattr_destroy()	---
pthread_cond_wait()	**cond_wait()**
pthread_cond_timedwait()	**cond_timedwait()**
pthread_cond_signal()	**cond_signal()**
pthread_cond_broadcast()	**cond_broadcast()**
pthread_cond_destroy()	**cond_destroy()**

Reader/Writer Locking

---	**rwlock_init()**
---	**rw_rdlock()**
---	**rw_tryrdlock()**
---	**rw_wrlock()**
---	**rw_trywrlock()**
---	**rw_unlock()**
---	**rwlock_destroy()**

Semaphore

sem_init()	**sema_init()**
sem_open()	---
sem_close()	---
sem_wait()	**sema_wait()**
sem_trywait()	**sema_trywait()**
sem_post()	**sema_post()**
sem_getvalue()	---
sem_unlink()	---
sem_destroy()	**sema_destroy()**

fork() Cleanup Handling

pthread_atfork() ---

Limits

pthread_once() ---

LOCKING

Synchronization

Multithreaded behavior is asynchronous and, therefore, optimized for concurrent and parallel processing. Since threads, always from within the same process and sometimes from multiple processes, share global data with each other, they are not guaranteed exclusive access to the shared data at any point in time. Securing mutually exclusive access to shared data requires synchronization among the threads. Solaris implements four synchronization mechanisms:

- mutex
- condition variable
- reader/writer locking (*optimized frequent-read occasional-write mutex*)
- semaphore

POSIX implements all but reader/writer locking.

Synchronizing multiple threads diminishes their concurrency. The coarser the grain of synchronization, that is, the larger the block of code that is locked, the lesser the concurrency.

MT fork()

If a multithreaded program calls **fork**(2), it implicitly calls **fork1**(2), which replicates only the calling thread. Should there be any outstanding mutexes throughout the process, the application should call **pthread_atfork**(3T), to wait for and acquire those mutexes, prior to calling **fork()**.

FILES

POSIX

/usr/include/pthread.h
/lib/libpthread.*
/lib/libposix4.*

Solaris

/usr/include/thread.h
/usr/include/sched.h
/lib/libthread.*

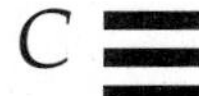

SEE ALSO

fork(2), **intro**(3), **pthread_atfork**(3T), **pthread_create**(3T).

ERRORS

In a multithreaded application, linked with **libpthread** or **libthread**, **EINTR** may be returned whenever another thread calls **fork**(2), which calls **fork1**(2) instead.

NAME

cancellation, pthread_cancel, pthread_setcancelstate, pthread_setcanceltype, pthread_testcancel, pthread_cleanup_push, pthread_cleanup_pop – canceling execution of a thread

SYNOPSIS

cc [*flag* ...] *file* ... **–lpthread** [*library* ...]

#include <pthread.h>

int pthread_cancel(pthread_t *target_thread***);**

int pthread_setcancelstate(int *state***, int** **oldstate***);**
int pthread_setcanceltype(int *type***, int** **oldtype***);**
void pthread_testcancel();

void pthread_cleanup_push(void (**handler***)(void *) void** **arg***);**
void pthread_cleanup_pop(int *execute***);**

MT-LEVEL

MT-Safe

DESCRIPTION

Thread cancellation enables a thread to terminate the execution of any thread in the process. When the notice of cancellation is acted upon, the target thread (the thread being cancelled) is allowed to hold pending cancellation requests in several ways and to perform application-specific cleanup processing.

As a thread acquires resources around areas where it may get cancelled (i.e., before a cancellation point), it needs to push cancellation cleanup handlers along with the acquisition of these resources. The cleanup handlers release these resources and are invoked only if the thread were to be cancelled. As the thread leaves the last cancellation point before releasing a resource, it needs to pop the cleanup handler it had pushed earlier for this resource.

When a thread is cancelled, all the currently stacked cleanup handlers are executed and thread execution is terminated when the last cancellation cleanup handler returns. Its exit status of **PTHREAD_CANCELED** is then available to any threads joining with the cancelled target thread.

The thread's cancellation state and type determine when a thread could get cancelled.

State

PTHREAD_CANCEL_DISABLE
All cancellation requests to the *target_thread* are held pending.

PTHREAD_CANCEL_ENABLE
Cancellation requests are acted upon, depending upon the thread's cancellation type:

PTHREAD_CANCEL_ASYNCHRONOUS
If the cancellation state is enabled, new or pending cancellation requests may be acted upon at any time.

PTHREAD_CANCEL_DEFERRED
Cancellation requests are held pending until a cancellation point (see below) is reached.

Disabling cancellation will cause the setting of the cancellation type to be ineffective because all cancellation requests are held pending; however, when cancellation is enabled again, the new type will be in effect. The cancellation state is set to enabled, by default.

Type

When the cancellation state is disabled, a thread's cancellation *type* is meaningless. The following cancellation types behave as follows when enabled:

PTHREAD_CANCEL_ASYNCHRONOUS
Receipt of a **pthread_cancel**() call will result in an immediate cancellation.

PTHREAD_CANCEL_DEFERRED
Cancellation will not occur until the target thread reaches a cancellation point (see below). Receipt of a **pthread_cancel**() call will result in an immediate cancellation at this cancellation point.

The cancellation type is set to **PTHREAD_CANCEL_DEFERRED**, by default.

Cancellation Points

Cancellation begins at a point in a thread's execution when pending cancellation requests are tested and the cancellation state is found to be enabled. This is called the cancellation point.

A cancellation point can be explicitly set by inserting a call to the **pthread_testcancel**() function.

In addition to explicit **pthread_testcancel**() cancellation points, implicit cancellation points occur at a defined list of system entry points. Typically, any call that might require a long term wait should be a cancellation point. Operations need only check for pending cancellation requests when the operation is about to block indefinitely. This includes threads waiting in **pthread_cond_wait**(3T) and **pthread_cond_timedwait**(3T), threads waiting for the termination of another thread in **pthread_join**(3T), and threads blocked on **sigwait**(2).

POSIX has also defined several other functions (in **libc** and **libposix4**), as implicit cancellation points. In general, these are functions in which threads may block:

aio_suspend(3R), **close**(2), **creat**(2), **fcntl**(2), **fsync**(3C), **mq_receive**(3R), **mq_send**(3R), **msync**(3C), **nanosleep**(3R), **open**(2), **pause**(2), **pthread_cond_timedwait**(3T), **pthread_cond_wait**(3T), **pthread_join**(3T), **pthread_testcancel**(), **read**(2), **sem_wait**(3R), **sigwaitinfo**(3R), **sigsuspend**(2), **sigtimedwait**(3R), **sigwait**(2), **sleep**(3C), **system**(3S), **tcdrain**(3), **wait**(2), **waitpid**(2), and **write**(2).

A cancellation point may also occur when a thread is executing the following functions:

closedir(3C), **ctermid**(3S), **fclose**(3S), **fcntl**(2), **fflush**(3S), **fgetc**(3S), **fgets**(3S), **fopen**(3S), **fprintf**(3S), **fputc**(3S), **fputs**(3S), **fread**(3S), **freopen**(3S), **fscanf**(3S), **fseek**(3S), **ftell**(3S), **fwrite**(3S), **getc**(3S), **getc_unlocked**(3S), **getchar**(3S), **getchar_unlocked**(3S), **getcwd**(3C), **getgrgid**(3C), **getgrgid_r**(3C), **getgrnam**(3C), **getgrnam_r**(3C), **getlogin**(3C), **getlogin_r**(3C), **getpwnam**(3C), **getpwnam_r**(3C), **getpwuid**(3C), **getpwuid_r**(3C), **gets**(3S), **lseek**(2), **opendir**(3C), **perror**(3C), **printf**(3S), **putc**(3S), **putc_unlocked**(3S), **putchar**(3S), **putchar_unlocked**(3S), **puts**(3S), **readdir**(3C), **remove**(3C), **rename**(3C), **rewind**(3C), **rewinddir**(3C), **scanf**(3S), **tmpfile**(3S), **tmpname**(3S), **ttyname**(3C), **ttyname_r**(3C), **ungetc**(3S), and **unlink**(2).

Cleanup Handling

An application should set up a cancellation cleanup handling function to restore any resources before a thread reaches a cancellation point. Specified cancellation points allow programmers to easily keep track of actions needed in a cancellation cleanup handler. A thread should only be made asynchronously cancelable when it is not in the process of acquiring or releasing resources (or locks), or otherwise, not in a difficult or impossible recover state.

When a cancellation request is acted upon, the routines in the list are invoked one-by-one in LIFO (last-in, first-out) order. When a scope's cancellation cleanup handler is invoked, the storage for that scope remains valid.

pthread_cancel

pthread_cancel() requests that *target_thread* be canceled. If the *target_thread*'s cancellation state is enabled, the cancellation will happen immediately, if the target thread has the **PTHREAD_CANCEL_ASYNCHRONOUS** type set. If the target thread has the **PTHREAD_CANCEL_DEFERRED** type set, the cancellation will be deferred until the target thread reaches a cancellation point. By default, the cancellation type is set to **PTHREAD_CANCEL_DEFERRED**. Cancellation cleanup handlers for *target_thread* are called when the cancellation is acted on. Upon return of the last cancellation cleanup handler, the thread-specific data destructor functions are called for *target_thread*. *target_thread* is terminated when the last destructor function returns.

pthread_setcancelstate

pthread_setcancelstate() atomically sets the calling thread's cancellation state to the specified *state* and, if *oldstate* is not **NULL**, stores the previous cancellation state in *oldstate*.

A cancellation point occurs in the calling thread once the state is set if **pthread_setcancelstate()** is called with **PTHREAD_CANCEL_ENABLE**, and *type* is **PTHREAD_CANCEL_ASYNCHRONOUS**.

pthread_setcanceltype

pthread_setcanceltype() atomically sets the calling thread's cancellation type to the specified *type* and, if *oldtype* is not **NULL** stores the previous cancellation type in *oldtype*.

Legal values for *state* are **PTHREAD_CANCEL_ENABLE** and **PTHREAD_CANCEL_DISABLE**. Legal values for *type* are **PTHREAD_CANCEL_DEFERRED** and **PTHREAD_CANCEL_ASYNCHRONOUS**. The cancellation state and type for newly created threads, including the thread in which **main()** was first invoked, are **PTHREAD_CANCEL_ENABLE** and **PTHREAD_CANCEL_DEFERRED**, respectively.

pthread_testcancel

pthread_testcancel() creates a cancellation point in the calling thread; it has no effect if cancellation is disabled.

pthread_cleanup_push

pthread_cleanup_push() pushes the specified cancellation cleanup handler routine, *handler*, onto the cancellation cleanup stack of the calling thread. When a thread exits and its cancellation cleanup stack is not empty, the cleanup handlers are invoked with the argument *arg* in LIFO order from the cancellation cleanup stack. The thread acts upon a cancellation request, or the thread calls **pthread_cleanup_pop()** with a non-zero *execute* argument.

pthread_cleanup_pop

pthread_cleanup_pop() removes the cleanup handler routine at the top of the cancellation cleanup stack of the calling thread and executes it if *execute* is non-zero.

If there are any calls to **pthread_cleanup_push()** or **pthread_cleanup_pop()** made without the matching call after the jump buffer is full, the effect of calling **longjmp**(3C) or **siglongjmp**(3C) is undefined.

Calls to **longjmp()** or **siglongjmp()** from within a cancellation cleanup handler is also undefined unless the jump buffer was also filled in the cancellation cleanup handler.

RETURN VALUES

If successful, **pthread_cancel()**, **pthread_setcancelstate()**, and **pthread_setcanceltype()** returns **0**; otherwise, an error number is returned.

pthread_testcancel(), **pthread_cleanup_push()**, and **pthread_cleanup_pop()** are statements and do not return anything.

ERRORS

For each of the following conditions, **pthread_cancel()** returns the corresponding error number if the condition is detected:

ESRCH No thread was found corresponding to that specified by the *target_thread* ID.

For each of the following conditions, **pthread_setcancelstate()** returns the corresponding error if the condition is detected:

EINVAL The specified state is not **PTHREAD_CANCEL_ENABLE** or **PTHREAD_CANCEL_DISABLE**.

For each of the following conditions, **pthread_setcanceltype()** returns the corresponding error if the condition is detected:

EINVAL The specified type is not **PTHREAD_CANCEL_DEFERRED** or **PTHREAD_CANCEL_ASYNCHRONOUS**.

SEE ALSO

condition(3T), **pthread_exit**(3T), **pthread_join**(3T), **setjmp**(3C).

NOTES

Please see **Intro**(3) for the notion of cancel-safety, deferred-cancel-safety, and asynchronous-cancel-safety. All libraries that have cancellation points but do not push/pop cancellation cleanup handlers are cancel-unsafe. If they push/pop cancellation handlers around cancellation points, they would become deferred-cancel-safe, but could still be asynchronous-cancel-unsafe.

In general, on Solaris, unless stated otherwise, all libraries are asynchronous-cancel-unsafe and they may always remain so, because it may be too expensive for the common case (which is deferred cancellation) to make them asynchronous-cancel-safe.

Libraries that do not have cancellation points are, by definition, deferred-cancel-safe. Libraries that do have cancellation points but do not acquire any resources, such as locks or memory around these cancellation points, are also deferred-cancel-safe.

Those libraries which acquire locks and/or other resources before cancellation points are deferred-cancel-unsafe. Currently, there does not exist any labeling of libraries on Solaris about their cancel-safety status.

Applications can ensure cancel-safety of libraries by disabling cancellation before entering the library and restoring the old cancellation state on exit from the library.

Solaris threads do not offer this functionality.

Use of asynchronous cancellation while holding resources that need to be released may result in resource loss. Similarly, cancellation scopes may be safely manipulated (pushed and popped) only when the thread is in the deferred or disabled cancellation states.

For every **pthread_cleanup_push()** there must be a **pthread_cleanup_pop()** to compile the application.

NAME

condition, pthread_cond_init, pthread_cond_wait, pthread_cond_timedwait, pthread_cond_signal, pthread_cond_broadcast, pthread_cond_destroy, cond_init, cond_wait, cond_timedwait, cond_signal, cond_broadcast, cond_destroy – condition variables

SYNOPSIS

POSIX

cc [*flag* **...]** *file* **... –lpthread [** *library* **...]**

#include <pthread.h>

int pthread_cond_init(pthread_cond_t **cond*, **const pthread_condattr_t** **attr*);

pthread_cond_t *cond* **= PTHREAD_COND_INITIALIZER;**

int pthread_cond_wait(pthread_cond_t **cond*, **pthread_mutex_t** **mutex*);

int pthread_cond_timedwait(pthread_cond_t **cond*, **pthread_mutex_t** **mutex*,
const struct timespec **abstime*);

int pthread_cond_signal(pthread_cond_t **cond*);

int pthread_cond_broadcast(pthread_cond_t **cond*);

int pthread_cond_destroy(pthread_cond_t **cond*);

Solaris

cc [*flag* **...]** *file* **... –lthread [** *library* **...]**

#include <thread.h>
#include <synch.h>

int cond_init(cond_t **cvp*, **int type, int** *arg*);

int cond_wait(cond_t **cvp*, **mutex_t** **mp*);

int cond_timedwait(cond_t **cvp*, **mutex_t** **mp*, **timestruc_t** **abstime*);

int cond_signal(cond_t **cvp*);

int cond_broadcast(cond_t **cvp*);

int cond_destroy(cond_t **cvp*);

MT-LEVEL

MT-Safe

DESCRIPTION

Occasionally, a thread running within a mutex needs to wait for an event, in which case, it blocks or sleeps. When a thread is waiting for another thread to communicate its disposition, it uses a condition variable in conjunction with a mutex. Although a mutex is exclusive and the code it protects is sharable (at certain moments), condition variables enable the synchronization of differing events that share a mutex, but not necessarily data. Several condition variables may be used by threads to signal each other when a task is complete, which then allows the next waiting thread to take ownership of the mutex.

A condition variable enables threads to atomically block and test the condition under the protection of a mutual exclusion lock (mutex) until the condition is satisfied. If the condition is false, a thread blocks on a condition variable and atomically releases the mutex that is waiting for the condition to change. If another thread changes the condition, it may wake up waiting threads by signaling the associated condition variable. The waiting threads, upon awakening, reacquire the mutex and re-evaluate the condition.

Initialize

Condition variables and mutexes should be global. Condition variables that are allocated in writable memory can synchronize threads among processes if they are shared by the cooperating processes (see **mmap**(2)) and are initialized for this purpose.

The scope of a condition variable is either intraprocess or interprocess. This is dependent upon whether the argument is passed implicitly or explicitly to the initialization of that condition variable. A condition variable does not need to be explicitly initialized. A condition variable is initialized with all zeros, by default, and its scope is set to within the calling process. For interprocess synchronization, a condition variable must be initialized once, and only once, before use.

A condition variable must not be simultaneously initialized by multiple threads or re-initialized while in use by other threads.

Condition variables attributes may be set to the default or customized at initialization. POSIX threads even allow the default values to be customized. Establishing these attributes varies depending upon whether POSIX or Solaris threads are used. Similar to the distinctions between POSIX and Solaris thread creation, POSIX condition variables implement the default, intraprocess, unless an attribute object is modified for interprocess prior to the initialization of the condition variable. Solaris condition variables also implement as the default, intraprocess; however, they set this attribute according to the argument, *type*, passed to their initialization function.

POSIX Initialize

POSIX condition variables mutexes, and threads use attributes objects in the same manner; they are initialized with the configuration of an attributes object (see **pthread_condattr_init**(3T)). The **pthread_cond_init()** function initializes the condition variable referenced by *cond* with attributes referenced by *attr*. If *attr* is **NULL**, the default condition variable attributes are used, which is the same as passing the address of a default condition variable attributes object. When the initialization is complete, the state of the condition variable is then initialized. If a default condition variable is used, then only threads created within the same process can operate on the initialized condition variable.

A condition variable can possess two different types of shared-scope behavior, which is determined by the second argument to **pthread_condattr_setpshared**(3T). This argument can be set to either of the following:

PTHREAD_PROCESS_PRIVATE
: The condition variable can synchronize threads only in this process. The **PTHREAD_PROCESS_PRIVATE** POSIX setting for process scope is equivalent to the **USYNC_THREAD** flag to **cond_init()** in the Solaris API. This is the default.

PTHREAD_PROCESS_SHARED
: The condition variable can synchronize threads in this process and other processes. Only one process should initialize the condition variable. The **PTHREAD_PROCESS_SHARED** POSIX setting for system-wide scope is equivalent to the **USYNC_PROCESS** flag to **cond_init()** in the Solaris API.

Initializing condition variables can also be accomplished by allocating-in zeroed memory (default), in which case, **PTHREAD_PROCESS_PRIVATE** is assumed. The same condition variable must not be simultaneously initialized by multiple threads nor re-initialized while in use by other threads.

If default condition variable attributes are used, statically allocated condition variables can be initialized by the macro **PTHREAD_COND_INITIALIZER**. The effect is the same as a dynamic initialization by a call to **pthread_cond_init()** with parameter *attr* specified as **NULL**, except error checks are not performed.

Default condition variable initialization (intraprocess):

```
pthread_cond_t cvp;
pthread_condattr_t cv_attr;

pthread_cond_init(&cvp, NULL);  /* initialize cv with defaults */

OR

pthread_condattr_init(&cv_attr);  /* initialize cv_attr with defaults */
pthread_cond_init(&cvp, &cv_attr);  /* initialize cv with default cv_attr */

OR

pthread_condattr_setpshared(&cv_attr, PTHREAD_PROCESS_PRIVATE);
pthread_cond_init(&cvp, &cv_attr);  /* initialize cv with defaults */

OR

pthread_cond_t cond = PTHREAD_COND_INITIALIZER;
```

OR

pthread_cond_t cond;

cond = calloc(1, sizeof (pthread_cond_t));

Customized condition variable initialization (interprocess):

```
pthread_condattr_init(&cv_attr); /* init cv_attr with defaults */
pthread_condattr_setpshared(&cv_attr, PTHREAD_PROCESS_SHARED);
pthread_cond_init(&cvp, &cv_attr); /* init cv with interprocess scope */
```

Solaris Initialize

cond_init() initializes the condition variable pointed to by *cvp*. A condition variable can have several different types of behavior, specified by *type*. No current type uses *arg* although a future type may specify additional behavior parameters via *arg*. *type* may be one of the following:

USYNC_THREAD
The condition variable can synchronize threads only in this process. The **USYNC_THREAD** Solaris condition variable type for process scope is equivalent to the POSIX condition variable attribute setting **PTHREAD_PROCESS_PRIVATE**. *arg* is ignored.

USYNC_PROCESS
The condition variable can synchronize threads in this process and other processes. Only one process should initialize the condition variable. The **USYNC_PROCESS** Solaris condition variable type for system-wide scope is equivalent to the POSIX condition variable attribute setting **PTHREAD_PROCESS_SHARED**. *arg* is ignored.

Initializing condition variables can also be accomplished by allocating in zeroed memory, in which case, a *type* of **USYNC_THREAD** is assumed.

If default condition variable attributes are used, statically allocated condition variables can be initialized by the macro **DEFAULTCV**.

Default condition variable initialization (intraprocess):

cond_t cvp;

cond_init(&cvp, NULL, NULL); /* initialize cv with default */

OR

cond_init(&cvp, USYNC_THREAD, NULL);

OR

cond_t cond = DEFAULTCV;

Customized condition variable initialization (interprocess):

cond_init(&cvp, USYNC_PROCESS, NULL); /* init w interproc. scope */

Condition Wait

The condition wait interface allows a thread to wait for a condition and atomically release the associated mutex that it needs to hold to check the condition. The thread waits for another thread to make the condition true and that thread's resulting call to signal and wake up the waiting thread.

POSIX Wait

pthread_cond_wait() and **pthread_cond_timedwait()** block on a condition variable, which atomically releases the mutex pointed to by *mp* and causes the calling thread to block on the condition variable pointed to by *cond*. The blocked thread may be awakened by **pthread_cond_signal()**, **pthread_cond_broadcast()**, or interrupted by a **UNIX** signal.

These functions atomically release the *mutex*, causing the calling thread to block on the condition variable *cond*.

Upon successful completion, the mutex is locked and owned by the calling thread.

pthread_cond_timedwait() is the same as **pthread_cond_wait()**, except an error is returned if the system time equals or exceeds the time specified by *abstime* before the condition *cond* is signaled or broadcasted, or if the absolute time specified by *abstime* has already passed at the time of the call. When time-outs occur, **pthread_cond_timedwait()** releases and reacquires the mutex referenced by *mutex*.

When using condition variables, there is always a boolean predicate involving shared variables related to each condition wait that is true, if the thread should proceed. Since the return from **pthread_cond_wait()** or **pthread_cond_timedwait()** does not indicate anything about the value of this predicate, the predicate should be reevaluated on return. Unwanted wakeups from **pthread_cond_wait()** or **pthread_cond_timedwait()** may occur.

The functions **pthread_cond_wait()** and **pthread_cond_timedwait()** are cancellation points. If a cancellation request is acted upon while in a condition wait when the cancellation enable state of a thread is set to **PTHREAD_CANCEL_DEFERRED**, the mutex will be reacquired before calling the first cancellation cleanup handler. In other words, the thread is unblocked, allowed to execute up to the point of returning from the call to **pthread_cond_wait()** or **pthread_cond_timedwait()**, but then notices the cancellation request and, instead of returning to the caller of **pthread_cond_wait()** or **pthread_cond_timedwait()**, it starts the thread cancellation activities including cancellation cleanup handlers.

A thread that is unblocked because it was canceled while blocked in a call to **pthread_cond_wait()** or **pthread_cond_timedwait()** does not awaken anyone else asleep on the condition.

Solaris Wait

cond_wait() atomically releases the mutex pointed to by *mp* and causes the calling thread to block on the condition variable pointed to by *cvp*. The blocked thread may be awakened by **cond_signal()**, **cond_broadcast()**, or when interrupted by delivery of a **UNIX** signal or a **fork()**.

cond_wait() and **cond_timedwait()** always return with the mutex locked and owned by the calling thread even when returning an error.

Condition Signaling

A condition signal allows a thread to unblock the next thread waiting on the condition variable, whereas, a condition broadcast allows a thread to unblock all threads waiting on the condition variable.

POSIX Signal and Broadcast

pthread_cond_signal() and **pthread_cond_broadcast()** unblock threads blocked on a condition variable.

pthread_cond_signal() unblocks at least one thread blocked on the specified condition variable *cond*, if any threads are blocked on *cond*.

pthread_cond_broadcast() unblocks all threads blocked on the condition variable *cond*.

pthread_cond_signal() and **pthread_cond_broadcast()** have no effect if there are no threads blocked on *cond*.

pthread_cond_signal() or **pthread_cond_broadcast()** may be called by a thread regardless of whether it owns the mutex which threads calling **pthread_cond_wait()** or **pthread_cond_timedwait()** have associated with the condition variable during their waits. However, if predictable scheduling behavior is required, then that mutex should be locked by the thread calling **pthread_cond_signal()** or **pthread_cond_broadcast()**.

Solaris Signal and Broadcast

cond_signal() unblocks one thread that is blocked on the condition variable pointed to by *cvp*.

cond_broadcast() unblocks all threads that are blocked on the condition variable pointed to by *cvp*.

If no threads are blocked on the condition variable, then **cond_signal()** and **cond_broadcast()** have no effect.

Both functions should be called under the protection of the same mutex that is used with the condition variable being signaled. Otherwise, the condition variable may be signaled between the test of the associated condition and blocking in **cond_wait()**. This can cause an infinite wait.

Destroy

The condition destroy functions destroy any state, but not the space, associated with the condition variable.

POSIX Destroy

pthread_cond_destroy() destroys the condition variable specified by *cond*. The space for destroying the condition variable is not freed.

Solaris Destroy

cond_destroy() destroys any state associated with the condition variable pointed to by *cvp*. The space for storing the condition variable is not freed.

RETURN VALUES

0 is returned when any of these functions are successful. A non-zero value indicates an error, except **pthread_timedwait()**, which returns **ETIME**.

ERRORS

These functions fail and return the corresponding value if any of the following conditions are detected:

EFAULT *cond*, *attr*, *cvp*, *arg*, *abstime*, or *mutex* point to an illegal address.

EINVAL For **cond_init()**, *type* is not a recognized type.

pthread_cond_init() fails and returns the corresponding value if any of the following conditions are detected:

EINVAL The value specified for *attr* is invalid.

ENOMEM The system lacked the memory to initialize the condition variable.

EAGAIN The system lacked the resources to initialize the condition variable.

EBUSY The system detected an attempt to reinitialize an active condition variable.

pthread_cond_destroy() fails and returns the corresponding value if any of the following conditions are detected:

EBUSY The system detected an attempt to destroy an active condition variable.

cond_wait() or **cond_timedwait()** fails and returns the corresponding value if any of the following conditions are detected:

EINTR The wait was interrupted by a signal or **fork()**.

cond_timedwait() fails and returns the corresponding value if any of the following conditions are detected:

ETIME *abstime* The time specified by *abstime* has passed.

EINVAL *abstime* is invalid.

pthread_cond_wait() or **pthread_cond_timedwait**() fails and returns the corresponding value if any of the following conditions are detected:

ETIMEDOUT The time specified by *abstime* has passed.

EINVAL *abstime* is invalid.

EINVAL Different mutexes are in use with the same condition variable.

EINVAL The mutex is not owned by the calling thread.

SEE ALSO

mmap(2), **fork**(2), **signal**(3C), **mutex**(3T), **pthread_condattr_init**(3T).

NOTES

The only policy currently supported is **SCHED_OTHER**. In Solaris, under the **SCHED_OTHER** policy, there is no established order in which threads are unblocked.

If more than one thread is blocked on a condition variable, the order in which threads are unblocked is determined by the scheduling policy. When each thread, unblocked as a result of a **pthread_cond_signal**() or **pthread_cond_broadcast**(), returns from its call to **pthread_cond_wait**() or **pthread_cond_timedwait**(), the thread owns the mutex with which it called **pthread_cond_wait**() or **pthread_cond_timedwait**(). The thread(s) that are unblocked compete for the mutex according to the scheduling policy, and as if each had called **pthread_mutex_lock**(3T).

When **cond_wait**() returns the value of the condition is indeterminate and must be reevaluated.

cond_timedwait() is similar to **cond_wait**(), except that the calling thread will not wait for the condition to become true past the absolute time specified by *abstime*. Note that **cond_timedwait**() may continue to block as it tries to reacquire the mutex pointed to by *mp*, which may be locked by another thread. If *abstime* then **cond_timedwait**() returns because of a timeout, it returns the error code **ETIME**.

NAME

mutex, pthread_mutex_init, pthread_mutex_lock, pthread_mutex_trylock, pthread_mutex_unlock, pthread_mutex_destroy, mutex_init, mutex_lock, mutex_trylock, mutex_unlock, mutex_destroy – mutual exclusion locks

SYNOPSIS

POSIX

cc [*flag* **...]** *file* **... –lpthread [** *library* **...]**

#include <pthread.h>

int pthread_mutex_init(pthread_mutex_t **mp*,
    const pthread_mutexattr_t **attr*);

pthread_mutex_t *mutex* **= PTHREAD_MUTEX_INITIALIZER;**

int pthread_mutex_lock(pthread_mutex_t **mp*);

int pthread_mutex_trylock(pthread_mutex_t **mp*);

int pthread_mutex_unlock(pthread_mutex_t **mp*);

int pthread_mutex_destroy(pthread_mutex_t **mp*);

Solaris

cc [*flag* **...]** *file* **... –lthread [** *library* **...]**

#include <thread.h>
#include <synch.h>

int mutex_init(mutex_t **mp*, **int type, void** **arg*);

int mutex_lock(mutex_t **mp*);

int mutex_trylock(mutex_t **mp*);

int mutex_unlock(mutex_t **mp*);

int mutex_destroy(mutex_t **mp*);

MT-LEVEL

MT-Safe

DESCRIPTION

Mutual exclusion locks (mutexes) prevent multiple threads from simultaneously executing critical sections of code which access shared data (i.e., mutexes are used to serialize the execution of threads). All mutexes must be global. A successful call for a mutex lock via **pthread_mutex_lock**( ) or **mutex_lock**( ) will cause another thread that is also trying to lock the same mutex to block until the owner thread unlocks it via **pthread_mutex_unlock**( ) or **mutex_unlock**( ). Threads within the same process or within other processes can share mutexes.

Mutexes can synchronize threads within the same process or in other processes. Mutexes can be used to synchronize threads between processes if the mutexes are allocated in writable memory and shared among the cooperating processes (see **mmap**(2)), and have been initialized for this task.

Initialize

Mutexes are either intraprocess or interprocess, depending upon the argument passed implicitly or explicitly to the initialization of that mutex. A statically allocated mutex does not need to be explicitly initialized; by default, a statically allocated mutex is initialized with all zeros and its scope is set to be within the calling process. For POSIX portability of statically allocated mutexes, use the **PTHREAD_MUTEX_INITIALIZER** macro (see below).

For interprocess synchronization, a mutex needs to be allocated in memory shared between these processes. Since the memory for such a mutex must be allocated dynamically, the mutex needs to be explicitly initialized using **mutex_init**() or **pthread_mutex_init**() with the appropriate attribute that indicates interprocess use.

POSIX Initialize

POSIX mutexes, threads, and condition variables use attributes objects in the same manner; they are initialized with the configuration of an attributes object (see **pthread_mutexattr_init**(3T)). The **pthread_mutex_init**() function initializes the mutex referenced by *mp* with attributes specified by *attr*. If *attr* is **NULL**, the default mutex attributes are used, which is the same as passing the address of a default mutex attributes object. Upon initialization, the state of the mutex is initialized and unlocked. If default mutex attributes are used, then only threads created within the same process can operate on the initialized mutex variable.

In POSIX, the attributes of a mutex may be specified via the attribute object created via **pthread_mutexattr_init**() and modified using the **pthread_mutexattr_***() functions. To explicitly specify whether a mutex is or is not shared between processes, it can be initialized with an attribute object modified via **pthread_mutexattr_setpshared**(3T). The second argument to this function can be either of the following:

PTHREAD_PROCESS_PRIVATE
The mutex can synchronize threads within this process. The **PTHREAD_PROCESS_PRIVATE** POSIX mutex type for process scope is equivalent to the **USYNC_THREAD** flag to **mutex_init()** in the Solaris API (see below).

PTHREAD_PROCESS_SHARED
The mutex can synchronize threads in this process and other processes. Only one process should initialize the mutex. The **PTHREAD_PROCESS_SHARED**

POSIX mutex type for system-wide scope is equivalent to the **USYNC_PROCESS** flag to **mutex_init()** in the Solaris API (see below).

Initializing mutexes can also be accomplished by allocating in zeroed memory (default), in which case, **PTHREAD_PROCESS_PRIVATE** is assumed. The same mutex must not be simultaneously initialized by multiple threads, nor should a mutex lock be re-initialized while in use by other threads.

If default mutex attributes are used, statically allocated mutexes can be initialized by the macro **PTHREAD_MUTEX_INITIALIZER**. The effect is the same as a dynamic initialization by a call to pthread_mutex_init() with parameter *attr* specified as **NULL**, except error checks are not performed.

Default mutex initialization (intraprocess):

```
pthread_mutex_t mp;
pthread_mutexattr_t mattr;

pthread_mutex_init(&mp, NULL);
```

OR

```
pthread_mutexattr_init(&mattr);
pthread_mutex_init(&mp, &mattr);
```

OR

```
pthread_mutexattr_setpshared(&mattr, PTHREAD_PROCESS_PRIVATE);
pthread_mutex_init(&mp, &mattr);
```

OR

```
pthread_mutex_t  mp  =  PTHREAD_MUTEX_INITIALIZER;
```

OR

```
pthread_mutex_t mp;

mp = calloc (1, sizeof (pthread_mutex_t));
```

Customized mutex initialization (interprocess):

```
pthread_mutexattr_init(&mattr);
pthread_mutexattr_setpshared(&mattr, PTHREAD_PROCESS_SHARED);
pthread_mutex_init(&mp, &mattr);
```

Solaris Initialize

The equivalent Solaris API used to initialize a mutex so that it has several different types of behavior is the *type* argument passed to **mutex_init**(). No current type uses *arg* although a future type may specify additional behavior parameters via *arg*. *type* may be one of the following:

USYNC_THREAD

The mutex can synchronize threads only in this process. *arg* is ignored. The **USYNC_THREAD** Solaris mutex type for process scope is equivalent to the POSIX mutex attribute setting **PTHREAD_PROCESS_PRIVATE**.

USYNC_PROCESS

The mutex can synchronize threads in this process and other processes. Only one process should initialize the mutex. *arg* is ignored. The **USYNC_PROCESS** Solaris mutex type for process scope is equivalent to the POSIX mutex attribute setting **PTHREAD_PROCESS_SHARED**.

Initializing mutexes can also be accomplished by allocating in zeroed memory (default), in which case, a *type* of **USYNC_THREAD** is assumed. The same mutex must not be simultaneously initialized by multiple threads. A mutex lock must not be re-initialized while in use by other threads.

If default mutex attributes are used, the macro **DEFAULTMUTEX** can be used to initialize mutexes that are statically allocated.

Default mutex initialization (intraprocess):

```
mutex_t mp;
mutex_init(&mp, NULL, NULL);
```

OR

```
mutex_init(&mp, USYNC_THREAD, NULL);
```

OR

```
mutex_t mp = DEFAULTMUTEX;
```

OR

```
mutex_t mp;
mp = calloc(1, sizeof (mutex_t));
```

OR

```
mutex_t mp;
mp = malloc(sizeof (mutex_t));
memset(mp, 0, sizeof (mutex_t));
```

Customized mutex initialization (interprocess):

```
mutex_init(&mp, USYNC_PROCESS, NULL);
```

Lock and Unlock

A critical section of code is enclosed by a the call to lock the mutex and the call to unlock the mutex to protect it from simultaneous access by multiple threads. Only one thread at a time may possess mutually exclusive access to the critical section of code that is enclosed by the mutex-locking call and the mutex-unlocking call, whether the mutex's scope is intraprocess or interprocess. A thread calling to lock the mutex either gets exclusive access to the code starting from the successful locking until its call to unlock the mutex, or it waits until the mutex is unlocked by the thread that locked it.

Mutexes have ownership, unlike semaphores. Although any thread, within the scope of a mutex, can get an unlocked mutex and lock access to the same critical section of code, only the thread that locked a mutex can unlock it.

If a thread waiting for a mutex receives a signal, upon return from the signal handler, the thread resumes waiting for the mutex as if there was no interrupt. A mutex protects code, not data; therefore, strongly bind a mutex with the data by putting both within the same structure, or at least within the same procedure.

POSIX/Solaris Locking

A call to **pthread_mutex_lock**() or **mutex_lock**() locks the mutex object referenced by *mp*. If the mutex is already locked, the calling thread blocks until the mutex is freed; this will return with the mutex object referenced by *mp* in the locked state with the calling thread as its owner. If the current owner of a mutex tries to relock the mutex, it will result in deadlock.

pthread_mutex_trylock() and **mutex_trylock**() is the same as **pthread_mutex_lock**() and **mutex_lock**(), respectively, except that if the mutex object referenced by *mp* is locked (by any thread, including the current thread), the call returns immediately with an error.

pthread_mutex_unlock() or **mutex_unlock**() are called by the owner of the mutex object referenced by *mp* to release it. The mutex must be locked and the calling thread must be the one that last locked the mutex (the owner). If there are threads blocked on the mutex object referenced by *mp* when **pthread_mutex_unlock**() is called, the *mp* is freed, and the scheduling policy will determine which thread gets the mutex. If the calling thread is not the owner of the lock, no error status is returned, and the behavior of the program is undefined.

Destroy

Either **pthread_mutex_destroy**() or **mutex_destroy**() destroys the mutex object referenced by *mp*; the mutex object becomes uninitialized. The space used by the destroyed mutex variable is not freed. It needs to be explicitly reclaimed.

RETURN VALUES

If successful, all of these functions return **0**; otherwise, an error number is returned.

pthread_mutex_trylock() or **mutex_trylock**() returns **0** if a lock on the mutex object referenced by *mp* is obtained; otherwise, an error number is returned.

ERRORS

These functions fail and return the corresponding value if any of the following conditions are detected:

EFAULT *mp* or *attr* points to an illegal address.

pthread_mutex_init() or **mutex_init**() fails and returns the corresponding value if any of the following conditions are detected:

EINVAL The value specified by *mp* or *attr* is invalid.

ENOMEM The system lacked the memory to initialize the mutex.

EAGAIN The system lacked the resources to initialize the mutex.

EBUSY The system detected an attempt to reinitialize an active mutex.

pthread_mutex_trylock() or **mutex_trylock**() fails and returns the corresponding value if any of the following conditions occur:

EBUSY The mutex was already locked.

pthread_mutex_lock() fails and returns the corresponding value if any of the following conditions are detected:

EDEADLK The mutex was already locked and is owned by the calling thread.

pthread_mutex_lock() or **pthread_mutex_trylock**() fails and returns the corresponding value if any of the following conditions occur:

EINVAL The mutex has been initialized with a protocol of **PTHREAD_PRIO_PROTECT** and the calling thread's priority is higher than the mutex's priority ceiling.

pthread_mutex_unlock() fails and returns the corresponding value if any of the following conditions are detected:

EPERM The calling thread does not own the mutex.

SEE ALSO

mmap(2), **pthread_create**(3T), **pthread_mutexattr_init**(3T).

NOTES

Currently, the only supported policy is **SCHED_OTHER**. In Solaris, under the **SCHED_OTHER** policy, there is no established order in which threads are unblocked.

In the current implementation of threads, **pthread_mutex_lock**(), **pthread_mutex_unlock**(), **mutex_lock**(), **mutex_unlock**(), **pthread_mutex_trylock**(), and **mutex_trylock**() do not validate the mutex type. Therefore, an uninitialized mutex or a mutex with an invalid type does not return **EINVAL**. Interfaces for mutexes with an invalid type have unspecified behavior.

Uninitialized mutexes which are allocated locally may contain junk data. Such mutexes need to be initialized using **pthread_mutex_init**() or **mutex_init**().

By default, if multiple threads are waiting for a mutex, the order of acquisition is undefined.

NAME

pthread_atfork – register fork handlers

SYNOPSIS

cc [*flag* **...]** *file* **... –lpthread [** *library* **...]**

#include <sys/types.h>

int pthread_atfork (void (**prepare***)(void), void (****parent***)(void), void (****child***)(void));**

MT-LEVEL

MT-Safe

DESCRIPTION

pthread_atfork() declares fork handlers to be called prior to and following **fork**(), within the thread that called **fork**(). The order of calls to **pthread_atfork**() is important.

Before **fork**() processing begins, the *prepare* fork handler is called. The *prepare* handler is not called if its address is **NULL**.

The *parent* fork handler is called after **fork**() processing finishes in the parent process, and the *child* fork handler is called after **fork**() processing finishes in the child process. If the address of *parent* or *child* is **NULL**, then its handler is not called.

The *prepare* fork handler is called in LIFO (last-in first-out) order, whereas the *parent* and *child* fork handlers are called in FIFO (first-in first-out) order. This calling order allows applications to preserve locking order.

RETURN VALUES

Upon successful completion, **pthread_atfork**() returns **0**; otherwise, an error number is returned.

ERRORS

ENOMEM Insufficient table space exists to record the fork handler addresses.

SEE ALSO

fork(2), **atexit**(3C).

NOTES

Solaris threads do not offer this functionality, although a call to this interface may be used by a Solaris thread program since the two thread APIs are inter-operable.

NAME

pthread_attr_init, pthread_attr_destroy, pthread_attr_setscope, pthread_attr_getscope, pthread_attr_setdetachstate, pthread_attr_getdetachstate, pthread_attr_setstacksize, pthread_attr_getstacksize, pthread_attr_setstackaddr, pthread_attr_getstackaddr, pthread_attr_setschedparam, pthread_attr_getschedparam, pthread_attr_setschedpolicy, pthread_attr_getschedpolicy, pthread_attr_setinheritsched, pthread_attr_getinheritsched – thread creation attributes

SYNOPSIS

cc [*flag* **...]** *file* **... –lpthread [** *library* **...]**

#include <pthread.h>

int pthread_attr_init(pthread_attr_t ***_attr_);**

int pthread_attr_destroy(pthread_attr_t ***_attr_);**

int pthread_attr_setscope(pthread_attr_t ***_attr_, int** *contentionscope***);**

int pthread_attr_getscope(const pthread_attr_t ***_attr_, int ***_contentionscope_**);**

int pthread_attr_setdetachstate(pthread_attr_t ***_attr_, int** *detachstate***);**

int pthread_attr_getdetachstate(const pthread_attr_t ***_attr_, int ***_detachstate_**);**

int pthread_attr_setstacksize(pthread_attr_t ***_attr_, size_t** *stacksize***);**

int pthread_attr_getstacksize(const pthread_attr_t ***_attr_, size_t ***_stacksize_**);**

int pthread_attr_setstackaddr(pthread_attr_t ***_attr_, void ***_stackaddr_**);**

int pthread_attr_getstackaddr(const pthread_attr_t ***_attr_, void ****_stackaddr_**);**

int pthread_attr_setschedparam(pthread_attr_t ***_attr_,**
const struct sched_param ***_param_);**

int pthread_attr_getschedparam(const pthread_attr_t ***_attr_,**
struct sched_param ***_param_);**

int pthread_attr_setschedpolicy(pthread_attr_t ***_attr_, int** *policy***);**

int pthread_attr_getschedpolicy(const pthread_attr_t ***_attr_, int ***_policy_**);**

int pthread_attr_setinheritsched(pthread_attr_t ***_attr_, int** *inheritsched***);**

int pthread_attr_getinheritsched(const pthread_attr_t ***_attr_, int ***_inheritsched_**);**

MT-LEVEL

MT-Safe

DESCRIPTION

The pthread approach to setting attributes for threads is to request the initialization of an attribute object, *attr*, and pass the initialized attribute object to

pthread_create(3T). The convention in Solaris is to pass these attributes as flags to **thr_create**(3T).

All attributes in *attr* are independent of one another and may be singularly modified or retrieved. *attr*, itself, is independent of any thread and can be modified or used to create new threads. However, any change to *attr* after a thread is created will not affect that thread.

init

The **pthread_attr_init**() function initializes a thread attributes object (*attr*) with the default value for each attribute as follows:

Attribute	Default Value	Meaning of Default
contentionscope	**PTHREAD_SCOPE_PROCESS**	resource competition within process
detachstate	**PTHREAD_CREATE_JOINABLE**	joinable by other threads
stackaddr	**NULL**	stack allocated by system
stacksize	**NULL**	1 megabyte
priority	---	priority of parent (calling) thread
policy	**SCHED_OTHER**	determined by system
inheritsched	**PTHREAD_EXPLICIT_SCHED**	scheduling policy and parameters not inherited but explicitly defined by the attribute object

NOTE: Attribute objects should be destroyed before an initialized attribute object is re-initialized.

destroy

pthread_attr_destroy() destroys a thread attributes object (*attr*), which cannot be reused until it is reinitialized.

contentionscope

The **pthread_attr_setscope**() and **pthread_attr_getscope**() functions set and get the *contentionscope* thread attribute in the *attr* object. The *contentionscope* value may be set to the following:

PTHREAD_SCOPE_SYSTEM
Indicates system scheduling contention scope. This thread is permanently "bound" to an LWP, and is also called a bound thread. This value is equivalent to **THR_BOUND** in Solaris threads (see **thr_create**(3T)).

PTHREAD_SCOPE_PROCESS
Indicates process scheduling contention scope. This thread is not "bound" to an

LWP, and is also called an unbound thread. **PTHREAD_SCOPE_PROCESS**, or unbound, is the default.

detachstate

The **pthread_attr_setdetachstate**() and **pthread_attr_getdetachstate**() functions set and get the *detachstate* attribute in the *attr* object. The *detachstate* attribute determines whether the thread is created in a detached state or not. The *detachstate* may be set to the following values:

PTHREAD_CREATE_DETACHED
Creates a new detached thread. A detached thread disappears without leaving a trace. The thread ID and any of its resources are freed and ready for reuse. **pthread_join**(3T) and **thr_join**(3T) cannot wait for a detached thread.

PTHREAD_CREATE_JOINABLE
Creates a new non-detached thread. The thread ID and its user-defined stack, if specified at thread creation time, is not freed until **pthread_join**(3T) or **thr_join**(3T) are called. **pthread_join**(3T) or **thr_join**(3T) must be called to release any resources associated with the terminated thread.

stacksize and stackaddr

The **pthread_attr_setstacksize()** and **pthread_attr_getstacksize()** functions set and get the *stacksize* thread attribute in the *attr* object. The *stacksize* default argument is **NULL**, and a thread default stack size is 1 megabyte.

The **pthread_attr_setstackaddr()** and **pthread_attr_getstackaddr()** functions set and get the *stackaddr* thread attribute in the *attr* object. The *stackaddr* default is **NULL**. (See **pthread_create**(3T).)

schedparam (priority)

The **pthread_attr_setschedparam()** and **pthread_attr_getschedparam()** functions set and get the scheduling parameter thread attributes in the *attr* argument, determined by the scheduling policy set in the *attr* object. The only required member of the *param* structure for the **SCHED_OTHER**, **SCHED_FIFO**, and **SCHED_RR** policies is *sched_priority* (see **NOTES** section below). You can use these functions to get and set the priority of the thread to be created. The sched_priority of the *param* structure is **NULL**, by default, which means the newly created thread inherits the priority of its parent thread.

schedpolicy

The **pthread_attr_setschedpolicy()** and **pthread_attr_getschedpolicy()** functions set and get the *schedpolicy* thread attribute in the *attr* argument.

Values for the *policy* attribute are **SCHED_FIFO**, **SCHED_RR**, or the default value **SCHED_OTHER** (see **NOTES** section below and **sched_setschedparam**(3R)).

RETURN VALUES

Upon successful completion, the following functions return 0; otherwise, an error number is returned to indicate the error: **pthread_attr_init**(), **pthread_attr_destroy**(), **pthread_attr_setstacksize**(), **pthread_attr_getstacksize**(), **pthread_attr_setstackaddr**(), **pthread_attr_getstackaddr**(), **pthread_attr_setdetachstate**(), **pthread_attr_getdetachstate**(), **pthread_attr_setscope**(), **pthread_attr_getscope**(), **pthread_attr_setinheritsched**(), **pthread_attr_getinheritsched**(), **pthread_attr_setschedpolicy**(), and **pthread_attr_getschedpolicy**().

ERRORS

If any of the following conditions occur, **pthread_attr_init**() returns the corresponding error number:

ENOMEM Insufficient memory exists to create the thread attributes object.

If any of the following conditions occur, **pthread_attr_setstacksize**() returns the corresponding error number:

EINVAL The value of *stacksize* is less than **PTHREAD_STACK_MIN** or exceeds a system-imposed limit.

If any of the following conditions occur, **pthread_attr_destroy**(), **pthread_attr_setstacksize**(), **pthread_attr_getstacksize**(), **pthread_attr_setstackaddr**(), **pthread_attr_getstackaddr**(), **pthread_attr_setdetachstate**(), **pthread_attr_getdetachstate**(), **pthread_attr_setscope**(), **pthread_attr_getscope**(), **pthread_attr_setschedparam**(), **pthread_attr_getschedparam**(), **pthread_attr_setinheritsched**(), **pthread_attr_getinheritsched**(), **pthread_attr_setschedpolicy**(), and **pthread_attr_getschedpolicy**() return the corresponding error number:

EINVAL The value of *attr* is not valid.

If any of the following conditions occur, **pthread_attr_setstacksize**() returns the corresponding error number:

EINVAL The value of *stacksize* is less than **PTHREAD_STACK_MIN**.

If any of the following conditions occur, **pthread_attr_setdetachstate**() returns the corresponding error number:

EINVAL The value of *detachstate* is not valid.

If any of the following conditions occur, **pthread_attr_setscope**() returns the corresponding error number:

EINVAL The value of *contentionscope* is not valid.

If any of the following conditions occur, **pthread_attr_setschedparam()** returns the corresponding error number:

EINVAL The value of the **sched_priority** member of the *param* structure is less than or equal to **0**.

If any of the following conditions occur, **pthread_attr_getstacksize()** returns the corresponding error number:

EINVAL The value of *stacksize* is **NULL**.

If any of the following conditions occur, **pthread_attr_getstackaddr()** returns the corresponding error number:

EINVAL The value of *stackaddr* is **NULL**.

If any of the following conditions occur, **pthread_attr_getdetachstate()** returns the corresponding error number:

EINVAL The value of *detachstate* is **NULL**.

If any of the following conditions occur, **pthread_attr_getscope()** returns the corresponding error number:

EINVAL The value of *contentionscope* is **NULL**.

If any of the following conditions occur, either **pthread_attr_setschedparam()** and **pthread_attr_getschedparam()** returns the corresponding error number:

EINVAL The value of *param* is **NULL**.

For each of the following conditions, if the condition is detected, **pthread_attr_setinheritsched()** and **pthread_attr_setschedpolicy()** return the corresponding error number:

ENOTSUP An attempt was made to set the attribute to an unsupported *policy* or *inheritsched*.

For each of the following conditions, if the condition is detected, **pthread_attr_getinheritsched()** and **pthread_attr_getschedpolicy()** return the corresponding error number:

EINVAL *policy* or *inheritsched* is **NULL**.

SEE ALSO

sched_setschedparam(3R), **pthread_create**(3T), **pthread_join**(3T), **thr_create**(3T).

NOTES

Currently, the only policy supported is **SCHED_OTHER**. Attempting to set policy as **SCHED_FIFO** or **SCHED_RR** will result in the error **ENOTSUP**.

The attribute object is part of the POSIX threads interface. There is no Solaris threads counterpart to the POSIX threads attribute object.

NAME

pthread_condattr_init, pthread_condattr_setpshared, pthread_condattr_getpshared, pthread_condattr_destroy – condition variable initialization attributes

SYNOPSIS

cc [*flag* ...] *file* ... **–lpthread** [*library* ...]

#include <pthread.h>

int pthread_condattr_init(pthread_condattr_t **attr***);**

int pthread_condattr_setpshared(pthread_condattr_t **attr***, int** *process-shared***);**

int pthread_condattr_getpshared(const pthread_condattr_t **attr***,**
    int **process-shared***);**

int pthread_condattr_destroy(pthread_condattr_t **attr***);**

MT-LEVEL

MT-Safe

DESCRIPTION

Initialize

The function **pthread_condattr_init()** initializes a condition variable attributes object *attr* with the default value for all the attributes.

At present, the only attribute available is the scope of condition variables, specified by *process-shared*.

The default value of the *process-shared* attribute is **PTHREAD_PROCESS_PRIVATE**, which only allows the condition variable to be operated upon by threads created within the same process as the thread that initialized the condition variable. If threads from other processes try to operate on this condition variable, the behavior is undefined.

The *process-shared* attribute may be set to **PTHREAD_PROCESS_SHARED**, which allows a condition variable to be operated upon by any thread with access to the memory allocated to the condition variable, even if the condition variable is allocated in memory that is shared by multiple processes.

Attempts to initialize previously initialized condition variable attributes object will leave the storage allocated by the previous initialization unallocated.

Once a condition variable attributes object initializes one or more condition variables, any function affecting the attributes object (including destruction) will not effect any previously initialized condition variables.

Set/Get Scope

pthread_condattr_setpshared() sets the *process-shared* attribute in an initialized attributes object referenced by *attr*. **pthread_condattr_getpshared()** obtains the value of the *process-shared* attribute from the attributes object referenced by *attr*.

Destroy

pthread_condattr_destroy() destroys a condition variable attributes object; the object becomes uninitialized. A destroyed condition variable attributes object can be reinitialized with **pthread_condattr_init()**; however, the results of referencing the object after it has been destroyed are undefined.

RETURN VALUES

pthread_condattr_init(), **pthread_condattr_destroy()**, and **pthread_condattr_setpshared()** return 0 upon a successful return; otherwise, an error number is returned.

pthread_condattr_getpshared() returns 0 upon a successful return, and stores the value of the *process-shared* attribute of *attr* in the object referenced by the *process-shared* parameter; otherwise, an error number is returned.

ERRORS

pthread_condattr_init() returns an error number if any of the following conditions are detected:

ENOMEM Insufficient memory exists to initialize the condition variable attributes object.

pthread_condattr_destroy(), **pthread_condattr_getpshared()**, and **pthread_condattr_setpshared()** return an error number if the following condition is detected:

EINVAL The value specified by *attr* is invalid.

pthread_condattr_setpshared() returns an error number if the following condition is detected:

EINVAL The new value specified for the attribute is outside the range of legal values for that attribute.

SEE ALSO

cond_init(3T), **pthread_create**(3T), **pthread_cond_init**(3T), **pthread_mutex_init**(3T).

NAME

pthread_create, thr_create – thread creation

SYNOPSIS

POSIX

cc [*flag* **...]** *file* **... –lpthread [** *library* **...]**

#include <pthread.h>

int pthread_create(pthread_t **new_thread_ID*, **const pthread_attr_t** **attr*,
void * (**start_func***)(void *), void** **arg***);**

Solaris

cc [*flag* **...]** *file* **... –lthread [** *library* **...]**

#include <thread.h>

int thr_create(void **stack_base*, **size_t** *stack_size*, **void *(****start_func***)(void *),**
void **arg*, **long** *flags*, **thread_t** **new_thread_ID***);**

MT-LEVEL

MT-Safe

DESCRIPTION

Thread creation adds a new thread of control to the current process. The procedure **main**(), itself, is a single thread of control. Each thread executes simultaneously with all the other threads within the calling process, and with other threads from other active processes.

A newly created thread shares all of the calling process's global data with the other threads in this process; however, it has its own set of attributes and private execution stack. The new thread inherits the calling thread's signal mask, possibly, and scheduling priority. Pending signals for a new thread are not inherited and will be empty.

The call to create a thread takes the address of a user-defined function, specified by *start_func*, as one of its arguments, which is the complete execution routine for the new thread.

The lifetime of a thread begins with the successful return from **pthread_create()** or **thr_create**(), which calls *start_func*() and ends with either:

- the normal completion of *start_func*(),
- the return from an explicit call to **pthread_exit**(3T) or **thr_exit**(3T),
- a thread cancellation (see **pthread_cancel**(3T)). or
- the conclusion of the calling process (see **exit**(2)).

The new thread performs by calling the function defined by *start_func* with one argument, *arg*. If more than one argument needs to be passed to *start_func*, the arguments can be packed into a structure, and the address of that structure can be passed to *arg*.

If *start_func* returns, the thread will terminate with the exit status set to the *start_func* return value (see **pthread_exit**(3T) or **thr_exit**(3T)).

Note that when the thread returns in which **main()** originated from, the effect is the same as if there were an implicit call to **exit()** using the return value of **main()** as the exit status. This differs from a *start_func* return. However, if **main()** itself calls either **pthread_exit**(3T) or **thr_exit**(3T), only the main thread exits, not the entire process.

If the thread creation itself fails, a new thread is not created and the contents of the location referenced by the pointer to the new thread are undefined.

Attributes

The configuration of a set of attributes defines the behavior of a thread. At creation, each attribute of a new thread may be user-defined or set to the default. All attributes are defined upon thread creation, however, some may be dynamically modified after creation. Establishing these attributes varies depending upon whether POSIX or Solaris threads are used. Both implementations offer a few attributes the other does not.

The available attributes are:

Attribute	Description	API
contentionscope	Scheduled by threads library (local scope) or scheduled by the OS (global scope)	both
detachstate	Allows other threads to wait for a particular thread to terminate	both
stackaddr	Sets a pointer to the thread's stack	both
stacksize	Sets the size of the thread's stack	both
concurrency	Elevates concurrency, if possible	Solaris
priority	Sets ranking within the policy (scheduling class)	both
policy	Sets scheduling class; **SCHED_OTHER**	POSIX
inheritsched	Determines whether scheduling parameters are inherited or explicitly defined	POSIX
suspended	Sets thread to runnable vs. suspended	Solaris
daemon	Defines a thread's behavior to be like a daemon	Solaris

POSIX

pthread_create() creates a new thread within a process with attributes defined by *attr*. Default attributes are used if *attr* is **NULL**. If any attributes specified by *attr* are changed in the attribute object prior to the call to **pthread_create**(), the new thread will acquire those changes. However, if any attributes specified by *attr* are changed after the call to **pthread_create**(), the attributes of existing threads will not be affected. Since **pthread_create**() can use an attribute object in its call, a user-defined thread creation must be preceded by a user-defined attribute object (see **pthread_attr_init**(3T)). Upon successful completion, and if the return value is not **NULL**, **pthread_create**() will store the ID of the created thread in the location referenced by *new_thread_ID*.

It is recommended that for POSIX thread creation, all attribute objects, *attr*s, which will be used later during creation calls, be initialized and modified in the early stages of program execution.

The default creation attributes for **pthread_create**(3T) are:

Attribute	Default Value	Meaning of Default Value
contentionscope	**PTHREAD_SCOPE_PROCESS**	Resource competition within process
detachstate	**PTHREAD_CREATE_JOINABLE**	Joinable by other threads
stackaddr	**NULL**	Allocated by system
stacksize	**NULL**	1 megabyte
priority	**NULL**	Parent (calling) thread's priority
policy	**SCHED_OTHER**	Determined by system
inheritsched	**PTHREAD_EXPLICIT_SCHED**	Scheduling attributes explicitly set, e.g., policy is **SCHED_OTHER**.

Default thread creation:

```
pthread_t tid;

void *start_func(void *), *arg;
pthread_create(&tid, NULL, start_func, arg);
```

This would have the same effect as:

```
pthread_attr_t attr;

pthread_attr_init(&attr); /* initialize attr with default attributes */
pthread_create(&tid, &attr, start_func, arg);
```

User-defined thread creation:

To create a thread that is scheduled on a system-wide basis (i.e., a bound thread, as per the Solaris API), use:

pthread_attr_init(&attr); /* initialize attr with default attributes */
pthread_attr_setscope(&attr, PTHREAD_SCOPE_SYSTEM); /* sys-wide */
pthread_create(&tid, &attr, start_func, arg);

To customize the attributes for POSIX threads, see **pthread_attr_init**(3T).

A new thread created with **pthread_create**() uses the stack specified by the *stackaddr* attribute, and the stack continues for the number of bytes specified by the *stacksize* attribute. By default, the stack size is 1 megabyte (see **pthread_attr_setstacksize**(3T)). If the default is used for both the *stackaddr* and *stacksize* attributes, **pthread_create**() creates a stack for the new thread with at least 1 megabyte. (For customizing stack sizes, see **NOTES**).

Solaris

In the Solaris API, **thr_create**() either results in the creation of a default thread or a thread whose attributes are defined by the *flags* passed to **thr_create**(). There is no attribute object to configure, as there is in POSIX. The attributes are either the separate arguments, *stackaddr* or *stacksize*, or the result of bitwise inclusive OR-ing the possible values for *flags*.

The creation attributes for **thr_create**(3T) are:

Attribute	Default Value	Meaning of Default Value	Specified Via
contentionscope	NULL	Resource competition within process	flags
detachstate	NULL	Joinable by other threads	flags
stackaddr	NULL	Allocated by system	separate argument
stacksize	NULL	1 megabyte	separate argument
priority	NULL	Parent (calling) thread's priority	
concurrency	NULL	Determined by system	flags
suspended	NULL	Runnable, not suspended	flags
daemon	NULL	Not a daemon	flags

flags specifies which attributes are modifiable for the created thread. The value in *flags* is determined by the bitwise inclusive OR of the following:

THR_BOUND
This flag affects the contentionscope attribute of the thread. The new thread is created permanently bound to an LWP (i.e., it is a *bound thread*). This thread will

now contend among system-wide resources. The bind flag is equivalent to setting the *contentionscope* to the **PTHREAD_SCOPE_SYSTEM** in POSIX.

THR_DETACHED
This flag affects the detachstate attribute of the thread. The new thread is created detached. The exit status of a detached thread is not accessible to other threads. Its thread ID and other resources may be re-used as soon as the thread terminates. **thr_join**(3T) (nor **pthread_join**(3T)) will not wait for a detached thread. This is equivalent to **PTHREAD_CREATE_DETACHED** in POSIX, which is the default for POSIX.

THR_NEW_LWP
This flag affects the concurrency attribute of the thread. The desired concurrency level for unbound threads is increased by one. This is similar to incrementing concurrency by one via **thr_setconcurrency**(3T). Typically, this adds a new LWP to the pool of LWPs running unbound threads.

THR_SUSPENDED
This flag affects the suspended attribute of the thread. The new thread is created suspended and will not execute *start_func* until it is started by **thr_continue()**.

THR_DAEMON
This flag affects the daemon attribute of the thread. The thread is marked as a daemon. The process will exit when all non-daemon threads exit. **thr_join**(3T) will not wait for a daemon thread. Daemon threads do not interfere with the exit conditions for a process. A process will terminate when all regular threads exit or the process calls **exit()**. Daemon threads are most useful in libraries that want to use threads.

Default thread creation:

```
thread_t tid;

void *start_func(void *), *arg;
thr_create(NULL, NULL, start_func, arg, NULL, &tid);
```

User-defined thread creation:

To create a thread scheduled on a system-wide basis (i.e., a bound thread), use:

```
thr_create(NULL, NULL, start_func, arg, THR_BOUND, &tid);
```

Another example of customization is, if both **THR_BOUND** and **THR_NEW_LWP** are specified then, typically, two LWPs are created, one for the bound thread and another for the pool of LWPs running unbound threads.

```
thr_create(NULL, NULL, start_func, arg,
    THR_BOUND | THR_NEW_LWP, &tid);
```

With **thr_create()**, the new thread will use the stack starting at the address specified by *stack_base* and continuing for *stack_size* bytes. *stack_size* must be greater than the value returned by **thr_min_stack**(3T). If *stack_base* is **NULL** then **thr_create()** allocates a stack for the new thread with at least *stack_size* bytes. If *stack_size* is zero then a default size is used. If *stack_size* is not zero, it must be greater than the value returned by **thr_min_stack**(3T) (see **NOTES**).

When *new_thread_ID* is not **NULL**, it points to a location where the ID of the new thread is stored if **thr_create()** is successful. The ID is only valid within the calling process.

RETURN VALUES

Zero indicates a successful return and a non-zero value indicates an error.

ERRORS

If any of the following conditions occur, these functions fail and return the corresponding value:

EAGAIN The system-imposed limit on the total number of threads in a process has been exceeded or some system resource has been exceeded (e.g., too many LWPs were created).

EINVAL The value specified by *attr* is invalid.

If any of the following conditions are detected, **pthread_create()** fails and returns the corresponding value:

ENOMEM Not enough memory was available to create the new thread.

If any of the following conditions are detected, **thr_create()** fails and returns the corresponding value:

EINVAL *stack_base* is not **NULL** and *stack_size* is less than the value returned by **thr_min_stack**(3T).

stack_base is **NULL** and *stack_size* is not zero and is less than the value returned by **thr_min_stack**(3T).

SEE ALSO

_lwp_create(2), **exit**(2), **exit**(3C), **pthread_attr_init**(3T), **pthread_cancel**(3T), **pthread_exit**(3T), **pthread_join**(3T), **thr_suspend**(3T), **thr_min_stack**(3T), **thr_setconcurrency**(3T), **threads**(3T).

NOTES

MT application threads execute independently of each other, thus their relative behavior is unpredictable. Therefore, it is possible for the thread executing **main()** to finish before all other user application threads.

Using **thr_join**(3T) in the following syntax:

```
while (thr_join(NULL, NULL, NULL) == 0)
    ;
```

will cause the invoking thread (which may be **main()**) to wait for the termination of all other undetached and non-daemon threads; however, the second and third arguments to **thr_join**(3T) need not necessarily be **NULL**.

pthread_join(3T), on the other hand, must specify the terminating thread (IDs) for which it will wait.

A thread has not terminated until **thr_exit**() has finished. The only way to determine this is by **thr_join**(). When **thr_join**() returns a departed thread, it means that this thread has terminated and its resources are reclaimable. For instance, if a user specified a stack to **thr_create**(), this stack can only be reclaimed after **thr_join**() has reported this thread as a departed thread. It is not possible to determine when a *detached* thread has terminated. A detached thread disappears without leaving a trace.

Typically, thread stacks allocated by **thr_create**() begin on page boundaries and any specified (a red-zone) size is rounded up to the next page boundary. A page with no access permission is appended to the top of the stack so that most stack overflows will result in a **SIGSEGV** signal being sent to the offending thread. Thread stacks allocated by the caller are used as is.

Using a default stack size for the new thread, instead of passing a user-specified stack size, results in much better **thr_create**() performance. The default stack size for a user-thread is 1 megabyte, in this implementation.

A user-specified stack size must be greater than the value **THR_MIN_STACK** or **PTHREAD_STACK_MIN**. A minimum stack size may not accommodate the stack frame for the user thread function *start_func*. If a stack size is specified, it must accommodate *start_func* requirements and the functions that it may call in turn, in addition to the minimum requirement.

It is usually very difficult to determine the runtime stack requirements for a thread. **THR_MIN_STACK** or **PTHREAD_STACK_MIN** specifies how much stack storage is required to execute a **NULL** *start_func*. The total runtime requirements for stack storage are dependent on the storage required to do runtime linking, the amount of storage required by library runtimes (like **printf**()) that your thread calls. Since these storage parameters are not known before the program runs, it is best to use default stacks. If you know your runtime requirements or decide to use stacks that are larger than the default, then it makes sense to specify your own stacks.

NAME

pthread_detach – dynamically detaching a thread

SYNOPSIS

POSIX

cc [*flag* **...]** *file* **... –lpthread [** *library* **...]**

#include <pthread.h>

int pthread_detach(pthread_t *threadID***);**

MT-LEVEL

MT-Safe

DESCRIPTION

pthread_detach() can dynamically reset the detachstate attribute of a thread to **PTHREAD_CREATE_DETACHED**. For example, a thread could detach itself as follows:

pthread_detach(**pthread_self**());

RETURN VALUES

Upon successful completion, 0 is returned; otherwise, a non-zero value indicates an error.

ERRORS

These functions fail and return the corresponding value, if any of the following conditions are detected:

EINVAL The value specified by *threadID* is not a joinable thread.

ESRCH The value specified by *threadID* is not an existing thread ID.

SEE ALSO

pthread_create(3T), **pthread_join**(3T).

NAME

pthread_equal – compare thread IDs

SYNOPSIS

cc [*flag* **...]** *file* **... –lpthread [** *library* **...]**

#include <pthread.h>

int pthread_equal(pthread_t *t1*, **pthread_t** *t2***);**

MT-LEVEL

MT-Safe

DESCRIPTION

The **pthread_equal**() function compares the thread IDs *t1* and *t2*.

RETURN VALUES

If *t1* and *t2* are equal, **pthread_equal**() returns a non-zero value; otherwise, 0 is returned.

If either *t1* or *t2* is an invalid thread ID, the result is unpredictable.

SEE ALSO

pthread_create(3T), **pthread_self**(3T).

NOTES

Solaris thread IDs do not require an equal function because the **thread_t** structure is really an unsigned int.

NAME

pthread_exit, thr_exit – thread termination

SYNOPSIS

POSIX

cc [*flag* ...] *file* ... **–lpthread** [*library* ...]

#include <pthread.h>

void pthread_exit(void **status***);**

Solaris

cc [*flag* ...] *file* ... **–lthread** [*library* ...]

#include <thread.h>

void thr_exit(void **status***);**

MT-LEVEL

MT-Safe

DESCRIPTION

pthread_exit() and **thr_exit**() terminates the calling threads, similar to how **exit**(3C) terminates calling processes. If the calling thread is not detached, then the thread's ID and the exit status specified by *status* are retained. The value *status* is then made available to any successful join with the terminating thread (see **pthread_join**(3T)); otherwise, *status* is disregarded allowing the thread's ID to be reclaimed immediately.

Upon thread termination, all thread-specific data bindings are released (see **pthread__key_create**(3T)), and its cancellation routines are called, but application visible process resources, including, but not limited to, mutexes and file descriptors are not released.

The cleanup handlers are called before the thread-specific data bindings are released (see **pthread_cancel**(3T)). Any cancellation cleanup handlers that have been pushed and not yet popped will be popped in reverse order of when they were pushed and then executed. If the thread still has any thread-specific data after all cancellation cleanup handlers have been executed, appropriate destructor functions will be called in an unspecified order. If any thread, including the **main()** thread, calls **pthread_exit**(), only that thread will exit.

If **main**() returns or exits (either implicitly or explicitly), or any thread explicitly calls **exit**(), the entire process will exit.

If any thread (except the **main()** thread) implicitly or explicitly returns, the result is the same as if the thread called **pthread_exit()** and it will return the value of *status* as the exit code.

The process will terminate with an exit status of 0 after the last thread has terminated (including the **main()** thread). This action is the same as if the application had called **exit()** with a zero argument at any time.

RETURN VALUES

pthread_exit() or **thr_exit()** does not return to its caller.

SEE ALSO

exit(3C), **pthread_cancel**(3T), **pthread_create**(3T), **pthread_join**(3T), **pthread_key_create**(3T), **pthread_cancel**(3T).

NOTES

Although only POSIX implements cancellation, cancellation can be used with Solaris threads, due to their interoperability.

Do not call **pthread_exit()** from a cancellation cleanup handler or destructor function that will be invoked as a result of either an implicit or explicit call to **pthread_exit()**.

status should not reference any variables local to the calling thread.

NAME

pthread_join, thr_join – wait for thread termination

SYNOPSIS

POSIX

cc [*flag* ...] *file* ... **–lpthread** [*library* ...]

#include <pthread.h>

int pthread_join(pthread_t *target_thread*, **void** ***status*);

Solaris

cc [*flag* ...] *file* ... **–lthread** [*library* ...]

#include <thread.h>

int thr_join(thread_t *target_thread*, **thread_t** **departed*, **void** ***status*);

MT-LEVEL

MT-Safe

DESCRIPTION

The **pthread_join()** and **thr_join()** functions suspend processing of the calling thread until the target *target_thread* completes. *target_thread* must be a member of the current process and it cannot be a detached or daemon thread (see **pthread_create**(3T)).

Several threads cannot wait for the same thread to complete; one thread will complete successfully and the others will terminate with an error of **ESRCH**. **pthread_join()** or **thr_join()** will not block processing of the calling thread if the target *target_thread* has already terminated.

pthread_join() or **thr_join()** will return successfully when the target *target_thread* terminates.

POSIX

If a **pthread_join()** call returns successfully with a non-null *status* argument, the value passed to **pthread_exit**(3T) by the terminating thread will be placed in the location referenced by *status*.

If the **pthread_join()** calling thread is cancelled, then the target *target_thread* will remain joinable by **pthread_join()**. However, the calling thread may set up a cancellation cleanup handler on *target_thread* prior to the join call, which may detach the target thread by calling **pthread_detach**(3T). (See **pthread_detach**(3T) and **pthread_cancel**(3T).)

pthread_join() does not return the *target_thread*'s ID, as does the Solaris threads' function **thr_join()**, and it does not cause the calling thread to wait for detached threads. **pthread_join()** returns **ESRCH** if the target is detached.

Solaris

If a **thr_join()** call returns successfully with a non-null *status* argument, the value passed to **thr_exit**(3T) by the terminating thread will be placed in the location referenced by *status*.

If the target *target_thread* ID is 0, **thr_join()** waits for any undetached thread in the process to terminate.

If *departed* is not **NULL**, it points to a location that is set to the ID of the terminated thread if **thr_join()** returns successfully.

RETURN VALUES

If successful, both **pthread_join()** and **thr_join()** would return 0; otherwise, an error number is returned to indicate the error.

ERRORS

ESRCH No undetached thread could be found corresponding to that specified by the given thread ID.

EDEADLK A deadlock was detected or the value of *target_thread* specifies the calling thread. (See **NOTES** section below.)

SEE ALSO

wait(2), **pthread_create**(3T), **pthread_exit**(3T), **pthread_join**(3T).

NOTES

Using **thr_join**(3T) in the following syntax:

```
while (thr_join(NULL, NULL, NULL) == 0)
    ;
```

will wait for the termination of all other undetached and non-daemon threads; after which, **EDEADLK** will be returned.

pthread_join(3T), on the other hand, must specify the *target_thread* ID for whose termination it will wait.

Calling **pthread_join()** also "detaches" the thread, that is, **pthread_join()** includes the effect of **pthread_detach()**. Hence, if a thread were to be cancelled when blocked in **pthread_join()**, an explicit detach would have to be done in the cancellation cleanup handler. In fact, the routine **pthread_detach()** exists mainly for this reason.

NAME

pthread_key_create, pthread_setspecific, pthread_getspecific, pthread_key_delete, thr_keycreate, thr_setspecific, thr_getspecific – thread-specific-data functions

SYNOPSIS

POSIX

cc [*flag* **...]** *file* **... –lpthread [** *library* **...]**

#include <pthread.h>

int pthread_key_create(pthread_key_t ***_keyp_, void (***_destructor_**)(void *value));**

int pthread_setspecific(pthread_key_t *key*, **const void ***_value_**);**

void *pthread_getspecific(pthread_key_t *key***);**

int pthread_key_delete(pthread_key_t *key***);**

Solaris

cc [*flag* **...]** *file* **... –lthread [** *library* **...]**

#include <thread.h>

int thr_keycreate(thread_key_t ***_keyp_, void (***_destructor_**)(void ***_value_**));**

int thr_setspecific(thread_key_t *key*, **void ***_value_**);**

int thr_getspecific(thread_key_t *key*, **void ****_valuep_**);**

MT-LEVEL

MT-Safe

DESCRIPTION

Create Key

In general, thread key creation allocates a key that locates data specific to each thread in the process. The key is global to all threads in the process, which allows each thread to bind a value to the key once the key has been created. The key independently maintains specific values for each binding thread. **pthread_key_create()** or **thr_keycreate()** allocates a global *key* name space, pointed to by *keyp*, that is visible to all threads in the process. Each thread is initially bound to a private element of this *key*, which allows access to its thread-specific data.

Upon key creation, a new key is assigned the value **NULL** for all active threads. Additionally, upon thread creation, all previously created keys in the new thread are assigned the value **NULL**.

Optionally, a destructor function, *destructor*, may be associated with each *key*. Upon thread exit, if a *key* has a non-**NULL** *destructor* function and the thread has a non-**NULL** *value* associated with that *key*, the *destructor* function is called with the current associated *value*. If more than one *destructor* exists for a thread when it exits, the order of destructor calls is unspecified.

Set Value

Once a key has been created, each thread may bind a new *value* to the key using **pthread_setspecific()** or **thr_setspecific()**. The values are unique to the binding thread and are individually maintained. These values continue for the life of the calling thread.

Proper synchronization of *key* storage and access must be ensured by the caller. The *value* argument to either **pthread_setspecific()** or **thr_setspecific()** is generally a pointer to a block of dynamically allocated memory reserved by the calling thread for its own use.

At thread exit, the *destructor* function, which is associated at time of creation, is called and it uses the specific key value as its sole argument.

POSIX Get Value

pthread_getspecific() returns the current value bound to the designated *key* specified by the calling thread. If the key has no value bound to it, the value **NULL** is returned. (see "Warnings" section below).

Solaris Get Value

thr_getspecific() stores the current value bound to *key* for the calling thread into the location pointed to by *valuep*.

POSIX Delete Key

pthread_key_delete() deletes a thread-specific data key formerly created by **pthread_key_create()** or **thr_keycreate()**. At the time **pthread_key_delete()** is called, the thread-specific data values associated with *key* do not have to be **NULL**. It is the application's responsibility to perform cleanup actions related to the deleted key or associated thread-specific data in any threads. Cleanup can be done either before or after calling **pthread_key_delete()**. **pthread_key_delete()** does not invoke a destructor function.

Although **pthread_key_create()**'s or **thr_keycreate()**'s *destructor* function should clean-up the *key*'s thread-specific-data storage, **pthread_key_delete()** needs to be used to free the storage associated with the *key*.

Solaris threads do not have a similar delete function.

RETURN VALUES

POSIX/Solaris

If successful, **pthread_key_create()**, **pthread_setspecific()**, **pthread_key_delete()**, **thr_keycreate()**, **thr_setspecific()**, or **thr_getspecific()**

returns **0**; otherwise, an error number is returned to indicate the error. **pthread_getspecific**() does not return any errors.

ERRORS

If the following conditions occur, **pthread_key_create**() or **thr_keycreate**() return the corresponding error number:

EAGAIN The system lacked the necessary resources to create another thread-specific data key, or the number of keys exceeds the per-process limit of **PTHREAD_KEYS_MAX**.

ENOMEM Insufficient memory exists to create the key.

If the following conditions occur, **pthread_key_create**(), **pthread_setspecific**(), **thr_keycreate**(), or **thr_setspecific**() return the corresponding error number:

ENOMEM Insufficient memory exists to associate the value with the key.

For each of the following conditions, if the condition is detected, **pthread_setspecific**(), **thr_setspecific**(), or **pthread_key_delete**() return the corresponding error number:

EINVAL The *key* value is invalid.

SEE ALSO

pthread_exit(3T).

WARNINGS

pthread_setspecific(), **pthread_getspecific**(), **thr_setspecific**(), and **thr_getspecific**(), may be called either explicitly, or implicitly from a thread-specific data destructor function. However, calling **pthread_setspecific**() or **thr_setspecific**() from a destructor may result in lost storage or infinite loops.

NAME

pthread_kill, thr_kill – send a signal to a thread

SYNOPSIS

POSIX

cc [*flag* ...] *file* ... **–lpthread** [*library* ...]

#include <signal.h>
#include <pthread.h>

int pthread_kill(pthread_t *thread*, **int** *sig*);

Solaris

cc [*flag* ...] *file* ... **–lthread** [*library* ...]

#include <signal.h>
#include <thread.h>

int thr_kill(thread_t *thread*, **int** *sig*);

MT-LEVEL

MT-Safe

Async-Signal-Safe

DESCRIPTION

pthread_kill() sends the *sig* signal to the thread designated by *thread*. *thread* must be a member of the same process as the calling thread. *sig* must be one of the signals listed in signal(5); with the exception of **SIGLWP**, **SIGCANCEL**, and **SIGWAITING** being reserved and off limits to **thr_kill()** or **pthread_kill()**. If *sig* is **0**, a validity check is done for the existence of the target thread; no signal is sent.

thr_kill() performs the same function as **pthread_kill()**.

RETURN VALUES

Upon successful completion, **pthread_kill()** and **thr_kill()** return **0**; otherwise, they return an error number. In the event of failure, no signal is sent.

ERRORS

ESRCH No thread was found that corresponded to the thread designated by *thread* ID.

EINVAL The *sig* argument value is not zero and is an invalid or an unsupported signal number.

SEE ALSO

kill(2), **sigaction**(2), **pthread_self**(3T), **pthread_sigmask**(3T), **raise**(3C), **signal**(5).

NOTES

Although **pthread_kill()** is async-signal-safe with respect to the Solaris environment, this safeness is not guaranteed to be portable to other POSIX domains.

NAME

pthread_mutex_setprioceiling, pthread_mutex_getprioceiling – change the priority ceiling of a mutex

SYNOPSIS

cc [*flag* **...**] *file* **... –lpthread** [*library* **...**]

#include <pthread.h>

int pthread_mutex_getprioceiling(const pthread_mutex_t **mutex***,**
int **prioceiling***);**

int pthread_mutex_setprioceiling(pthread_mutex_t **mutex***,**
int *prioceiling***, int** **old_ceiling***);**

MT-LEVEL

MT-Safe

DESCRIPTION

In the current implementation, **{_POSIX_THREAD_PRIO_PROTECT}** is undefined and the functions **pthread_mutex_setprioceiling**() and **pthread_mutex_getprioceiling**() return **ENOSYS**.

SEE ALSO

pthread_mutex_init(3T).

NAME

pthread_mutexattr_init, pthread_mutexattr_destroy, pthread_mutexattr_setpshared, pthread_mutexattr_getpshared, pthread_mutexattr_setprotocol, pthread_mutexattr_getprotocol, pthread_mutexattr_setprioceiling, pthread_mutexattr_getprioceiling – mutex initialization attributes

SYNOPSIS

cc [*flag* **...**] *file* **... –lpthread** [*library* **...**]

#include <pthread.h>

int pthread_mutexattr_init(pthread_mutexattr_t **attr*);

int pthread_mutexattr_destroy(pthread_mutexattr_t **attr*);

int pthread_mutexattr_setpshared(pthread_mutexattr_t **attr*,
    int *process-shared*);

int pthread_mutexattr_getpshared(const pthread_mutexattr_t **attr*,
    int **process-shared*);

MT-LEVEL

MT-Safe

DESCRIPTION

Initialize

pthread_mutexattr_init() initializes a mutex attributes object, *attr*, with the default value for its attribute, which is **PTHREAD_PROCESS_PRIVATE**. If the *process-shared* attribute is **PTHREAD_PROCESS_PRIVATE**, only threads created within the same process as the thread that initialized the mutex can access the mutex. If threads of differing processes attempt to access the mutex, the behavior is unpredictable.

Attempts to initialize an already initialized mutex variable attributes object will leave the storage allocated by the previous initialization unallocated.

Once a mutex attributes object is used to initialize one or more mutexes, any function that affects the attributes object (including destruction) will not affect any previously initialized mutexes.

Destroy

pthread_mutexattr_destroy() destroys a mutex attributes object; the object will then become uninitialized. A destroyed mutex attributes object can be reinitialized using **pthread_mutexattr_init()**. The results of referencing the object after it has been destroyed are undefined.

Set/Get Scope

pthread_mutexattr_setpshared() and **pthread_mutexattr_getpshared()** sets the *process-shared* attribute in an initialized attributes object pointed to by *attr*, and gets the value of the *process-shared* attribute from the attributes object pointed to by *attr*, respectively.

At present, only the attribute *process-shared* is defined.

Unsupported Interfaces

Currently, the following interfaces, which are optional under POSIX, are not supported:

int pthread_mutexattr_setprotocol (pthread_mutexattr_t *attr, int protocol);

RETURN VALUES

Upon successful completion, **pthread_mutexattr_init()**, **pthread_mutexattr_destroy()**, **pthread_mutexattr_setprotocol()**, **pthread_mutexattr_getprotocol()**, **pthread_mutexattr_setprioceiling()**, **pthread_mutexattr_getprioceiling()**, and **pthread_mutexattr_setpshared()** return **0**; otherwise, an error number is returned.

Upon successful completion, **pthread_mutexattr_getpshared()** returns **0** and stores the value of the *process-shared* attribute of *attr* in the object pointed to by the *process-shared* parameter; otherwise, an error number is returned.

ERRORS

The function **pthread_mutexattr_init()** returns an error number if the following condition is detected:

ENOMEM Insufficient memory exists to initialize the mutex attributes object.

The functions **pthread_mutexattr_destroy()**, **pthread_mutexattr_getpshared()**, and **pthread_mutexattr_setpshared()** return an error number if the following condition is detected:

EINVAL The value specified by *attr* is invalid.

The function **pthread_mutexattr_setpshared()** returns an error number if the following condition is detected:

EINVAL The new value specified for the attribute is outside the range of legal values for that attribute.

Currently, the functions **pthread_mutexattr_setprotocol()**, **pthread_mutexattr_getprotocol()**, **pthread_mutexattr_setprioceiling()**, and **pthread_mutexattr_getprioceiling()** always return the following error code:

ENOSYS These optional interfaces are not supported.

SEE ALSO

pthread_cond_init(3T), **pthread_create**(3T), **pthread_mutex_init**(3T).

NOTES

The functions **pthread_mutexattr_setprotocol**(), **pthread_mutexattr_getprotocol**(), **pthread_mutexattr_setprioceiling**(), and **pthread_mutexattr_getprioceiling**() return **ENOSYS** in the current implementation, i.e., this function is not currently implemented.

NAME

pthread_once – dynamic package initialization

SYNOPSIS

cc [*flag* **...]** *file* **... –lpthread [** *library* **...]**

#include <pthread.h>

pthread_once_t *once_control* **= PTHREAD_ONCE_INIT;**

int pthread_once(pthread_once_t **once_control*, **void (****init_routine***)(void));**

MT-LEVEL

MT-Safe

DESCRIPTION

If any thread in a process with a *once_control* parameter makes a call to **pthread_once**(), the first call will summon the *init_routine*(), but subsequent calls will not. The *once_control* parameter determines whether the associated initialization routine has been called. The *init_routine*() is complete upon return of **pthread_once**().

pthread_once() is not a cancellation point; however, if the function **init_routine()** is a cancellation point and is canceled, the effect on *once_control* is the same as if **pthread_once**() had never been called.

The constant **PTHREAD_ONCE_INIT** is defined in the <pthread.h> header.

If *once_control* has automatic storage duration or is not initialized by **PTHREAD_ONCE_INIT**, the behavior of **pthread_once**() is undefined.

RETURN VALUES

pthread_once() returns **0** upon successful completion; otherwise, an error number is returned.

ERRORS

EINVAL *once_control* or *init_routine* is **NULL.**

NOTES

Solaris threads do not offer this functionality.

NAME

pthread_self, thr_self – get calling thread's ID

SYNOPSIS

POSIX

cc [*flag* ...] *file* ... –lpthread [*library* ...]

#include <pthread.h>

pthread_t pthread_self(void);

Solaris

cc [*flag* ...] *file* ... –lthread [*library* ...]

#include <thread.h>

thread_t thr_self(void)

MT-LEVEL

MT-Safe

DESCRIPTION

thr_self() returns the thread ID of the calling thread.

pthread_self() performs the same function as **thr_self**().

SEE ALSO

pthread_create(3T), **pthread_equal**(3T).

NAME

pthread_setschedparam, pthread_getschedparam, thr_setprio, thr_getprio – dynamic access to thread scheduling

SYNOPSIS

POSIX

cc [*flag* ...] *file* ... **–lpthread** [*library* ...]

#include <pthread.h>

int pthread_setschedparam(pthread_t *target_thread*, **int** *policy*,
    const struct sched_param **param*);

int pthread_getschedparam(pthread_t *target_thread*, **int** **policy*,
    struct sched_param **param*);

Solaris

cc [*flag* ...] *file* ... **–lthread** [*library* ...]

#include <thread.h>

int thr_setprio(thread_t *target_thread*, **int** *priority*);

int thr_getprio(thread_t *target_thread*, **int** **priority*);

MT-LEVEL

MT-Safe

DESCRIPTION

Thread scheduling is controlled by three attributes: its scope of contention, being either interprocess or intraprocess (bound vs. unbound), (see **priocntl**(2)); a relative scheduling priority; and a scheduling policy.

Contentionscope

Bound threads, which are interprocess, compete system-wide for scheduling resources and must be set at creation, for example:

```
pthread_attr_setscope(&attr, PTHREAD_SCOPE_SYSTEM);
pthread_create(NULL, &attr, thread_routine, arg);
```

OR

```
thr_create(NULL, NULL, thread_routine, arg, THR_BOUND, NULL);
```

A bound thread is bound to an LWP and its scheduling is dependent upon the scheduling of the LWP to which it is bound. LWPs compete with other LWPs in other processes, however, their scheduling may be dynamically controlled by **priocntl**(2), or **sched_setscheduler**(3R).

By default, the scope for newly created threads are unbound, or intraprocess, and their setting is **PTHREAD_SCOPE_PROCESS** or **NULL**. An unbound thread is scheduled by libthread or libpthread on an underlying LWP, which competes with other LWPs in the same process.

The following dynamic scheduling functions should be used only with unbound threads: **pthread_setschedparam()**, **pthread_getschedparam()**, **thr_setprio()**, and **thr_getprio()**.

Priority

Priority scheduling is determined as follows:

- Higher priority threads are scheduled before lower priority threads.
- Both POSIX and Solaris assume that the priority is inherited across a thread create.
- POSIX can modify priority at creation time (see **pthread_attr_setschedparam**(3T)). Equivalently, a Solaris thread can be created suspended and its priority can be modified.

pthread_setschedparam() and **thr_setprio()** can dynamically modify an unbound thread's priority, and **pthread_getschedparam()** and **thr_getprio()** can read an unbound thread's priority.

Policy

The scheduling *policy* setting is:

SCHED_OTHER
(*system default, often time-sharing*)
Competing threads in this class are multiplexed according to their relative *priority*.

NOTE: POSIX specifies, under an option, the additional policies, **SCHED_FIFO** and **SCHED_RR**. Solaris has chosen to not implement these options at this time. Equivalent functionality may be obtained by creating bound threads (i.e., threads with the **PTHREAD_SCOPE_SYSTEM** value for the *contentionscope* attribute), which use **priocntl**(2). See **pthread_create**(3T) and **priocntl**(2).

POSIX Scheduling

The **pthread_setschedparam()** and **pthread_getschedparam()** functions allow the scheduling policy and scheduling priority parameters to be retrieved and set for individual threads within a multithreaded process.

The **pthread_setschedparam()** function sets the scheduling policy and related scheduling priority for the thread ID given by *target_thread* to the policy and associated priority provided in *policy*, and the **sched_priority** member of *param*, respectively.

No scheduling parameters are changed for the target thread if **pthread_setschedparam**() fails.

For **SCHED_OTHER**, the affected scheduling parameter is the *sched_priority* member of the **sched_param** structure.

Presently, **SCHED_OTHER** is the only policy supported. An **ENOTSUP** error will occur following an attempt to set policy as **SCHED_FIFO** or **SCHED_RR**. (The latter two policies are optional under POSIX.)

The **pthread_getschedparam**() function retrieves the scheduling policy and scheduling priority parameters for the thread ID given by *target_thread*, and then stores the values in *policy* and the **sched_priority** member of *param*, respectively.

Solaris Scheduling

Solaris scheduling may only dynamically affect *priority*. There is no functionality to alter the *policy* of any thread; by default, a Solaris thread's schedule is equivalent to **SCHED_OTHER**, which is the only available Solaris policy.

thr_setprio() changes the priority of the thread, specified by *target_thread*, within the current process to the priority specified by *priority*. Currently, by default, threads are scheduled based on fixed priorities that range from zero, the least significant, to 127. The *target_thread* will preempt lower priority threads, and will yield to higher priority threads in their contention for LWPs, not CPUs.

The function **thr_getprio**() stores the current priority for the thread specified by *target_thread* in the location pointed to by *priority*. Note that thread priorities regulate access to LWPs, not CPUs, and hence are different from realtime priorities, which regulate and enforce access to CPU resources. A thread's priority set via these functions is more like a hint in terms of guaranteed access to execution resources. Programs that need access to "real" priorities should use bound threads in the realtime class (see **priocntl**(2)).

RETURN VALUES

Zero is returned upon successful completion; otherwise, an error number is returned.

ERRORS

For each of the following conditions, these functions return an error number if the condition is detected.

ESRCH The value specified by *target_thread* does not refer to an existing thread.

For each of the following conditions, **pthread_setschedparam**() and **pthread_getschedparam**() return an error number if the condition is detected.

ENOTSUP The only policy supported is **SCHED_OTHER**. Attempts to set policy as **SCHED_FIFO** or **SCHED_RR** will result in the error **ENOTSUP**.

EINVAL The *policy* or *param* specified value is invalid.

For each of the following conditions, if the condition is detected, **thr_setprio()** returns an error number.

EINVAL The value of *priority* makes no sense for the scheduling class associated with the *target_thread*.

SEE ALSO

priocntl(2), **sched_setparam**(3R), **sched_setscheduler**(3R), **pthread_attr_init**(3T), **pthread_create**(3T), **thr_suspend**(3T), **thr_yield**(3T).

NOTES

Currently, the only supported policy is **SCHED_OTHER**. Attempts to set policy as **SCHED_FIFO** or **SCHED_RR** will result in the error **ENOTSUP**.

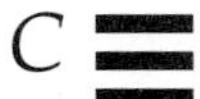

NAME

pthread_sigmask, thr_sigsetmask – change and/or examine calling thread's signal mask

SYNOPSIS

POSIX

cc [*flag* **...]** *file* **... –lpthread [** *library* **...]**

#include <pthread.h>
#include <signal.h>

int pthread_sigmask(int *how*, **const sigset_t** **set*, **sigset_t** **oset*);

Solaris

cc [*flag* **...]** *file* **... –lthread [** *library* **...]**

#include <thread.h>
#include <signal.h>

int thr_sigsetmask(int *how*, **const sigset_t** **set*, **sigset_t** **oset*);

MT-LEVEL

MT-Safe

Async-Signal-Safe

DESCRIPTION

pthread_sigmask() and **thr_sigsetmask()** changes and/or examines a calling thread's signal mask. Each thread has its own signal mask. A new thread inherits the calling thread's signal mask and priority, however, pending signals are not inherited. Signals pending for a new thread will be empty.

If the value of the argument *set* is not **NULL**, *set* points to a set of signals that can modify the currently blocked set. If the value of *set* is **NULL**, the value of *how* is insignificant and the thread's signal mask is unmodified; thus, **pthread_sigmask()** or **thr_sigsetmask()** can be used to inquire about the currently blocked signals.

The value of the argument *how* specifies the method in which the set is changed. *how* takes one of the following values:

SIG_BLOCK *set* corresponds to a set of signals to block. They are added to the current signal mask.

SIG_UNBLOCK *set* corresponds to a set of signals to unblock. These signals are deleted from the current signal mask.

SIG_SETMASK *set* corresponds to the new signal mask. The current signal mask is replaced by *set*.

If the value of *oset* is not **NULL**, it points to the location where the previous signal mask is stored.

RETURN VALUES

Zero is returned upon successful completion; otherwise, a non-zero value indicates an error.

ERRORS

If any of the following conditions occur, **pthread_sigmask()** or **thr_sigsetmask()** fails and returns the corresponding value:

EINVAL *set* is not **NULL** and the value of *how* is not defined.

If any of the following conditions are detected, **pthread_sigmask()** or **thr_sigsetmask()** fails and returns the corresponding value:

EFAULT *set* or *oset* are not valid addresses.

SEE ALSO

sigaction(2), **sigprocmask**(2), **sigwait**(2), **sigsetops**(3C), **pthread_cancel**(3T), **pthread_create**(3T), **pthread_exit**(3T), **pthread_join**(3T), **pthread_kill**(3T), **pthread_self**(3T).

NOTES

It is not possible to block signals that cannot be ignored (see **sigaction**(2)). If using the threads library, it is not possible to block the signals **SIGLWP** or **SIGCANCEL**, which are reserved by the threads library. Additionally, it is impossible to unblock the signal **SIGWAITING**, which is always blocked on all threads. This restriction is quietly enforced by the threads library.

Using **sigwait**(2) in a dedicated thread allows asynchronous signals to be managed synchronously; however, **sigwait**(2) should never be used to manage synchronous signals. Synchronous signals (i.e., exceptions or traps) are sent by the process itself, such as **SIGFPE**, **pthread_kill**(3T), **pthread_exit**(3T), **pthread_cancel**(3T), **thr_kill**(3T), or **thr_exit**(3T), rather than device interrupts or signals sent by other processes.

Synchronous signals are exceptions that are generated by a thread and are directed at the thread causing the exception. Since **sigwait()** blocks waiting for signals, the blocking thread will not generate any synchronous signals.

If **sigprocmask**(2) is used in a multithreaded program, it will be the same as if **thr_sigsetmask()** or **pthread_sigmask()** has been called. Note that POSIX leaves the semantics of the call to **sigprocmask**(2) unspecified in a multithreaded process, so programs that care about POSIX portability should not depend on this semantic.

If a signal is delivered while a thread is waiting on a condition variable, the **cond_wait()** will be interrupted and the handler will be executed. The handler should assume that the lock protecting the condition variable is held.

Although **pthread_sigmask()** is Async-Signal-Safe with respect to the Solaris environment, this safeness is not guaranteed to be portable to other POSIX domains.

NAME

rwlock, rwlock_init, rwlock_destroy, rw_rdlock, rw_wrlock, rw_tryrdlock, rw_trywrlock, rw_unlock – multiple readers, single writer locks

SYNOPSIS

cc [*flag* **...]** *file* **... –lthread –lc [** *library* **...]**

#include <synch.h>

int rwlock_init(rwlock_t ****rwlp*, **int *type*, **void *** *arg*);

**int rwlock_destroy(rwlock_t ****rwlp*);

**int rw_rdlock(rwlock_t ****rwlp*);

**int rw_wrlock(rwlock_t ****rwlp*);

**int rw_unlock(rwlock_t ****rwlp*);

**int rw_tryrdlock(rwlock_t ****rwlp*);

**int rw_trywrlock(rwlock_t ****rwlp*);

MT-LEVEL

MT-Safe

DESCRIPTION

Many threads can have simultaneous read-only access to data, while only one thread can have write access at any given time. Multiple read access with single write access is controlled by locks, which are generally used to protect data that is frequently searched.

Readers/writer locks can synchronize threads in this process and other processes if they are allocated in writable memory and shared among cooperating processes (see **mmap**(2)), and are initialized for this purpose.

Additionally, readers/writer locks must be initialized prior to use. **rwlock_init**() The readers/writer lock pointed to by *rwlp* is initialized by **rwlock_init**(). A readers/writer lock is capable of having several types of behavior, which is specified by *type*. *arg* is currently not used, although a future type may define new behavior parameters via *arg*.

type may be one of the following:

USYNC_PROCESS

The readers/writer lock can synchronize threads in this process and other processes. The readers/writer lock should be initialized by only one lock. *arg* is ignored.

USYNC_THREAD
The readers/writer lock can synchronize threads in this process, only. *arg* is ignored.

Additionally, readers/writer locks can be initialized by allocation in zeroed memory. A *type* of **USYNC_THREAD** is assumed in this case. Multiple threads must not simultaneously initialize the same readers/writer lock. And a readers/writer lock must not be re-initialized while in use by other threads.

The following are default readers/writer lock initialization (intraprocess):

rwlock_t rwlp;

rwlock_init(&rwlp, NULL, NULL);

OR

rwlock_init(&rwlp, USYNC_THREAD, NULL);

OR

rwlock_t rwlp = DEFAULTRWLOCK;

The following is a customized readers/writer lock initialization (interprocess):

rwlock_init(&rwlp, USYNC_PROCESS, NULL);

Any state associated with the readers/writer lock pointed to by *rwlp* are destroyed by **rwlock_destroy**() and the readers/writer lock storage space is not released.

rw_rdlock() gets a read lock on the readers/writer lock pointed to by *rwlp*. If the readers/writer lock is currently locked for writing, the calling thread blocks until the write lock is freed. Multiple threads may simultaneously hold a read lock on a readers/writer lock.

rw_tryrdlock() tries to get a read lock on the readers/writer lock pointed to by *rwlp*. If the readers/writer lock is locked for writing, it returns an error; otherwise, the read lock is acquired.

rw_wrlock() gets a write lock on the readers/writer lock pointed to by *rwlp*. If the readers/writer lock is currently locked for reading or writing, the calling thread blocks until all the read and write locks are freed. At any given time, only one thread may have a write lock on a readers/writer lock.

rw_trywrlock() tries to get a write lock on the readers/writer lock pointed to by *rwlp*. If the readers/writer lock is currently locked for reading or writing, it returns an error.

rw_unlock() unlocks a readers/writer lock pointed to by *rwlp*, if the readers/writer lock is locked and the calling thread holds the lock for either reading or writing. One of the other threads that is waiting for the readers/writer lock to be freed will be unblocked, provided there is other waiting threads. If the calling thread does not hold the lock for either reading or writing, no error status is returned, and the program's behavior is unknown.

RETURN VALUES

Upon successful completion, **0** is returned; otherwise, a non-zero value indicates an error.

ERRORS

These functions fail and return the corresponding value if any of the following conditions are detected.

EINVAL Invalid argument.

EFAULT *rwlp* or *arg* point to an illegal address.

rw_tryrdlock() or **rw_trywrlock**() fails and returns the corresponding value if any of the following conditions are detected.

EBUSY The readers/writer lock pointed to by *rwlp* was already locked.

SEE ALSO

mmap(2).

NOTES

These interfaces also available via:

#include <thread.h>

If multiple threads are waiting for a readers/writer lock, the acquisition order is random by default. However, some implementations may bias acquisition order to avoid depriving writers. The current implementation favors writers over readers.

NAME

semaphore, sema_init, sema_destroy, sema_wait, sema_trywait, sema_post – semaphores

SYNOPSIS

cc [*flag* **...]** *file* **... –lthread –lc [** *library* **...]**

#include <synch.h>

int sema_init(sema_t **sp*, **unsigned int** *count*, **int** *type*, **void *** *arg***);**

int sema_destroy(sema_t **sp***);**

int sema_wait(sema_t **sp***);**

int sema_trywait(sema_t **sp***);**

int sema_post(sema_t **sp***);**

MT-LEVEL

MT-Safe

sema_post() is Async-Signal-Safe

DESCRIPTION

A semaphore is a non-negative integer count and is generally used to coordinate access to resources. The initial semaphore count is set to the number of free resources, then threads slowly increment and decrement the count as resources are added and removed. If the semaphore count drops to zero, which means no available resources, threads attempting to decrement the semaphore will block until the count is greater than zero.

Semaphores can synchronize threads in this process and other processes if they are allocated in writable memory and shared among the cooperating processes (see **mmap**(2)), and have been initialized for this purpose.

Semaphores must be initialized before use; a semaphore pointed to by *sp* is initialized to *count* by **sema_init()**. *type* can assign several different types of behavior to a semaphore. No current type uses *arg* although it may be used in the future.

type may be one of the following:

USYNC_PROCESS
The semaphore can synchronize threads in this process and other processes. Initializing the semaphore should be done by only one process. *arg* is ignored.

USYNC_THREAD
The semaphore can synchronize threads only in this process. *arg* is ignored.

A semaphore must not be simultaneously initialized by multiple threads, nor re-initialized while in use by other threads.

Default semaphore initialization (intraprocess):

```
sema_t sp;
sema_init(&sp, NULL, NULL);
```

OR

```
sema_init(&sp, USYNC_THREAD, NULL);
```

OR

```
sema_t sp = DEFAULTSEMA;
```

Customized semaphore initialization (interprocess):

```
sema_init(&sp, USYNC_PROCESS, NULL);
```

sema_destroy() destroys any state related to the semaphore pointed to by *sp*. The semaphore storage space is not released.

sema_wait() blocks the calling thread until the semaphore count pointed to by *sp* is greater than zero, and then it atomically decrements the count.

sema_trywait() atomically decrements the semaphore count pointed to by *sp*, if the count is greater than zero; otherwise, it returns an error.

sema_post() atomically increments the semaphore count pointed to by *sp*. If there are any threads blocked on the semaphore, one will be unblocked.

The semaphore functionality described on this man page is for the Solaris threads implementation. For the POSIX-compliant semaphore interface documentation, see **sem_open**(3R), **sem_init**(3R), **sem_wait**(3R), **sem_post**(3R), **sem_getvalue**(3R), **sem_unlink**(3R), **sem_close**(3R), **sem_destroy**(3R)).

RETURN VALUES

Upon successful completion, **0** is returned; otherwise, a non-zero value indicates an error.

ERRORS

These functions fail and return the corresponding value if any of the following conditions are detected:

EINVAL Invalid argument.

EFAULT *sp* or *arg* points to an illegal address.

sema_wait() fails and returns the corresponding value if any of the following conditions are detected:

EINTR The wait was interrupted by a signal or **fork()**.

sema_trywait() fails and returns the corresponding value if any of the following conditions are detected:

EBUSY The semaphore pointed to by *sp* has a zero count.

SEE ALSO

mmap(2), **sem_open**(3R), **sem_init**(3R), **sem_wait**(3R), **sem_post**(3R), **sem_getvalue**(3R), **sem_unlink**(3R), **sem_close**(3R), **sem_destroy**(3R).

NOTES

These interfaces are also available via:

#include <thread.h>

If multiple threads are waiting for a semaphore, by default, there is no defined order of unblocking.

NAME

thr_min_stack – returns the minimum-allowable size for a thread's stack

SYNOPSIS

cc [*flag* **...**] *file* **... –lthread** [*library* **...**]

#include <thread.h>

size_t thr_min_stack(void);

MT-LEVEL

MT-Safe

DESCRIPTION

When a thread is created with a user-supplied stack, the user must reserve enough space to run this thread. In a dynamically linked execution environment, it is very hard to know what the minimum stack requirements are for a thread. The function **thr_min_stack**() returns the amount of space needed to execute a null thread. This is a thread that was created to execute a null procedure. A thread that does something useful should have a stack size that is **thr_min_stack() +** *<some increment>*.

Most users should not be creating threads with user-supplied stacks. This functionality was provided to support applications that wanted complete control over their execution environment.

Typically, users should let the threads library manage stack allocation. The threads library provides default stacks which should meet the requirements of any created thread.

thr_min_stack() will return the unsigned int **THR_MIN_STACK**, which is the minimum-allowable size for a thread's stack.

In this implementation the default size for a user-thread's stack is one megabyte. If the second argument to **thr_create**(3T) is **NULL**, then the default stack size for the newly created thread will be used. Otherwise, you may specify a stack size that is at least **THR_MIN_STACK**, yet less than the size of your machine's virtual memory.

It is recommended that the default stack size be used.

SEE ALSO

pthread_attr_init(3T), **pthread_create**(3T).

NOTES

The POSIX threads interface provides equivalent minimum stack information by calling:

(size_t) sysconf(_SC_THREAD_STACK_MIN);

NAME

thr_setconcurrency, thr_getconcurrency – get/set thread concurrency level

SYNOPSIS

cc [*flag* ...] *file* ... **–lthread** [*library* ...]

#include <thread.h>

int thr_setconcurrency(int *new_level***);**

int thr_getconcurrency(void);

MT-LEVEL

MT-Safe

DESCRIPTION

Unbound threads in a process (see **thr_create**(3T)) may or may not be required to be simultaneously active. By default, the threads system ensures that a sufficient number of threads are active so that the process can continue to make progress. While this conserves system resources, it may not produce the most effective level of concurrency. **thr_setconcurrency**() permits the application to give the threads system a hint, specified by *new_level*, for the desired level of concurrency. The actual number of simultaneously active threads may be larger or smaller than this number. The value for the desired concurrency level may also be affected by creating threads with the **THR_NEW_LWP** flag set (see **thr_create**(3T)).

If *new_level* is zero, the threads system will only ensure that a sufficient number of threads are active so that the process can continue to make progress.

thr_getconcurrency() returns the current value for the desired concurrency level. The actual number of simultaneously active threads may be larger or smaller than this number.

RETURN VALUES

thr_setconcurrency() returns zero when successful. A non-zero value indicates an error code.

thr_getconcurrency() always returns the current value for the desired concurrency level.

ERRORS

If any of the following conditions are detected, **thr_setconcurrency**() fails and returns the corresponding value:

EAGAIN The specified concurrency level would cause a system resource to be exceeded.

EINVAL *new_level* is negative.

SEE ALSO

thr_create(3T).

NOTES

The Solaris threads set/get concurrency functionality described on this man page are not implemented in the POSIX threads interface.

NAME

thr_suspend, thr_continue – suspend or continue thread execution

SYNOPSIS

cc [*flag* **...**] *file* **... –lthread** [*library* **...**]

#include <thread.h>

int thr_suspend(thread_t *target_thread***);**

int thr_continue(thread_t *target_thread***);**

MT-LEVEL

MT-Safe

DESCRIPTION

thr_suspend() immediately suspends the execution of the thread specified by *target_thread*. On successful return from **thr_suspend**(), the suspended thread is no longer executing. Once a thread is suspended, subsequent calls to **thr_suspend**() have no effect.

thr_continue() resumes the execution of a suspended thread. Once a suspended thread is continued, subsequent calls to **thr_continue**() have no effect.

A suspended thread will not be awakened by a signal. The signal stays pending until the execution of the thread is resumed by **thr_continue**().

RETURN VALUES

Zero is returned when successful. A non-zero value indicates an error.

ERRORS

If any of the following conditions are detected, **thr_suspend**() or **thr_continue**() fails and returns the corresponding value:

ESRCH *target_thread* cannot be found in the current process.

SEE ALSO

thr_create(3T).

NOTES

The are no POSIX counterparts to the Solaris threads suspend and continue functionality described on this man page.

NAME

thr_yield – thread yield to another thread

SYNOPSIS

cc [*flag* **...**] *file* **... –lthread** [*library* **...**]

#include <thread.h>

void thr_yield(void);

MT-LEVEL

MT-Safe

DESCRIPTION

thr_yield() causes the current thread to yield its execution in favor of another thread with the same or greater priority.

RETURN VALUES

thr_yield() returns nothing and does not set **errno**.

SEE ALSO

sched_yield(3R), **thr_setprio**(3T).

NOTES

The POSIX realtime function, **sched_yield**(3R) corresponds to **thr_yield**().

NAME

sched_get_priority_max, sched_get_priority_min, sched_rr_get_interval – get scheduling parameter limits

SYNOPSIS

cc [*flag* **...**] *file* **... –lposix4** [*library* **...**]

#include <sched.h>

int sched_get_priority_max(int *policy***);**

int sched_get_priority_min(int *policy***);**

int sched_rr_get_interval(pid_t *pid***, struct timespec** **interval***);**

```
struct timespec {
    time_t      tv_sec;         /* seconds */
    long        tv_nsec;        /* and nanoseconds */
};
```

MT-LEVEL

MT-Safe

DESCRIPTION

sched_get_priority_max() and **sched_get_priority_min()** return the appropriate maximum or minimum values, respectively, for the scheduling policy specified by *policy*.

sched_rr_get_interval() updates the **timespec** structure referenced by *interval* to contain the current execution time limit (i.e., time quantum) for the process specified by *pid* under the **SCHED_RR** policy. After that time limit expires, when another process at the same priority is ready to execute, a scheduling decision will be made. If *pid* is zero, the current execution time limit for the calling process is stored in *interval*.

The value of *policy* must be one of the scheduling policy values defined in **<sched.h>**: **SCHED_FIFO**, **SCHED_RR**, or **SCHED_OTHER**.

RETURN VALUES

If successful, **sched_get_priority_max()** or **sched_get_priority_min()** returns the appropriate maximum or minimum values, respectively.

If successful, **sched_rr_get_interval()** returns **0**.

If unsuccessful, these functions return **-1**, and set **errno** to indicate the error condition.

ERRORS

EINVAL The value of *policy* does not represent a defined scheduling policy.

ENOSYS **sched_get_priority_max(), sched_get_priority_min(),** and **sched_rr_get_interval()** are not supported by this implementation.

ESRCH No process can be found corresponding to that specified by *pid*.

SEE ALSO

sched_setparam(3R), **sched_setscheduler**(3R).

BUGS

In Solaris 2.5, these functions always return **–1** and set **errno** to **ENOSYS**, because this release does not support the Priority Scheduling option. It is Sun's intention to provide support for these interfaces in future releases.

NAME

sched_setparam, sched_getparam – set/get scheduling parameters

SYNOPSIS

cc [*flag* **...]** *file* **... –lposix4 [** *library* **...]**

#include <sched.h>

int sched_setparam(pid_t *pid*, **const struct sched_param** **param*);

int sched_getparam(pid_t *pid*, **struct sched_param** **param*);

```
struct sched_param {
    int   sched_priority;        /* process execution scheduling priority */
    ...
};
```

MT-LEVEL

MT-Safe

DESCRIPTION

sched_setparam() sets the scheduling parameters of the process specified by *pid* to the values specified by the **sched_param** structure referenced by *param*.

sched_getparam() stores the scheduling parameters of a process, specified by *pid*, in the **sched_param** structure pointed to by *param*.

If the target process has as its scheduling policy, **SCHED_FIFO** or **SCHED_RR**:

> If *pid* is zero, the scheduling parameters are set/stored for the calling process. Otherwise, if a process specified by *pid* exists and if the calling process has permission, the scheduling parameters are set/stored for the process whose process ID is equal to *pid*. The real or effective user ID of the calling process must match the real or saved (from **exec**(2)) user ID of the target process unless the effective user ID of the calling process is **0**. See **intro**(2).
>
> The target process, *pid*, whether it is running or not running, resumes execution after all other runnable processes of equal or greater priority have been scheduled to run.
>
> If the priority of the process, *pid*, is set higher than that of the lowest priority running process, and if process *pid* is ready to run, process *pid* preempts a lowest priority running process. Similarly, if the process calling **sched_setparam()** sets its own priority lower than that of one or more other non-empty process lists, the process that is the head of the highest priority list preempts the calling process. Thus, in either case, the originating process might not receive notification of the completion of the requested priority change until the higher priority process has executed.

The value of *param*->**sched_priority** must be an integer within the inclusive priority range for the current scheduling policy of the process specified by *pid*. Higher numerical values for the priority represent higher priorities.

RETURN VALUES

If successful, **sched_setparam**() and **sched_getparam**() returns **0**; otherwise, the priority remains unchanged, the function returns **-1,** and sets **errno** to indicate the error condition.

ERRORS

EINVAL One or more of **sched_setparam**()'s requested scheduling parameters is outside the range defined for the specified *pid*'s scheduling policy.

ENOSYS **sched_setparam**() and **sched_getparam**() are not supported by this implementation.

EPERM The requesting process does not have permission to set/get the scheduling parameters for the specified process, or does not have the appropriate privilege to invoke **sched_setparam**().

ESRCH No process can be found corresponding to that specified by *pid*.

SEE ALSO

intro(2), **exec**(2), **sched_setscheduler**(3R).

BUGS

In Solaris 2.5, these functions always return **–1** and set **errno** to **ENOSYS**, because this release does not support the Priority Scheduling option. It is Sun's intention to provide support for these interfaces in future releases.

NAME

sched_setscheduler, sched_getscheduler – set/get scheduling policy and scheduling parameters

SYNOPSIS

cc [*flag* **...**] *file* **... –lposix4** [*library* **...**]

#include <sched.h>

int sched_setscheduler(pid_t *pid*, **int** *policy*, **const struct sched_param** **param*);

int sched_getscheduler(pid_t *pid*);

```
struct sched_param {
     int sched_priority;    /* process execution scheduling priority */
     ...
};
```

MT-LEVEL

MT-Safe

DESCRIPTION

sched_setscheduler() sets the scheduling policy and scheduling parameters of the process specified by *pid* to *policy* and the parameters specified in the **sched_param** structure pointed to by *param*, respectively. The value of *param*->**sched_priority** must be any integer within the inclusive priority range for the scheduling policy specified by *policy*.

The possible values for the *policy* parameter are defined in the header file **<sched.h>**: **SCHED_FIFO**, **SCHED_RR**, or **SCHED_OTHER**.

If *pid* is zero, the scheduling policy and scheduling parameters are set for the calling process. Otherwise, if a process specified by *pid* exists and if the calling process has permission, the scheduling policy and scheduling parameters are set for the process whose process ID is equal to *pid*. The real or effective user ID of the calling process must match the real or saved (from **exec**(2)) user ID of the target process unless the effective user ID of the calling process is super-user. See **intro**(2).

To change the *policy* of any process to either of the realtime policies **SCHED_FIFO** or **SCHED_RR**, the calling process must either have the **SCHED_FIFO**, or **SCHED_RR** policy or have an effective user ID of **0**.

sched_getscheduler() returns the scheduling policy of the process specified by *pid*. If *pid* is zero, the scheduling policy is returned for the calling process. Otherwise, if a process specified by *pid* exists and if the calling process has permission, the scheduling policy is returned for the process whose process ID is equal to *pid*.

RETURN VALUES

If successful, **sched_setscheduler()** returns the former scheduling policy of the specified process (*pid*), which will be one of the following values:

SCHED_FIFO (realtime)
: First-In-First-Out; processes scheduled to this policy, if not preempted by a higher priority or interrupted by a signal, will proceed until completion.

SCHED_RR (realtime)
: Round-Robin; processes scheduled to this policy, if not preempted by a higher priority or interrupted by a signal, will execute for a time period, returned by **sched_rr_get_interval**(3R) or by the system.

SCHED_OTHER (time-sharing).

Otherwise, the policy and scheduling parameters remain unchanged, **sched_setscheduler()** returns **-1**, and sets **errno** to indicate the error condition. If successful, **sched_getscheduler()** returns the scheduling policy of the specified process; otherwise, it returns **-1**, and sets **errno** to indicate the error condition.

ERRORS

EINVAL The value of *policy* is invalid, or one or more of the parameters contained in **param** is outside the valid range for the specified scheduling policy.

ENOSYS **sched_setscheduler()** and **sched_getscheduler()** are not supported by this implementation.

EPERM **sched_setscheduler()** does not have permission to set either or both of the scheduling parameters or the scheduling policy of the specified process.

EPERM **sched_getscheduler()** does not have permission to determine the scheduling policy of the specified process.

ESRCH No process can be found corresponding to that specified by *pid*.

SEE ALSO

priocntl(1), **intro**(2), **exec**(2), **priocntl**(2), **sched_get_priority_max**(3R), **sched_setparam**(3R).

BUGS

In Solaris 2.5, these functions always return **–1** and set **errno** to **ENOSYS**, because this release does not support the Priority Scheduling option. It is Sun's intention to provide support for these interfaces in future releases.

NAME

sched_yield – yield processor

SYNOPSIS

cc [*flag* **...**] *file* **... –lposix4** [*library* **...**]

#include <sched.h>

int sched_yield(void);

MT-LEVEL

MT-Safe

DESCRIPTION

sched_yield() forces the running process to relinquish the processor until the process again becomes the head of its process list.

RETURN VALUES

If successful, **sched_yield**() returns **0**, otherwise, it returns **-1**, and sets **errno** to indicate the error condition.

ERRORS

ENOSYS sched_yield() is not supported by this implementation.

BUGS

In Solaris 2.5, these functions always return **–1** and set **errno** to **ENOSYS**, because this release does not support the Priority Scheduling option. It is Sun's intention to provide support for these interfaces in future releases.

NAME

sem_close – close a named semaphore

SYNOPSIS

cc [*flag* **...**] *file* **... –lposix4** [*library* **...**]

#include <semaphore.h>

int sem_close(sem_t **sem*);

typedef struct {

...

} sem_t; **/* opaque POSIX.4 semaphore */**

MT-LEVEL

MT-Safe

DESCRIPTION

sem_close() is used to indicate that the calling process is finished using the named semaphore *sem*. **sem_close**() deallocates any system resources for use by this process for this semaphore. If the semaphore has not been removed with a successful call to **sem_unlink**(3R), then **sem_close**() has no effect on the state of the semaphore. If **sem_unlink**(3R) has been successfully invoked for *name* after the most recent call to **sem_open**(3R) with **O_CREAT** for this semaphore, then when all processes that have opened the semaphore close it, the semaphore will no longer be accessible.

sem_close() should not be called for an unnamed semaphore initialized by **sem_init**(3R).

RETURN VALUES

If successful, **sem_close**() returns **0**, otherwise it returns **-1** and sets **errno** to indicate the error condition.

ERRORS

EINVAL *sem* is not a valid semaphore descriptor.

ENOSYS **sem_close**() is not supported by this implementation.

SEE ALSO

sem_init(3R), **sem_open**(3R), **sem_unlink**(3R).

BUGS

In Solaris 2.5, these functions always return **–1** and set **errno** to **ENOSYS**, because this release does not support the Semaphores option. It is Sun's intention to provide support for these interfaces in future releases.

NAME

sem_destroy – destroy an unnamed semaphore

SYNOPSIS

cc [*flag* ...] *file* ... **–lposix4** [*library* ...]

#include <semaphore.h>

int sem_destroy(sem_t **sem*);

typedef struct {

...

} sem_t; **/* opaque POSIX.4 semaphore */**

MT-LEVEL

MT-Safe

DESCRIPTION

sem_destroy() is used to destroy the unnamed semaphore, *sem*, which was initialized by **sem_init**(3R).

RETURN VALUES

If successful, **sem_destroy**() returns **0**, otherwise it returns **-1** and sets **errno** to indicate the error condition.

ERRORS

EINVAL	*sem* is not a valid semaphore.
ENOSYS	**sem_destroy**() is not supported by this implementation.
EBUSY	Other processes (or LWPs or threads) are currently blocked on the semaphore.

SEE ALSO

sem_init(3R), **sem_open**(3R).

BUGS

In Solaris 2.5, these functions always return **–1** and set **errno** to **ENOSYS**, because this release does not support the Semaphores option. It is Sun's intention to provide support for these interfaces in future releases.

NAME

sem_getvalue – get the value of a semaphore

SYNOPSIS

cc [*flag* ...] *file* ... **–lposix4** [*library* ...]

#include <semaphore.h>

int sem_getvalue(sem_t **sem*, **int** **sval*)**;**

```
typedef struct {
    ...
} sem_t;            /* opaque POSIX.4 semaphore */
```

MT-LEVEL

MT-Safe

DESCRIPTION

sem_getvalue() updates the location referenced by *sval* to have the value of the semaphore referenced by *sem* without affecting the state of the semaphore. The updated value represents an actual semaphore value that occurred at some unspecified time during the call to **sem_getvalue()**, but may not be the actual value of the semaphore when **sem_getvalue()** is returned to the caller.

The value set in *sval* may be zero or positive. If *sval* is zero, there may be other processes (or LWPs or threads) waiting for the semaphore; if *sval* is positive, no one is waiting.

RETURN VALUES

If successful, **sem_getvalue**() returns **0**, otherwise, it returns **-1**, and sets **errno** to indicate the error condition.

ERRORS

EINVAL	*sem* does not refer to a valid semaphore.
ENOSYS	**sem_getvalue**() is not supported by this implementation.

SEE ALSO

sem_post(3R), **sem_wait**(3R).

BUGS

In Solaris 2.5, these functions always return **–1** and set **errno** to **ENOSYS**, because this release does not support the Semaphores option. It is Sun's intention to provide support for these interfaces in future releases.

NAME

sem_init – initialize an unnamed semaphore

SYNOPSIS

cc [*flag* **...**] *file* **... –lposix4** [*library* **...**]

#include <semaphore.h>

int sem_init(sem_t **sem*, **int** *pshared*, **unsigned int** *value***);**

```
typedef struct {
    ...
} sem_t;            /* opaque POSIX.4 semaphore */
```

MT-LEVEL

MT-Safe

DESCRIPTION

sem_init() is used to initialize the unnamed semaphore, referred to by *sem*, to *value*. This semaphore may be used in subsequent calls to **sem_wait**(3R), **sem_trywait**(3R), **sem_post**(3R), and **sem_destroy**(3R). This semaphore remains usable until the semaphore is destroyed.

If *pshared* is non-zero, then the semaphore is sharable between processes. If the semaphore is not being shared between processes, the application should set *pshared* to **0**.

RETURN VALUES

If successful, **sem_init**() returns **0** and initializes the semaphore in *sem*; otherwise it returns **-1** and sets **errno** to indicate the error condition.

ERRORS

EINVAL — *value* exceeds **SEM_VALUE_MAX**.

ENOSPC — A resource required to initialize the semaphore has been exhausted. The resources have reached the limit on semaphores, **SEM_NSEMS_MAX**.

ENOSYS — **sem_init**() is not supported by this implementation.

EPERM — The calling process lacks the appropriate privileges to initialize the semaphore.

SEE ALSO

sem_destroy(3R), **sem_post**(3R), **sem_wait**(3R).

BUGS

In Solaris 2.5, these functions always return **–1** and set **errno ENOSYS**, because this release does not support the Semaphores option. It is Sun's intention to provide support for these interfaces in future releases.

NAME

sem_open – initialize/open a named semaphore

SYNOPSIS

cc [*flag* **...**] *file* **... –lposix4** [*library* **...**]

#include <semaphore.h>

sem_t *sem_open(const char ****name*, int** *oflag***,**
    /* unsigned long *mode***, unsigned int** *value* ***/ ...);**

```
typedef struct {
    ...
} sem_t;            /* opaque POSIX.4 semaphore */
```

MT-LEVEL

MT-Safe

DESCRIPTION

sem_open() establishes a connection to a semaphore, *name*, returning the address of the semaphore to the calling process (or LWP or thread) for subsequent calls to **sem_wait**(3R), **sem_trywait**(3R), **sem_post**(3R), and **sem_close**(3R). The semaphore remains usable by this process until the semaphore is closed.

name points to a string naming a semaphore object. The *name* argument should conform to the construction rules for a pathname. If a process makes multiple successful calls to **sem_open**() with the same value for *name*, the same semaphore address will be returned for each such successful call, provided that there have been no calls to **sem_unlink**(3R) for this semaphore.

oflag determines whether the semaphore is created or merely accessed by the call to **sem_open().** The three valid values for *oflag* are **0**, **O_CREAT**, or the bitwise inclusive OR of **O_CREAT** and **O_EXCL**. Setting the *oflag* bits to **O_CREAT** will create the semaphore if it does not already exist. Setting both **O_CREAT** and **O_EXCL** will fail if the semaphore already exists. The check for the existence of the semaphore and the creation of the semaphore if it does not exist is atomic with respect to other processes executing **sem_open**(). After the semaphore named *name* has been created by **sem_open()** with the **O_CREAT** flag, other processes can connect to this semaphore by calling **sem_open()** with the same value of *name*, and no bits set in *oflag*.

Using the **O_CREAT** flag requires a third and a fourth argument: *mode* and *value*. The semaphore is created with an initial count of *value*. *value* must be less than or equal to **{SEM_VALUE_MAX}**. The semaphore's user ID acquires the effective user ID of the process; the semaphore's group ID is set to a system default group ID or to the effective group ID of the process. The semaphore's permission bits is set to the value

 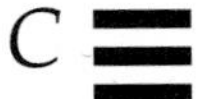

of *mode*, modified by clearing all bits set in the file creation mask of the process (see **umask**(2)).

RETURN VALUES

If successful, **sem_open()** returns the address of the semaphore, otherwise it returns **-1** and sets **errno** to indicate the error condition.

ERRORS

EACCES	The named semaphore exists and the **O_RDWR** permissions are denied, or the named semaphore does not exist and permission to create the named semaphore is denied.
EEXIST	**O_CREAT** and **O_EXCL** are set and the named semaphore already exists.
EINTR	**sem_open()** was interrupted by a signal.
EINVAL	*name* is not a valid name. **O_CREAT** was set in *oflag* and *value* is greater than **{SEM_VALUE_MAX}**.
EMFILE	The number of open semaphore descriptors in this process exceeds **{SEM_NSEMS_MAX}**. The number of open file descriptors in this process exceeds **{OPEN_MAX}**.
ENAMETOOLONG	The string-length of *name* exceeds **{PATH_MAX}**, or a pathname component is longer than **{NAME_MAX}** while **_POSIX_NO_TRUNC** is in effect.
ENFILE	The system file table is full.
ENOENT	**O_CREAT** is not set and the named semaphore does not exist.
ENOSPC	There is insufficient space for the creation of the new named semaphore.
ENOSYS	**sem_open()** is not supported by this implementation.

SEE ALSO

exec(2), **exit**(2), **umask**(2), **sysconf**(3C), **sem_close**(3R), **sem_post**(3R), **sem_unlink**(3R), **sem_wait**(3R).

BUGS

In Solaris 2.5, these functions always return **–1** and set **errno** to **ENOSYS**, because this release does not support the Semaphores option. It is Sun's intention to provide support for these interfaces in future releases.

NAME

sem_post – increment the count of a semaphore

SYNOPSIS

cc [*flag* ...] *file* ... **–lposix4** [*library* ...]

#include <semaphore.h>

int sem_post(sem_t **sem*);

```
typedef struct {
    ...
} sem_t            /* opaque POSIX.4 semaphore */
```

MT-LEVEL

Async-Signal-Safe

DESCRIPTION

If, prior to the call to **sem_post(),** the value of *sem* was **0**, and other processes (or LWPs or threads) were blocked waiting for the semaphore, then one of them will be allowed to return successfully from its call to **sem_wait**(3R). The process to be unblocked will be chosen in a manner appropriate to the scheduling policies and parameters in effect for the blocked processes. In the case of the policies **SCHED_FIFO** and **SCHED_RR**, the highest priority waiting process is unblocked, and if there is more than one highest-priority process blocked waiting for the semaphore, then the highest priority process which has been waiting the longest is unblocked.

If, prior to the call to **sem_post**(), no other processes (or LWPs or thread) were blocked for the semaphore, then its value is incremented by one.

sem_post() is reentrant with respect to signals (ASYNC-SAFE), and may be invoked from a signal-catching function. The semaphore functionality described on this man page is for the POSIX threads implementation. For the documentation of the Solaris threads interface, see **semaphore**(3T)).

RETURN VALUES

If successful, **sem_post**() returns **0**, otherwise it returns **-1**, and sets **errno** to indicate the error condition.

ERRORS

EINVAL	*sem* does not refer to a valid semaphore.
ENOSYS	**sem_post**() is not supported by this implementation.

EXAMPLES

(see **sem_wait**(3R))

SEE ALSO

sched_setscheduler(3R), **sem_wait**(3R), **semaphore**(3T).

NOTES

sem_wait(3R) and **sem_trywait**(3R) decrement the semaphore upon their successful return.

BUGS

In Solaris 2.5, these functions always return **–1** and set **errno** to **ENOSYS**, because this release does not support the Semaphores option. It is Sun's intention to provide support for these interfaces in future releases.

NAME

sem_unlink – remove a named semaphore

SYNOPSIS

cc [*flag* **...**] *file* **... –lposix4** [*library* **...**]

#include <semaphore.h>

int sem_unlink(const char **name***);**

MT-LEVEL

MT-Safe

DESCRIPTION

sem_unlink() removes the semaphore named by the string *name*. If the semaphore, *name*, is currently referenced by other processes, **sem_unlink()** has no effect on the state of the semaphore. If one or more processes have the semaphore open when **sem_unlink()** is called, destruction of the semaphore is postponed until all references to the semaphore have been destroyed by calls to **sem_close**(3R), **exit**(2), or **exec**(2). Calls to **sem_open**(3R) to re-create or re-connect to the semaphore will refer to a new semaphore after **sem_unlink()** is called. **sem_unlink()** does not block until all references have been destroyed; rather, it returns immediately.

RETURN VALUES

If successful, **sem_unlink()** returns **0**; otherwise, the function returns **-1**, sets **errno** to indicate the error condition, and the semaphore is left unchanged.

ERRORS

EACCES	Permission is denied to unlink the named semaphore.
ENAMETOOLONG	The string-length of *name* exceeds **{PATH_MAX}**, or a pathname component is longer than **{NAME_MAX}** while **_POSIX_NO_TRUNC** is in effect.
ENOENT	The named semaphore does not exist.
ENOSYS	**sem_unlink()** is not supported by this implementation.

SEE ALSO

exec(2), **exit**(2), **sem_close**(3R), **sem_open**(3R).

BUGS

In Solaris 2.5, these functions always return **–1** and set **errno** to **ENOSYS**, because this release does not support the Semaphores option. It is Sun's intention to provide support for these interfaces in future releases.

NAME

sem_wait, sem_trywait – acquire or wait for a semaphore

SYNOPSIS

cc [*flag* **...**] *file* **... –lposix4** [*library* **...**]

#include <semaphore.h>

int sem_wait(sem_t **sem***);**

int sem_trywait(sem_t **sem***);**

```
typedef struct {
    ...
} sem_t              /* opaque POSIX.4 semaphore */
```

MT-LEVEL

MT-Safe

DESCRIPTION

sem_wait() and **sem_trywait**() are the functions by which a calling thread waits or proceeds depending upon the state of a semaphore. A synchronizing process can proceed only if the value of the semaphore it accesses is currently greater than **0**.

If at the time of a call to either **sem_wait**() or **sem_trywait**(), the value of *sem* is positive, these functions decrement the value of the semaphore, return immediately, and allow the calling process to continue.

If the semaphore's value is **0**:

> **sem_wait**() blocks, awaiting the semaphore to be released by another process (or LWP or thread).
>
> **sem_trywait**() fails, returning immediately.

RETURN VALUES

If at the time of a call to either **sem_wait**() or **sem_trywait**(), the value of *sem* is positive, these functions return **0** on success. If the call was unsuccessful, the state of the semaphore is unchanged, the calling function returns **-1**, and sets **errno** to indicate the error condition.

ERRORS

EAGAIN	The value of *sem* was **0** when **sem_trywait**() was called.
EINVAL	*sem* does not refer to a valid semaphore.
EINTR	**sem_wait**() was interrupted by a signal.
ENOSYS	**sem_wait**() and **sem_trywait**() are not supported by this implementation.

EDEADLK A deadlock condition was detected; i.e., two separate processes are waiting for an available resource to be released via a semaphore "held" by the other process.

SEE ALSO

sem_post(3R).

NOTES

sem_wait() can be interrupted by a signal, which may result in its premature return.

sem_post(3R) increments the semaphore upon its successful return.

BUGS

In Solaris 2.5, these functions always return **–1** and set **errno** to **ENOSYS**, because this release does not support the Semaphores option. It is Sun's intention to provide support for these interfaces in future releases.

NAME

sigwaitinfo, sigtimedwait – wait for queued signals

SYNOPSIS

cc [*flag* ...] *file* ... **–lposix4** [*library* ...]

#include <signal.h>

int sigwaitinfo(const sigset_t **set*, **siginfo_t** **info*);

int sigtimedwait(const sigset_t **set*, **siginfo_t** **info*, **const struct timespec** **timeout*);

```
typedef struct siginfo {
    int si_signo;              /* signal from signal.h */
    int si_code;               /* code from above      */
    int si_value;
    ...
} siginfo_t;

struct timespec {
    time_t      tv_sec;        /* seconds */
    long        tv_nsec;       /* and nanoseconds */
};
```

MT-LEVEL

Async-Safe

DESCRIPTION

sigwaitinfo() and **sigtimedwait()** select the pending signal from the set specified by *set*. When multiple signals are pending, the lowest numbered one will be selected. The selection order between realtime and non-realtime signals, or between multiple pending non-realtime signals, is unspecified.

If no signal in *set* is pending at the time of the call, **sigwaitinfo()** suspends the calling process until one or more signals in *set* become pending or until it is interrupted by an unblocked, caught signal. **sigtimedwait()**, on the other hand, suspends itself for the time interval specified in the **timespec** structure referenced by *timeout*. If the **timespec** structure pointed to by *timeout* is zero-valued, and if none of the signals specified by *set* are pending, then **sigtimedwait()** returns immediately with the error **EAGAIN**.

If, while **sigwaitinfo()** or **sigtimedwait()** is waiting, a signal occurs which is eligible for delivery (i.e., not blocked by the process signal mask), that signal is handled asynchronously and the wait is interrupted.

If *info* is non-**NULL**, the selected signal number is stored in **si_signo**, and the cause of the signal is stored in the **si_code**. If any value is queued to the selected signal, the first such queued value is dequeued and, if *info* is non-**NULL**, the value is stored in the **si_value** member of *info*. The system resource used to queue the signal is released and made available to queue other signals.

If the value of the **si_code** member is **SI_NOINFO**, only the **si_signo** member of **siginfo_t** is meaningful, and the value of all other members is unspecified. If no further signals are queued for the selected signal, the pending indication for that signal is reset. RETURN VALUES

If one of the signals specified by *set* is either pending or generated, **sigwaitinfo**() or **sigtimedwait**() returns the selected signal number. Otherwise, the function returns **-1** and sets **errno** to indicate the error condition.

ERRORS

EINTR The wait was interrupted by an unblocked, caught signal.

ENOSYS **sigwaitinfo**() or **sigtimedwait**() is not supported by this implementation.

The following errors relate to only **sigtimedwait**():

EAGAIN No signal specified by *set* was delivered within the specified timeout period.

EINVAL *timeout* specified a **tv_nsec** value less than 0 or greater than 1,000,000,000.

SEE ALSO

time(2), **sigqueue**(3R), **siginfo**(5), **signal**(5).

NAME

sigwait – wait until a signal is posted

SYNOPSIS

POSIX

cc [*flag* **...]** *file* **... -D_POSIX_PTHREAD_SEMANTICS** [*library* **...]**

#include <signal.h>

int sigwait(const sigset_t ***set, int ***sig**);**

Solaris

#include <signal.h>

int sigwait(const sigset_t ***set);**

DESCRIPTION

sigwait() selects a signal in *set* that is pending on the calling thread or LWP. If no signal in *set* is pending, then **sigwait()** blocks until a signal in *set* becomes pending. The selected signal is cleared from the set of signals pending on the calling thread or LWP and the number of the signal is returned. The selection of a signal in *set* is independent of the signal mask of the calling thread or LWP. This means a thread or LWP can synchronously wait for signals that are being blocked by the signal mask of the calling thread or LWP.

If **sigwait()** is called on an ignored signal, then the occurrence of the signal will be ignored, even though **sigwait()** was called for this signal.

If more than one thread or LWP waits for the same signal, only one is unblocked when the signal arrives.

RETURN VALUES

Upon successful completion, **sigwait()** returns a signal number. Otherwise, it returns a value of **–1** and sets **errno** Upon successful completion, the POSIX version of **sigwait()** returns zero and stores the signal number at the location pointed to by sig. Otherwise, it returns the error number.

ERRORS

If any of the following conditions are detected, **sigwait()** fails and returns an error:

EINVAL *set* contains an unsupported signal number.

EFAULT *set* points to an invalid address.

SEE ALSO

sigaction(2), **sigpending**(2), **sigprocmask**(2), **sigsuspend**(2), **pthread_sigmask**(3T), **signal**(5).

NOTES

sigwait() cannot be used to wait for signals that cannot be caught (see **sigaction**(2)). This restriction is silently imposed by the system.

In Solaris 2.4 and earlier releases, the call to **sigwait()** from a multithreaded process overrode the signal's ignore disposition; even if a signal's disposition was **SIG_IGN**, a call to **sigwait()** resulted in catching the signal, if generated. This is incorrect behavior from the standpoint of the POSIX 1003.1c spec.

In SOlaris 2.5, the behavior of **sigwait()** was corrected, so that it does not override the signal's ignore disposition. This change can cause applications which rely on the old behavior, to break. The applications should employ **sigwait()** as follows: Install a dummy signal handler, thereby changing the disposition from **SIG_IGN** to having a handler. Then any calls to **sigwait()** for this signal would catch it on generation.

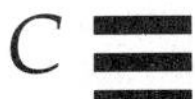

NAME

ctime, ctime_r, localtime, localtime_r, gmtime, gmtime_r, asctime, asctime_r, tzset, tzsetwall – convert date and time to string

SYNOPSIS

#include <time.h>

char *ctime(const time_t ***clock*);**

struct tm *localtime(const time_t ***clock*);**

struct tm *localtime_r(const time_t ***clock*, struct tm ***res***);**

struct tm *gmtime(const time_t ***clock*);**

struct tm *gmtime_r(const time_t ***clock*, struct tm ***res***);**

char *asctime(const struct tm ***tm*);**

extern time_t timezone, altzone;
extern int daylight;
extern char *tzname[2];

void tzset(void);

void tzsetwall(void);

POSIX

cc [*flag* **...]** *file* **... -D_POSIX_PTHREAD_SEMANTICS [** *library* **...]**

char *ctime_r(const time_t ***clock*, char ***buf***);**

char *asctime_r(const struct tm ***tm*, char ***buf***);**

Solaris

char *ctime_r(const time_t ***clock*, char ***buf***, int** *buflen***);**

char *asctime_r(const struct tm ***tm*, char ***buf***, int** *buflen***);**

MT-LEVEL

See the **NOTES** section of this page.

DESCRIPTION

ctime(), **localtime**(), and **gmtime**() accept arguments of type **time_t**, pointed to by **clock**(), representing the time in seconds since 00:00:00 UTC, January 1, 1970. **ctime**() returns a pointer to a 26-character string as shown below. Time zone and daylight savings corrections are made before the string is generated. The fields are constant in width:

Fri Sep 13 00:00:00 1986\n\0

ctime_r() has the same functionality as **ctime()** except that the caller must supply a buffer to store the result. *buf* must be at least 26 bytes. The POSIX **ctime_r()** routine does not take a buflen parameter.

localtime() and **gmtime()** return pointers to **tm** structures (see below). **localtime()** corrects for the main time zone and possible alternate (daylight savings) time zone; **gmtime()** converts directly to Coordinated Universal Time (UTC), which is what the UNIX system uses internally.

localtime_r() and **gmtime_r()** have the same functionality as **localtime()** and **gmtime()** respectively, except that the caller must supply a buffer for storing the result.

asctime() converts a **tm** structure to a 26-character string, as shown in the above example, and returns a pointer to the string.

asctime_r() has the same functionality as **asctime()** except that the caller must supply a buffer *buf* with length *buflen* for the result to be stored. *buf* must be at least 26 bytes. The POSIX **asctime_r()** routine does not take a *buflen* parameter. **asctime_r()** returns a pointer to *buf* upon success. In case of failure, **NULL** is returned and **errno** is set.

Declarations of all the functions and externals, and the **tm** structure, are in the **time.h** header. The members of the **tm** structure are:

```
int tm_sec;      /* seconds after the minute — [0, 61] */
                 /* for leap seconds */
int tm_min;      /* minutes after the hour — [0, 59] */
int tm_hour;     /* hour since midnight — [0, 23] */
int tm_mday;     /* day of the month — [1, 31] */
int tm_mon;      /* months since January — [0, 11] */
int tm_year;     /* years since 1900 */
int tm_wday;     /* days since Sunday — [0, 6] */
int tm_yday;     /* days since January 1 — [0, 365] */
int tm_isdst;    /* flag for alternate daylight */
                 /* savings time */
```

The value of **tm_isdst** is positive if daylight savings time is in effect, zero if daylight savings time is not in effect, and negative if the information is not available. (Previously, the value of **tm_isdst** was defined as non-zero if daylight savings was in effect.)

The external **time_t** variable **altzone** contains the difference, in seconds, between Coordinated Universal Time and the alternate time zone. The external variable **timezone** contains the difference, in seconds, between UTC and local standard time. The external variable **daylight** indicates whether time should reflect daylight savings time. Both **timezone** and **altzone** default to 0 (UTC). The external variable **daylight** is non-zero if an alternate time zone exists. The time zone names are contained in the external variable **tzname**, which by default is set to:

char *tzname[2] = { "GMT", " " };

These functions know about the peculiarities of this conversion for various time periods for the U.S. (specifically, the years 1974, 1975, and 1987). They handled the new daylight savings time starting with the first Sunday in April 1987.

tzset() uses the contents of the environment variable **TZ** to override the value of the different external variables. The function **tzset()** is called by **asctime()** and may also be called by the user. See **environ**(5) for a description of the **TZ** environment variable.

Starting and ending times are relative to the current local time zone. If the alternate time zone start and end dates and the time are not provided, the days for the United States that year will be used and the time will be 2 AM. If the start and end dates are provided but the time is not provided, the time will be 2 AM. The effects of **tzset()** change the values of the external variables **timezone**, **altzone**, **daylight**, and **tzname**.

Note that in most installations, **TZ** is set to the correct value by default when the user logs on, using the local **/etc/default/init** file (see **TIMEZONE**(4)).

tzsetwall() sets things up so that **localtime()** returns the best available approximation of local wall clock time.

LC_TIME determines how these functions handle date and time formats. In the "C" locale, date and time handling follow the U.S. rules.

ERRORS

ctime_r() and **asctime_r()** will fail if the following is true:

ERANGE length of the buffer supplied by caller is not large enough to store the result.

EXAMPLES

tzset() scans the contents of the environment variable and assigns the different fields to the respective variable. For example, the most complete setting for New Jersey in 1986 could be:

EST5EDT4,116/2:00:00,298/2:00:00

or simply

EST5EDT

An example of a southern hemisphere setting such as the Cook Islands could be:

KDT9:30KST10:00,63/5:00,302/20:00

In the longer version of the New Jersey example of TZ, **tzname**[*0*] is EST, **timezone** will be set to 5*60*60, **tzname**[*1*] is EDT, **altzone** will be set to 4*60*60, the starting date of the alternate time zone is the 117th day at 2 AM, the ending date of the alternate time zone is the 299th day at 2 AM (using zero-based Julian days), and **daylight** will be set positive. Starting and ending times are relative to the current local time zone. If the alternate time zone start and end dates and the time are not provided, the days for the United States that year will be used and the time will be 2 AM. If the start and end dates are provided but the time is not provided, the time will be 2 AM. The effects of **tzset()** are thus to change the values of the external variables **timezone**, **altzone**, **daylight**, and **tzname**. **ctime()**, **localtime()**, **mktime()**, and **strftime()** will also update these external variables as if they had called **tzset()** at the time specified by the **time_t** or **struct tm** value that they are converting.

FILES

/usr/lib/locale/*locale***/LC_TIME/time**
file containing locale specific date and time information

SEE ALSO

time(2), **getenv**(3C), **mktime**(3C), **printf**(3S), **putenv**(3C), **setlocale**(3C), **strftime**(3C), **TIMEZONE**(4), **environ**(5).

NOTES

When compiling multithread applications, the **_REENTRANT** flag must be defined on the compile line. This flag should only be used in multithread applications.

The return values for **ctime()**, **localtime()**, and **gmtime()** point to static data whose content is overwritten by each call.

Setting the time during the interval of change from **timezone** to **altzone** or vice versa can produce unpredictable results. The system administrator must change the Julian start and end days annually.

asctime(), **ctime()**, **gmtime()** and **localtime()** are unsafe in multithread applications. **asctime_r()**, **ctime_r()**, **gmtime_r()** and **localtime_r()** are MT-Safe, and should be used instead. **tzset()** and **tzsetwall()** are unsafe in multithread applications.

NAME

directory, opendir, readdir, readdir_r, telldir, seekdir, rewinddir, closedir – directory operations

SYNOPSIS

#include <dirent.h>

DIR *opendir(const char ****filename*);**

struct dirent *readdir(DIR ****dirp*);**

long telldir(DIR ****dirp*);**

void seekdir(DIR ****dirp*, long** *loc***);**

void rewinddir(DIR ****dirp*);**

int closedir(DIR ****dirp*);**

POSIX

cc [*flag* **...]** *file* **... -D_POSIX_PTHREAD_SEMANTICS [** *library* **...]**

int *readdir_r(DIR ****dirp*, struct dirent ****ent***, struct dirent *****res***);**

Solaris

struct dirent *readdir_r(DIR ****dirp*, struct dirent ****ent***);**

MT-LEVEL

See the **NOTES** section of this page.

DESCRIPTION

opendir() opens the directory named by *filename* and associates a directory stream with it. **opendir**() returns a pointer to be used to identify the directory stream in subsequent operations. The directory stream is positioned at the first entry. A null pointer is returned if *filename* cannot be accessed or is not a directory, or if it cannot **malloc**(3C) enough memory to hold a **DIR** structure or a buffer for the directory entries.

readdir() returns a pointer to a structure representing the directory entry at the current position in the directory stream to which *drip* refers, and positions the directory stream at the next entry, except on read-only file systems. It returns a **NULL** pointer upon reaching the end of the directory stream, or upon detecting an invalid location in the directory. **readdir**() will not return directory entries containing empty names. It is unspecified whether entries are returned for dot or dot-dot. The pointer returned by **readdir**() points to data that may be overwritten by another call to **readdir**() on the same directory stream. This data will not be overwritten by another call to **readdir**() on a different directory stream. **readdir**() may buffer several directory entries per actual read operation; **readdir()** marks for update the *st_atime* field of the directory each time the directory is actually read.

readdir_r() has the equivalent functionality as **readdir()** except that a buffer *ent* must be supplied by the caller to store the result. The size of *ent* must be at least **sizeof (struct dirent)** + {NAME_MAX} (i.e., **pathconf(_PC_NAME_MAX)**) + **1**. When the end of the directory is reached the Solaris version of **readdir_r()** returns **NULL**. Otherwise it returns the value of *ent*. When the end of the directory is reached the POSIX version of **readdir_r()** sets the location pointed to by *res* to **NULL**. Otherwise, it sets **res* to the value of *ent*.

telldir() returns the current location associated with the named directory stream.

seekdir() sets the position of the next **readdir()** operation on the directory stream. The new position reverts to the position associated with the directory stream at the time the **telldir()** operation that provides *loc* was performed. Values returned by **telldir()** are good only for the lifetime of the **DIR** pointer from which they are derived. If the directory is closed and then reopened, the **telldir()** value may be invalidated due to undetected directory compaction. It is safe to use a previous **telldir()** value immediately after a call to **opendir()** and before any calls to **readdir**.

rewinddir() resets the position of the named directory stream to the beginning of the directory. It also causes the directory stream to refer to the current state of the corresponding directory, as a call to **opendir()** would.

closedir() closes the named directory stream and frees the **DIR** structure.

RETURN VALUES

opendir(), **readdir()**, return **NULL** on failure and set **errno** to indicate the error. **telldir()**, **seekdir()**, and **closedir()** return **–1** on failure and set **errno** to indicate the error. The POSIX version of **readdir_r()** returns the error number of failure and zero otherwise. The Solaris version of **readdir_r()** returns **NULL** on failure and set **errno** to indicate the error.

ERRORS

opendir() will fail if one or more of the following are true:

EACCES	Read permission is denied on the specified directory.
EFAULT	*filename* points outside the allocated address space.
ELOOP	Too many symbolic links were encountered in translating *filename*.
ENOTDIR	A component of *filename* is not a directory.
EMFILE	The maximum number of file descriptors are currently open.
ENFILE	The system file table is full.

ENAMETOOLONG The length of the *filename* argument exceeds **{PATH_MAX}**, or the length of a *filename* component exceeds **{NAME_MAX}** while **{_POSIX_NO_TRUNC}** is in effect.

ENOENT A component of *filename* does not exist or is a null pathname.

EACCES A component of *filename* denies search permission.

readdir() and **readdir_r**() will fail if one or more of the following are true:

EAGAIN Mandatory file/record locking was set, **O_NDELAY** or **O_NONBLOCK** was set, and there was a blocking record lock.

EAGAIN Total amount of system memory available when reading using raw I/O is temporarily insufficient.

EAGAIN No data is waiting to be read on a file associated with a tty device and **O_NONBLOCK** was set.

EAGAIN No message is waiting to be read on a stream and **O_NDELAY** or **O_NONBLOCK** was set.

EBADF The file descriptor determined by the **DIR** stream is no longer valid. This results if the **DIR** stream has been closed.

EBADMSG Message waiting to be read on a stream is not a data message.

EDEADLK The **read**() was going to go to sleep and cause a deadlock to occur.

EFAULT *buf* points to an illegal address.

EINTR A signal was caught during the **read**() or **readv**() function.

EINVAL Attempted to read from a stream linked to a multiplexor.

EIO A physical I/O error has occurred, or the process is in a background process group and is attempting to read from its controlling terminal, and either the process is ignoring or blocking the **SIGTTIN** signal or the process group of the process is orphaned.

ENOENT The current file pointer for the directory is not located at a valid entry.

ENOLCK The system record lock table was full, so the **read**() or **readv**() could not go to sleep until the blocking record lock was removed.

ENOLINK *fildes* is on a remote machine and the link to that machine is no longer active.

ENXIO — The device associated with *fildes* is a block special or character special file and the value of the file pointer is out of range.

telldir(), **seekdir()**, and **closedir()** return **0** on success and will fail if one or more of the following are true:

EBADF — The file descriptor determined by the **DIR** stream is no longer valid. This results if the **DIR** stream has been closed.

EXAMPLES

Here is a sample program that prints the names of all the files in the current directory:

```
#include <stdio.h>
#include <dirent.h>

int
main()
{
    DIR *dirp;
    struct dirent *direntp;

    dirp = opendir(".");
    while ((direntp = readdir( dirp )) != NULL)
        (void) printf("%s\n", direntp->d_name );
    (void) closedir(dirp);
    return (0);
}
```

SEE ALSO

getdents(2), **dirent**(4).

NOTES

When compiling multithread applications, the **_REENTRANT** flag must be defined on the compile line. This flag should only be used in multithread applications.

readdir() is unsafe in multithread applications. **readdir_r()** is safe and should be used instead. **closedir()**, **directory()**, **opendir()**, **rewinddir()**, **seekdir()**, and **telldir()** are safe in multithread applications.

NAME

getgrnam, getgrnam_r, getgrent, getgrent_r, getgrgid, getgrgid_r, setgrent, endgrent, fgetgrent, fgetgrent_r – get group entry

SYNOPSIS

#include <grp.h>

struct group *getgrnam(const char ***name*);**

int getgrnam_r(const char ***name*, struct group ***grp***, char ***buf***, int** *len***,**
struct group ****result*);**

struct group *getgrent(void);

int getgrent_r(struct group ***grp*, char ***buf***, int** *len***, struct group ****result***);**

struct group *getgrgid(gid_t *gid***);**

int getgrgid_r(gid_t *gid,* **struct group ***grp***, char ***buf***, int** *len***,**
struct group ****result*);**

void setgrent(void);

void endgrent(void);

struct group *fgetgrent(FILE ***f*);**

int fgetgrent_r(FILE ***f,* **struct group ***grp*, char ***buffer***, int** *buflen***,**
struct group ****result*);**

POSIX

cc [*flag* **...]** *file* **... -D_POSIX_PTHREAD_SEMANTICS [** *library* **...]**

int getgrnam_r(const char ***name*, struct group ***grp***, char ***buf***, int** *len***,**
struct group ****res*);**

int getgrgid_r(gid_t *gid,* **struct group ***grp***, char ***buf***, int** *len***,**
struct group ****res*);**

Solaris

struct group *getgrnam_r(const char ***name*, struct group ***grp***, char ***buf***,**
int *len***);**

struct group *getgrgid_r(gid_t *gid,* **struct group ***grp***, char ***buf***, int** *len***);**

MT-LEVEL

See the subsection “Reentrant Interfaces” in the **DESCRIPTION** section of this page.

DESCRIPTION

These functions are used to obtain entries describing user groups. Entries may come from any of the sources for **group** specified in the **/etc/nsswitch.conf** file (see **nsswitch.conf**(4)).

getgrnam() searches for an entry with the group name specified by the character string parameter *name*.

getgrgid() searches for an entry with the (numeric) group id specified by *gid*.

The functions **setgrent()**, **getgrent()**, and **endgrent()** are used to enumerate group entries from the database. **setgrent()** sets (or resets) the enumeration to the beginning of the set of group entries. This function should be called before the first call to **getgrent()**. Calls to **getgrnam()** and **getgrgid()** leave the enumeration position in an indeterminate state. Successive calls to **getgrent()** return either successive entries or NULL, indicating the end of the enumeration.

endgrent() may be called to indicate that the caller expects to do no further group entry retrieval operations; the system may then close the group file, deallocate resources it was using, and so forth. It is still allowed, but possibly less efficient, for the process to call more group functions after calling **endgrent()**.

fgetgrent(), unlike the other functions above, does not use **nsswitch.conf**; it reads and parses the next line from the stream *f*, which is assumed to have the format of the **group** file (see **group**(4)).

Reentrant Interfaces

The functions **getgrnam()**, **getgrgid()**, **getgrent()**, and **fgetgrent()** use static storage that is re-used in each call, making them unsafe for use in multithreaded applications.

The functions **getgrnam_r()**, **getgrgid_r()**, **getgrent_r()**, and **fgetgrent_r()** provide reentrant interfaces for these operations. Each reentrant interface performs the same operation as its non-reentrant counterpart, named by removing the "_r" suffix. The reentrant interfaces, however, use buffers supplied by the caller to store returned results, and are safe for use in both single-threaded and multithreaded applications.

Each reentrant interface takes the same parameters as its non-reentrant counterpart, as well as the following additional parameters. The parameter *grp* must be a pointer to a **struct group** structure allocated by the caller. The parameter *buf* must be a pointer to a buffer supplied by the caller of size *len*. This buffer is used as storage space for returned group data. When the function completes successfully, all of the pointers within the **struct group** *grp* point to data stored within this buffer. The buffer must be large enough to hold all of the data associated with the group entry. The required size is returned by **sysconf(_SC_GETGR_R_SIZE_MAX)**. The POSIX versions store the value of *grp* into the location pointed to by *res*, if they complete successfully.

For enumeration in multithreaded applications, the position within the enumeration is a process-wide property shared by all threads. **setgrent()** may be used in a multithreaded application but resets the enumeration position for all threads. If multiple threads interleave calls to **getgrent_r()**, the threads will enumerate disjoint subsets of the group database.

Like their non-reentrant counterparts, **getgrnam_r()** and **getgrgid_r()** leave the enumeration position in an indeterminate state.

RETURN VALUES

Group entries are represented by the **struct group** structure defined in **<grp.h>**:

```
struct group {
    char *gr_name;      /* the name of the group */
    char *gr_passwd;    /* the encrypted group password */
    gid_t gr_gid;       /* the numerical group ID */
    char **gr_mem;      /* vector of pointers to member names */
};
```

The functions **getgrnam()**, **getgrgid()**, **getgrent()**, **fgetgrent()**, and the Solaris versions of **getgrnam_r()**, and **getgrgid_r()** each return a pointer to a **struct group** if they successfully locate the requested entry; otherwise they return **NULL**.

The POSIX versions of **getgrnam_r()**, **getgrgid_r()**, and the functions **getgrent_r()**, and **fgetgrent_r()** each return **0** if they are successful; otherwise they return an error code.

The functions **getgrnam()**, **getgrgid()**, **getgrent()**, and **fgetgrent()** use static storage, so returned data must be copied before a subsequent call to any of these functions if the data is to be saved.

ERRORS

getgrnam_r(), **getgrgid_r()**, **getgrent_r()**, and **fgetgrent_r()** will return the following errors if the condition is detected:

ERANGE The length of the buffer supplied by caller is not large enough to store the result.

FILES

/etc/group

SEE ALSO

getpwnam(3C), **group**(4), **passwd**(4).

NOTES

Programs that use the interfaces described in this manual page cannot be linked statically since the implementations of these functions employ dynamic loading and linking of shared objects at run time.

Use of the enumeration interfaces **getgrent()** and **getgrent_r()** is discouraged. In general enumeration is not efficient and may not be supported for all database sources.

NAME

getlogin, getlogin_r – get login name

SYNOPSIS

#include <stdlib.h>

char *getlogin(void);

POSIX

cc [*flag* **...]** *file* **... -D_POSIX_PTHREAD_SEMANTICS [** *library* **...]**

int getlogin_r(char ***name*****, size_t** *namesize***);**

Solaris

int getlogin_r(char ***name*****, int** *namelen***);**

MT-LEVEL

See the **NOTES** section of this page.

DESCRIPTION

getlogin() returns a pointer to the login name as found in **/var/adm/utmp**. It may be used in conjunction with **getpwnam()** to locate the correct password file entry when the same user id is shared by several login names.

If **getlogin()** is called within a process that is not attached to a terminal, it returns a null pointer. The correct procedure for determining the login name is to call **cuserid**(), or to call **getlogin**() and if it fails to call **getpwuid**().

getlogin_r() has the same functionality as **getlogin**() except that a buffer *name* with length *namesize* (*namelen* for the Solaris version) has to be supplied by the caller to store the result. *name* must be at least **LOGIN_NAME_MAX** bytes in size (defined in **<limits.h>**).

RETURN VALUES

getlogin() returns **NULL** if the login name is not found. **getlogin_r**() returns **0** if successful. Otherwise it returns an error number.

ERRORS

getlogin_r() will fail and return an error if the following is true:

ERANGE The size of the buffer is smaller than the result to be returned.

ESRCH *fildes* does not describe a terminal device in directory **/dev**.

FILES

/var/adm/utmp

SEE ALSO

cuserid(3S), **getgrnam**(3C), **getpwnam**(3C), **utmp**(4).

NOTES

When compiling multithread applications, the **_REENTRANT** flag must be defined on the compile line. This flag should only be used in multithread applications.

The return values point to static data whose content is overwritten by each call.

getlogin() is unsafe in multithread applications. **getlogin_r()** should be used instead.

NAME

getpwnam, getpwnam_r, getpwent, getpwent_r, getpwuid, getpwuid_r, setpwent, endpwent, fgetpwent, fgetpwent_r – get password entry

SYNOPSIS

#include <pwd.h>

struct passwd *getpwnam(const char ***name*);**

struct passwd *getpwent(void);

int getpwent_r(struct passwd ***pwd*, char ***buf***, int** *len***, struct passwd ***result***);**

struct passwd *getpwuid(uid_t *uid***);**

void setpwent(void);

void endpwent(void);

struct passwd *fgetpwent(FILE ***f*);**

int fgetpwent_r(FILE ***f*, struct passwd ***pwd***, char ***buf***, int** *len***,**
struct passwd ***result*);**

POSIX

cc [*flag* **...]** *file* **... -D_POSIX_PTHREAD_SEMANTICS [** *library* **...]**

int getpwnam_r(const char ***name*, struct passwd ***pwd***, char ***buf***, int** *len***,**
struct passwd ***res*);**

int getpwuid_r(uid_t *uid***, struct passwd ***pwd***, char ***buf***, int** *len***,**
struct passwd ***res*);**

Solaris

struct passwd *getpwnam_r(const char ***name*, struct passwd ***pwd***,**
char ***buf*, int** *len***);**

struct passwd *getpwuid_r(uid_t *uid***, struct passwd ***pwd***, char ***buf***, int** *len***);**

MT-LEVEL

See the subsection "Reentrant Interfaces" in the **DESCRIPTION** section of this page.

DESCRIPTION

These functions are used to obtain password entries. An entry may come from any of the sources for **passwd** specified in the **/etc/nsswitch.conf** file. See **nsswitch.conf**(4).

getpwnam() searches for a password entry with the login name specified by the character string parameter *name*.

getpwuid() searches for a password entry with the (numeric) user id specified by the parameter *uid*.

The functions **setpwent**(), **getpwent**(), and **endpwent**() are used to enumerate password entries from the database.

setpwent() sets (or resets) the enumeration to the beginning of the set of password entries. This function should be called before the first call to **getpwent**(). Calls to **getpwnam**() and **getpwuid**() leave the enumeration position in an indeterminate state.

Successive calls to **getpwent**() return either successive entries or NULL, indicating the end of the enumeration.

endpwent() may be called to indicate that the caller expects to do no further password retrieval operations; the system may then close the password file, deallocate resources it was using, and so forth. It is still allowed, but possibly less efficient, for the process to call more password functions after calling **endpwent**().

fgetpwent(), unlike the other functions above, does not use **nsswitch.conf**; it reads and parses the next line from the stream *f*, which is assumed to have the format of the **passwd** file. See **passwd**(4).

Reentrant Interfaces

The functions **getpwnam**(), **getpwuid**(), **getpwent**(), and **fgetpwent**() use static storage that is re-used in each call, making these routines unsafe for use in multithreaded applications.

The functions **getpwnam_r**(), **getpwuid_r**(), **getpwent_r**(), and **fgetpwent_r**() provide reentrant interfaces for these operations. Each reentrant interface performs the same operation as its non-reentrant counterpart, named by removing the "**_r**" suffix. The reentrant interfaces, however, use buffers supplied by the caller to store returned results, and are safe for use in both single-threaded and multithreaded applications.

Each reentrant interface takes the same parameters as its non-reentrant counterpart, as well as the following additional parameters. The parameter *pwd* must be a pointer to a **struct passwd** structure allocated by the caller. The parameter *buf* must be a pointer to a buffer supplied by the caller of size *len*. This buffer is used as storage space for the password data. When the function completes successfully, all of the pointers within the **struct passwd** *pwd* point to data stored within this buffer. The buffer must be large enough to hold all of the data associated with the password entry. The required size is returned by **sysconf(_SC_GETPW_R_SIZE_MAX)**. The POSIX versions store the value of *pwd* into the location pointed to by *res*, if they complete successfully.

For enumeration in multithreaded applications, the position within the enumeration is a process-wide property shared by all threads. **setpwent()** may be used in a multithreaded application but resets the enumeration position for all threads. If multiple threads interleave calls to **getpwent_r()**, the threads will enumerate disjoint subsets of the password database.

Like their non-reentrant counterparts, **getpwnam_r()** and **getpwuid_r()** leave the enumeration position in an indeterminate state.

RETURN VALUES

Password entries are represented by the **struct passwd** structure defined in **<pwd.h>**:

```
struct passwd {
    char *pw_name;       /* user's login name */
    char *pw_passwd;     /* no longer used */
    uid_t pw_uid;        /* user's uid */
    gid_t pw_gid;        /* user's gid */
    char *pw_age;        /* not used */
    char *pw_comment;    /* not used */
    char *pw_gecos;      /* typically user's full name */
    char *pw_dir         /* user's home dir */
    char *pw_shell;      /* user's login shell */
};
```

The functions **getpwnam()**, **getpwuid()**, **getpwent()**, and **fgetpwent()**, and the Solaris versions of **getpwnam_r()**, and **getpwuid_r()** each return a pointer to a **struct passwd** if they successfully locate the requested entry; otherwise they return **NULL**.

The POSIX versions of **getpwnam_r()**, **getpwuid_r()**, and the functions **getpwent_r()**, and **fgetpwent_r()** each return **0** if they are successful; otherwise they return an error code.

The functions **getpwnam()**, **getpwuid()**, **getpwent()**, and **fgetpwent()** use static storage, so returned data must be copied before a subsequent call to any of these functions if the data is to be saved.

ERRORS

getpwnam_r(), **getpwuid_r()**, **getpwent_r()**, and **fgetpwent_r()** will return the following errors if the condition is detected:

ERANGE The length of the buffer supplied by caller is not large enough to store the result.

FILES

/etc/passwd
/etc/shadow

SEE ALSO

passwd(1), **intro**(2), **intro**(3), **getgrnam**(3C), **getlogin**(3C), **getspnam**(3C), **cuserid**(3S), **passwd**(4), **shadow**(4).

NOTES

The **pw_passwd** field in the **passwd** structure should not be used as the encrypted password for the user; use **getspnam()** or **getspnam_r()** instead. See **getspnam**(3C).

Programs that use the interfaces described in this manual page cannot be linked statically since, the implementations of these functions employ dynamic loading and linking of shared objects at run time.

Use of the enumeration interfaces **getpwent()** and **getpwent_r()** is discouraged. In general enumeration is not efficient and may not be supported for all database sources.

If a password entry contains an empty *gecos*, *home directory*, or *shell* field, **getpwnam**() and **getpwnam_r**() return a pointer to a null string in the respective field of the **passwd** structure.

If the shell field is empty, **login**(1) automatically assigns the default shell. See **login**(1).

NAME

rand, srand, rand_r – simple random-number generator

SYNOPSIS

#include <stdlib.h>

int rand(void);

void srand(unsigned int *seed***);**

int rand_r(unsigned int **seed***);**

MT-LEVEL

See the **NOTES** section of this page.

DESCRIPTION

rand() uses a multiplicative congruential random-number generator with period 2^{32} that returns successive pseudo-random numbers in the range from **0** to **RAND_MAX**.

The function **srand()** uses the argument *seed* as a seed for a new sequence of pseudo-random numbers to be returned by subsequent calls to the function **rand().** If the function **srand()** is then called with the same *seed* value, the sequence of pseudo-random numbers will be repeated. If the function **rand()** is called before any calls to **srand()** have been made, the same sequence will be generated as when **srand()** is first called with a *seed* value of **1**.

rand_r() has the same functionality as **rand()** except that a pointer to a *seed* must be supplied by the caller.

SEE ALSO

drand48(3C).

NOTES

When compiling multithread applications, the **_REENTRANT** flag must be defined on the compile line. This flag should only be used in multithread applications.

The spectral properties of **rand()** are limited. **drand48**(3C) provides a much better, though more elaborate, random-number generator.

rand() is unsafe in multithread applications. **rand_r()** is MT-Safe, and should be used instead. **srand()** is unsafe in multithread applications.

NAME

string, strcasecmp, strncasecmp, strcat, strncat, strchr, strrchr, strcmp, strncmp, strcpy, strncpy, strcspn, strspn, strdup, strlen, strpbrk, strstr, strtok, strtok_r – string operations

SYNOPSIS

#include <string.h>

int strcasecmp(const char ***s1*****, const char** ***s2*****);**

int strncasecmp(const char ***s1*****, const char** ***s2*****, int** *n***);**

char *strcat(char ***dst*****, const char** ***src*****);**

char *strncat(char ***dst*****, const char** ***src*****, size_t** *n***);**

char *strchr(const char ***s*****, int** *c***);**

char *strrchr(const char ***s*****, int** *c***);**

int strcmp(const char ***s1*****, const char** ***s2*****);**

int strncmp(const char ***s1*****, const char** ***s2*****, size_t** *n***);**

char *strcpy(char ***dst*****, const char** ***src*****);**

char *strncpy(char ***dst*****, const char** ***src*****, size_t** *n***);**

size_t strcspn(const char ***s1*****, const char** ***s2*****);**

size_t strspn(const char ***s1*****, const char** ***s2*****);**

char *strdup(const char ***s1*****);**

size_t strlen(const char ***s*****);**

char *strpbrk(const char ***s1*****, const char** ***s2*****);**

char *strstr(const char ***s1*****, const char** ***s2*****);**

char *strtok(char ***s1*****, const char** ***s2*****);**

char *strtok_r(char ***s1*****, const char** ***s2*****, char** ****lasts*****);**

MT-LEVEL

See the **NOTES** section of this page.

DESCRIPTION

The arguments *s*, *s1*, *s2*, *src*, and *dst* point to strings (arrays of characters terminated by a null character). The functions **strcat**(), **strncat**(), **strcpy**(), **strncpy**(), **strtok**(), and **strtok_r**() all alter their first argument. These functions do not check for overflow of the array pointed to by the first argument.

strcasecmp() and **strncasecmp**() are case-insensitive versions of **strcmp**() and **strncmp**() respectively, described below. **strcasecmp**() and **strncasecmp**() assume the ASCII character set and ignore differences in case when comparing lower and upper case characters.

strcat() appends a copy of string *src*, including the terminating null character, to the end of string *dst*. **strncat()** appends at most *n* characters. Each returns a pointer to the null-terminated result. The initial character of *src* overrides the null character at the end of *dst*.

strchr() returns a pointer to the first occurrence of *c* (converted to a **char**) in string *s*, or a null pointer if *c* does not occur in the string. **strrchr()** returns a pointer to the last occurrence of *c*. The null character terminating a string is considered to be part of the string.

strcmp() compares two strings byte-by-byte, according to the ordering of your machine's character set. The function returns an integer greater than, equal to, or less than 0, if the string pointed to by *s1* is greater than, equal to, or less than the string pointed to by *s2* respectively. The sign of a non-zero return value is determined by the sign of the difference between the values of the first pair of bytes that differ in the strings being compared. **strncmp()** makes the same comparison but looks at a maximum of *n* bytes. Bytes following a null byte are not compared.

strcpy() copies string *src* to *dst* including the terminating null character, stopping after the null character has been copied. **strncpy()** copies exactly *n* bytes, truncating *src* or adding null characters to *dst* if necessary. The result will not be null-terminated if the length of *src* is *n* or more. Each function returns *dst*.

strcspn() returns the length of the initial segment of string *s1* that consists entirely of characters not from string *s2*. **strspn()** returns the length of the initial segment of string *s1* that consists entirely of characters from string *s2*.

strdup() returns a pointer to a new string that is a duplicate of the string pointed to by *s1*. The space for the new string is obtained using **malloc**(3C). If the new string cannot be created, a null pointer is returned.

strlen() returns the number of bytes in *s*, not including the terminating null character.

strpbrk() returns a pointer to the first occurrence in string *s1* of any character from string *s2*, or a null pointer if no character from *s2* exists in *s1*.

strstr() locates the first occurrence of the string *s2* (excluding the terminating null character) in string *s1*. **strstr()** returns a pointer to the located string, or a null pointer if the string is not found. If *s2* points to a string with zero length (that is, the string ""), the function returns *s1*.

strtok() can be used to break the string pointed to by *s1* into a sequence of tokens, each of which is delimited by one or more characters from the string pointed to by *s2*. **strtok()** considers the string *s1* to consist of a sequence of zero or more text tokens separated by spans of one or more characters from the separator string *s2*. The first call (with pointer *s1* specified) returns a pointer to the first character of the first token, and will have written a null character into *s1* immediately following the returned token. The function keeps track of its position in the string between separate calls, so that subsequent calls (which must be made with the first argument being a null pointer) will work through the string *s1* immediately following that token. In this way subsequent calls will work through the string *s1* until no tokens remain. The separator string *s2* may be different from call to call. When no token remains in *s1*, a null pointer is returned.

strtok_r() has the same functionality as **strtok()** except that a pointer to a string placeholder *lasts* must be supplied by the caller. The *lasts* pointer is to keep track of the next substring in which to search for the next token.

SEE ALSO

malloc(3C), **setlocale**(3C), **strxfrm**(3C).

NOTES

When compiling multithread applications, the **_REENTRANT** flag must be defined on the compile line. This flag should only be used in multithread applications.

All of these functions assume the default locale "C." For some locales, **strxfrm()** should be applied to the strings before they are passed to the functions.

strtok() is unsafe in multithread applications. **strtok_r()** should be used instead.

string(), **strcasecmp()**, **strcat()**, **strchr()**, **strcmp()**, **strcpy()**, **strcspn()**, **strdup()**, **strlen()**, **strncasecmp()**, **strncat()**, **strncmp()**, **strncpy()**, **strpbrk()**, **strrchr()**, **strspn()**, and **strstr()**, are MT-Safe in multithread applications.

NAME

sysconf – get configurable system variables

SYNOPSIS

#include <unistd.h>

long sysconf(int *name***);**

MT-LEVEL

MT-Safe, Async-Signal-Safe

DESCRIPTION

The **sysconf()** function provides a method for an application to determine the current value of a configurable system limit or option (variable).

The *name* argument represents the system variable to be queried. The following table lists the minimal set of system variables from **<limits.h>** and **<unistd.h>** that can be returned by **sysconf()**, and the symbolic constants, defined in **<unistd.h>** that are the corresponding values used for *name*.

Name	Return Value	Meaning
_SC_ARG_MAX	ARG_MAX	Max combined size of **argv[]** and **envp[]**
_SC_CHILD_MAX	CHILD_MAX	Max processes allowed to any UID
_SC_CLK_TCK	CLK_TCK	Ticks per second (**clock_t**)
_SC_NGROUPS_MAX	NGROUPS_MAX	Max simultaneous groups one may belong to
_SC_OPEN_MAX	OPEN_MAX	Max open files per process
_SC_PASS_MAX	PASS_MAX	
_SC_PAGESIZE	PAGESIZE	System memory page size
_SC_JOB_CONTROL	_POSIX_JOB_CONTROL	Job control supported (boolean)
_SC_SAVED_IDS	_POSIX_SAVED_IDS	Saved ids (**seteuid()**) supported (boolean)
_SC_VERSION	_POSIX_VERSION	Version of the POSIX.1 standard supported
_SC_XOPEN_VERSION	_XOPEN_VERSION	
_SC_LOGNAME_MAX	LOGNAME_MAX	

Name	Return Value	Meaning
_SC_NPROCESSORS_CONF		Number of processors (CPUs) configured
_SC_NPROCESSORS_ONLN		Number of processors online
_SC_PHYS_PAGES		The total number of pages of physical memory in the system
_SC_AVPHYS_PAGES		The number of pages of physical memory not currently in use by the system
_SC_AIO_LISTIO_MAX	AIO_LISTIO_MAX	Maximum number of I/O operations in a single list I/O call supported by the implementation
_SC_AIO_MAX	AIO_MAX	Maximum number of outstanding asynchronous I/O operations supported by the implementation
_SC_AIO_PRIO_DELTA_MAX	AIO_PRIO_DELTA_MAX	The maximum amount by which a process can decrease its asynchronous I/O priority level from its own scheduling priority
_SC_DELAYTIMER_MAX	DELAYTIMER_MAX	Maximum number of timer expiration overruns
_SC_GETGR_R_SIZE_MAX		Maximum size of group entry buffer
_SC_GETPW_R_SIZE_MAX		Maximum size of password entry buffer
_SC_LOGIN_NAME_MAX	LOGIN_NAME_MAX	Maximum size of login name

Name	Return Value	Meaning
_SC_MQ_OPEN_MAX	MQ_OPEN_MAX	The maximum number of open message queue descriptors a process may hold
_SC_MQ_PRIO_MAX	MQ_PRIO_MAX	The maximum number of message priorities supported by the implementation
_SC_RTSIG_MAX	RTSIG_MAX	Maximum number of realtime signals reserved for application use in this implementation
_SC_SEM_NSEMS_MAX	SEM_NSEMS_MAX	Maximum number of semaphores that a process may have
_SC_SEM_VALUE_MAX	SEM_VALUE_MAX	The maximum value a semaphore may have
_SC_SIGQUEUE_MAX	SIGQUEUE_MAX	Maximum number of queued signals that a process may send and have pending at the receiver(s) at any time
_SC_THREAD_DESTRUCTOR_ITERATIONS	PTHREAD_DESTRUCTOR_ITERATIONS	Minimum number of attempts to call TSD destructor
_SC_THREAD_KEYS_MAX	PTHREAD_KEYS_MAX	Maximum number of TSD keys per process
_SC_THREAD_STACK_MIN	PTHREAD_STACK_MIN	Minimum thread stack size
_SC_THREAD_THREADS_MAX	PTHREAD_THREADS_MAX	Maximum number of threads per process
_SC_TIMER_MAX	TIMER_MAX	Maximum number of timers per process supported by the implementation
_SC_TTY_NAME_MAX	TTY_NAME_MAX	Maximum size of tty name

Name	Return Value	Meaning
_SC_ASYNCHRONOUS_IO	_POSIX_ASYNCHRONOUS_IO	Supports asynchronous input and output
_SC_FSYNC	_POSIX_FSYNC	Supports file synchronization
_SC_MAPPED_FILES	_POSIX_MAPPED_FILES	Supports memory mapped files
_SC_MEMLOCK	_POSIX_MEMLOCK	Supports process memory locking
_SC_MEMLOCK_RANGE	_POSIX_MEMLOCK_RANGE	Supports range memory locking
_SC_MEMORY_PROTECTION	_POSIX_MEMORY_PROTECTION	Supports memory protection
_SC_MESSAGE_PASSING	_POSIX_MESSAGE_PASSING	Supports message passing
_SC_PRIORITIZED_IO	_POSIX_PRIORITIZED_IO	Supports prioritized input and output
_SC_PRIORITY_SCHEDULING	_POSIX_PRIORITY_SCHEDULING	Supports process scheduling
_SC_REALTIME_SIGNALS	_POSIX_REALTIME_SIGNALS	Supports realtime signals extension
_SC_SEMAPHORES	_POSIX_SEMAPHORES	Supports semaphores
_SC_SHARED_MEMORY_OBJECTS	_POSIX_SHARED_MEMORY_OBJECTS	Supports shared memory objects
_SC_SYNCHRONIZED_IO	_POSIX_SYNCHRONIZED_IO	Supports synchronized input and output
_SC_THREADS	_POSIX_THREADS	Supports Pthreads
_SC_THREAD_ATTR_STACKADDR	_POSIX_THREAD_ATTR_STACKADDR	Supports stack address thread attribute
_SC_THREAD_ATTR_STACKSIZE	_POSIX_THREAD_ATTR_STACKSIZE	Supports stack size thread attribute
_SC_THREAD_PRIORITY_SCHEDULING	_POSIX_THREAD_PRIORITY_SCHEDULING	Supports thread priority scheduling
_SC_THREAD_PRIO_INHERIT	_POSIX_THREAD_PRIO_INHERIT	Supports thread priority inheritance protocol
_SC_THREAD_PRIO_PROTECT	_POSIX_THREAD_PRIO_PROTECT	Supports thread priority ceiling protocol
_SC_THREAD_SAFE_FUNCTIONS	_POSIX_THREAD_SAFE_FUNCTIONS	Supports POSIX thread-safe functions

Name	Return Value	Meaning
_SC_THREAD_PROCESS_SHARED	_POSIX_THREAD_PROCESS_SHARED	Supports inter-process thread synchronization
_SC_TIMERS	_POSIX_TIMERS	Supports timers

RETURN VALUES

If *name* is an invalid value, **sysconf**() will return **–1** and set **errno** to indicate the error. If **sysconf**() fails due to a value of *name* that is not defined on the system, the function will return a value of **–1** without changing the value of **errno**.

SEE ALSO

fpathconf(2), **seteuid**(2), **setrlimit**(2).

NOTES

A call to **setrlimit()** may cause the value of **OPEN_MAX** to change.

Multiplying **sysconf(_SC_PHYS_PAGES)** or **sysconf(_SC_AVPHYS_PAGES)** by **sysconf(_SC_PAGESIZE)** to determine memory amount in bytes can exceed the maximum values representable in a long or unsigned long.

_SC_PHYS_PAGES and **_SC_AVPHYS_PAGES** are specific to Solaris 2.3 and later releases.

The value of **CLK_TCK** may be variable and it should not be assumed that **CLK_TCK** is a compile-time constant.

NAME

ttyname, ttyname_r, isatty – find name of a terminal

SYNOPSIS

#include <stdlib.h>

char *ttyname(int *fildes*);

int isatty(int *fildes*);

POSIX

cc [*flag* ...] *file* ... **-D_POSIX_PTHREAD_SEMANTICS** [*library* ...]

int ttyname_r(int *fildes*, **char** **name*, **size_t** *namesize*);

Solaris

int ttyname_r(int *fildes*, **char** **name*, **int** *len*);

MT-LEVEL

See the **NOTES** section of this page.

DESCRIPTION

ttyname() returns a pointer to a string containing the null-terminated path name of the terminal device associated with file descriptor *fildes*.

ttyname_r() has the equivalent functionality to **ttyname**() except that a buffer *name* with length *namesize* (*len* in the Solaris version) must be supplied by the caller to store the result. *name* must be at least **TTY_NAME_MAX** in size (defined in **<limits.h>**).

isatty() returns **1** if *fildes* is associated with a terminal device, **0** otherwise.

RETURN VALUES

ttyname() returns a **NULL** pointer if *fildes* does not describe a terminal device in directory **/dev**. **ttyname_r**() returns **0** if successful. Otherwise it returns an error number.

ERRORS

ttyname_r() will fail and return an error if the following is true:

ERANGE The size of the buffer is smaller than the result to be returned.

ESRCH *fildes* does not describe a terminal device in directory **/dev**.

FILES

/dev/*

SEE ALSO

gettext(3I), **setlocale**(3C).

NOTES

When compiling multithread applications, the **_REENTRANT** flag must be defined on the compile line. This flag should only be used in multithread applications.

If the application is linked with **–lintl**, then messages printed from this function are in the native language specified by the **LC_MESSAGES** locale category; see **setlocale**(3C).

The return value points to static data whose content is overwritten by each call.

ttyname() is unsafe in multithread applications. **ttyname_r**() is MT-Safe, and should be used instead. **isatty**() is MT-Safe in multithread applications.

Annotated Bibliography

[Anderson 89] T.E. Anderson, E.D. Lazowska, H.M. Levy, *The Performance Implications of Thread Management Alternatives for Shared Memory Multiprocessors,* IEEE Transactions on Computers, December 1989.

[Anderson 90] T.E. Anderson, *The Performance of Spin Lock Alternatives for Shared Memory Multiprocessors,* IEEE Transactions on Parallel and Distributed Systems, January 1990.

Compares spin waiting algorithms.

[Anderson 91] T.E. Anderson, E.D. Lazowska, B.N. Bershad, H.M. Levy, *Scheduler Activations: Effective Kernel Support for the User-Level Management of Parallelism.* Proceedings of the Thirteenth ACM Symposium on Operating Systems Principles, October 1991.

A way of unifying user-level and kernel-supported threads.

[Bailey 94] M.L. Bailey, J.V. Briner Jr., R.D. Chamberlain, *Parallel Logic Simulation of VLSI Systems,* ACM Computing Surveys, September 1994.

[Ben-Ari 82] M. Ben-Ari, *Principles of Concurrent Programming,* Prentice-Hall, 1982.

Dekker's algorithm, dining philosophers, proofs, semaphores, monitors, rendezvous.

[Birrell 91] A. Birrell, *An Introduction to Programming with Threads,* in *Systems Programming with Modula-3,* Greg Nelson, ed., Prentice-Hall, 1991.

A wonderful, small explanation of threads programming. Required reading.

[Carriero 89] N. Carriero, D. Gelertner, *Linda in Context*, Communications of the ACM, 32(4):444–458, April 1989.

[Dijkstra 68] E. W. Dijkstra, *GOTO Statements Considered Harmful*, Communications of the ACM, March 1968.

The original structured technique.

[Ellis 90] M.A. Ellis, B. Stroustrup, *The Annotated C++ Reference Manual*, Addison-Wesley, 1990.

[Eykholt 92] J.R. Eykholt, S.R. Kleiman, S. Barton, R. Faulkner, A. Shivalingiah, M. Smith, D. Stein, J. Voll, M. Weeks, D. Williams, *Beyond Multiprocessing: Multithreading the SunOS Kernel*, Proceedings USENIX, Summer 1992.

Details on how threads are implemented in Solaris and are used by the kernel itself.

[Ferrari 78] D. Ferrari, *Computer Systems Performance Evaluation*, Prentice-Hall Inc., 1978.

A good review of computer performance analysis techniques. Contains an introduction to queuing theory and discrete event simulation as applied to computer performance evaluation. The examples are somewhat dated.

[Foley 90] J.D. Foley, A. van Dam, S.K. Feiner, and J.F. Hughes, *Computer Graphics: Principles and Practice*, second edition, Addison-Wesley, 1990.

[Gallmeister 95] B. Gallmeister, *POSIX.4 Programming for the Real World*, O'Reilly & Associates, Inc., 1995.

[Gehani 88] N. Gehani, A.D. McGettrick, *Concurrent Programming*, Addison-Wesley, 1988.

A good review of distributed and language-based concurrent programming techniques.

[Gharachorloo 91] K. Gharachorloo, A. Gupta, J. Hennessy, *Performance Evaluation of Memory Consistency Models for Shared Memory Multiprocessors*, Proceedings of the Fourth International Conference on Architectural Support for Programming Languages and Operating Systems, ACM, April 1991.

[Geist 94] A. Geist, A. Beguelin, J. Dongarra, W. Jiang, R. Manchek, V. Sunderam, *PVM: Parallel Virtual Machine,* MIT Press, Cambridge, Mass., 1994.

[Gropp 94] W. Gropp, E. Lusk, and A. Skjellum, *Using MPI: Portable Parallel Programming with the Message-Passing Interface,* MIT Press, Cambridge, Mass., 1994.

[Haddon 77] B.K. Haddon, *Nested Monitor Calls*, Operating System Review 11-4, ACM, October 1977.

[Hauser 93] C.Hauser, C. Jacobi, M. Theimer, B. Welsh, and M. Weiser, *Using threads in Interactive Systems: A Case Study,* Proceedings of the Fourteenth ACM Symposium on Operating Systems Principles, December 1993.

A wonderful summary of the thread paradigms useful in an interactive system. The case study is based on an implementation of the Xerox Portable Common Runtime running Xerox programming environments.

[Herlihy 90] M. Herlihy, *A Methodology for Implementing Highly Concurrent Data Objects*, Proceedings of the Second Annual ACM SIGPLAN Symposium on Principles and Practices of Parallel Programming, ACM, March 1990.

[Herlihy 91] M. Herlihy, *Wait-Free Synchronization*, ACM Transactions on Programming Languages and Systems, January 1991.

Seminal paper on wait-free synchronization.

[Hoare 74] C.A.R. Hoare, *Monitors: An Operating System Structuring Concept*. Communications of the ACM., October 1974.

A seminal paper on monitors.

[IEEE 95A] Institute of Electrical and Electronic Engineers, Inc., *Information Technology - Portable Operating Systems Interface (POSIX)- Part 1: System Application Program Interface (API) - Amendment 1: Realtime Extension [C Language]*, IEEE Standard 1003.1c-1995, IEEE, New York, N.Y., Also ISO/IEC 9945-1:1990b.

[IEEE 95B] Institute of Electrical and Electronic Engineers, Inc., *Information Technology - Portable Operating Systems Interface (POSIX)- Part 1: System Application Program Interface (API) - Amendment 2: Threads Extension [C Language]*, IEEE Standard 1003.1c-1995, IEEE, New York, N.Y., Also ISO/IEC 9945-1:1990c.

[Jones 91] M.B. Jones, *Bringing the C Libraries with Us into a Multi-Threaded Future*. Proceedings Winter 1991 USENIX Conference, January 1991.

[Karlin 91] A.R. Karlin, K. Li, M.S. Manasse, S. Owicki, *Empirical Studies of Competitive Spinning for a Shared Memory Multiprocessor,* Proceedings of the Thirteenth ACM Symposium on Operating System Principles, ACM, October 1991.

[Kernighan 88] B.W. Kernighan, D.M. Ritchie, *The C Programming Language*, Prentice-Hall Inc. 1988.

[Kleiman 95] S.R. Kleiman, J.R. Eykholt, *Interrupts as Threads*, ACM Operating System Review, April 1995.

[Kleinrock 75] L. Kleinrock, *Queuing Systems, Volume 1: Theory,* John Wiley & Sons, 1975.

[Knuth 73] D.E. Knuth, *The Art of Computer Programming,* Volume 3, *Sorting and Searching*, Addison-Wesley, Reading, Mass., 1973.

[Lampson 80] B. Lampson, D. Redell, *Experience with Processes and Monitors in Mesa*, Communications of the ACM., February 1980.

[Leighton XX] F.T. Leighton, *Introduction to Parallel Algorithms and Architectures*, Morgan Kaufmann, 1991.

A comprehensive treatment of parallel algorithms, oriented toward supercomputer and massive parallelism.

[Lister 77] A. Lister, *The Problem of Nested Monitor Calls*, Operating System Review 11-3, ACM, July 1977.

[McJones 89] P. McJones, G. Swart, *Evolving the UNIX System Interface to Support Multi-threaded Programs*, Proceedings Winter 1989 USENIX Conference, January 1989.

[Miller 90] B.P. Miller, M. Clark, J. Hollingsworth, S. Kierstead, S. Lim and T. Torzewski, *IPS-2: The Second Generation of a Parallel Program Measurement System*, IEEE Transactions on Parallel and Distributed Systems, April 1990.

[Mitchell 79] J.G. Mitchell, W. Maybury, R. Sweet. *Mesa Language Manual, Version 5.0*, Xerox Palo Alto Research Center Report CSL-79-3, April 1979.

[Newman 79] W.M. Newman and R.F. Sproull, *Principles of Interactive Computer Graphics*, second edition, McGraw-Hill, 1979.

[Novell 95] Novell Inc., *UnixWare 2.0 Operating System API Reference Manual*, Novell Inc., 1995.

[Parnas 78] D.L. Parnas, *The Non-problem of Nested Monitor Calls*, Operating System Review 12-1, ACM, January 1978.

Response to [Lister 77] and [Haddon 77]. Explains that monitor should not be interpreted in the strict linguistic sense of [Hoare 74]. Instead they should be used as a useful technique. A classic flame.

[Powell 91] M.L. Powell, S.R. Kleiman, S. Barton, D. Shah, D. Stein, M. Weeks, *The SunOS Multi-thread Architecture*. Proceedings Winter 1991 USENIX Conference January, 1991.

[Rao 91] M.R. Rao, *Performance Efficient Parallel Programming*, unpublished Ph.D. dissertation, Dept. of Electrical and Computer Engineering, Carnegie Mellon University, February 1991. Available from University Microfilms.

[Smaalders 92] B. Smaalders, B. Warkentine and K. Clarke, *Prototyping MT-Safe Xt and XView Libraries*, 6th Annual X Technical Conference, Boston, Mass., January 1992.

[Sterling 93] N. Sterling, *Warlock: A Static Data Race Analysis Tool*, Proceedings USENIX, Summer 1993.

This tool became `lock_lint` on Solaris.

[Upstill 90] S. Upstill, *The RenderMan Companion*, Addison-Wesley, 1990.

[Xu 89] Z. Xu and K. Hwang, *Molecule: A Language Construct for Layered Development of Parallel Programs*, IEEE Transactions on Software Engineering, 15(5):587- 599, 1989.

[Yang 88] C. Yang and B.P. Miller, *Critical Path Analysis for the Execution of Parallel and Distributed Programs*, 8th International Conference on Distributed Computing Systems, San Jose, Calif., June 1988.

Index

Symbols

A

B

E

F

G

H

I

J

K

L

M

N

O

P

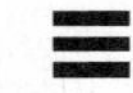

Q

R

S

T